RUSSIA AND NATIONALISM
IN CENTRAL ASIA

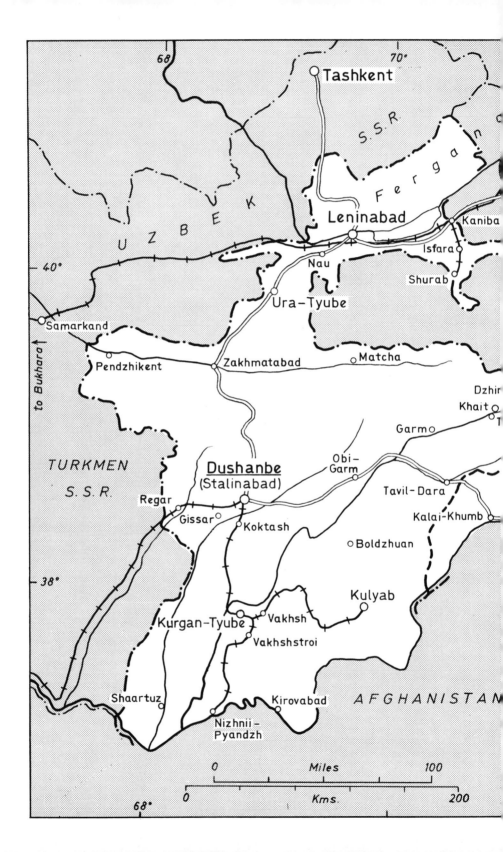

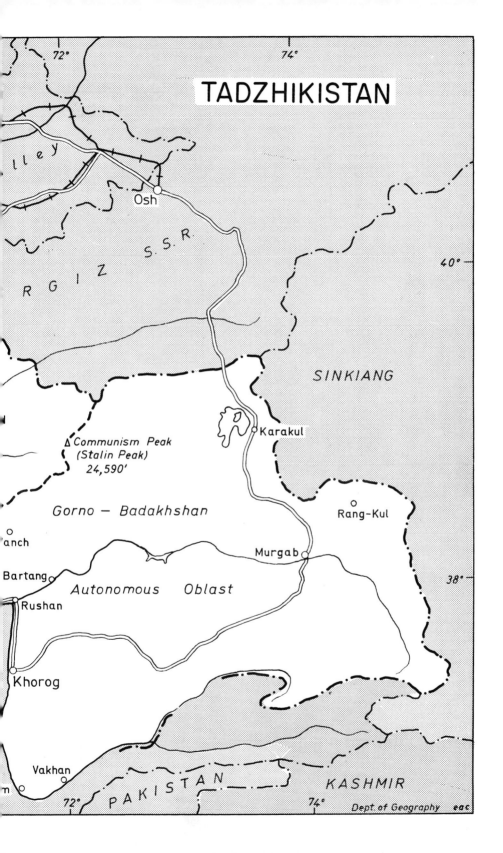

TADZHIKISTAN

lle y

72°   74°

○ Osh

R G I Z   S. S. R.

40°

SINKIANG

○ Karakul

△ Communism Peak
(Stalin Peak)
24,590'

Gorno — Badakhshan

○ Rang-Kul

○ 'anch

Bartang ○   Murgab ○

Autonomous   Oblast

○ Rushan   38°

○ Khorog

○ Vakhan

○ *m*

72°   *P A K I S T A N*   74°   *KASHMIR*

Dept. of Geography *eac*

RUSSIA AND NATIONALISM IN CENTRAL ASIA

THE CASE OF TADZHIKISTAN

TERESA RAKOWSKA-HARMSTONE

PUBLISHED IN COOPERATION WITH THE INSTITUTE
FOR SINO-SOVIET STUDIES
THE GEORGE WASHINGTON UNIVERSITY

THE JOHNS HOPKINS PRESS
BALTIMORE AND LONDON

Copyright © 1970 by The Johns Hopkins Press
All rights reserved
Manufactured in the United States of America

The Johns Hopkins Press, Baltimore, Maryland 21218
The Johns Hopkins Press Ltd., London

Library of Congress Catalog Card Number 69–13722

Standard Book Number 8018–1021–3

To Andrew

Workers of Tadzhikistan! Advance the culture of your land, develop its economy, assist the toilers of the city and the village, rally around you the best sons of the fatherland. Show the whole East that it is you, vigorously holding in your hands the banners of liberation, who are the most worthy heirs of your ancestors.

J. V. STALIN, *at the occasion of the proclamation of the Tadzhik Autonomous Soviet Socialist Republic, in March 15, 1925*

PREFACE

My interest in Soviet Central Asia dates back to my 1954–56 participation in a project on Soviet Central Asia under the sponsorship of the Human Relations Area Files—Washington Branch, an interest that later developed into a doctoral thesis, which, in turn, has served as the point of departure for this monograph. My greatest debt is to Professor Merle Fainsod of Harvard University, under whose direction it was my privilege to work. His scholarship has been a source of guidance and inspiration, and his advice and encouragement was of the greatest value in the preparation of this manuscript. He is, of course, in no way responsible for any of its shortcomings. For the early stages of the research I am also indebted to the original team of the HRAF project, especially to its director, Dr. Lawrence Krader, who introduced me to the methodology of ethnic "name-reading," and to Mrs. Natalie Frenkley for fruitful exchange of information and for unfailing friendship.

A fellowship grant from the American Association of University Women (1963–64) enabled me to pursue the research on this project, and a publication grant from Carleton University, Ottawa, Canada, made possible last minute research and the preparation of the manuscript. For the latter, special thanks are due to Dean D. M. L. Farr, Associate Dean G. C. Merrill, and Professor P. V. Lyon. I am also indebted to Professor Adam Bromke for friendship and encouragement. Professor Kurt London, Director of the Institute for Sino-Soviet Studies of The George Washington

University in Washington, D.C., has made the publication of this manuscript possible through the Institute's generous assistance. Last, but not least, special thanks are due to William Y. Elliott, Professor Emeritus at Harvard University, but for whose interest, advice, and encouragement this project might never have been begun. The final shape of the manuscript owes much to the editorial assistance and advice of John Gallman and Mrs. Carol Lee Zimmerman of the Johns Hopkins Press. My thanks are also due to Mrs. Judith Benn who edited the early manuscript, Miss Mary Ann Bacon who wrote the index, and to the able and longsuffering ladies who did the typing, Mrs. Carolyn Kappes and Mrs. Agnes Simpson. During the preparation of the manuscript my family exhibited qualities of patience and forbearance which deserve a better reward than an acknowledgment here. My thanks go to my family and especially to my son, to whom this book is dedicated, for uncritical love and understanding beyond his years.

NOTE ON TRANSLITERATION

Transliteration of Russian names follows the Library of Congress usage, except for generally accepted spellings of geographic and other names. Russian capitalization usage in transliterating titles of books and articles is retained, but Russian nouns are given anglicized plural forms when practicable. Names of territorial-administrative units, and some economic and political terms such as *kolkhoz* (collective farm), *obkom* (province Party committee), and *Komsomol* (Young Communist League), are also kept in the original Russian. Persian and Arabic names are transliterated from Russian spelling. The Tadzhik capital, originally Dushambe (Monday), was called Stalinabad until 1961 when the original name was restored in a new spelling, Dushanbe. The name Stalinabad is used here as the appropriate one for the period.

T.R.-H.

CONTENTS

TABLES

CHARTS

ABBREVIATED TITLE GUIDE

AN TSSR, *Istoriia, III, Book 1*—Akademiia Nauk Tadzhikskoi SSR, Institut Istorii im. A. Donisha, *Istoriia Tadzhikskogo Naroda,* vol. III, Book 1, *Perekhod k sotsializmu (1917–1937),* ed. B. A. Antonenko (Moscow: Izd. "Nauka," 1964).

AN TSSR, *Istoriia, III, Book 2*—Akademiia Nauk Tadzhikskoi SSR, Institut Istorii im. A. Donisha, *Istoriia Tadzhikskogo Naroda,* vol. III, Book 2, *Period sotsializma i perekhod k kommunizmu (1938–1963 gg.),* eds. S. A. Radzhabov and Iu. A. Nikovaev (Moscow: Izd. "Nauka," 1965).

BSE, 1st ed., LIII—*Bol'shaia Sovetskaia Entsiklopediia* (1st ed., 1946, Tadzhik SSR), vol. LIII.

BSE, 2d ed., XLI—*Bol'shaia Sovetskaia Entsiklopediia* (2d ed., Moscow, 1956), vol. XLI.

GBAO—Gorno-Badakhshan Autonomous Oblast

Ezhegodnik BSE—*Ezhegodnik Bol'shoi Sovetskoi Entsiklopedii* (Moscow: "Sovetskaia Entsiklopediia").

KPSS, *Tadzhikskaia SSR*—KPSS Vysshaia Partiinaia Shkola, Kafedra ekonomicheskoi i politicheskoi geografii i zarubezhnykh gosudarstv. *Tadzhikskaia SSR: Uchebnyi Material.* (Moscow: Gospolitizdat, 1953).

KPT v dokumentakh—*Kommunisticheskaia Partiia Tadzhikistana v dokumentakh i tsifrakh (1924–1963 gg.); Sbornik dokumentov i materialov o roste i regulirovanii sostava partiinoi organizatsii,* ed. Kozachkovskii. (Institut Istorii Partii, Dushanbe: "Irfon," 1965).

KT—*Kommunist Tadzhikistana* (Stalinabad).

TsK KPT, *Tadzhikskaia SSR za 25 let*—Tsentral'nyi Komitet KP Tadzhikistana, Institut Istorii Partii, *Tadzhikskaia SSR za 25 let* (Stalinabad: Tadzhikgosizdat, 1955).

TSSR. Nar. Khoz. 1957—Tadzhikskaia SSR. Statisticheskoe Upravlenie. *Narodnoe Khoziaistvo Tadzhikskoi SSR: Statisticheskii Sbornik* (Stalinabad: Gosstatizdat, 1957).

TSSR. Nar. Khoz. 1961—Tadzhikskaia SSR. Sovet Ministrov. Tsentral'noe Statisticheskoe Upravlenie, *Narodnoe Khoziaistvo Tadzhikskoi SSR v 1961 godu: Kratkii Statisticheskii Sbornik* (Dushanbe: Gosstatizdat, 1962).

VKP(b) *Perepis'1927 goda*—Vsesoiuznaia Kommunisticheskaia Partiia (bol'shevikov), Tsentral'nyi Komitet, Statisticheskii Otdel. *Vsesoiuznaia partiinaia perepis'1927 goda,* nos. 1–8 (Moscow: TsK VKP (b), 1927).

Russia and Nationalism in Central Asia

INTRODUCTION

Treaty-making and conquest made a colony of Russian Turkestan. Like most other non-Russian areas of the empire, it knew the first stirrings of nationalist agitation when the revolution came in 1917. The few members of the educated elite capable of formulating a modern nationalist message were reared in the Islamic tradition and looked for inspiration to the Young Turks rather than to the Russian revolutionaries. The Bolshevik revolutionaries recognized the right of the border peoples of the empire to national self-determination but modified it by the higher right of the revolutionary proletarian unity. In the process of the consolidation of power, the Pan-Turkic, Pan-Islamic nationalist aspirations in Central Asia were submerged and the area was reincorporated into the Soviet Union, successor to the empire. Under Soviet rule the cultural and political unity of Central Asia was broken, and the nationalities of Turkestan, Khiva, and Bukhara were each given constitutional recognition in the form of a union or autonomous republic within the political system which concentrated the essential powers in the hands of the federal government *de jure* and placed a *de facto* monopoly of political power in the hands of the highly centralized Communist Party.

In this century of nationalism and nationalist-led anticolonial revolution, it is legitimate to ask whether the Soviet Asians shared in the general process of national awakening brought about by the impact of colonial rule and modernization in Asia and Africa, or whether the revolution has prevented their revolutionary na-

1

tionalist potential from developing by giving them equal partner-
ship in place of colonial servitude. Can Soviet Central Asia still be
regarded as a colonial area? Did the nationalistic aspirations of the
people of Turkestan fail to develop? Or have they been suppressed? Or have they found satisfaction within the Soviet federal
system?

Soviet leaders admit that the Soviet political system is ideologically motivated and seeks a total transformation of society through
a process initiated and defined by the Russian-dominated ruling
bodies of the Party and the state. Is the Russian component strong
enough to mean Russification for the non-Russians in the process
of transformation from a traditional into a Soviet society? Do the
Russians share with the British and the French the sense of a
civilizing mission? If so, how does it affect the well-being and the
attitudes of the Asians in the borderlands?

The process of rapid modernization enforced from the top
under Soviet rule had far-reaching consequences in Central Asia
as it altered the economic base, transformed the social structure,
extended the benefits of mass education and communication systems to the Asian peoples, and created a modern Asian elite. Are
the members of the new Soviet Asian elite committed to the system
that gave them education and new opportunities? Do they share in
its goals? How do they participate in the political process and what
is their attitude toward the Russians, whose influx is an inescap-
able concomitant of the new system? Were they able to escape the
colonial-nationalist syndrome developed by similar Western-edu-
cated elites in the other ex-colonial areas of Asia and Africa?

An attempt is made here to seek answers to these and related
questions, and in the process to examine the ramifications of the
Soviet nationality policy, the dimensions and quality of the change,
and the process of formation of the new elite, whose attitudes and
behavior will influence the direction of the future growth of the
country.

In order to permit investigation in depth, I have made no attempt to cover the subject in time and space, but rather I have
examined a representative sample: a selected area (Tadzhikistan),
in a specific time period (the 1946–56 decade). The Soviet nationality policy has been the same in all non-Russian areas, with adjust-

ments made in the general pattern to accommodate some local variations. It requires the imposition of central political control by the Party, directed from Moscow, and a common institutional pattern within which national areas are granted a formal autonomy. The policy also demands a Moscow-determined social and economic transformation, and a cultural reorientation designed to familiarize the people with the message of the revolution and "proletarian" rule. National languages and other forms of cultural expression were preserved and cultivated as the media through which the new messages and policies reached the people; the traditional political and social institutions and usages were suppressed, subverted, and eventually eradicated. The common past and the centuries-old Islamic unity made for a uniform response to the nationality policy in Central Asia. The initial differences between the oases dwellers and the nomads disappeared quickly under the impact of collectivization, industrialization, and mass socialization, as the traditional fabric of society was disrupted and the leaders were eliminated. This study is concerned with the impact of the policy in Tadzhikistan, but its findings have broad validity because the impact-response dynamics charted here developed on the same pattern throughout Central Asia. Information available on the area as a whole from Western and Soviet sources (supported by the author's own research) indicates that specific developments and changes in Tadzhikistan were accompanied by parallel developments and changes in the other Central Asian republics, and problems and tensions present in Tadzhikistan were also found in the other republics. The findings also indicate certain basic similarities with the changes and developments in other postcolonial modernizing societies.

I chose Tadzhikistan as the locale for my investigation because of the relative lack of research in this area, as compared with Uzbekistan, for example, and because certain of its unique geographic, historical, and cultural features place the process of social and political transformation in sharper focus. The Tadzhik Soviet Socialist Republic, located in the southeast corner of Soviet Central Asia, is one of the smallest, least populous, most conservative, and most isolated of the union republics and has had the shortest period of exposure to Western influence. Unlike the Turkic people of the rest of Soviet Central Asia, the Tadzhiks are Iranians. They preserved their Iranian speech and some cultural characteristics under the heavy overlay of Islam, but they shared in the general Pan-Islamic unity of the area and, before the Soviet period, had no sense of a separate national consciousness.

The decade following the end of World War II seemed a logical period to choose for my investigation because it was the period in which the Stalinist nationality policy reached its final expression. The 1920's were devoted to political consolidation of Soviet rule, while the 1930's were dominated by the struggle for collectivization, and by industrialization. The early 1940's were spent under the shadow of tremendous war effort. Although the cut-off date for this investigation was 1956, much of the research has been clarified by information made available after that date, and the development of the major trends has been checked against the context of the late 1950's and the early 1960's.

A background chapter, which traces the establishment of Soviet power in Tadzhikistan and briefly describes the transformation of the country from the traditional to the Soviet pattern in the first two decades of Communist rule, serves as a point of departure for the main lines of investigation: discussion of the theory of the Tadzhik nationhood and its practical implications; examination of the pattern of ethnic stratification in the power structure and in the society at large; analysis of the composition, behavior, and attitudes of the new Tadzhik elite; study of the patterns of political socialization, and of its most important component, the new Tadzhik culture, which combines the traditional and the Soviet elements; and finally, the evaluation of the findings.

Throughout the study analysis will focus on the development of a new sense of national identity, awakened in the Tadzhiks by the cultivation of national forms and traditions required by the nationality policy, and on the bearers of this new national identity, the modern Tadzhik elite. In a pattern of development reminiscent of that in other postcolonial societies, the new elite's values have been shaped by interaction between the traditional agents of socialization such as the family and the native village and the modern ones such as the new soviet schools, collective farms, offices, and factories, and the resulting ambivalence in outlook and behavior. The outstanding aspect of the process of value formation of the new elite has been its relationship with its Russian teachers, supervisors, and colleagues. The crucial implication of this relationship is the growth of a national potential which, while capable of evolving into a positive force in the future development of soviet politics and society, may also prove to be highly disruptive.

1

❀

THE SETTING

Tadzhikistan, which has an area of 142,500 square kilometers,[1] is located in the southeast corner of Central Asia, bordering in the east on Chinese Sinkiang and in the south on Afghanistan; its internal boundaries are shared with the Uzbek and Kirgiz republics. The country's topography is dominated by towering mountain ranges: the central and eastern part of the Kopet Dagh system, the Pamir system, which includes the desert plateau of eastern Pamir (elevation 5,000 meters), and the central and southern arcs of the Tyan-Shan chain. The Soviet Union's two highest mountains, Peak Communism and Peak Lenin, are found in Tadzhikistan. Flowing out of the mountains westward and southward, rivers cut deep gorges in the rock and emerge into broad fertile valleys opening onto the desert plains which stretch between the mountains and the landlocked Aral and Caspian seas. To the north the area is bounded by the Syr-Darya River (the ancient Jaxartes), to the south by the Amu-Darya River (the ancient Oxus); Tadzhikistan occupies the easternmost part of Transoxiana, including a part of the Fergana Valley of the Syr-Darya, and the valleys of the tributaries of the Amu-Darya—the Vakhsh, Kafirnigan, and Zeravshan. The Zeravshan Valley is shared with Uzbekistan. Aridity and extremes in temperature are characteristic of the climate: temperatures range from 45° C. in the Vakhsh Valley to −50° C. in east-

---

[1] Tadzhikskaia SSR. Statisticheskoe Upravlenie. *Narodnoe Khoziaistvo Tadzhikskoi SSR: Statisticheskii Sbornik* (Stalinabad: Gosstatizdat, 1957), p. 7. Henceforth referred to as *TSSR. Nar. Khoz. 1957.*

ern Pamir. The average annual precipitation is less than 200 mm. Vegetation ranges from tropical crops, grown in southern valleys, to Alpine meadow plants.[2]

The mountains have traditionally been a formidable barrier to human interchange, and there are still many almost completely isolated pockets of habitation. Even in the 1960's there were few railroads and roads in Tadzhikistan, and snow and ice made mountain roads impassable from November through April. The airplane, linking Dushanbe (Stalinabad), the capital, with regional centers and the outside world, was the major passenger and freight carrier, but most of the traveling in the mountains was done on foot or by horse, ass, or camel over perilous mountain trails.[3] In contrast, the valleys were the crossroads of many peoples and the melting-pot of many cultures. Their fertile soil formed the base for the still predominantly agricultural economy; but the low precipitation made a well-developed irrigation network a necessity. The mountains guard still largely unexplored mineral resources, while the tremendous power potential of the falling rivers began to be developed only during the 1960's.

The indigenous people of the area are the Iranian Tadzhiks, considered to be the most ancient racial group in Central Asia. The mountain Tadzhiks of Western Pamir, such as the Iagnob, Iazgulem, Rushan, Shugnan, Vakhan, and Vanch clans, represent an almost pure ancient Iranian stock. Some non-Iranian admixture is found among the Galcha—the Tadzhiks of the Darvaz and Kara- tegin mountains. The Tadzhiks of the plains, who mixed freely with numerous invaders, have many Mongoloid racial features and are frequently indistinguishable in physical type from the Turkic-speaking Uzbeks, their Iranian language alone marking them as Tadzhiks.[4] A nineteenth-century traveler in Bukhara char-

[2] Lev Semenovich Berg, *Natural Regions of the USSR*, trans. Olga Adler Titel- baum, eds. J. A. Morrison and C. C. Nikiforoff (New York: Macmillan, 1950); Pavel Luknitsky, *Soviet Tadzhikistan* (Moscow: Foreign Languages Publishing House, 1954); *Bol'shaia Sovetskaia Entsiklopediia* (2d ed., Moscow, 1956), vol. XLI. Hence- forth referred to as *BSE, 2d ed., XLI.*

[3] *Kommunist Tadzhikistana* (Stalinabad), June 20, 1954, p. 2 and *passim.* Hence- forth referred to as *KT.*

[4] L. V. Oshanin, *Etnogenez Tadzhikov po dannym sravnitel'noi antropologii Tiurkskikh i Iranskikh narodov Srednei Azii* (Akademiia Nauk Tadzhikskoi SSR, Institut Istorii, Arkheologii i Etnografii, Works. (Stalinabad: AN Tadzhikskoi SSR, 1954), XXVII, 13–24; V. V. Ginzburg, "Antropologicheskie materialy k etnogenezu

acterized the Tadzhiks as handsome, polished, intelligent, accommodating, and willing to adjust to rule by a superior force,[5] a judgment that appears to hold true also in modern circumstances. Most Tadzhiks are Sunni Moslems, but in their religion are many survivals of pre-Moslem beliefs, including the worship of the forces of nature. The Pamir Tadzhiks are Ismailites, followers of the Aga Khan. Among the Pamir and Galcha Tadzhiks, traces of the ancient Iranian fire worship have survived into the Soviet period.[6]

The second most important national group in Tadzhikistan is the Uzbeks, also Sunni Moslems, the descendants of the Turkish nomads who conquered the area in the fifteenth century. Other nationalities include the pastoral Kirgiz and Turkmen and, Russians, and other immigrants from European Russia. Relations between the Uzbeks and the Tadzhiks have traditionally been hostile because the former ruled the country before the revolution, treating their Tadzhik subjects with cruelty and contempt. In the plains the Tadzhik upper classes transmitted some of their culture to the Uzbeks, but they were disliked and distrusted by the Uzbek conquerors. An Uzbek proverb, "When a Tadzhik tells the truth he has a fit of colic," illustrates the conquerors' attitude.[7] The attitude of local nationalities toward the Russians has been shaped by the colonial past and by the fact that from the Russian conquest through the Soviet era, the Russians have formed a *de facto* ruling elite in the area.

Pre-Soviet Historical Background

Eastern Transoxiana was the meeting place of peoples and cultures long before the beginning of the Christian era. An ancient

Tadzhikov," *Kratkie soobshcheniia o dokladakh i polevykh issledovaniiakh Instituta Istorii Material'noi Kul'tury* (Moscow: AN SSSR, Institut Istorii Material'noi Kul'tury), no. 61 (1956), 45–47; V. V. Ginzburg, *Gornye Tadzhiki. Materialy po antropologii Tadzhikov Karategina i Darvaza* (AN SSSR, Institut Antropologii, Etnografii i Arkheologii, Works), Anthropological Series #2 (Moscow: AN SSSR, 1937), XVI, 16.

[5] A Hungarian nineteenth-century anthropologist, Ujfalvy, as quoted in F. H. Skrine and E. D. Ross, *The Heart of Asia: A History of Russian Turkestan and the Central Asian Khanates from the Earliest Times* (London: Methuen & Co., 1899), pp. 364–65.

[6] Aleksandr Mikhailovich Briskin, *Strana Tadzhikov* (Moscow: Gosizdat, 1930), pp. 18–23; see also Walter Kolarz, *Religion in the Soviet Union* (New York: St. Martin's Press, 1962), Chap. xiii.

[7] Skrine and Ross, *The Heart of Asia*, pp. 364–65.

center and trading crossroad of cultivated lands and glamorous
cities, it has been the prize of conquerors from time immemorial.
Peace, a strong unified government, irrigation, and trade were the
functions of its growth and power; conquest, political fragmentation and internecine wars, a standstill in trade, and the destruction
of the irrigation network caused its decline. The area formed a
meeting ground; nomads and settlers waged armed struggles and
exchanged their women, goods, and services there. While invading
hordes stormed across plains, valleys, and foothills, the mountains
served as a refuge from invaders and a shelter behind which to
preserve ancient habits and beliefs.

Archeological evidence records the existence of settled societies
in Tadzhikistan as early as 3000 B.C., but the first historical record
of eastern Iranian kingdoms dates from the last millenium B.C. On
the upper Oxus [8] was Bactria, the home of Zoroaster and of Rox-
anne, who married Alexander the Great. Sogd (Sogdiana) extended along the middle Oxus. Alexander, who conquered both
Sogd and Bactria in 329 B.C., left a legacy of Greek culture and a
legend which survives to this day. He also left new cities as tangible
evidence of his rule, among them Khodzhent (now Leninabad) and
Kulyab. The Greco-Bactrian kingdom of Alexander's successors
fell in the second century B.C. at the onslaught of a Tatar tribe,
the nomadic Tokhari, who founded the Great Kushan empire.
The Kushan ruled Central Asia for the next five hundred years;
its conquest by the White Huns (Ephtalides) in the third century
A.D. marked the beginning of political fragmentation of the area
which was exacerbated by a new invasion of nomadic Turks three
hundred years later.

The Arab conquest in the seventh century A.D. was a milestone
in the history of Central Asia. The dynamic religion of Islam, replacing and eradicating other faiths such as Zoroastrianism, Buddhism, and Nestorian Christianity remained the dominant cultural
and social force in the area until modern times. It molded diverse
peoples into a uniform social pattern; it was strong enough to be
adopted by successive invaders and so resistant to change that it
ultimately led to social and political stagnation. The conquest

---

[8] In modern times the upper flow of the Oxus (Amu-Darya) is known as the Panj
(Pyandzh) River, now a boundary between Tadzhikistan and Afghanistan.

restored old cultural ties with the Middle East and the Mediterranean basin and sparked the growth of a splendid civilization.

Resistance to the Arabs was initially spirited, requiring several campaigns and the suppression of various local rebellions, the most important of which was a revolt of A.D. 776–83. Its leader, Mukanna, is now enshrined in the Soviet Tadzhik pantheon as a fighter for popular freedom. As the authority of the Baghdad caliphate in Central Asia declined, political power came to be exercised by powerful local families. The local dynasties of the Takharides (821–73) and the Saffarides (873–903) were followed by that of the Samanides (903–99). The Samanid rule ushered in a period of unprecedented economic prosperity and cultural development, the fruits of which are still considered the highest achievement of Persian culture.

The Samanid empire had an efficient and highly centralized government. Its irrigated agriculture produced cereals, cotton, and fruits, and supported animal husbandry, viniculture, and sericulture. Mines in the mountains produced silver, lead, mercury, iron, copper, gold, and precious stones. Craftsmen of the cities became world famous for their textiles, paper (the technique imported from China), leather goods, arms, tools, and pottery. Caravan routes dissected Central Asia; its cities grew rich in the trade. Arts developed rapidly, and the Samanid capital of Bukhara became a great center of learning in the Moslem world. A sophisticated Farsi language, the language of the great medieval Persian literature of the ninth and tenth centuries represented by such poets as Rudaki and Firdousi, was formed by the impact of Arabic on the Iranian Dari language (Soviet historians now call Farsi the Tadzhik language). The great scientists of the period, led by Avicenna (Abuali ibn Sina), wrote in Arabic, the *lingua franca* of the Islamic world.

By the end of the tenth century, however, internal unrest and the growth of religious heresies had undermined the power of the Samanides. The dynasty was toppled by another Turkish invasion, of the Karakhanides, who were followed in the twelfth century by the Seljuk Turks. Both tribes were assimilated and adopted Islam. Political fragmentation resulted but economic prosperity was not seriously affected, and learning and culture continued to flourish

under the impact of new religious movements. Ismailism originated as a resistance movement against the Seljuk rulers; Sufizm,
a rebellion against orthodoxy, injected into Islam a strong mystical
element which manifested itself in the court literature of the period.

The thirteenth-century Mongol invasion of Genghis Khan was
the second milestone in the history of Central Asia, but instead of
building, it destroyed. Bukhara, Samarkand, and Khodzhent fell
after heroic resistance in 1220, and by 1221 the Mongols had
reached across the Oxus, to rule all of what is now northern Afghanistan, except for the Badakhshan mountains. Cities and the
irrigation network were reduced to ruins; population was deci-
mated. The splendid civilization that fell was never to recover,
despite subsequent periods of prosperity and cultural growth. For
Central Asia the Dark Ages began in the thirteenth century, and
there has been no Renaissance. Cut off from the West, the people
of eastern Iran mixed with the Turks, and the blended culture
that emerged differed from that on the Iranian plateau across the
Oxus. The Pan-Iranian unity of the Samanid empire was irretriev-
ably lost.

After the death of Genghis Khan his heirs divided the empire,
and a measure of prosperity returned to Central Asia. Timur
(Tamerlane), the great conqueror of the fourteenth century, enriched his capital of Samarkand with the spoils of war; he built
roads and canals, developed trade, and encouraged the work of
artisans, artists, and scientists. There was a revival of literature,
this time written in the Turkic language (later claimed as the
Uzbek heritage in the Soviet period). Timur's grandson, Ulug-Beg,
himself a noted astronomer, was a patron of arts and learning, but
under his successors a weakening of the central authority precipi-
tated a general decline. The last major invasion before the coming
of the Russians occurred in the fifteenth century when the Uzbeks, Turkic nomads who were a part of the Golden Horde, swept
through Central Asia. They established a decentralized khanate
and supplied the last ethnic element to the people who now bear
their name. By the mid-eighteenth century the khanate was again
broken up into independent principalities: Bukhara, Khiva,
Kokand, Gissar, and Badakhshan. These engaged in a continuous

war that led to population losses, destruction of the rebuilt irrigation network, and a general social and economic upheaval. Cultural activity was carried out primarily by court sycophants in the service of various khans. Expressions of independent spirit were suppressed by the powerful and increasingly conservative Moslem clergy.

Under Uzbek rule the Tadzhiks, distinguished from their conquerors by their Iranian language, dispersed throughout the many principalities in the area. Farsi was adopted as the court language by the various khans. Many Tadzhiks lived in the cities of the Bukhara and Kokand khanates and in the Fergana Valley. In the mountains they were grouped in the semiautonomous principalities of Gissar, Kulyab, Zeravshan, Darvaz, Karategin, Shugnan, Vakhan, Rushan, and others, most of which paid tribute to the Bukhara emirate. Other Tadzhiks lived in the Khiva and Kazakh khanates, in Chinese Turkestan, in northern India and Afghanistan, and in Persian Khorassan.[9]

Western penetration of Central Asia began in the late eighteenth century. The British, established in India and hoping to extend their influence to Afghanistan, advanced from the southeast; the Russians came from the northwest. For both powers the area was of military and political importance; their agents were military and intelligence officers rather than merchants or missionaries.

The Russian conquest of Central Asia began in the 1860's. It was prompted by the need for cotton to replace the supply cut off by the American Civil War and by the desire to protect Russian settlers and trade from nomadic raids. Chimkent and Tashkent were taken in 1865 as were parts of the Bukhara khanate, including Khodzhent, in 1866. The Russian province of Turkestan was formed in 1867. By 1868 the Russians held the Zeravshan Valley

[9] Discussion in this section was based on: Bobodzhan Gafurovich Gafurov, *Istoriia Tadzhikskogo naroda v kratkom izlozhenii,* vol. I. *S drevneishikh vremen do Velikoi Oktiabr'skoi Sotsialisticheskoi Revoliutsii 1917 g.,* 3d corrected and enlarged ed. (AN Tadzhikskoi SSR. Institut Istorii, Moscow: Gospolitizdat, 1955); William Montgomery McGovern, *The Early Empires of Central Asia: A Study of the Scythians and the Huns and the Part They Played in World History* (Chapel Hill: University of North Carolina Press, 1939); Skrine and Ross, *The Heart of Asia;* Briskin, *Strana Tadzhikov;* Richard Nelson Frye, *Bukhara: The Medieval Achievement* (Norman, Okla.: University of Oklahoma Press, 1965).

and Samarkand and had forced Bukhara to accept their protectorate. Khiva met a similar fate in 1873, while Kokand was incorporated into Russian Turkestan in 1876 as the Fergana Province. All three khanates offered resistance, but they were no match for Russia's modern armies. By 1884 the Russians had also subdued the Turkmen and arrived within striking distance of Persia and Afghanistan, areas regarded by the British as their sphere of influence. The two powers negotiated a demarcation line between their respective spheres of influence in the 1880's and 1890's. It left the Pamirs west of the Sarykol range and north of the river Panj under Russian influence.

At the beginning of the twentieth century the area of modern Tadzhikistan was divided between the khanate of Bukhara and the Samarkand and Fergana provinces of Russian Turkestan. Governed by military governors under a governor general, Turkestan became a Russian colonial dependency. Peace and growth of trade brought renewed prosperity. Cotton cultivation began on a large scale with new irrigation works; railroads were built, and rudimentary industries were established. Russian colonists, officials, merchants, and farmers followed. They formed a distinct privileged minority, living in separate quarters and having no contacts with the Moslems. Traditional Moslem agencies of authority served as intermediaries between the Asians and the Russian government. The Moslem community continued its traditional way of life largely undisturbed, on the condition that it fulfill the requirements of the new government.

Under a protectorate agreement with the Emir of Bukhara, the Russians assumed the right to represent the khanate in foreign affairs and received economic and extraterritorial concessions. Slavery was abolished. In all other matters the Emir retained his powers, limited only by Islamic law and the power of the conservative clergy. Provinces and districts of the khanate were governed by Emir-appointed *beks* and *amlakdars,* respectively. Each village (*kishlak*) had a headman (*aksakal*). There were special officials for the collection of taxes (*haradzh,* the field tax; *amin,* the tax on livestock and livestock products bought and sold in a bazaar; and *ziaket,* the tax on all other goods bought and sold in a bazaar). Most of the cultivated land was either a religious endowment (*vakf*) or belonged to the Emir or the beks; the remaining land was in the hands of a few wealthy landlords (*bai*). Most peasants (*dekhkans*) were tenant farmers or hired laborers. Justice was administered according to the Shariat (the Islamic code of law) by a *kazi*, an Emir-appointed judge; public morals were guided by the universally hated special officials called *rais*. Fines, beatings, and torture were usual modes of punishment. Judicial and administrative decisions depended on the disposition of the magistrates, the social class of the petitioners or defendants, and the amount of payment received. Officials received no salary, but gained their livelihood from payments exacted from the population. Only boys who were members of wealthier families were educated. Mosque schools (*mektebe*) taught the children how to chant the Koran; higher schools (*medresse*) taught the Koran and Shariat. With the exception of the clergy and a few members of the upper classes, illiteracy was universal.[10]

The Moslem clergy exercised strict control over the life of the community. In every village the mosque was a place of worship, a meeting hall, and a guest house. The *mullah* (priest) was usually the most powerful person in a kishlak. He was a spiritual teacher, a judge in local matters, and a leader in all aspects of life; he held the key to a better life in the hereafter. Those who challenged the clergy were frequently lynched by fanatical crowds. Mullahs and *ishans* (heads of the Sufi orders) were the base of authority in the khanate. Polygamy and child marriage were common. Women were bought and sold like chattels or beasts of burden; they were veiled and did not participate in communal life. Their life was somewhat easier in the mountains where the veil was not required and their freedom of movement was less restricted. Poor peasants formed the largest social class in the khanate; there were also a few landlords, a large and powerful group of fanatical and well-organized clergy, and the officials of the Emir. Craftsmen lived in the cities and larger kishlaks.[11]

The various mountain principalities of eastern Bukhara such as Darvaz, Karategin, and Gissar were, until the 1870's, ruled by hereditary beks who recognized the sovereignty of Bukhara only

[10] Gafurov, *Istoriia*, Chap. xxi; Briskin, *Strana Tadzhikov*, pp. 17–35.
[11] *Ibid.*

nominally. When the Russians extended their protectorate over
Bukhara, the Emir took advantage of assistance offered by the
imperial army to subdue and oust mountain rulers and to appoint
new beks from among his Uzbek chiefs. They were supported by
mountain Uzbek tribesmen in exchange for special privileges.
Mountain Tadzhiks resented Uzbek rule and the exactions imposed, but their rebellions were quelled by brutality and blood-
shed.[12]

The Moslem masses of Bukhara and Turkestan were not affected by the revolutionary ferment of the first two decades of the
twentieth century in Russia. In Turkestan the conservative Moslem majority, dominated by the clergy, wanted only to preserve
its old way of life. A few educated members of the middle class,
known as Jadidists, advocated westernization and modern educational facilities; they started the so-called new method schools in
Turkestan. The Jadidists became an increasingly political Pan-
Islamic and Pan-Turkic group after the 1906 elections to the
Duma. The Russians, who initially supported the movement, became alarmed and joined forces with Moslem conservatives to
curtail its activities. This was relatively easy because the Jadidists
were essentially middle-class liberals who had no supporters
among the peasant masses.[13]

The movement for educational reform also penetrated to the
khanate of Bukhara, where it appealed to wealthy merchants and
students of Islam. The Khodzha and Maksum families supplied
many Jadidist leaders, some of whom later became prominent in
the Soviet governments of Uzbekistan and Tadzhikistan. A Tadzhik, Sadriddin Aini, Moslem scholar and later the founder of the
Soviet Tadzhik literature, was one of the movement's leaders. Reformed schools were opened only in the extraterritorial areas held

[12] Briskin, *Strana Tadzhikov*, p. 17; and B. Kh. Karmysheva, *Uzbeki–Lokaitsy
iuzhnogo Tadzhikistana*, no. 1. *Istoriko-etnograficheskii ocherk zhivotnovodstva v
dorevoliutsionnyi period.* (AN Tadzhikskoi SSR, Institut Istorii, Arkheologii i Etnografii. Works. XXVIII, Stalinabad: AN Tadzhikskoi SSR, 1954), 122–31.
[13] Discussion in this section was based on: Serge A. Zenkovsky, *Pan-Turkism and
Islam in Russia* (Cambridge, Mass.: Harvard University Press, 1960), *passim;* Serge
A. Zenkovsky, "Kulturkampf in Pre-Revolutionary Central Asia," *American Slavic
and East European Review,* XIV, no. 1 (1955), 15–41; Richard Pipes, *The Formation
of the Soviet Union: Communism and Nationalism, 1917–1923* (Cambridge, Mass.:
Harvard University Press, 1954), pp. 86–93.

by the Russians, because of the opposition of the clergy. The success of such schools led the Emir to give permission to open one in Bukhara. The first one, with Tadzhik as the language of instruction, opened in October, 1908; by 1914 there were ten reformed schools in the city, but all were closed with the outbreak of the war, when the Jadidist leaders fled or were imprisoned. One reason for the suppression of the movement was its demand for political reform. Some of the persecuted leaders found themselves in Turkey, where they were favorably impressed by the Young Turks movement.[14]

The war had an adverse effect on the economy of Turkestan. At first it did not directly affect the Moslem population, but in 1916 the Russian government decided to conscript Moslems for labor in the army. Forcible conscription caused resistance in Khodzhent, Fergana, Samarkand, and other places; it was suppressed by the Russian army. The resistance movement subsequently became known as the revolt of 1916. In Bukhara unrest was also provoked by the use of peasant labor for the construction of the Bukhara-Termez railroad.[15] The Jadidists opposed conscription of labor and were sympathetic to resistance, but they remained inactive in 1916. The unrest of 1916, which was sporadic and limited in scope, was a direct reaction to unpopular measures taken by the Russian government and had no broader revolutionary significance for the Moslem masses or the Moslem leaders.

[14] Zenkovsky, *Kulturkampf*, pp. 34–39.
[15] Gafurov, *Istoriia*, pp. 479–83.

2

THE FORMATION OF SOVIET TADZHIKISTAN

THE REVOLUTION AND CONSOLIDATION
OF SOVIET POWER

Soviet and Western sources alike agree that Russian Turkestan
and the neighboring khanates were not ready for a revolution in
the second decade of the twentieth century. It was only because
of the presence of a determined Russian minority, consisting of
people who participated in the general stream of Russian revolutionary activity, that Turkestan had a revolution at all. The revolution eventually engulfed the khanates, changed the life of the
indigenous population, and set them apart from their conationals
and coreligionists in neighboring countries. The short drama of
the revolution in Turkestan was played out among the Russians
fighting each other; the Moslem masses were inert, the politically
fragmented Moslem elite was unable, and largely unwilling, to
act. When the importance of the change and the accompanying
possibilities became clear to Moslem leaders, the new regime was
already established, with its commanding posts in Russian hands.
The Russians were the new rulers; the Moslems could only sur-
render or rebel. From the very beginning this significant fact has
determined the dominant role played by the Russians in the establishment and perpetuation of Soviet rule throughout Central
Asia.

The revolutionary authority in Turkestan was represented first
by the Turkestan Committee of the Petrograd Provisional Govern-

18

ment and, after October, 1917, by the Tashkent Soviet. Both were composed of local Russians and neither was willing to grant political autonomy to the Moslems, as requested by the Turkestan Moslem Central Council formed by liberal Moslem leaders in response to the news of the revolution. Convinced that they had to act themselves, the council leaders, who were joined by some of the conservatives grouped in the Association of Ulema, called a congress in Kokand in late November, 1917, to proclaim the territorial autonomy of Turkestan and elect a council to serve as a Moslem provisional government. Even at this point, however, there was no declaration of independence from Russia, which shows the weakness of separatist tendencies and the absence of a unified Moslem policy.[1]

The few Moslem socialists in Turkestan (members of the Union of Toiling Moslems in Fergana and the Ittihad in Samarkand) joined the soviets as they were formed, but were numerically too weak to play any significant role. Moreover, most of them were Mensheviks or Socialist Revolutionaries and thus were used but not trusted by the Bolsheviks. The Tadzhiks as a group were not involved in the Kokand government. At this stage of development there was little, if any, sense of distinct national identity among the educated Tadzhiks which would have separated them from their fellow Uzbeks in terms of political activity.

The Kokand Provisional Government proved to be a head without a body. Few localities recognized its authority; it found no allies among the White Russians because of its insistence on Turkestan's autonomy. The Emir of Bukhara was hostile to it because it was dominated by the liberals, and, moreover, he wished to remain neutral in the civil war. Attacked by Russian troops sent by the Tashkent Soviet government, the Kokand government fell in February, 1918.[2] Its failure to gain support among the people shows the extent of the gap that existed between the few modern leaders and the tradition-bound masses.

In Bukhara, meanwhile, the most enterprising Jadidists organized themselves into a "Young Bukhara" movement, a clandestine organization modeled on the Young Turks and dedicated

[1] Pipes, *Formation,* pp. 86–93.
[2] *Ibid.,* pp. 174–76.

to the removal of the Emir. Late in 1917 they contacted the Soviet Tashkent government and with the assistance of its troops attempted a combined internal coup and military attack in March, 1918. The attempt failed, largely because of the fierce resistance of the people, roused to the "holy war" by the clergy. Russians in Bukhara were massacred, as were all the Young Bukhara members except those who managed to escape to Soviet Turkestan. Discouraged, the Tashkent government recognized the independence of the Bukhara khanate.[3]

In the Tadzhik-inhabited areas of Turkestan soviets were established in 1918, in Khodzhent, Isfara, Ura-Tyube, and Kanibadam. In contrast, except for the abortive coup in the city of Bukhara, there was no revolutionary agitation or activity in eastern Bukhara, which remained securely in the grip of the Emir's officials and the conservative clergy.[4] Jadidists made absolutely no inroads there.

In the first three years of revolutionary struggle, Turkestan's Russian leaders remained almost completely isolated from other revolutionary centers. The Russian attitude toward the local population was colored by the prerevolutionary colonial attitude and a sense of cultural superiority. On the part of the Bolsheviks this was augmented by a contempt for religious obscurantism and a crusading spirit that urged them to free the Moslem masses from their religious domination and "class yoke." During the time when power in Tashkent was passing from the hands of Tsarist officials to the short-lived representation of the Petrograd Provisional Government to the Bolshevik-dominated Tashkent Soviet, the Moslems were treated as inferiors and were subjected to forcible exactions and persecutions by the Russian minority.[5]

From 1917 the Bolsheviks in Central Asia have strived to extend and consolidate the Soviet order in the region, but their interpretation of the principle was colored by the social atmosphere in which they operated. Existing as tiny European islands amid an alien sea of Turkic peoples, fearful lest these peoples unite to destroy them,

[3] *Ibid.*, p. 177; and Zenkovsky, *Kulturkampf, passim.*
[4] G. A. Aliev, *Uspekhi razvitiia ekonomiki i kul'tury Tadzhikskoi SSR. K 40–letiiu Velikoi Oktiabr'skoi Sotsialisticheskoi Revoliutsii* (Moscow: Izd. "Znanie," 1957), p. 7.
[5] Pipes, *Formation*, pp. 174–84; and Alexander G. Park, *Bolshevism in Turkestan, 1917–1927* (New York: Columbia University Press, 1957), pp. 34–37 and 155–204.

they were inclined at the outset to interpret the class struggle as a conflict between Moslem and European and to minimize class differences within the European community for the sake of solidarity against the greater danger.[6]

Mikhail Frunze, one of the emissaries in Turkestan of the Central Committee of the Russian Communist Party (Bolsheviks), remarked at the time on the typically colonial attitude of local Russian Communists:

> European Communists, mainly railway workers . . . maintained the principle of pure dictatorship of the proletariat and attempted to apply this principle to life in spite of the fact that this actually meant the dictatorship of a small group of the local European population over the Muslim masses.[7]

Thirty years later, Soviet Central Asian leaders also felt free to criticize the initial policy. Writing in the central Party journal, Bobodzhan Gafurov, then First Secretary of the Tadzhik Communist Party, singled out for criticism such practices of the local Party organizations in Turkestan in the early days as the refusal to allow local nationals to participate in the organs of Soviet power, and the segregation of soviets by nationality.[8]

The early policy of suppression and abuse fostered dislike and hatred of the new government among the local population. Roused, the people followed the conservative leaders' call to resistance, and a guerilla movement known as the *Basmachi* was born. The backbone of the resistance was provided by the conservative elite seeking the restoration of the status quo; the people flocked to them in their anxiety to preserve their religion and traditional customs. Among the Jadidists and Young Bukharans,

[6] Park, *Bolshevism in Turkestan*, pp. 156–57.

[7] M. V. Frunze, "Communist Difficulties in Turkestan, 1920," quoted in X. J. Eudin and R. C. North, *Soviet Russia and the East, 1920–1927. A Documentary Survey* (Stanford: Stanford University Press, 1957), p. 49. The 1964 Tadzhik official history relates that many Russian Communists did not want to recruit local nationals into Party-soviet work. AN Tadzhikskoi SSR, Institut Istorii im. A. Donisha, *Istoriia Tadzhikskogo Naroda*, III, Book I, *Perekhod k sotsializmu (1917–1937)*, ed. B. A. Antonenko (Moscow: Izd. "Nauka," 1964), 72–73. Henceforth referred to as AN TSSR, *Istoriia*, III, Book 1.

[8] B. G. Gafurov, "V. I. Lenin i pobeda sovetskoi vlasti v Srednei Azii," *Kommunist*, XXXII, no. 6 (1955), 74–90, 80.

only the left faction supported the Soviet government, while many others joined the conservatives in overt rebellion. The tragedy of the liberal-educated Moslems was that as reform-seeking representatives of a nascent middle class they cooperated with Russian revolutionaries and thus became tainted in the popular eye. Russian colonial policies alienated even the Moslem Communists, who proclaimed a desire to establish a "Turkic republic" and a "Turkic Communist Party." [9]

The growth of Moslem resistance in Turkestan caused some uneasiness to the Bolshevik government in Moscow. On October 8, 1919, it appointed a special Commission for Turkestan Affairs (Turkkomissiia) to supervise local soviet authorities.[10] Anxious to gain adherence among the Moslems and to undercut their aspirations to independence, the Commission sent back to Russia the "open chauvinists and colonizers" who were the most vocal exponents of the "European" viewpoint,[11] and launched a new policy of cooperation. Moslems were asked to join the Party and the government; their right to trade freely was restored and repressions ceased. The new policy temporarily halted the spread of the Basmachi, who, by the summer of 1920, controlled a considerable part of the Fergana Valley.[12]

The continued existence of the independent khanates of Khiva and Bukhara, which supported the Basmachi movement, was regarded as a thorn in the flesh of Soviet Turkestan. The Turkestan Commission therefore decided to destroy them; Khiva fell in February, 1920, and the People's Republic of Khorezm was established in its place. The campaign against Bukhara was prepared with the cooperation of the left faction of the Young Bukharans. Having gained control of the movement, it staged an uprising against the Emir in Chardzhou in August, 1920, and asked for the help of the

---

[9] Frunze, "Communist Difficulties," quoted in Eudin and North, *Soviet Russia,* p. 49.

[10] Its full name was *Kommissiia VTsIK po delam Turkestana.* It was composed of Sh. Z. Eliava, chairman; M. V. Frunze, commander-in-chief of the Fourth Army; V. V. Kuibyshev; F. I. Goloshchekin; Ia. E. Rudzutak; and G. I. Bokii. AN TSSR, *Istoriia,* III, Book 1, 72. Pipes (*Formation,* p. 181) gives the date of the establishment of the commission as January, 1919.

[11] AN TSSR, *Istoriia,* III, Book 1, 72–73; and Frunze, "Communist Difficulties," quoted in Eudin and North, *Soviet Russia,* p. 49.

[12] Zenkovsky, *Pan-Turkism and Islam,* p. 206.

Red Army. The help duly arrived, led by M. V. Frunze, Commander-in-chief of Soviet forces in Turkestan, and after a five-day
battle the city of Bukhara was captured on September 2, 1920. Said
Alim Khan, the last Mangit ruler of the khanate, fled to eastern
Bukhara.[13]

The Soviet interpretation of these events is somewhat different.
A 1930 source simply states that the Young Bukharans, many of
whom were members of the Communist Party, called at a conference in Chardzhou for an uprising to overthrow the Emir, and
that they succeeded in the task with the help of the Red Army.[14] A
more elaborate version, published in 1955, claimed that the Emir
had become a menace to Soviet Central Asia because of the help
he received from the British, and that he was destroyed, with assistance from the Red Army, by a revolution begun by the Bukharan Communist Party.[15]

A people's republic like that in Khiva was established in Bukhara (Bukharskaia Narodnaia Sovetskaia Respublika, BNSR). Its
government was made up of Jadidists and Young Bukharans, its
nucleus controlled by the left faction of the young Bukharans,
run by its Communist members. Then, as now, a people's republic
was officially considered a transition form for a country not yet
ready for a Communist government. It was nominally independent; its formal ties with the Russian Socialist Federated Soviet
Republic (RSFSR) were based on a treaty of military, economic,
and political alliance concluded on March 4, 1921. In fact the
BNSR was militarily and politically dependent on the Soviet authorities in Turkestan.[16]

The Emir's flight to eastern Bukhara transformed the area (its
terrain ideally suited to guerilla warfare) into the center of Basmachi operations for the next decade. The Emir established temporary headquarters in Dushambe and rapidly collected an army
of 30,000 to 40,000 men.[17] The Bukhara government summoned

---

[13] Pipes, *Formation*, pp. 183–84.

[14] Briskin, *Strana Tadzhikov*, p. 33.

[15] Tsentral'nyi Komitet KP Tadzhikistana, Institut Istorii Partii, *Tadzhikskaia SSR za 25 let* (Stalinabad: Tadzhikgosizdat, 1955), p. 27. Henceforth referred to as TsK KPT, *Tadzhikiskaia SSR za 25 let*.

[16] Pipes, *Formation*, p. 255.

[17] Aliev, *Uspekhi razvitiia*, p. 8; and AN TSSR, *Istoriia*, III, Book 1, 99.

the Red Army which, with its Gissar Expeditionary Force, succeeded in forcing the Emir to flee to Afghanistan, and by May,
1921 in clearing eastern Bukhara of Basmachi troops.[18] The BNSR
government followed this success by sending representatives to
eastern Bukhara to attempt to establish revolutionary committees
throughout the area. V. V. Kuibyshev, one of the members of the
Turkestan Commission, also arrived in eastern Bukhara, where
he was "of great assistance in the development of the Party and
Soviet work." [19]

The pacification by the Red Army was the first exposure the
Tadzhiks of eastern Bukhara had to the Russians and the new rule.
The Tadzhik peasants had had little love for the Emir and the
ruling Uzbeks and were glad to see them expelled, which made the
task of the Red soldiers much easier. However, the Red Army behaved with exceptional brutality and disregard for local customs
and sensitivities, and the Basmachi movement began to revive
almost immediately. Locally, their leadership was provided by the
most influential elements in the kishlak: the mullah, the bai, and
the local officials. The Uzbek tribes of Gissar, Lokai, and Mangit
were the first to revive the resistance. Unwilling to lose their
privileges, the leaders rallied the clans around them by an appeal
based on religion and familial ties (Uzbeks, like other Turkic
tribes, based their social organization on the blood ties of a clan).
Bands were organized on the basis of clan ties; religious sanctions
were used to force people to join.[20] The Lokai formed the strongest bands and produced the best-known leaders, among them
Ibrahim Bek. Said to have been a horse thief and a leader of a
robber band before the revolution, he commanded a large unit of
Basmachi and was appointed "Commander-in-Chief of the Armies
of Islam" by the fleeing Emir.[21]

The Basmachi movement spread in the summer and fall of 1921
as a result of religious agitation and the absence of a strong government and army in the BNSR. Tadzhiks formed bands to defend

[18] TsK KPT, *Tadzhikskaia SSR za 25 let*, pp. 27–34.
[19] AN TSSR, *Istoriia*, III, Book 1, 103.
[20] Briskin, *Strana Tadzhikov*, pp. 36–37; and Karmysheva, *Uzbeki-Lokaitsy*, pp.
52–53.
[21] Karmysheva, *Uzbeki-Lokaitsy*, p. 45.

themselves from the Uzbeks, as did other nationalities such as the Turkmen and the Kirgiz, and there was much internecine fighting. The Basmachi bands lacked unity, but by the end of 1921, when Ibrahim Bek was able to oust the Russian garrison from Dushambe, they numbered about 20,000. In the words of a Soviet chronicler, the Red Army situation was not enviable:

> With a tremendous percentage of malaria sickness in the army (in some areas the number of the sick reached up to 90 or 95 per cent of the total), without provisions, and faced with the generally hostile attitude of the fanatic population, our units began a planned westward retreat.[22]

Although they were in effective control of eastern Bukhara, the Basmachi lacked leadership and unity. Unity was also absent in the beleaguered and largely ineffectual government of the BNSR, divided between Young Bukharans and Young Bukharan Communists, the latter acting as agents for Communist penetration. In November, 1921, Enver Pasha, a former leader of the Young Turks movement, now in the Soviet service, came to Bukhara. Well known among the Moslems, he was sent to pacify the Basmachi, but he decided to seek glory as a Moslem leader rather than as a Soviet stooge. Thinking to unite Turkestan and to lead it toward independence, he defected, prevailed upon the Emir to appoint him the Basmachi commander-in-chief, and made an attempt to unify the movement. Several members of the BNSR government, including Usman Khodzhaev, the chairman of its Central Executive Committee, and the ministers of war and the interior, defected with him. Enver cleared eastern Bukhara of Red troops but was unable to gain the adherence of the many diverse elements of the Basmachi. Ibrahim Bek and other commanders refused to recognize his authority, and the Emir himself was distrustful. Surprised by a Red Army ambush at Khovaling in Kulyab, Enver Pasha was killed on August 4, 1922. His death ended the prospect of Moslem unity; the strength of the Basmachi declined, and Ibrahim Bek again became their most important leader.[23]

In line with Lenin's New Economic Policy (NEP) in 1922 the

---

[22] Briskin, *Strana Tadzhikov,* p. 38.
[23] *Ibid.,* pp. 38–40; and Pipes, *Formation,* pp. 257–59.

Soviet attitude toward Moslems in Central Asia became more conciliatory. Economic exactions and political repressions ceased, and private trade was restored. The Islamic clergy recovered some of their former powers; church lands were returned, and Moslem schools and Shariat courts were allowed to reopen. The economic and religious concessions considerably weakened the popular resistance to the regime and reduced the Basmachi following.[24] Nevertheless, the movement survived. In 1923 and 1924 three major bases of Basmachi activity remained in eastern Bukhara: Matcha, Darvaz, and Karategin. Sending emissaries who preached holy war against the infidel, the Basmachi conducted propaganda warfare throughout the country. Ibrahim Bek was well informed about Soviet moves because of his many sympathizers in the Soviet government apparatus. His money and arms came from Afghanistan from the Emir, and reportedly from the British.[25]

The Soviet administration in Central Asia was reorganized with the adoption of the first Soviet federal constitution in 1924. The reorganization became known as national delimitation (*natsional 'noe razmezhevanie*). The People's Republics of Khorezm and Bukhara were first transformed into Soviet Socialist Republics in order to become eligible to join the USSR, and were then divided, together with Turkestan, into new federal units. The Kazakh and Kirgiz areas remained in the RSFSR as autonomous units; two new union republics, Turkmenia and Uzbekistan, were formed. The Tadzhik areas were given autonomous status within the latter as the Tadzhik Autonomous Soviet Socialist Republic (TASSR). This included parts of the Samarkand and Fergana provinces, all of eastern Bukhara and the Pamirs. In 1925 the Pamirs gained formal autonomy as the Gorno-Badakhshan Autonomous Oblast (GBAO).[26]

[24] Pipes, *Formation*, pp. 257–59.
[25] Briskin, *Strana Tadzhikov*, pp. 40–42. All Soviet sources insist that the Basmachi received British assistance via Afghanistan.
[26] Discussion in this section was based on: AN TSSR, *Istoriia*, III, Book 1, 157–58; *Bol'shaia Sovetskaia Entsiklopediia* (1st ed., 1946, Tadzhik SSR), Vol. LIII, henceforth referred to as *BSE, 1st ed., LIII;* and *BSE, 2d ed., XLI;* Merle Fainsod, *How Russia is Ruled*, rev. ed. (Cambridge, Mass.: Harvard University Press, 1964), pp. 359–70; TsK KPT, *Tadzhikskaia SSR za 25 let, passim;* and *KT* (Stalinabad), February 28, 1947, p. 1.

Ostensibly, the process of delimitation was designed to grant political autonomy to major ethnic groups, in line with the stated policy of the right to national self-determination; the degree of formal autonomy granted depended on the degree of political development. Other reasons for the delimitation, equally important if not explicitly stated, were the Russian desires to facilitate the All-Union (federal) control and to keep local nationalities apart by the application of the "divide and rule" policy. The new system established a uniform territorial-administrative structure that allowed centralized control from Moscow. It attempted to undermine the Pan-Islamic unity of Central Asia and to prevent transformation of the nascent Pan-Turkism of the local leaders into politically potent anti-Russian movements.

The policies of granting temporary concessions to the Moslem way of life and of new national delimitation were accompanied by a strong emphasis on the education of local cadres and the rapid entry of native workers into the Party and government apparatus (*korenizatsiia*). The general encouragement by the NEP of trade and small private enterprise strengthened the Russian entrepreneurial elements in Turkestan; among the Moslems much power was restored to the traditional village power hierarchy of mullahs and bai, and traders and craftsmen prospered.[27]

The concern with education and promotion of native cadres was genuine. Stalin, as well as other Soviet spokesmen, repeatedly emphasized the need to have local people in the Party and in the soviets in order to "bring the apparatus . . . close to the people.":

> If it is the task of our party to convince the masses that the Soviet system is their own system, then this can only be done when that system is understood by them. . . . Local people who are familiar with the language and customs of the population must be appointed to the management of state institutions in the Republics.[28]

Nevertheless, a general shortage of qualified local cadres led to

[27] Park, *Bolshevism in Turkestan,* pp. 155–204.
[28] Joseph Stalin, "Report at the Fourth Conference of the Central Committee with Nationalities Officials, June 10, 1923, on the Practical Measures for Applying the Resolution on the National Question of the Twelfth Party Congress," quoted in Rudolf Schlesinger, ed., *The Nationalities Problem and Soviet Administration. Selected Readings on the Development of Soviet Nationalities Policies* (London: Routledge & Kegan Paul, 1956), p. 65.

the influx of European (primarily Russian) officials. As Stalin made clear in 1923 when he answered criticism by minority Communist leaders directed at the Russian members' hegemony in the republican hierarchical apparatus, "time does not stand still, you must build and run the administration, while cadres of local people are maturing slowly." Still, he admitted, the presence of Russian Communists in the administration of the borderlands was an irritant in relationships with local native leaders:

> I know that in the Republics and provinces a proportion of leading officials, mainly Russians, sometimes stands in the way of officials from the local people, impedes their promotion to certain posts, and refuses to give them a chance.[29]

The special role of the Russians was nevertheless justified by the fact that local Communists generally proved ideologically unreliable; thus the Russian influx continued. The first of a series of purges swept the Turkestani and Bukhara Party organizations in 1920. Gafurov relates that after the purge, the Central Committee of the Russian Communist Party sent "leading cadres" from Russia to "heal" the two Party organizations; in one year, between the summers of 1920 and 1921, more than 400 Russian Communists experienced in the work of Party and government apparatus arrived in Central Asia.[30] Some of them—probably a small number in keeping with the importance of the Tadzhik area as compared with others in Central Asia—were put to work with the Tadzhiks.

Tadzhik areas were included in the general korenizatsiia policy gradually, as they came under Soviet authority, but there were

[29] *Ibid.*, p. 74. In his theses on the national question delivered to the Twelfth Congress, Stalin also complained of "an arrogant, negligent and soullessly bureaucratic attitude on the part of Russian Soviet officials towards the needs and requirements of the national republics," Joseph Stalin, *Marxism and the National Question. Selected Writings and Speeches* (New York: International Publishers, 1942), p. 131. The contemptuous Russian attitude toward the Tadzhiks is illustrated by a conversation Egon Kisch had with a Russian buyer for a leather trust who was going to Tadzhikistan; he said that the Uzbeks and Tadzhiks were "unfit to govern themselves." Egon Erwin Kisch, *Changing Asia,* trans. Rita Reil (New York: Alfred A. Knopf, 1935), p. 36. In 1935 an official source complained of the "scant regard" with which republican government organs treated local national cadres, quoted in Schlesinger, *The Nationalities Problem,* p. 230.

[30] Gafurov, "V. I. Lenin i pobeda," p. 85.

even fewer Tadzhiks who met the minimal requirements for work in the agencies of power than there were Uzbeks. Even after the establishment of the Tadzhik ASSR the government consisted only of revolutionary committees wherever such committees were able to establish themselves effectively. In February, 1925, the Revolutionary Committee (*Revkom*) of the Tadzhik ASSR was superimposed on the network of the local committees to coordinate their work until pacification, and it gradually formed a central state administration. It maintained itself precariously in conditions of civil war and suffered from an "acute shortage" of native cadres.[31]

In early 1925 the Basmachi again spread through the Tadzhik countryside. Fifty-seven bands with approximately 1,370 warriors found support and refuge in the kishlaks and were able to infiltrate even the agencies of the soviet government:

> The apparatus of the soviets was infected by alien, counter-revolutionary elements; in its substance it was really the apparatus of the Basmachi. There were cases when leaders of lower soviets went over to Ibrahim Beg. . . . Basmachi sympathizers in soviets and Revkoms twisted the meaning of every measure passed by the central government. . . .[32]

The continuous war brought depopulation and economic destruction. Cultivated land decreased to less than one-half of the pre-1920 level, and about 26 per cent of the population of eastern Bukhara, mostly from the border regions, emigrated to Afghanistan.[33]

In energetic action the Revkom combined economic concessions and propaganda with stepped-up military action, a purge, and harsh punitive measures directed at Basmachi supporters. Local units, the so-called Red Sticks (*Krasnopalochniki*), were organized to help the Red Army fight the Basmachi. The new policy brought results. By October, 1925, the Basmachi warriors were reduced by two-thirds and as their prestige declined, that of the government increased. Many people lost faith in an eventual Basmachi victory and withheld their support. After the government's promise of

[31] AN TSSR, *Istoriia*, III, Book 1, 159–60.
[32] Briskin, *Strana Tadzhikov*, pp. 43–44.
[33] *Ibid.*, p. 42; and AN TSSR, *Istoriia*, III, Book 1, 159.

amnesty, defections multiplied, not only among the warriors but also among the leaders.[34]

Basmachi bands were still strong, however, and a poor harvest and the resulting famine favored the rebels. A new Basmachi offensive began in the fall of 1925 with the slogan: "Hunger is the punishment of God for cooperation with Bolsheviks." The government retaliated with an energetic campaign of repression. By the end of 1926 the movement in central and southern Tadzhikistan was liquidated, even though in the Pamirs Soviet power remained extremely tenuous. Ibrahim Bek fled to Afghanistan.[35]

In addition to military measures, the government used both the carrot and the stick techniques. It extended massive economic assistance to the dekhkans, including the distribution of food and products and an exemption from taxes. Pressure was exerted to organize the peasants into agricultural associations, while a simultaneous massive political purge was carried out in the lower soviet apparatus, the "purge of 50 per cent." Vacancies were filled by representatives of the "poor masses." A regular local militia was established. In addition, an extensive campaign of propaganda and indoctrination was extended to remote areas by Communist agitators.[36]

When pacification was successfully completed, on August 14, 1926, the Revkom of the Tadzhik ASSR announced the end of the civil war and called for elections of deputies to local soviets, who were later to meet as the first Congress of the Soviets in Tadzhikistan. The elections took place in September and October, 1926; the electoral campaign was a struggle between Soviet agitators and the still powerful Basmachi supporters who apparently used all types of pressure to ensure the election of their own candidates. Electoral results favored government candidates; in areas where "alien elements" gained control, the Soviets were dissolved and new elections were called by local revkoms. The newly elected soviets, composed primarily of the so-called middle and poor elements, replaced the revkoms as organs of local government.[37]

[34] Briskin, *Strana Tadzhikov*, pp. 45–47.

[35] *Ibid.*, pp. 47–48; and Kisch, *Changing Asia*, pp. 170–71.

[36] Briskin, *Strana Tadzhikov*, pp. 48–50.

[37] *KT*, February 28, 1947, p. 4; AN TSSR, *Istoriia*, III, Book 1, 174–75; Briskin *Strana Tadzhikov*, pp. 50–52.

The founding congress (*Andzhuman*), of the soviets of Tadzhikistan met on December 1, 1926, and formally declared the establishment of the Tadzhik Autonomous Republic. It formed the
Central Executive Committee with a Presidium and a Council of
People's Commissars, and entrusted to the committee the task of
preparing a new constitution. A series of decrees was designed to
restructure the social and economic base of the society: land, water
resources, and forests were nationalized; women were declared free
of the restrictions imposed on them by the Shariat; and the principle of universal education was proclaimed.[38] The congress
marked the beginning of the Soviet era in Tadzhikistan; the battle
for the implementation of the new system filled the following
decade.

It took six years of bitter fighting before the Soviet rule was
finally established in Tadzhikistan and resistance destroyed. The
attitudes formed during the period were to weigh heavily on
future relations between the Russians and the Tadzhiks. Tadzhik
support for the Basmachi resulted from several factors. No initial
hostility toward the Russians had existed in the country, but the
Red Army's excesses in the 1920–21 campaign had earned it
popular hatred which was later transferred to the Russians at large
and to the new Soviet government. By an official admission it was
the Red Army (composed almost exclusively of Russians and other
Slavs), and not the few local Communist supporters, who had
"played the major role in the liquidation of the Basmachi bands"
and "conducted an unwavering struggle against the counter-revolu-
tion and foreign intervention."[39] An eyewitness who was an undercover agent of the Cheka in Bukhara at the time claims that the
strong support the local population gave to Enver Pasha and to
the Basmachi was due to their hatred of the Red Army and its
"depredations" rather than to any love they had for the escaped
Emir or for Enver.[40]

The Bolshevik attack on religion and on the traditional mode
of life was another powerful factor in the resistance. Resentment

---

[38] AN TSSR, *Istoriaa*, III, Book 1, 176–77.

[39] *Ibid.*, p. 170.

[40] Georges Agabekov, *OGPU: The Russian Secret Terror*, trans. Henry W. Bunn
(New York: Brentano's, 1931), pp. 23–24.

of Russian behavior and widespread devotion to Islam made it easy for the representatives of the *ancien régime* and members of the kishlak power structure to rally the people, using religious slogans stressing the Soviet menace to Islam and local traditions. They particularly emphasized the threat to the traditional status of women and to private land ownership.[41]

An official Tadzhik source attributes the "colossal difficulties" of the pacification and the lengthy local resistance to the "political backwardness" of the masses who "did not comprehend the beneficial nature of the Soviet power" and were "slaves of religious fanaticism." V. V. Kuibyshev is quoted as saying that at the time "among Tadzhiks and Uzbeks only isolated individuals were communists-revolutionaries."[42]

A review of available historical evidence makes it clear, therefore, that the Soviet rule in Tadzhikistan was established by Russian military action largely against the wishes of the local population, which resisted it for a number of years, and that civilian authorities formed in the aftermath of military victory were dominated by Russian elements and faced a population still largely hostile to the new regime.

Transformation and Adjustment

The exceptional economic and cultural backwardness of Tadzhikistan made the task of the new soviet government truly formidable. Even though the Basmachi were militarily defeated, the background and attitudes which had fostered and supported their movement remained. Five years of civil war had left destruction, desolation, and bitterness.

The first years after pacification were devoted to preparation for economic reform, to social transformation, and political indoctrination. The irrigation network had to be rebuilt, crafts and agricultural skills had to be restored, and industries had to be initiated. The solid Moslem anti-Soviet front of the kishlak had to be broken, the poor had to be alienated from the rich, the clergy had to be discredited, women had to be released from bondage, and children and adults had to be taught how to read.

[41] See *The Proclamation of Ibrahim Beg*, Appendix of this volume.
[42] AN TSSR, *Istoriia*, III, Book 1, 103.

The first schools for children and adults (*likbezy*) were opened in 1926–27, though there were virtually no buildings, textbooks, or teachers. The first Tadzhik newspaper was published in Dushambe in 1926. Preparations for economic and social reform were made in 1927. State assistance was made available to poor and middle peasants, and the first agricultural cooperatives were introduced. It proved impossible, however, to enforce the land and water nationalization decree, because both the economy and soviet power were too weak. Land ownership was still primarily in the hands of the bai. Numbering 6.6 per cent of all peasant households, they owned 31 per cent of irrigated land, 22 per cent of dry land, and 11.5 per cent of draft animals. Throughout Tadzhikistan, land cultivation was carried on by primitive methods with the wooden plow, wooden hoe, and sickle.[43]

A wide range of economic measures was aimed at facilitating the transition to collectivized agriculture. A graduated progressive agricultural tax victimized rich bai,[44] while special agricultural credits were made available to the poor peasants. Mosque lands and the lands that belonged to the Emir and his officials were distributed to landless peasants on government tenure. The new emphasis on cotton cultivation required settlement of the southern valleys. The forcible resettlement of mountain villages met with resistance, and many new "settlers" managed to return to their old homes. Some of the new cultivators came from Uzbekistan; others returned from Afghanistan, lured by promises of irrigated land and government assistance; returning officials and bai were prosecuted. It is reported that of the 43,000 households that fled with the Basmachi, some 7,000 had returned by 1930.[45] Fifty new kishlaks, most of them in southern Tadzhikistan, had been established through resettlement by the end of 1929. Membership in the various agricultural cooperatives (general and specialized) was made economically advantageous, and many households joined. In 1930

---

[43] B. A. Antonenko, "Podgotovka massovoi kollektivizatsii v Tadzhikistane," *Ocherki po istorii Tadzhikistana*, I (Stalinabad: Ministerstvo Prosveshcheniia Tadzhikskoi SSR, Stalinabadskii Gosudarstvennyi Pedagogicheskii Institut im. T. G. Shevchenko, 1957), 99–101.

[44] Kisch, in *Changing Asia*, p. 152, gives a definition of a bai as "anyone who has more than 300 sheep and more than 15 acres of cotton, and who employs labor."

[45] *Ibid.*, pp. 149–52; Briskin, *Strana Tadzhikov*, p. 60.

some 155,000 households, that is, 75 per cent of all peasant households in the Tadzhik ASSR, belonged to cooperatives.[46]

The Communist Party governed through the soviets and
through the newly established mass political organizations. Elections to the soviets were carried under an unwieldy if specific
slogan: "Struggle and victory of the farmhands and poor peasants
in alliance with the middle peasant, against the bai, and for the
full takeover of the lower Soviet apparatus!" The three favored
social categories won 83 per cent of the total number of deputies
in the 1927–28 elections, and 97 per cent in the 1928–29 elections.[47] A mass organization designed to foster collectivization was
the Union of Peasants (*Dzhuftgaron, Koshchi* in Uzbek). Although
the poor and landless peasants were the special target of the drive
for membership, the organization was comprised mainly of middle
peasants. Purged in May, 1929, the union was renamed the Union
of the Poor (*Ittifoki, Kambagalon* in Uzbek), but the change of
name did not make the organization any more successful, and
it was dissolved in 1931.

Training local cadres for Party and government work became
possible only after the establishment of the Tadzhik ASSR. Suit-
able local candidates were difficult to find because of the almost
total absence of local intelligentsia and "literate Soviet people."
In 1925 and 1926, however, short courses were offered by the Tadzhik commissariats of education, internal affairs, and health, and
some Tadzhiks were sent to school in Uzbekistan. Russian cadres
continued to arrive. In 1925–26, at the invitation of the Tadzhik
government, ". . . thousands of Party and Soviet workers, and
economic and cultural specialists, came from other Soviet republics. Most of them were Russians."[48] The Russian influx is illustrated by changes in the ethnic composition of the Tadzhik Party
organization. In 1925 Tadzhiks constituted 53 per cent of the total
membership, Russians and other Europeans 15 per cent, and Uzbeks 15 per cent; members of other nationalities made up the re-

[46] Antonenko, *Ocherki,* pp. 107–15. The *vakf* lands were not confiscated in the
Khodzhent region, then in the Uzbek SSR, until 1928.
[47] *Ibid.,* p. 116. The ratio was 70 per cent in 1926, according to Briskin, *Strana
Tadzhikov,* p. 50; AN TSSR, *Istoriia,* III, Book 1, 187–88.
[48] AN TSSR, *Istoriia,* III, Book 1, 163–64.

mainder of the total of 435.[49] By January, 1927, when the member-ship had doubled (to a total of 795), the percentage of Tadzhiks had decreased to 41, while that of the Europeans had risen to 28 per cent of the total; the Uzbeks' share remained unchanged.[50]

Although Russians were still few in numbers, they were most frequently found in the key posts of the Party's central apparatus, while government agencies were staffed largely by local people. Egon Kisch, a German Communist visiting Tadzhikistan in 1930, reported that all members of the Central Executive Committee were local peasants, and that none could understand Russian except the chairman, Nasratullah Maksum, "who could read printed Russian with difficulty"; all members of the Tadzhik Council of People's Commissars were Tadzhiks except the Commissar of Education, who was an Afghan revolutionary. The Party's First Secretary, Gusseinov, a Turko-Tatar, was not a local man.[51] The government apparatus at the lower level was from 75 to 90 per cent "nativized."[52] The prevalent illiteracy of the Tadzhik cadres made business difficult to conduct. Most Tadzhiks were illiterate in any language and did not speak Russian; Russians did not speak Tadzhik and could not read or write Arabic script. An NKVD source relates that "enemies of the people" such as mullahs, bai, and ex-officials of the emirate were used by local soviets as secretaries, sometimes with interesting results when instructions were intentionally misread and the contents of letters altered.[53]

The power of the "enemies of the people" in the local apparatus

[49] *Kommunisticheskaia Partiia Tadzhikistana v dokumentakh i tsifrakh (1924–1963 gg.); Sbornik dokumentov i materialov o roste i regulirovanii sostava partiinoi organizatsii*, ed. Kozachkovskii (Institut Istorii Partii, Dushanbe: "Irfon," 1965), p. 37. Henceforth referred to as *KPT v dokumentakh*. See Table 4–1. Except for the 1927 Party census this was the first official information published on the ethnic breakdown of the KPT.

[50] Vsesoiuznaia Kommunisticheskaia Partiia (bol'shevikov), Tsentral'nyi Komitet, Statisticheskii otdel. *Vsesoiuznaia partiinaia perepis' 1927 goda*, nos. 1–8 (Moscow: TsK VKP(b), 1927), no. 7, 56. Henceforth referred to as VKP(b) *Perepis' 1927 goda*. Russians accounted for 25 per cent, and Ukrainians for 3 per cent, of the European group.

[51] Kisch, *Changing Asia*, p. 91.

[52] Briskin, *Strana Tadzhikov*, p. 56.

[53] D. Fanian, *K istorii sovetskogo stroitel'stva v Tadzhikistane (1920–1929 gg.)*, Part I (Stalinabad: Arkhivnyi Otdel NKVD Tadzhikskoi SSR, 1940), p. 20.

is also confirmed by Kisch, who quotes a Russian functionary on the subject:

> In many districts the clergy and the kulaks have taken the Soviet apparatus into their own hands. Some of them have even joined the Party and exercise their corrupt reign of terror in the name of the Soviet, extorting registration fees, levying taxes, and cooly pocketing the money.[54]

The peasants submitted to this kind of abuse because, being illiterate, they were easily persuaded that the people's commissariat had decreed it. Local notables were also known to apply sanctions to, and even to kill, resistant peasants. After his visit to the interior, Kisch also reported that in the Pamirs the earliest soviets were composed of former officials of the Emir, who were ousted only after 1929.[55]

The government's political and economic measures met resistance, which centered around the so-called counter-revolutionary bourgeois nationalist elements; in retrospect, the phrase seems to apply not only to the representatives of the *ancien régime* but also to Tadzhik and Uzbek Party members and officials who resented and tried to modify the ruthless implementation of policies conceived in and directed by Moscow. Among those critical of Russian leadership were the Uzbek Commnists Khodzhaev and Ikramov, who at the time supervised the Tadzhik Party and were models for and patrons of many of its leaders. Both are quoted as saying that only a change of a signboard differentiated Tsarist Turkestan from Soviet Turkestan, as both were run by the Russians.[56] Characteristically, the objection was widespread among the local cadres. At a Samarkand Party meeting held in the late 1920's to discuss counter-revolutionary activities, the following note was handed to the speaker:

> Our Uzbekization proceeds in such a way that Uzbeks sit at the head of the institutions, and Uzbeks are the coachmen: some are

[54] Kisch, *Changing Asia*, pp. 36–37.
[55] *Ibid.*, p. 171.
[56] The citation comes from Stalin, who criticized the two leaders in 1923; Stalin, *Marxism and the National Question*, p. 166. Khodzhaev and Ikramov were among the victims of the 1938 purge of rightists and nationalist deviationists, along with many of their protegees in the Tadzhik Communist Party—see below p. 41.

riding, some are driving, but the work is directed by the Russians. Is this Uzbekization? Is this not (rather) colonization by the Russians? [57]

The same question might well have been asked by Tadzhik Communists in the same period and in the following one.

By 1929 it was decided in Moscow that Tadzhikistan had advanced enough on the "road to socialism" to become a union republic. On June 22, 1929, the Presidium of the Central Executive Committee of the USSR adopted a decree transforming the Tadzhik ASSR into a union republic. A third special Congress of the Soviets of Tadzhikistan met, and on October 16 of that year it adopted a declaration approving the change.[58] The Khodzhent region of Uzbekistan was added to the new republic. The official reason given was that its population was primarily Tadzhik, but the economic importance of this piece of Fergana Valley to the well-being of the new republic was probably the decisive reason; without it, Tadzhikistan could not have met the necessary conditions for becoming a union republic. The change of status emancipated the Tadzhik Party from Uzbek supervision. By a November 25, 1929, decision of the Politbureau of the All-Union Party, the Tadzhik regional Party organization within the Uzbek Party was transformed into the republican Tadzhik Communist Party (KPT), directly subordinated to the All-Union Central Committee.[59]

Collectivization, which was instituted experimentally in 1927–29,[60] triggered another attempt by the Basmachi to renew the civil war. The ex-Emir is reported to have made plans for an armed invasion and appealed to the population to overthrow the Communist government. In April, 1929, Fuzail Maksum, former Bek of Karategin, crossed the border from Afghanistan and occupied his old domain. The pro-Soviet elements were massacred in Kalai-Khumb, Tavil-Dara, Khait, and Garm, but airlifted Red troops

[57] P. Rysakov, "The Practice of Chauvinism and Local Nationalism," *Revoliutsiia i Natsional'nosti*, no. 8 (1930), quoted in Schlesinger, *The Nationalities Problem*, p. 177.

[58] AN TSSR, *Istoriia*, III, Book 1, 216–17.

[59] *KPT v dokumentakh*, p. 36.

[60] Antonenko, *Ocherki*, p. 122. By October 1, 1929, Tadzhikistan had 209 kolkhozes with 2,888 households, and 5 state farms.

defeated Maksum and chased him back across the border. Another
and final attempt was made in April, 1931, by Ibrahim Beg, who
crossed the border with 2,000 fighters. This time, however, he
found little support among the people, even among his own Lokai
tribe. Tired of fighting in a hopeless cause, they had come to
terms with the new regime. Kisch, who was in the area at the time,
has written that many of Ibrahim's ex-followers who had become
Soviet officials and Party members turned out to hunt him. Ibrahim issued a proclamation which stressed the same old religious
grievances, but it seems to have evoked little response. He was
captured on June 23, 1931, and was subsequently executed.[61] With
the capture of its leader, the Basmachi movement ended. Exiled
writers indicated that the resistance to collectivization occasionally
assumed proportions of open rebellion, and that rebel units continued to operate in Central Asia until 1935.[62]

Mass collectivization in Tadzhikistan began in the early 1930's
and was basically completed by 1934. By 1940 the country's economy had been transformed from one of primitive subsistence agriculture to one of specialized agriculture with a single technical
crop, cotton, and grain, fruits, and livestock products as subsidi-
ary commodities. Economically the two major features introduced by collectivization, conversion to cotton and irrigation,
complemented each other.

Mass resistance to collectivization was as determined in Tadzhikistan as it was in other parts of Russia. The bitterness of the
struggle and the use of force on both sides is reflected in Soviet
sources. Peasants were herded into kolkhozes by force (a method
which, after it had done the job, was condemned as a deviation
from the Party line); "middle peasants" were classified as bai
and treated accordingly, that is, they were shot; and the 1926
decree on the nationalization of land and water rights was at last
ruthlessly enforced. In March, 1930, one-half year after the beginning of the mass collectivization drive, there were 418 kolkhozes

    [61] Kisch, *Changing Asia*, pp. 127, 134. See Appendix of this volume.
    [62] Devlet, "Natsional'no-osvoboditel'naia bor'ba v Turkestane," *Türkeli,* no. 1
(September, 1951), 13–32; and Rachman, "The Anti-Bolshevik Struggle in Turkestan," *The Strength and Weakness of Red Russia,* Congress of Delegates of Independence Movements within the USSR, held in Edinburgh, June 12–14, 1950 (Edinburgh: Scottish League for European Freedom, 1950).

with 27,000 households, and 4 Motor Tractor Stations (MTS) in the TSSR. By December, 1933, 50 per cent of all agriculture had been collectivized, with MTS, greatly increased in numbers, playing the crucial role in the campaign. They served as propaganda and indoctrination centers; their members trained and distributed cadres, and later were instrumental in purging the kolkhozes of "alien elements" and liquidating the bai. The personnel of the newly established state farms assisted the MTS cadres in these tasks.[63]

Many members of the Tadzhik Party and government apparatus, especially leaders of local origin, were opposed to collectivization and tried to slow it down and to lessen its impact on the people. Soviet sources complain of "the furious resistance on the part of bourgeois nationalists." It is said that the collectivization campaign was carried out

> . . . in the bitter struggle with the enemies, who deliberately damaged the development of the national economy by their wrecking activities, who damaged irrigation networks, killed off the livestock, and distributed the best lands to kulak elements. They deliberately placed followers of bai and clergy in kolkhozes, made up fictitious kolkhozes the economy of which actually remained in private hands, and at the same time allowed the economically and organizationally strong kolkhozes to fall apart.[64]

The struggle was reflected in the internal Party and Soviet apparatus, which was, by the Soviet's own admission, infected by "alien elements." There was a purge of the Soviet organizations in 1927–28, and a purge of the Party apparatus in 1929–30.[65] The first wholesale purge of "bourgeois nationalists" was carried out by the Second Congress of the Tadzhik Communist Party in January, 1934, at the behest of the Central Committee of the All-Union Communist Party (VKP[b]), which, as quoted in a 1964 Tadzhik source: ". . . helped the Tadzhik Communists to unmask in the Party and government apparatus a group of backsliders into nationalist deviation, who, with their conciliatory attitude

[63] TsK KPT, *Tadzhikskaia SSR za 25 let,* pp. 59, 61, 64, 66.
[64] *Ibid.,* p. 53.
[65] AN TSSR, *Istoriia,* III, Book 1, 181, 254.

toward the bai and other anti-Soviet elements, favored the awakening of bourgeois-nationalist tendencies and thus were hostile to the national policy of the Party." [66]

Many in this group of national deviationists "occupied important positions in the Party and the government." They "violated the principles of Leninist nationality policy, nourished bourgeois-nationalist tendencies, and caused major harm to the economic and cultural construction in Tadzhikistan." [67] The group included the two top leaders of the Tadzhik government, both of them ethnic Tadzhiks: Nasratullah Maksum, chairman of the Central Executive Committee (TsIK of the TSSR), and Abdurakhim Khodzhibaev, chairman of the Council of People's Commissars.[68] Maksum apparently advocated getting rid of the Russians in the government apparatus, while Khodzhibaev wanted to create a "Greater Tadzhikistan" at the expense of "sister" republics. Both denied the need for a class struggle in Tadzhikistan.[69] In their resistance to centrally-determined policies, the political leaders were joined by the new group of Tadzhik and Uzbek writers who resented the newly introduced cultural Russification.

The expulsion of Maksum and Khodzhibaev from their posts was followed by an extensive purge of both Party and government. The extent of the purge became fully known only after the death of Stalin. Between January 1, 1933, and January 1, 1935, the membership of the KPT fell from 14,329 to 4,791, a loss of almost 10,000 members! [70] The Party virtually ceased to exist in many localities. This situation is now considered to have damaged the Soviet cause and is blamed on the excesses of Stalin's "cult of personality." [71] It is significant that even though the sources from the

---

[66] *Ibid.*, p. 280.
[67] *Ibid.*, p. 328.
[68] TsK KPT, *Tadzhikskaia SSR za 25 let*, p. 68.
[69] Walter Kolarz, *Russia and Her Colonies* (New York: Praeger, 1952), pp. 289–90. The denial of the validity of the Marxist concept of class struggle in "feudal" Tadzhikistan is comparable to the similar argument advanced now by Marxist-oriented African leaders in respect to their own economically underdeveloped countries which, like Tadzhikistan, have neither a middle class nor a proletariat.
[70] See Table 4–1.
[71] AN TSSR, *Istoriia*, III, Book 1, 329–30; see also *KPT v dokumentakh*, p. 67.

1960's quoted here and above deplore the excesses committed, they do not question the purge itself, and they sharply condemn the "bourgeois nationalist deviation" of the purged leaders. Purged officials and functionaries were replaced by newly arrived Russian Party activists. Put in the position of local leadership in the soviets, the Russians "led the struggle with recalcitrant peasants and local officials" in the battle for collectivization.[72]

The second team of Tadzhik Communist leaders installed in office after the 1933–34 purge were also apparently prone to the vice of bourgeois nationalism. Their deviationism manifested itself in a desire for greater autonomy and in support for the embattled intellectuals. They were swept away in the new purge of September, 1937, a part of the Great Purge of the Right Opposition of Bukharin and Rykov. The Tadzhik purge was closely connected with that of the Uzbek leaders Akmal Ikramov and Faizulla Khodzhaev. The Tadzhik victims included the chairman of the Presidium of the Supreme Soviet, Shotemor; the chairman of the Council of People's Commissars, Rakhimbaev; members of the Council, and three secretaries of the Central Committee in addition to many lesser lights.[73] The purge also included numerous Russians. Unlike the victims of the 1933–34 purge, the leaders who fell in 1937–38 were gradually rehabilitated in the 1960's: Akmal Ikramov among the Uzbeks,[74] and Shotemor, Rakhimbaev, various Central Committee secretaries, and many others among the leaders of the Tadzhik Party and government.[75] At present they are represented as good Party workers who suffered unjustly because of the "cult of personality." The two purges virtually denuded the Tadzhik Party and government of the local cadres, and the republic was in effect placed under direct Russian tutelage. The new first secretary of the Tadzhik Party, Dmitri Zakharovich Protopopov, appointed in October, 1937, was a Russian from Voronezh

[72] TsK KPT, *Tadzhikskaia SSR za 25 let*, p. 59.
[73] Kolarz, *Russia and Her Colonies*, pp. 289–90; and Zbigniew K. Brzezinski, *The Permanent Purge: Politics of Soviet Totalitarianism* (Cambridge, Mass.: Harvard University Press, 1956), p. 81.
[74] *Pravda* (Moscow), April 9, 1964, p. 4.
[75] *KPT v dokumentakh*, p. 68.

and a professional Chekist,[76] and the apparatus was staffed by Russians at lower levels in a return to a frankly colonial pattern.

The struggle for collectivization, and the proven ideological "unreliability" of local cadres, placed the policy of *korenizatsiia* (nativization) in different perspective and introduced far-reaching changes. When it was initiated in the early 1920's, korenizatsiia had had two major objectives in the borderlands: to secure an efficient administration loyal to Moscow and to recruit natives into the Party as a means of consolidating and spreading the revolution. However, because Moscow would not allow modification of centrally determined policies in order to accommodate local preferences, local needs were sacrificed in favor of central requirements, and the need for a loyal and efficient administration came to the forefront in the policy toward cadres. While native recruitment continued, placement of local nationals was affected by the need to maintain Russians in the position of leadership. Alien to the area, the Russians were not affected by local pressures and were thus more reliable in the eyes of the central leadership. The effort to educate local cadres continued in the 1930's, but the emphasis was shifted from educating leaders to educating specialists and technicians, and from reeducating the older intelligentsia to educating young people.[77]

The new policy concerning national cadres was based on the assumptions that the old native intelligentsia was disloyal and that a new one should be trained primarily as technicians rather than intellectuals:

> The bulk of the old national intelligentsia . . . is alien to the Soviet regime (and) . . . the vast proportion of its members are clearly unfit to accomplish the tasks inherent in socialist reconstruction and in the intensified class struggle. . . . What we have to do now is to train not an intelligentsia in general but, firstly, our own cadres of the proletarian intelligentsia from the various nationalities of the USSR, and, secondly, such cadres as would, above all, be the exponents of definite technical and industrial knowledge.[78]

[76] See Chap. 5 for further discussion of Mr. Protopopov.

[77] The categories emphasized were: teachers, artists, medical workers, agronomists, mechanics, irrigation technicians, agricultural technicians, and chairmen of local soviets (TsK KPT, *Tadzhikskaia SSR za 25 let,* p. 97).

[78] K. Tobolov, "On National Cadres," *Sovetskoe Stroitel'stvo,* nos. 7–8 (1933), quoted in Schlesinger, *The Nationalities Problem,* pp. 214–15, 218.

In the 1920's the presence of the Russian cadres in the border-lands was regarded as temporary, but in the 1930's the continuous political leadership of the central cadres—consisting mostly of ethnic Russians—came to be regarded as a permanent feature.

Russians continued to flow into Central Asia. Some, like the town workers of Moscow, Ivanovo-Voznesensk, and other Russian cities, came voluntarily to help with collectivization; others brought the skills necessary for modernization in exchange for economic gain and prestige. The 1930's also witnessed an arrival of political exiles demoted to provincial Party, government, and managerial posts, and political prisoners deported for forced labor. Walter Kolarz reports that between 1926 and 1939 1,700,000 Russian settlers came to Central Asia from European Russia, most of them settling in cities and new industrial centers.[79] Fewer Russians migrated to Tadzhikistan than to any of its sister republics, but the influx was sufficient to bring them from less than 1 per cent of the total population in 1926 to 9 per cent in 1939. By the end of the 1930's ethnic Russians constituted one-fourth of the membership of the Tadzhik Communist Party.[80]

After collectivization was completed, other aspects of the "building of socialism" were stressed. Bases for local industry were established in the late 1930's, especially in the construction material and cotton processing industries. The reported rate of industrial growth was fantastic, but because the base had been almost non-existent, the development in absolute terms was modest.

The new "Stalin" constitution was adopted by the USSR in 1936, and union republics followed suit, changing their constitutions accordingly. The Tadzhik SSR adopted a new constitution on March 1, 1937, at the fourth special session of the Congress of the Soviets. Public information media, particularly the press, developed at a great rate, as did the network of new schools. The government also began to enforce measures designed to improve the position of women. The movement toward better education and female emancipation elicited the strongest popular resistance, backed by the Moslem clergy. Many new schools were burned and teachers were murdered. Most women who had removed the veil

[79] Kolarz, *Russia and Her Colonies,* p. 14.
[80] See Tables 2–1 and 4–1.

were ostracized; some were murdered by their own families, anxious to erase the shame.[81] Once introduced, however, social change began to leave its mark on society.

The literacy rate improved rapidly, though probably not as fast as the official statistics indicated. (The 1939 census gave the Tadzhik literacy rate as 71.7 per cent, an optimistic figure.) [82] In 1935, 38 per cent of the Tadzhik chairmen of village soviets were described as "almost illiterate." [83] In 1938, 65 per cent of the members of the Tadzhik Communist Party had had only a primary education, or were described as being "literate but without primary education"; the latter category constituted almost 30 per cent of the total membership.[84] Among the common people literacy must have been much lower.

The script in which the Tadzhik language was written was changed twice in the prewar period. Similar changes took place in other Central Asian republics. In 1929 the Arabic alphabet was replaced by the Latin alphabet; in 1940 the Latin script was replaced by Cyrillic script. The first change was justified on the grounds of simplification in the interest of literacy. It also proved extremely useful to the Russians in censoring the printed word. The second change facilitated the influence of the Russian language and made it easier to teach local children Russian—a compulsory subject after 1938. The cultural offensive in the thirties was directed at creating a "Tadzhik socialist culture." Great emphasis was placed on the Tadzhik cultural heritage, but only on selective aspects, while at the same time Russian cultural models were introduced for compulsory emulation, and political indoctrination supplied the "correct interpretation." The offensive met determined resistance on the part of Tadzhik intellectuals of the old Jadidist school and created an atmosphere described later as the

---

[81] TsK KPT, *Tadzhikskaia SSR za 25 let,* pp. 75–99; Boris Pil'nyak (B. Wogau), *Tadzhikistan: ocherki, materialy k romanu* (Leningrad: Izd. Pisatelei, 1931), *passim;* and *KT,* 1945–55, *passim.*

[82] Frank Lorimer, *The Population of the Soviet Union* (Geneva: League of Nations, 1946), p. 199.

[83] Telikhanov, "On National Cadres," *Revoliutsiia i Natsional'nosti,"* no. 12 (1935), quoted in Schlesinger, *The Nationalities Problem,* p. 229.

[84] *KPT v dokumentakh,* p. 99.

"cultural struggle with bourgeois nationalists." The "nationalist" intellectuals disappeared in the purges.

The German invasion of Russia in 1941, and the Soviet entry into the war, increased the Russification of Central Asia. In Tadzhikistan the influx of Russian Party functionaries, security agents, and military personnel increased and was augmented by the flow of war refugees and deportees. Since the days of the civil war, because it is a border republic, Tadzhikistan had been heavily garrisoned by the Red Army, the Internal Commissariat's Border Guards, and the State Security Services. The strength of the latter two increased with the withdrawal of the regular troops to the front, especially because the republic became a place for deportation of "politically unreliable" elements.

During the war the emphasis on creating a "socialist Tadzhik culture" was reduced as intensely patriotic pro-Russian and anti-German propaganda increased. In local terms, the cause of the Soviet Union was linked to that of the traditional Tadzhik resistance to invaders, while Germans were compared to historical conquerors from Alexander the Great to Genghis Khan. Economic pressure was applied for an increased production of food and other products to meet the needs of the front. Numerous campaigns were organized to borrow money in war loans and to collect and send food and clothing to the front and to the refugee population in the hinterland. Some firms from European Russia with their work forces were resettled in Tadzhikistan. Tadzhik men were mobilized for the army and labor brigades, and women were forced to take their places at work.

Like members of other Soviet nationalities, Tadzhik army draftees were dispersed throughout regular units. This dispersal prevented the possible defection of entire units. Service with the Russians provided the soldiers with an excellent opportunity for learning the Russian language and new attitudes. In order to mobilize popular support for the war, the Tadzhiks at home were given guardianship (shefstvo) of certain Red Army units which thus became objects of their special care. There was a tank column named Tadzhik Kolkhoznik and an air squadron called Soviet Tadzhikistan. There was also a cavalry division, apparently formed in Tadzhikistan, famous for its exploits in the Caucasus. The units above appear to have been predominantly Russian in their membership.[85] More than 50,000 of the soldiers from Tadzhikistan who partici- pated in the war received decorations, and 30 became Heroes of the Soviet Union.[86] Some 40,000 Tadzhik Komsomols were re- ported to have served in the armed forces during the war. There was substantial loss in Komsomol membership between 1940 and 1946. Since there was no purge in this period, the data on the length of membership of members in 1946 indicate a very high rate of military casualties among them; more than 50 per cent dis- appeared.[87]

The postwar period in Tadzhikistan was officially designated the period of "struggle for Communism," with the emphasis placed on two major areas of endeavor, economic development and cultural sovietization. When the first crop of students from Soviet schools in Tadzhikistan came of age, the graduates began to fill the Party and government apparatus and to swell the ranks of intellectuals, while their Russian mentors again dropped back into less obtrusive, if no less important, positions. But, in contrast to the situation in the 1920's, the new Soviet-educated Asians found that the pattern had been set and that some positions were *de facto* reserved for the Russian representatives of the central apparatus. A massive effort was put into economic development, particularly in agriculture and its major crop, long-fiber cotton, which was of great importance to the whole Union. In the cultural field, mass education and mass indoctrination became the primary tasks, and the development of the Tadzhik Soviet culture was given renewed emphasis.

[85] TsK KPT, *Tadzhikskaia SSR za 25 let*, p. 127; Luknitsky, *Soviet Tadzhikistan*, p. 83; and *KT*, 1945–55, *passim*, especially the issues published on the anniversaries of World War II battles. War stories often related exploits of military units named for Tadzhikistan. The names of the officers and soldiers mentioned were mostly Slavic.

[86] Luknitsky, *Soviet Tadzhikistan*, p. 83; Aliev, *Uspekhi razvitiia*, p. 14.

[87] *KT*, December 25, 1946, p. 2. As disclosed by the Tadzhik Komsomol's First Secretary, the 1946 membership was 55,000, of which 50 per cent (i.e., some 27,000), were admitted after 1942. This means that only 27,000 of the 1946 members were also members in 1940. As it is known that Tadzhik Komsomol membership in 1940 was 65,000, 38,000 of them were no longer among the members in 1946. While reg- ular attrition in the ranks, routine purges, and transfer into the Party would account for a part of the loss, the decline is too high to have been so absorbed. The most likely explanation for it is the exceptionally high mortality (or captivity ?) rate among Tadzhik Komsomol members at the front.

THE NEW SETTING

The relatively short period of Soviet rule brought far-reaching changes in Tadzhikistan, transforming it from a feudal backwater into a modernizing polity. Tadzhikistan became part of the general dynamics of Soviet political and economic transformation, even if, as in the rest of Soviet Central Asia, the development indices lagged behind those of European Russia.

The Tadzhik population (2,500,000 in January, 1966) more than doubled under Soviet rule. Although the rate of natural increase in the republic was higher than the All-Union average,[88] the spectacular population growth was largely the result of immigration, and particularly affected the development of cities and industrialized areas: the urban population increased eightfold in the 1926–65 period. The rate of growth of the capital, Stalinabad,[89] equaled that of the Soviet industrial giants such as Karaganda and Magnitogorsk; in the forty years of Soviet rule its population increased by more than fifty-fold.[90] However, Tadzhikistan's urbanization lagged behind that of the rest of the Soviet Union; 65 per cent of the people lived in rural areas in the 1960's. Population distribution and density were extremely uneven. Almost 40 per cent of the people lived in the Leninabad oblast (the part of the Fergana Valley that was added to Tadzhikistan in 1929), whereas

[88] *TSSR. Nar. Khoz. 1957,* p. 343; and "Regional Economic Policy in the Soviet Union: The Case of Central Asia," *Economic Bulletin for Europe,* United Nations, no. 3 (November, 1957), 49–75. For the discussion of the trends in Central Asia as a whole see Anne Sheehy, "Population Trends in Central Asia and Kazakhstan 1959–1965," *Central Asian Review,* XIV, no. 4 (1966), 317–29.

[89] Originally Dushambe (Monday), the name of the capital was changed to Stalinabad. After 1956 it reverted to the original name in new spelling: Dushanbe. The name Stalinabad will be used in the book, however, because it was the official name of the city in the period discussed.

[90] A glimpse of the story behind the statistics is afforded by Boris Pil'nyak in his 1931 account of a trip to Tadzhikistan. Like the Klondike in the days of the Gold Rush, Stalinabad was a new frontier town. Its European camp was engulfing the original adobe kishlak, with people arriving from European Russia, India, Afghanistan, Caucasus, Turkestan, and the Tadzhik mountains. Peasants and dedicated "builders of socialism" mingled with speculators and aristocrats in hiding. There was a "larger than usual share of crooks," the "has-beens," "failures," imposters and "followers of long rubles" (pursuers of dishonest gain). A known crook was the head of the militia, and no eyebrows were raised over gunfights in bars. Pil'nyak, *Tadzhikistan,* pp. 99–101.

48   FORMATION OF SOVIET TADZHIKISTAN

Table 2-1. TSSR POPULATION (IN THOUSANDS)

Population	1926	1939	1956[a]	1965[b]
TSSR total	1,032[c]	1,485[c]	1,775	2,482
Oblasts and raions				
Leninabad oblast			598	
GBAO			62	
Raions under republican				
jurisdiction			992	
Urban total	106[d]	249[d]	558	865
Stalinabad city	5.6[e]	82.5[e]	123	312
Leninabad city			68	
Ura-Tyube city			23	
Kulyab city			21	
Kurgan-Tyube city			20	
Sovetabad			14	
Kanibadam			13	
Isfara			12	
Khorog			8	

[a] The figures for oblasts and Stalinabad city are as of April 1; city population figures, as of January 1. In 1953 the Stalinabad, Kulyab, and Garm oblasts were abolished and their raions were placed under republican jurisdiction (TSSR. *Nar. Khoz. 1957*), p. 8.

[b] Anne Sheehy, "Population Trends in Central Asia and Kazakhstan 1959–1965," *Central Asian Review*, XIV, no. 4 (1966), 317–29, 322–23, 325.

[c] Frank Lorimer, *The Population of the Soviet Union: History and Prospects* (Series of League of Nations Publications, II. Economic and Financial, 1946. II, A.3) (Geneva: League of Nations, 1946), p. 162. The 1926 total is calculated on the basis of the 1939 boundaries. Based on the 1926 boundaries, the TASSR population was 827,000 (*ibid.*, p. 64). Stalinabad city figure, p. 148.

[d] Tadzhikskaia SSR. Sovet Ministrov. Tsentral'noe Statisticheskoe Upravlenie. *Narodnoe Khoziaistvo Tadzhikskoi SSR v 1961 godu: Kratkii Statisticheskii Sbornik* (Dushanbe: Gosstatizdat, 1962), p. 10. Henceforth referred to as *TSSR. Nar. Khoz. 1961*.

[e] D. A. Chumichev, *Stalinabad, Stolitsa Tadzhikskoi SSR* (Moscow: Geografizdat, 1950), p. 23.

less than 4 per cent lived in the Pamirs. The Leninabad region also had five out of the nine Tadzhik cities and most of its industrial plants. (See Table 2-1.) Population density differed greatly from the empty wastes of the Pamirs to the cultivated valleys, crowded by more than 100 persons per square kilometer.[91]

The 1959 census gave the latest data on the ethnic composition of the population. The Tadzhiks formed the largest group, followed by the Uzbeks and the Russians as the second and third

[91] KPSS. Vysshaia Partiinaia Shkola. Kafedra ekonomicheskoi i politicheskoi geografii i zarubezhnykh gosudarstv. *Tadzhikskaia SSR: Uchebnyi Material* (Moscow: Gospolitizdat, 1953), p. 44.

Table 2-2. TSSR Population: Ethnic Breakdown (in thousands, rounded)

Ethnic Group	1926[a] Absolute Figure	1926[a] Percentage of Total	1929[b] Absolute Figure[e]	1929[b] Percentage of Total	1939[c] Absolute Figure[e]	1939[c] Percentage of Total	1959[d] Absolute Figure	1959[d] Percentage of Total
Tadzhiks	620.0[e]	75.0[f]	901.4	78.38	883.6	59.50	1,051.2	53.10
Uzbeks			206.3	17.94	353.6	23.80	454.4	23.00
Russians	5.6[g]	0.70			153.0[h]	10.30	262.6	13.30
Ukrainians							26.9	1.40
Kirgiz			22.8	1.98			25.6	1.30
Kazakh							12.6	0.60
Turkmen			16.4	1.43			7.1	0.40
Tatars							56.9	2.90
Germans							32.6	1.60
Jews							12.4	0.60
Mordva							6.7	0.30
Osetin							4.5	0.20
Bashkir							3.9	0.20
Armenians							2.9	0.10
Belorussians							2.8	0.10
Koreans							2.4	0.10
Others			3.1	0.27	95.0	6.40	14.4	0.8

[a] Within the 1926 boundaries.

[b] A. M. Briskin, *Strana Tadzhikov* (Moscow: Gosizdat, 1930), p. 12. The "Turkmen" category also includes Turks.

[c] *BSE*, 2d ed., XLI, p. 471.

[d] *TSSR. Nar. Khoz. 1961*, p. 15.

[e] Calculated on the basis of available figures.

[f] Lorimer, *Population of the Soviet Union*, p. 64.

[g] *Soviet Central Asia* (3 vols.; Subcontractor's Monograph, HRAF-49, American U.1) (New Haven: Human Relations Area Files, Inc., 1956), 1, p. 227.

[h] *Soviet Central Asia*, p. 227, gives the number of Great Russians in 1939 as 133,000 (9 per cent of the total population).

groups, respectively. There were many other smaller national groups (see Table 2-2). The Tadzhiks were the titular nationality in their republic. The ratio of Tadzhiks to outsiders in the total population was higher than that of any other titular nationality of the Central Asian republics. Nevertheless, their relative weight declined from 80 per cent of the total in 1929 to 50 per cent in 1959.

The Tadzhik group increased in absolute numbers during the years of Soviet rule. The steady growth curve was checked only by a temporary decline in 1929–39 caused by losses resulting from resistance to collectivization. Many Tadzhiks also lived in Uzbekistan, and outside the Soviet Union in Iran, Afghanistan, Jammu, Kashmir, and Chinese Turkestan. The total number of Tadzhiks, estimated to be 3,500,000 in 1939,[92] is now probably close to twice that figure.

The Uzbeks constituted almost one-quarter of the TSSR population in 1959. Between 1929 and 1959 their numbers increased in absolute terms, as well as in relative weight, primarily as the result of immigration. Some came to cultivate cotton, others came as teachers and specialists or members of the Party and government apparatus. The Russian share in the population increased from less than 1 per cent in 1926 to 13 per cent in 1959. Along with other immigrant groups from European Russia such as Ukrainians, Belorussians, Armenians, and Jews, they settled primarily in urban and industrial areas, and provided political and economic leadership and the much needed specialized manpower.

Among the remaining national groups in Tadzhikistan some were indigenous to the area and some were deportees. The Kirgiz, Kazakh, Turkmen, and a few Arabs and Afghans, had lived in the Tadzhik area before the revolution. In numbers and in relative weight the Turkmen group decreased sharply between 1929 and 1959. Kirgiz shepherds (a group estimated at 8,000 in 1939) inhabited the deserts of the eastern Pamirs and the northern Garm oblast (formerly Karategin).

Tatars and Volga Germans were deported to Tadzhikistan in World War II for alleged cooperation with the Nazis. Official statistics made available only in 1959 revealed that there were 57,000 Tatars and 33,000 Germans in Tadzhikistan. Some of the other small national groups listed may also have consisted of deportees.

A question arises of why there was a directed migration into the republic, when one considers that its natural rate of increase was higher, and its rate of economic growth lower, than the USSR average. A valid reason might have been the need to strenghen the non-Asian population in an area of traditional resistance to the Russians. The need to modernize the republic and to develop it economically were other reasons.

---

[92] *BSE, 1st ed., LIII*, 464; *BSE, 2d ed., XLI*, 405; and Geoffrey Wheeler, *The Modern History of Soviet Central Asia* (New York: Praeger, 1964), p. 153.

As Tadzhikistan entered the 1960's its people were still predominantly Asian in ethnic origin, despite heavy European immigration; all the European groups taken together accounted for less than 18 per cent of the total population. (See Table 2-2.)

The political structure of the Tadzhik Soviet Socialist Republic was like that of any other Union republic; the Pamir region had autonomous status as the GBAO. The structure was established by the 1937 Tadzhik constitution, a carbon copy of the 1936 USSR constitution, except for minor variations reflecting local peculiarities. The rights of women, for example, were specifically defined in the Tadzhik constitution, and the exercise of certain traditional Moslem rights in respect to women was made a constitutional offence punishable by law.[93]

In the period under review, major areas of industrial endeavor were under All-Union management, and the frequent changes in the organization of executive agencies followed similar changes at the All-Union level and in other republics. The division of power between the All-Union and republican authorities is best illustrated by the structure of the executive apparatus. The three major types of ministries corresponded to constitutionally delineated areas of jurisdiction. The All-Union ministries directly managed areas, primarily in the economic field, reserved for exclusive federal domain. Locally they operated their own agencies, attached but not subordinated to the local executive body. Areas under joint All-Union and republican jurisdiction were managed by Union-republic ministries. The Tadzhik ministries, which belonged in this category, were local counterparts of the Union-republican ministries in Moscow. Republican ministries, of which there were few, were formed to conduct affairs that were best managed locally; they had no counterpart at the federal level, but received detailed policy guidance from the All-Union authorities. Extensive administrative reorganization in Tadzhikistan in the postwar decade, especially in 1953, primarily affected the economic ministries and was a direct result of changes carried out at the

---

[93] Moslem practices singled out in this fashion included: "giving minors in marriage, bride purchase, resistance to women going to school, or engaging in agricultural, industrial, state or other social or political activities." Art. 109, *Constitution of the Tajik Soviet Socialist Republic of March 1, 1937*, as amended through May, 1948 (New York: American-Russian Institute, 1950).

federal level. Few, if any, changes were initiated locally, and then
only to reflect a dominant local need. At lower levels of territorial
administration, departments of executive committees of the local
soviets carried out tasks delegated to them by specific ministries.
The departments were formed selectively, on the basis of individual needs of a given area. Agencies of the Ministry of Internal
Affairs (MVD) and the Ministry of State Security (MGB) (both
Union-republic ministries), existed in all units of local territorial
administration.

Table 2-3. TSSR Territorial-Administrative Divisions

Units	1948	1957
Cities	7	14
Settlements	28	32
Urban raions	3	3
Oblasts	5	2
Rural raions	71	49
Kishlak soviets	469	256

Source: *TSSR. Nar. Khoz. 1957*, p. 7.
        KT, January 24, 1948, p. 1, and March 4, 1955, p. 1.

Changes in the territorial-administrative structure consisted in
the consolidation of rural soviets and raions and in the abolition of
all but two oblasts (Leninabad and GBAO) as superfluous links in
the chain of command (Table 2-3). Raions and cities of the abolished oblasts were placed directly under republican jurisdiction.
As a result of the reform, all the major cotton-growing raions except those in the Leninabad oblast came under direct republican
administration. The need for improved political control and the
need to improve economic indices were the decisive factors in the
reform. Gafurov, First Secretary of the Tadzhik Communist Party,
offered this explanation in his report to the Tenth Party Congress
in January, 1956:

> In the course of the period under review (1954–56) the Bureau of
> the Central Committee of the Party made all possible efforts to
> strengthen raion party organization. The Garm and Kulyab oblasts
> were abolished for this reason. The abolition enabled us to strengthen
> the leading cadres of the raions (by transferring oblast cadres into
> raion work) . . .[94]

[94] *KT*, January 27, 1956, p. 2.

Gafurov mentions only the Garm and Kulyab oblasts, abolished in August, 1955, but similar reasons probably motivated the abolition of the other three oblasts: Kurgan-Tyube and Ura-Tyube in January, 1947, and Stalinabad in April, 1951.

Elections to representative bodies took place frequently. Deputies to the local soviets (kishlak, settlement, raion, city, and oblast) were elected every two years; deputies to the Supreme Soviet of the Tadzhik SSR and to the Supreme Soviet of the USSR every four years. Electoral practice did not differ in any way from the general Soviet practice. Some 12,000 deputies (about one-half of them Party members) participated in the work of the local soviets; there were some 300 deputies in the Tadzhik Supreme Soviet. The republic sent 5 or 6 deputies to the Council of the Union, and 30 deputies to the Council of Nationalities of the USSR Supreme Soviet.

Economically, Tadzhikistan showed spectacular development in comparison with the pre-Soviet days, and with other Asian countries. On the eve of the revolution the economy of eastern Bukhara was based on primitive agriculture, but crafts such as silk-weaving, pottery, and leatherwork were highly developed, and there was a lively internal exchange of grain, livestock, animal and craft products, and textiles. The old economy was ruined by the civil war which accompanied the establishment of Soviet power, but slow recovery began after 1926, interrupted temporarily by the shock of collectivization. The new collectivized agriculture emphasized the growing of cotton, and no significant effort was made to industrialize until after World War II, when local manufacture began to fill the void left by the disappearance of handicraft work in the 1930's.[95] In view of the absence of any significant industrial plant before 1926, the high comparative percentage increases in industrial production in the period between the wars tended to obscure the small absolute increases. Significant industrial progress

[95] It is estimated that industrial workers in 1955 constituted a smaller part of the total population of Soviet Central Asia than had handicraft workers in the same area in 1897. In Russian Turkestan craftsmen constituted 5 per cent of the total population in 1897; it is assumed that a similar ratio would have been obtained in Bukhara. In 1955 industrial workers constituted 4 per cent of the total population of Soviet Central Asia (*Regional Economic Policy*, p. 52). In Tadzhikistan the ratio was lower: 3 per cent of the total population in 1956 (computed from *TSSR. Nar. Khoz. 1957*, p. 211).

was made only in the 1950's and 1960's, and even now the rate of
industrialization in Tadzhikistan, and elsewhere in Soviet Central
Asia, remains below that of the Soviet Union as a whole.[96]

The exchange between Soviet Central Asia and European Russia followed the typical colonial pattern, characterized by the export of raw materials and the import of capital goods and manu-
factures.

> Generally, . . . Central Asia can be characterized as a region equipped
> with a fairly broad range of consumer goods industries, producing
> for the local market but dependent on imports for nearly all capital
> goods, but with scarcely any export industries save crude processing
> such as cotton ginning, oil pressing and silk spinning. Apart from
> some exports of ores and mineral oil, the region is therefore com-
> pletely dependent on its agriculture, and above all on its cotton, to
> pay for necessary imports of cereals, timber, and industrial goods.[97]

Primary production played a dominant role in the Tadzhik
economy. In addition to cotton, the main crop, silk and wool were
also exported to European Russia. Except for fruits, food production was geared to home consumption. There was no local processing of coal and petroleum, and only crude dressing of polymetallic
ores. Capital goods and light manufactured products were imported from other parts of the USSR, though there was a steady
increase in consumer goods produced for the local market by the
developing light industry.

Regional economic development was extremely uneven. Leninabad oblast was the economic heartland of Tadzhikistan. In 1950
it accounted for 40 per cent of the industrial production of the republic, one-fourth of its cotton acreage, two-thirds of its production of silk cocoons, and two-thirds of all its orchards and vine-
yards. Leninabad city, with the largest textile mills, was the second
most important industrial center of the republic, after Stalinabad.
The oblast's other industrial centers were Kanibadam and Isfara,
the latter a center of coal, petroleum, and ore extraction, and also
famous for its fruits.[98] The area of the former Stalinabad and

---

[96] *Regional Economic Policy*, p. 54; Lydia Bott, "Recent Trends in the Economy
of Soviet Central Asia," *Central Asian Review*, XIII, no. 3 (1965), 199–204.

[97] *Regional Economic Policy*, p. 61.

[98] KPSS, *Tadzhikskaia SSR*, pp. 37–39; Luknitsky, *Soviet Tadzhikistan*, pp. 90–
106, 116, 125; and *BSE*, 2d ed., *XLI*, 482.

Kurgan-Tyube oblasts comprised the best cotton-growing regions of the republic—the Gissar Valley and the newly irrigated Vakhsh Valley. The great triumph of Soviet construction, the Vakhsh Valley project (*Vakhshstroi*), irrigated about 60,000 hectares of former desert. In the early 1950's the valley produced 40 per cent of all Tadzhik cotton, most of it the long fiber variety. Stalinabad, the capital city of the TSSR and its major industrial center, was located in the Gissar Valley, as was another industrial city, Or- dzhonikidzeabad. Kolkhozes in the foothills specialized in grain and livestock. The area also produced rice, oil-bearing flax, pea- nuts, sesame, fruits, and wine.[99] Livestock breeding was the main occupation of the mountains of Darvaz and Karategin (the former oblasts of Kulyab and Garm, respectively); the area also produced 25 per cent of the republic's output of silk cocoons. Grain, mostly wheat, was its major agricultural crop. The economy of the Pamirs was based on grain and fruit cultivation for domestic consump- tion, and on livestock breeding.[100] Exploitation of the rich mineral resources found in the mountains awaited the development of the tremendous regional hydroelectric power potential. A beginning was made in the 1960's with the start of the construction of Nurek hydroelectric station, one of the largest projects of this kind in the USSR.[101]

The distribution of Tadzhik industry was also very uneven. Industry was centered in Stalinabad city (almost 30 per cent of the total) and in the Leninabad oblast (about 40 per cent of the total).[102] The textile industry accounted for almost 50 per cent of total industrial production in 1956; of this, 33 per cent was devoted to cotton, and 12 per cent to silk textiles. Food processing con- stituted almost a quarter of the total; most of it consisted of dried and canned fruits exported to European Russia. Seven per cent of Tadzhik manufacture consisted of articles of clothing. The rest (20

[99] KPSS, *Tadzhikskaia SSR*, pp. 39–40; Luknitsky, *Soviet Tadzhikistan*, pp. 167, 181–82, 186; and *BSE, 2d ed., XLI*, 482.
[100] KPSS, *Tadzhikskaia SSR*, pp. 41–44; Luknitsky, *Soviet Tadzhikistan*, pp. 206–7, 221–26.
[101] Luknitsky, *Soviet Tadzhikistan*, p. 131. The Nurek hydroelectric station was planned to have a 2,700,000-kw. capacity. *KT*, December 15, 1963, p. 1. See also Bott, *Recent Trends*, p. 203.
[102] *TSSR. Nar. Khoz. 1957*, p. 21.

per cent of the total) included miscellaneous industrial items.[103] The construction material industry was relatively well developed for the local needs. Heavy industry was limited to coal and petroleum extractions (see Table 2-4); some lead and zinc were mined.

Table 2-4. INDUSTRIAL PRODUCTION. SELECTED COMMODITIES

Commodity	1913[a]	1940	1950	1954	1955
Coal[b]	30	200	400	500	600
Petroleum[b]	10	30	20	16	17
Cement[b]			17	23	24
Cotton fabrics[c]		0.2	16.6	42.9	40.9
Leather shoes[d]	n.d.[e]	455	769	955	1,098

Source: USSR. Council of Ministers, Central Statistical Administration, *The National Economy of the USSR: A Statistical Compilation* (Moscow: Gosstatizdat, 1956), pp. 61, 63, 75, 79, and 82.

[a] Within present boundaries.
[b] In thousands of tons.
[c] In millions of meters.
[d] In thousands of pairs.
[e] No data.

The 3,310,000 hectares of agricultural land in Tadzhikistan in 1954 (one-fourth of it cultivated) were divided among the collective farms (3,100,000 hectares), the state farms (160,000 hectares), and other state agricultural enterprises (50,000 hectares).[104] The bulk of the total sown area was under kolkhoz cultivation (728,000 hectares in 1956).[105] The expansion of cotton production at the expense of grain in the postwar period is illustrated by a comparison of the figures for the 1940 and the 1956 distribution of kolkhoz sown area (see Table 2-5). The area under fodder also expanded considerably during the same period. Sown area per inhabitant in Tadzhikistan (0.46 hectares) was comparable to the average in Soviet Central Asia (0.44 hectares), but was much lower than the

[103] *BSE, 2d ed., XLI*, 481.
[104] *USSR National Economy*, pp. 97–99.
[105] *TSSR. Nar. Khoz. 1957*, p. 52.

Table 2-5. DISTRIBUTION OF SOWN AREAS IN KOLKHOZES
(IN PERCENTAGES OF TOTAL KOLKHOLZ SOWN AREA)

Crop	1940	1953	1955	1956
Grain crops	72.0	57.9	56.2	54.8
Technical crops	20.1	34.8	33.6	34.6
Potatoes, vegetables, fruit	1.7	1.8	1.8	1.5
Fodder	6.2	5.5	8.4	9.7

Source: *TSSR. Nar. Khoz. 1957*, p. 53.

average for the USSR as a whole (0.94 hectares).[106] As the cotton-growing area was extended, the quality of the crop and its yields improved because of better agricultural methods: the use of fertilizers and insecticides and the change from dry to wet cultivation. Since 1947 the average cotton yield in the Tadzhik SSR has been the highest in the Soviet Union—28.1 tsentnars (1 tsentnar = 100 kg.) per hectare in 1953, and 26.7 tsentnars per hectare in 1965; its gross cotton output is second only to that of Uzbekistan.[107]

A steady stream of new settlers moved to cotton-growing valleys. Many of them were resettled mountain Tadzhiks, primarily the Galcha of Karategin. The resettlement was neither voluntary nor successful, because the mountaineers were ill prepared for specialized agricultural work in the heat of tropical valleys and were given little encouragement or assistance. Other new settlers (mainly voluntary, it seems) included many Uzbeks, a few Russians, and members of other ethnic groups. Most of them farmed their own nationally homogeneous kolkhozes; there were apparently few kolkhozes of mixed ethnic stock.[108]

Livestock breeding, especially the raising of sheep and goats, was an important part of the agricultural economy, but it was much less successful than cotton growing. The size and quality of Tadzhik herds never quite recovered from the disastrous effects of the

[106] The data for Central Asia and the USSR are from *Regional Economic Policy*, p. 54; for TSSR, it was calculated on the basis of the following figures: 1956 population, 1,775,000; 1955 total sown area, 811,000 (USSR. *National Economy, 1956*, p. 108).
[107] N. A. Kisliakov *et al. Kul'tura i byt Tadzhikskogo kolkhoznogo krestianstva: Po materialam kolkhoza im. G. M. Malenkova Leninabadskogo raiona Leninabadskoi oblasti Tadzhikskoi SSR.* (AN SSSR, Institut Etnografii im. N. N. Miklukho-Maklaia, Works, New Series) (Moscow, izd. AN SSSR, 1954) XXIV, p. 6; *KT*, January 30, 1955, p. 3; and *Pravda*, March 9, 1966, p. 2.
[108] Kisliakov, *Kul'tura i byt*, p. 6. Impressions based on *KT*, 1945-55, *passim*. See also Chap. 4.

civil war and from collectivization. There were more cattle, sheep, and goats in the Tadzhik area in 1928 than there were in 1956 (see Table 2-6). Pigs were not raised in Moslem Central Asia except by the immigrants, and efforts to convert Moslems into pig breeders were not successful.

Table 2-6. LIVESTOCK (IN THOUSANDS OF HEADS)

Stock	Summer 1916	Summer 1928	Jan. 1 1941	Jan. 1 1946	Oct. 1 1956
Cattle	800,5	915,4	580,0	534,6	588,8
Sheep	2,296,5[a]	3,011,4[a]	1,054,3	1,110,7	2,243,8
Goats			1,120,0	723,0	731,1
Pigs			20,8	3,7	55,3
Horses	116,3	103,1	124,2	96,8	123,2

Source: *TSSR. Nar. Khoz. 1957*, pp. 82–83.
[a] Sheep and goats.

The kolkhoz consolidation drive of the 1950's was designed to replace the numerous small kolkhozes by fewer larger units that would be more viable economically. In the 1940–55 period the number of kolkhozes was reduced sevenfold, while average area size, number of households, and other indices increased proportionately (see Table 2-7). The strengthening of the Party network

Table 2-7. KOLKHOZES

	1940	1949	1954	1955
Number of kolkhozes	3,093	2,685	506	453
Households[a]	197	155	175	175
Averages per kolkhoz				
Households	64	58	345	386
Able-bodied members[b]	134	123	724	810
Sown area (ha.)	248	306	1,504	1,690
Livestock heads				
Cattle	37	109	651	731
Pigs	3	0.1	0.4	19
Sheep and goats	208	700	4,148	4,723
Money income[c]	136	341	3,765	3,792

Source: *TSSR. Nar. Khoz. 1957*, p. 37.
[a] In thousands.
[b] Capable of full-time work.
[c] In thousands of rubles.

in rural areas was an important political byproduct of the consolidation. Although they were unrecognized in the official statistics, a few private farms apparently did remain. The 1954 budget listed an item referring to the payment of horse taxes by individual peasant homesteads (*edinolichie khoziaistva*).[109] In 1955 there were 31 state farms (*sovkhoz*) and 71 MTS in Tadzhikistan (there had been 21 and 51, respectively, in 1940).[110] The mechanization of agriculture in the republic made significant progress in comparison with the 1930's, and contrasted favorably with the primitive agricultural processes of the neighboring Asian countries. In the total agricultural picture it was still negligible, however, because it was limited almost exclusively to cotton cultivation. In dry agriculture and in the mountains, 85 per cent of the work in fulfillment of the 1948 kolkhoz plan was done by draft animals.[111] In 1955 only one-fourth of all Tadzhik kolkhozes were equipped with electricity.[112]

The Tadzhik labor force (including workers in state farms and MTS but not kolkhoz members) constituted 14 per cent of the total population in 1956. The number of workers and employees more than doubled in the 1945–56 period. Women constituted one-third of the labor force.[113] It is not clear whether the figure included female kolkhoz workers. The relatively high percentage of female industrial workers was the result of the traditional Russian preference for women workers in spinning and textiles. Generally, except in the kolkhozes, the majority of women workers and employees belonged to non-Moslem groups. In the postwar period there was a shortage of skilled labor and too many unskilled workers. The press frequently voiced complaints about the shortage; it also advertised skilled positions.

[109] *KT*, June 10, 1954, p. 2. Private farms existed in Turkmenia during the war. See Jan Dubicki, *Elements of Disloyalty in Turkestan* (Research Program on the USSR. East European Fund, Inc. Mimeographed series no. 53. Russian text.) (New York: East European Fund, Inc., n.d.).

[110] *TSSR. Nar. Khoz. 1957*, p. 133; and USSR. *National Economy 1956*, p. 114.

[111] *KT*, March 1, 1949, p. 3.

[112] *TSSR. Nar. Khoz. 1957*, p. 39.

[113] *TSSR. Nar. Khoz. 1957*, pp. 211 and 222.

Only fragmentary information was available on the living stand-ards in Tadzhikistan, but, as elsewhere in Soviet Central Asia, general consumption appeared to be lower than in the USSR as a whole. Higher than the average for Soviet agricultural areas be-cause of the higher earnings in specialized cotton kolkhozes, living standards were still much below the Soviet urban average.[114] Data available on kolkhoz workday earnings, which included payment in rubles and in produce, were almost exclusively limited to cot-ton-growing kolkhozes. In the 1945–56 period, the workday pay-ment recorded in the press ranged between 4 rubles and 0.5 kg. of grain to 45 rubles and 4 kg. of grain.[115] The range of payment for the same unit of work varied greatly, depending on the size, type, and efficiency of management of each individual kolkhoz. The giant cotton-growing kolkhozes of the valleys yielded very high earnings, while small, poor, mountain kolkhozes were barely able to subsist on raising grain and livestock.

An ethnographic study of a large consolidated cotton kolkhoz in the Leninabad raion revealed the following data for estimated annual average earnings of the kolkhozniks in 1951: about 4,450 rubles, 4,500 kg. of grain, and over 100 kg. of fruit. A similar esti-mate for a household of four was 6,500 rubles, 6,800 kg. of grain, and 160 kg. of fruit. The workday income was in addition to what-ever food and income a kolkhoz family derived from the produce of their private plots, which formed an important item in their budget. A diligent kolkhoznik who worked more than the average 200-plus workdays per year was able to earn an annual income of 9,000, 12,000, or 13,000 rubles (20,000 to 40,000 rubles if the whole family was working) and proportionately larger quantities of grain and fruits.[116] It was reported in 1954 that individual kolkhozniks

[114] Regional Economic Policy, pp. 63–65; and KT, passim.
[115] Kisliakov, Kul'tura i byt, pp. 109–10; Luknitsky, Soviet Tadzhikistan, pp. 97–98; and KT, passim.
[116] Kisliakov, Kul'tura i byt, pp. 109–11. In the 1950's 4,450 rubles equaled $1,112 at the official gold purchase price, $445 at the tourist exchange rate, and $66 at the domestic sale price of gold; 12,000 rubles equaled $3,000, $1,200, and $150, re-spectively. See Harry Schwartz, Russia's Soviet Economy, 2d ed. (New York: Prentice-Hall, Inc., 1954), pp. 475, 481–83. M. T. Florinsky, ed., McGraw-Hill Encyclo-pedia of Russia and the Soviet Union (New York: McGraw-Hill, 1961), p. 364.

in the Vakhsh Valley earned as much as 30,000 rubles annually, plus tons of produce.[117] The average income in the cotton-growing valleys, however, was undoubtedly lower, and the income in highland grain and livestock kolkhozes was very much lower. Workers with important positions were paid more per day than those who were lower in the kolkhoz hierarchy. Benefits derived from working private plots and raising privately owned livestock were generally greater than benefits from working the collective land. The press reported many instances of the peasants working only the bare required minimum for collective farms; many women did not work the communal fields at all. This appears to have been especially true in the late 1940's.

In comparison, miners in the Shurab coal mines were reported to be earning from 3,000 to 8,000 rubles a month (36,000 to 96,000 rubles annually) in the early 1950's—a very handsome wage by Soviet standards.[118] Wages of textile workers were lower. In 1953 about 80 per cent of the workers of the Stalinabad Textile Combine were earning an average monthly wage of 700 rubles (8,400 rubles annually), while 10 per cent earned between 700 and 1,500 rubles monthly, and 10 per cent earned more than 15,000 rubles monthly.[119] These workers received no additional income in produce but they did receive bonuses for overfulfillment of plans. The average wages of Tadzhik industrial workers were below the level of the Stalinabad combine. An average industrial wage for the whole of Central Asia in the 1950's was reported to have been approximately 7,000 rubles per year.[120] No information was available on the salaries of employees of the state and economic administration and Party officials. As elsewhere in Soviet Central Asia, immigrant specialists received preferential salaries.

Housing in Tadzhikistan, as in the rest of Soviet Central Asia,

[117] *KT*, March 25, 1954, p. 3.

[118] Luknitsky, *Soviet Tadzhikistan,* p. 114; 36,000 rubles equaled $9,000 at gold purchase price, $3,600 at the tourist exchange rate, and $450 at gold sale price; 96,000 rubles equaled $24,000 at gold purchase price, $9,600 at the tourist exchange rate, and $1,200 at gold sale price.

[119] *KT*, March 5, 1954, p. 3.

[120] *Regional Economic Policy,* p. 67; 7,000 rubles were worth $1,750 at gold purchase price, $700 at the tourist exchange rate, and $87.50 at gold sale price.

and indeed in the Soviet Union as a whole, was notoriously bad, and worse in the cities than in the countryside. The traditional flat-roofed abode houses still predominated. European-style houses were few and were apparently reserved *de facto* for the Western Slav minority and the ruling elite. Popular preference seemed to favor the traditional type of housing in any case. Housing construction was hampered by major shortages of building materials and by administrative abuses: hundreds and thousands of establishments were constructed in a "beggardly way" (*dedovskim sposobom*).[121] The shortage of dwelling space in Stalinabad was worse than in other Central Asian capitals because of the population explosion. The floor space per capita—five square meters—was the same in 1926 as in 1956.[122] The city also suffered from shortages of electricity and water. Little is known about conditions in other cities, but—except in Leninabad—they appear to have been worse than in the capital. Kurgan-Tyube city had no electricity and no water pipes in 1954.[123]

In terms of other social investment, Tadzhikistan shared in the general standards of Soviet Central Asia. A United Nations study in the 1950's concluded that "for most types of social investment the number of units per capita (in Soviet Central Asia) is generally two-thirds of the USSR average," and that "average living standards for the region as a whole are probably one-fifth to one-fourth lower than the Soviet average. . . ." It was further stated that, nevertheless, "living standards in Central Asia are on much higher levels than those in the neighboring Asian countries, and that they have improved very considerably in the three decades since the end of the Civil War." [124] Since urban living was much

---

[121] *KT*, March 25, 1954, p. 3. In the 1960's the Tadzhik press was full of disclosures of housing scandals. High officials were using state construction funds, materials, labor, and agencies to build private residences for themselves. *The Current Digest of the Soviet Press*, 1960–65, *passim*.

[122] The total floor space in Stalinabad was: 1926, 31,000 m.² (pop. 5,607); 1940, 457,000 m.² (pop. 82,540 in 1939); 1956, 1,100,000 m.² (pop. 191,000) *TSSR. Nar. Khoz. 1957*, pp. 169–70. The average floor space per inhabitant in Central Asia was 6 m.² (*Regional Economic Policy*, p. 67).

[123] *KT*, January 22, 1954, p. 2.

[124] *Regional Economic Policy*, p. 68.

more comfortable than rural living, the city-centered European population benefited most, but the local Asian intelligentsia and the ruling elite fully shared in these benefits and thus enjoyed higher living standards than the Asian majority.

The Soviet government made a major investment in the improvement of health standards in the republic. A network of medical services, nonexistent before the revolution, spread until in the fifties it was not far below the All-Union average. Where there had been nineteen doctors in 1913, there were 1,900 in 1956; and the number of hospital beds increased from 100 to 9,700.[125] Still, trained doctors, most of whom were Europeans, were in short supply, and the bulk of medical work was performed by *feldshers* (assistant doctors), midwives, nurses, and medical technicians (1 for approximately 340 people in the 1950's), all of whom were designated as "middle medical personnel." Medical personnel and facilities were still inadequate for the needs of the country. And their uneven distribution was an additional major problem: 82 per cent of all doctors in the republic and 80 per cent of all middle medical personnel lived in urban areas in 1954.[126] There was a shortage of specialists. Surgery was available only in oblast centers; some kolkhozes were never visited by a doctor. The absence of doctors in rural areas was caused not only by their unwillingness to bury themselves "in the sticks" but also in many cases by the lack of housing facilities and equipment. There were few pharmacies, and drug distribution was notoriously unsatisfactory.[127] In view of the pattern of population distribution, it seems that medical services available to rural Tadzhiks were much below the average Soviet standards and were definitely inferior to services available to the immigrant population centered in the cities. Complaints of poor sanitary habits of the rural Tadzhiks and their practice of folk medicine were scattered in the press, but it appears that the people scarcely had an alternative.

---

[125] *Ibid.*, p. 71; *USSR. National Economy 1956*, pp. 248–49, and *The Soviet Union in Facts and Figures*, 1958 ed. (London: Soviet News, 1958), p. 195.

[126] *KT*, April 1, 1954, p. 2.

[127] *Ibid.*, June 2, 1946, p. 1; April 12, 1947, p. 2; May 19, 1948, p. 3; and April 23, 1954, p. 3.

The development of the mass educational system compared favorably with that of the health network. Always high on the Soviet priority list, education has shown spectacular progress, especially when compared with other Asian countries. General education in Tadzhikistan schools (primary, seven-year, and secondary schools) grew from a few schools in the early 1920's to approximately 3,000 schools in the late 1950's and early 1960's, while the number of students increased from 1,000 to over 300,000 (see Table 2-8). There were approximately 20,000 teachers in the 1950's because the first higher educational facilities were directed at training teachers, especially among the local population. The Tadzhik schools were organized on a trilingual or sometimes quadrilingual basis. There were general education schools with Tadzhik, Russian, Uzbek, or sometimes Kirgiz as the language of instruction; in some cases a school accommodated different language groups in special classes. Instruction in higher education institutions (7 in the 1950's) and in technical and specialized schools (approximately 30 in the 1950's) was primarily in Russian, except when the school's area of specialization was concerned with teachers' training or a study of local language, literature, or art. Special evening schools served urban and rural working youth.[128]

The educational system in Tadzhikistan has had its problems, however. The major one, the result of a continuing failure to implement the laws on universal education in rural areas,[129] was pupil absenteeism and dropping out of school. Dropouts were particularly prevalent among Tadzhik and Uzbek girls. The quality of instruction was also a problem because teachers' training was still inadequate, and the shortage of buildings, equipment, and textbooks was endemic. Nevertheless, in the 1950's the Tadzhik educational ratio of 58 students per 10,000 population compared favorably with that of other Asian countries and even with Western Europe, a point of great pride to Soviet spokesmen.[130]

[128] Based on *KT;* and AN TSSR, *Istoriia,* III, Book 1, and AN TSSR, *Istoriia,* III, Book 2, *Period sotsializma i perekhod k kommunizmu (1938–1963* gg.), S. A. Radzhabov and Iu. A. Nikolaev, eds. (Moscow: Izd. "Nauka," 1965), *passim.*

[129] The universal seven-year education law was passed in 1950; the universal eight-year education law in 1963. The ten-year universal education in the cities was introduced in 1953. AN TSSR, *Istoriia,* III, Book 2, 126 and 166.

[130] KPSS, *Tadzhikskaia SSR,* p. 19.

Table 2-8. TSSR Schools

Year	General Education Schools[a]			Schools for Working Youth		Tekhnikums and Special Schools		Higher Educational Institutions	
	No.	Students	Teachers	No.	Students	No.	Students	No.	Students
1913[b]	13	860	20						
1926/27[c]	144	3,500							
1928/29[c]	382	18,600	718						
1929/30[d]	541	26,730	980						
1932/33[c]	2,319	125,050	3,795			16		4	
1937/38[c]	4,224	221,000	8,144			28		4	
1944/45[b]	2,344	250,000	12,455					5	2,000
1946/47[e]	3,000	281,300				25		7	
1949/50[f]	3,005	300,000				31		9	
1950/51[g]	3,092	307,375	15,027	280	12,000				
1951/52[h]	2,657	304,800							
1955[i]	2,547	320,500				29	13,400		
1957/58[j]		320,000	20,394	214	13,995	29	13,600	7	17,000

[a] Including primary, seven-year, and secondary (middle) schools.
[b] *KT*, July 13, 1945, p. 2.
[c] AN TSSR, *Istoriia*, III, Book 1, *Perekhod k sotsializmu (1917–1937)*, ed. B. A. Antonenko (Moscow: Izd. "Nauka," 1964), 172, 205, 266, 268, and 316.
[d] *KT*, April 8, 1951, p. 3.
[e] *Ibid.*, January 13, 1946, p. 3.
[f] *Ibid.*, October 11, 1949, p. 2.
[g] *Ibid.*, January 5, 1951, p. 3.
[h] AN TSSR, *Istoriia*, III, Book 2, *Period sotsializma i perekhod k kommunizmu (1938–1963 gg.)*, ed. S. A. Radzhabov and Iu A. Nikolaev (Moscow: Izd. "Nauka," 1965), 126.
[i] *TSSR. Nar. Khoz. 1957*, p. 321.
[j] AN TSSR, *Istoriia*, III, Book 2, 166–67.

The process of political, economic, and social change in Tadzhikistan began late, and though spectacular, it was by no means
completed even by the 1960's. The establishment of Soviet rule
took approximately a decade and was accompanied by a prolonged
and bitter civil war in which the new regime subdued the overwhelmingly hostile local population by force. The transformation
began in the 1930's, but it was punctuated by a frequently brutal
suppression of religious observances and traditional customs, by
a violent struggle for collectivization which caused human misery
and economic losses, and by a series of ruthless purges of native
leaders who resented and resisted the policies determined by Moscow. It was interrupted by the war, of which the effects were felt
even in this remote corner of Soviet Central Asia. The process of
building a new society began in earnest only after 1945. The economic base charted in the thirties was consolidated; an effort to
build a national "Soviet" culture was accompanied by accelerated
social change; a new Soviet-educated native elite with a commitment to the regime began to ascend in the power structure.

Traditional attitudes and patterns of behavior remained very
much alive, and frequently conflicted with the new values and requirements. The legacy of bitterness left by the 1920's and 1930's
continued to be a vital factor in the relations between Tadzhiks
and Russians. In the general process of change and development, institutional and legal changes were the result of administrative fiat
backed by force; economic change, though more gradual, was carried out by the implementation of new economic policies by the
regime in power. Social change, however, cannot be effected
rapidly. Attitudes and habits cannot be ruled by law, and the traditional culture still remained strong at the base of the new Tadzhik society.

3

✿

THE TADZHIK NATIONHOOD
AND THE RUSSIAN "ELDER BROTHER"

THE NATIONALITY POLICY which originated with Lenin but was shaped and developed largely by Stalin [1] was used by the Bolsheviks to shape the relationship between the Russians and other national groups. Known officially as "the proletarian solution of the nationality problem," the policy has also been described as the "best form of mutual assistance" and the "historically highest form of cooperation between peoples." [2] Given Lenin's unerring sense of political reality, the right to self-determination of the component nationalities of the Russian empire was recognized by the Bolsheviks from the very beginning. Although it was helpful in the breakdown of the empire, self-determination was not allowed to jeopardize the unity of the new Soviet state, which embodied the "proletarian unity of the oppressed," historically the higher right than that of national self-determination. In practice, unity was pursued by all methods, including the use of force. In theory, the apparent contradiction between the right of the national minorities to decide their own fate and the need for centralized control in the new Soviet state was solved by the application of the nationality policy. "National in form and socialist in content," the policy satisfied

---

[1] Official texts of the sixties reflect the results of de-Stalinization. Lenin is credited with the formulation of the policy, while Stalin's name appears only as one of the many who carried it out. Implementation of the policy is generally portrayed as a "collective effort." See, for example, S. I. Iakubovskaia, *Obrazovanie i razvitie sovetskogo mnogonatsional'nogo gosudarstva* (Moscow: Izd. "Znanie," 1966).

[2] M. Kim, "Torzhestvo ideologii druzhby narodov," *Kommunist*, XXIX, no. 22 (December, 1952), 53–54. For a discussion of early nationality policy in Turkestan see Park, *Bolshevism in Turkestan*, Chap. 10 and *passim*.

national aspirations within a formal federal state structure, while safeguarding union with Russia through the centralized leadership of the Communist Party.[3]

The role of the Communist Party was made explicit in the 1919 Party Program, which resolved that the Party's unitary structure should underlie the federal divisions of separate republics:

> The Eighth Congress . . . resolves: It is imperative to have a single centralized Communist Party with a single Central Committee to direct the entire work of the Party. . . . All the decisions of the Russian Communist Party and its leading institutions are absolutely obligatory for all sections of the Party, irrespective of their national composition. The central committees of the Ukrainian, Latvian, and Lithuanian communists enjoy the rights of regional committees of the Party, and are fully subordinate to the Central Committee of the Russian Communist Party.[4]

The principle of subordination of regional units of the Party to its central leadership has never been weakened.

The limitations imposed on the exercise of autonomy in the borderlands (apart from those inherent in the constitutional divisions of powers between the Union and the republics) can be seen from the following discussion of the basic formula of the nationality policy and its practical implications. The three basic principles of the policy are the right to national self-determination, including the right to secede, the territorial autonomy of national groups, and the full equality of those groups. National self-determination, however, actually meant the "voluntary" union of the working classes of the various nationalities within the USSR, based on the principle of "proletarian internationalism."[5] The autonomy was to be exercised by the working masses, as represented by the Party, and not by the bourgeoisie;[6] and the equality of all nationalities had to be adjusted in practice to the differences in their economic and cultural development, which made some of

---

[3] For a discussion of the decision-making role of the Communist Party see Fainsod, *How Russia is Ruled,* and other books on the Soviet political system.

[4] Quoted in Eudin and North, *Soviet Russian and the East,* p. 22.

[5] A. M. Ganin, "Teoriia i programma kommunisticheskoi partii po natsional'nomu voprosu," *KT,* July 13, 1954, pp. 2–3.

[6] A. Gorkin, "Stalin—sozdatel' i rukovoditel' mnogonatsional'nogo Sovetskogo gosudarstva," *Bol'shevik,* no. 23 (December, 1949), 50.

them "incapable of achieving a higher level of development" unless given "real and prolonged assistance" by a "more advanced"
nationality.[7]

The free exercise of the right to secede was bluntly denied by
Stalin in 1923:

> There are occasions when the right to self-determination conflicts
> with . . . the higher right—the right of a working class that has
> assumed power to consolidate its power. In such cases—this must be
> said bluntly—the right to self-determination cannot and must not
> serve as an obstacle to the exercise by the working class of its right
> to dictatorship. The former must give way to the latter.[8]

At the same time Stalin placed great emphasis on the cultural
aspects of national autonomy, such as the use of the local language
in schools and offices, and the recruitment of local cadres into Party
and government work. This was necessary in order to establish
"proper relations between the proletariat of the former sovereign
nation" and "the peasantry of the formerly oppressed nationalities," and to make the Soviet government (run by the Russian
"workers"—"the most cultural section of the proletariat") "com-
prehensible" to this peasantry and "near and dear" to them.[9]

The implementation of the nationality policy suffered from two
major deviations: "Great Russian chauvinism" and "bourgeois nationalism"; both were blamed by the central leaderships on the
machinations of class enemies aiming to undermine the Soviet system and to restore capitalism."[10] Great Russian chauvinism expressed the views of the Russian Communists who were committed
to a centralized Russian-dominated state and were impatient with
the niceties of national autonomy and demanded that the privileged status of the Russians in the borderlands be recognized *de
jure* as well as *de facto*. Bourgeois nationalism, a deviation characteristic of the native Communist cadres, expressed local aspirations
to political autonomy by a literal interpretation of the right to self-

[7] Joseph Stalin, "Report on National Factors in the Development of the Party
and the State" at the Twelfth Congress of the Russian Communist Party, April 23,
1923, in *Marxism and the National Question*, p. 131.

[8] *Ibid.*, p. 158.

[9] *Ibid.*, pp. 138–39.

[10] Stalin at the Seventeenth Congress of the Communist Party of the Soviet Union,
January 26, 1934, in *Marxism and the National Question*, p. 215.

determination and equality, and by hostile reaction to the Russian domination.

The implementation of the nationality policy in Tadzhikistan was similar to that in the other union republics. To judge by the stormy history of the establishment of Soviet power there, and by the ethnic pattern of power distribution in the republic,[11] the Party has not succeeded in making the Soviet government "near and dear" to the Tadzhik peasants. The Party has been successful, however, in establishing a viable government and in transforming and developing the region, considered vital from the viewpoint of long-range objectives.

As in the other border republics, bourgeois nationalist deviation plagued the new government. Bourgeois nationalists were blamed for resistance to collectivization and cultural sovietization in the 1930's, and were the target of all the major purges. The Tadzhik intelligentsia were also accused of this deviation in the postwar cultural purges.

Criticism of nationalist tendencies was frequently linked with charges of Pan-Islamism and Pan-Iranianism. All the vices of bourgeois-nationalist ideology condemned by a 1952 issue of *Kommunist* [12] were to be found in postwar Tadzhikistan, if the criticisms repeatedly aired by the Tadzhik press are valid. The Tadzhiks seemed to have made little progress in acquiring positive "Soviet" attitudes and in developing "Soviet patriotism" [13]—an in-

---

[11] See Chaps. 2 and 4.

[12] Kim, *Torzhestvo ideologii,* p. 66.

[13] An editorial in *Bol'shevik,* no. 5 (March 15, 1949) ("Razvivat' i kul'tivirovat' sovetskii patriotizm—vazhneishaia zadacha partiinykh organizatsii") gives the following definition of the Soviet patriot and patriotism: "To be a Soviet patriot—it means to be unreservedly devoted to the great work of the party of Lenin and Stalin, to the work of communism, to the struggle for the speedy establishment and development of the national economy of the country; to try to achieve an uninterrupted growth of labor productivity, severely to observe state discipline, to take care constantly of the development and strengthening of the socialist economy—the basis of the power of our Motherland. To be a Soviet patriot in the conditions of harsh struggle between the camp of socialism and democracy, and the camp of imperialist reaction, means to strengthen in all ways the economic and war potential of the socialist Motherland, to show wide-awake vigilance toward efforts of imperialist reaction. . . . (p. 4). See also P. Fedoseev, "Sotsialism i patriotizm," *Kommunist,* no. 9 (June, 1953), 22; and M. Morozov, "Natsional'nye traditsii narodov SSSR i vospitanie Sovetskogo patriotizma," *Bol'shevik* no. 7 (April 15, 1949), 35–47. In practical terms Soviet patriotism meant Russian patriotism seasoned with Marxist-Leninist ideology. To be a Soviet patriot meant to follow the current Party line.

tegral and indispensable part of the "Soviet content" of the nationality policy.

With the consolidation of Soviet rule in Central Asia and the differentiation between national groups there in line with the requirements of the nationality policy, the Tadzhik national identity was recognized in the 1924 national delimitation by the creation of the Tadzhik autonomous republic, which was subsequently given the status of a union republic and separated from Uzbekistan in 1929. There were few objective indications of Tadzhikistan's readiness to assume its new status at that time. Formally, the country met the three criteria for union membership: it was a border area, its leading nationality formed a compact majority, and, after the Khodzhent region was transferred from Uzbekistan to the new republic, its population reached the one million mark.[14] However, it had neither a well-developed economic base nor national and cultural cohesion, and pacification was barely completed. The constitutional advancement of the Tadzhiks was all the more surprising, because according to the Marxist criteria they were then only a "nationality" (*narodnost'*) that had failed to develop into a "bourgeois nation." Not until the mid-1930's had they officially attained the status of a "socialist nation."

Two plausible explanations come to mind. The constitutional recognition of the Tadzhiks was undoubtedly prompted by the Soviet divide-and-rule policy which, in Central Asia, was designed to undercut the hegemony of the Uzbeks there, and by the Communist desire to destroy the Pan-Islamic, Pan-Turkic unity of Turkestan. The Tadzhik case differed from that of the other minorities, however, because initially their separate identity did not appear to have been recognized by the Party leadership. As late as 1923 Stalin failed to distinguish between the Uzbeks and the Tadzhiks when he discussed Bukhara nationalities; condemning the excesses of Uzbek chauvinism at the Twelfth Party Congress he acknowledged only the Turkmen and the Kirgiz as persecuted minorities.[15] It must, therefore, have been the new recognition of

[14] Joseph Stalin, "Report to the Eighth All-Union Congress of the Soviets, November 25, 1936," pp. 220–21 in *Marxism and the National Question*.

[15] Joseph Stalin, "Theses on National Factors in the Development of the Party and the State," in *Marxism and the National Question*. At the Twelfth Congress of the Russian Communist Party (Bolsheviks) (RKP[b]), Stalin said: ". . . In some of

the Tadzhiks' potential importance in the export of Communist influence across the border that was the major factor in their political advancement to the union republic level.

Winning the East for Communism was regarded by Stalin as a prerequisite to the "definite triumph of socialism." The Soviet task was "to infect the workers and peasants" of the countries of the East "with the liberating spirit of the revolution, to rouse them to struggle against imperialism and in that way to deprive world imperialism of its 'most reliable' and 'inexhaustible' reserve." [16] In this endeavor Russian Turkestan served as a "bridge which connects the socialist Russia with the oppressed countries of the East," and the strengthening of the Soviet power there was considered to be "of major revolutionary significance for the whole East." [17] The weakness of Communism there, and the delay in the consolidation of Soviet power were major concerns of the Bolsheviks. The revolutionary significance of Turkestan was emphasized by Stalin at a conference with representatives of national republics in 1923:

> ... it is clear that, of all the Soviet republics, Turkestan is the most important from the point of view of revolutionizing the East, not only because Turkestan is a combination of nationalities *which have more links with the East than any others,* but also because, geographically, it cuts into the heart of that part of the East which is the most exploited and the most explosive in the struggle against the imperialism.[18]

The strategic importance of Tadzhikistan, located at the confluence of Afghanistan and British India, and the significant fact

---

the republics the population of which is made up of several nationalities, . . . the outright chauvinism of the stronger nationality is directed against the weaker nationalities. . . . Uzbek chauvinism in Bokhara and Khorezm [is directed] against the Turkmens and Kirghiz . . ." (p. 132). At the same congress, he said: "Take Bokhara: In Bokhara there are three nationalities—the Uzbeks, who constitute the principal nationality, the Turkmens, who from the point of view of Bokharan chauvinism are a 'less important' nationality, and the Kirghiz, who are few in number and are 'less important' " (p. 146).

[16] Joseph Stalin, "Do Not Forget the East," November 24, 1918, quoted in Eudin and North, *Soviet Russia,* p. 156.

[17] Stalin's letter to the Turkestan CP of February 12, 1919, quoted in *KT,* July 29, 1949, p. 2. A letter of very similar content was written to the Turkestan Party organization in November, 1919, by Lenin; quoted by Eudin and North, *Soviet Russia,* p. 77.

[18] Joseph Stalin, "Report at the Fourth Conference," quoted in Schlesinger, *The Nationalities Problem,* pp. 70–71. Italics mine.

that the Tadzhiks were Iranians, heirs with the Persians to the ancient Persian culture, and that their language was understood in Iran as well as in the parts of Northwest India and Afghanistan inhabited by other Iranians must have become increasingly clear in the 1920's. Characteristically, in a message that Stalin sent to Dushambe on March 25, 1925, on the occasion of the official proclamation of the Tadzhik Autonomous Soviet Socialist Republic (ASSR), the emphasis was all on the Tadzhik role *outside* the Soviet Union:

> Greetings to Tadzhikistan, the new soviet working people's republic *at the gates of Hindustan.* I ardently wish all the working people of Tadzhikistan success in converting their republic into *a model republic of the Eastern countries.*
>
> The Tadzhiks have a rich history; their great organizing and political abilities of the past are no secret to anyone.
>
> Workers of Tadzhikistan! Advance the culture of your land, develop its economy, assist the toilers of the city and the village, rally around you the best sons of the fatherland. *Show the whole East that it is you, vigorously holding in your hands the banners of liberation, who are the most worthy heirs of your ancestors.*[19]

The "international significance" of the formation of Soviet Tadzhikistan was also underscored in an official 1964 Tadzhik history:

> The establishment of the Tadzhik Soviet Socialist Republic at the border of the colonial East was of great international importance. It became a model of how the Soviet government has resolved the national problem, and a proof of the triumph of Leninist nationality policy. It demonstrated the great care which the Communist Party and the Soviet government have taken in the creation and development of national statehood of the previously oppressed backward colonial peoples.[20]

Obviously it was to the neighboring "oppressed" peoples that Soviet Tadzhikistan "demonstrated" the success of the Soviet system, and it was for them that it was to serve as a model. Walter Kolarz thinks that the immediate cause of the transformation of Tadzhikistan from an autonomous republic into a union

---

[19] Quoted in *KT*, December 13, 1946, p. 2, and numerous other issues; also in Luknitsky, *Soviet Tadzhikistan*, p. 20. Italics mine. It seems that it is the only "quotable quote" Stalin directed at the Tadzhiks, and it is quoted *ad nauseam.* This message, plus a meeting or two with cotton growers from Tadzhikistan, seems to have been the extent of Stalin's direct contact with the Tadzhiks.

[20] AN TSSR, *Istoriia*, III, Book 1, 218.

republic was the British-inspired dethronement of King Amanullah of Afghanistan (who was considered friendly to the Soviet
Union), and that Tadzhikistan was intended to provide a rallying
point for potential irredenta in neighboring countries.[21]

The early revolutionary hopes that the "Russian proletarian
Muslims . . . will be coming to the rescue of their brothers in
Persia, India, and Afghanistan"[22] faded in the 1920's, but the
importance of Soviet Central Asian republics as a source of propaganda and as a showcase remained. A cultural offensive seeking to
convince the local people, as well as the neighbors, of the superiority of the Soviet system began in the 1930's and developed in the
postwar period. After Stalin's death it was intensified and augmented by cultural exchanges. Tadzhik broadcasts are heard in
other countries, and literary works are available to and apparently
known to Iranian speakers in neighboring countries.

The material, social, and cultural progress made by the Tadzhiks under the Soviet rule, and the contrast Tadzhikistan presents to the backward nations of Asia, form the major propaganda
theme. Considered of vital importance for domestic as well as for
foreign consumption, this theme was vigorously pursued by Tadzhik literary figures. Representative among them was the first
poet of Soviet Tadzhikistan, Mirzo Tursun-Zade, who won Stalin's
prize for a book-length poem, the *Indian Ballad* (1948), which
contrasted the squalor and oppression of British India with
"happy" Soviet Tadzhikistan.

The excerpts below of Tursun-Zade's poem "I am from the Free
East" illustrate the theme:

I glory in the struggle and labor,
While you are degraded and always in need; why?
The light of happiness shines on me,
While you yearn for a day of ease; why?
I am free as a mountain eagle,
While you drag your chains; why?

. . . .

[21] Despite the fact that the king gave asylum to the ex-Emir of Bokhara. Walter
Kolarz, *Russia and Her Colonies*, p. 238. See also Eudin and North, *Soviet Russia*,
pp. 103–6.

[22] "Zhizn Natsional'nostei," no. 19 (27), May 26, 1919, quoted in Eudin and North,
Soviet Russia, p. 161.

Listen to me comrade, I am glad to answer you!
You are just the same as I.
You are just the same as I.
You are a man, and it means that
You and I are friends.
You are also born under the Eastern sky,
Son of the people known from ancient times.

. . . .

[but]
As before, your people slave
So that the overseas robber can increase his wealth.

. . . .

Here is where the difference is, friend,
Between you and me.
Here, one East is mine, another East is yours.

. . . .

The enemy sows discord day and night,
He sends ships from New York and London
Destroying and robbing your ancient people.

. . . .

Know:
With us the traces of oppression are erased.
Here all the peoples are equal in friendship, and in fame,
Their hearts beat like one, full of happiness.
The air is clean . . .
Like spreading rays Moscow sends the warmth of the new life
into each town and village . . .

. . . .

Here is where the difference is, friend . . .

Glory to our fathers in the reaches of the earth
For many years they fought with the enemy.
The Russian brother—he is our chief—
In the war years he helped
all the peoples of the country,

As always.

. . . .

Here is where the difference is, friend . . .[23]

The Tadzhik nation has been called "a child of October," and it may safely be assumed that without the 1917 revolution and Soviet rule the Tadzhik national consciousness would never have developed, or else would have been lost in the Islamic consciousness of the dominant Turkic majority. The official Soviet theory of the formation of the Tadzhik nation recognizes two stages of development: [24] the nationality (*narodnost'*) stage, which began in antiquity and continued until the modern times, and the nation (*natsiia*) stage, begun and completed in the Soviet period, when the Tadzhiks were able to progress directly from feudalism to socialism.

The Tadzhik nationality began to be formed in the fifth and sixth centuries, according to Soviet historians, and the process was completed within the tenth-century Samanid empire. The empire's dominant ethnic strain was Iranian, with an admixture of nomadic Turkic blood; its language was Farsi, formed on the basis of ancient Iranian dialects. With the Tadzhiks dispersed territorially, economically, and politically in the following centuries, their national development was arrested and their political and linguistic unity was gradually lost. At the beginning of the twentieth century:

> In Tadzhikistan the Tadzhiks did not represent one national entity in an exact sense, because they were divided among a whole range of bekstva and khanates, were separated from one another, and did not have a common economic life. There was no additional market, no economic or cultural national center. . . .

[23] Mirzo Tursun-Zade, "Ia s Vostoka Svobodnogo," a Russian translation in *KT*, October 9, 1951, p. 1. My translation.

[24] This paragraph and subsequent discussion are based on the following sources: A. M. Bogoutdinov, "Formirovanie i razvitie Tadzhikskoi sotsialisticheskoi natsii," *KT*, September 8, 1954, pp. 2–3, and September 9, 1954, p. 2; P. Kh. Khamrakulov, "Rukovodiashchaia rol' kommunisticheskoi partii Sovetskogo Soiuza v formirovanii Tadzhikskoi sotsialisticheskoi natsii," *ibid.*, February 6, 1954, p. 2; Khamrakulov, "O nekotorykh osobennostiiakh formirovaniia i razvitiia Tadzhikskoi sotsialisticheskoi natsii," pp. 526–51, in *Formirovanie sotsialisticheskikh natsii v SSSR* (Moscow: Gospolitizdat, 1962); A. M. Ganin, "Teoriia i programma kommunisticheskoi partii po natsional'nomu voprosu," *KT*, July 13, 1954, pp. 2–3; *BSE*, 2d ed., XLI, p. 464; *Tadzhikskaia SSR za 25 let*, pp. 101–3; Gafurov, *Istoriia*, Chap. ii and x; I. Verkhovtsev and I. Maiatnikov, "O natsiakh i putiakh ikh razvitiia," in *Formirovaniie sotsialisticheskikh natsii*, pp. 1–24; Dzhabar Rasulov, *40 let Kommunisticheskoi Partii Tadzhikistana* (Dushanbe: Izd. "Irfon," 1964).

Naturally, the elements characterizing Tadzhiks as a nation, the language, territory, and cultural unity, were formed and existed from ancient times. But before the Great October Revolution these elements were not developed, and existed at best only as a potential.[25]

The Tadzhiks became a socialist nation after the October revolution, but Lenin's criteria of nationhood (one language, a united territory, a shared economic life, and a common psychological outlook) were achieved only at the time of the conclusion of the first two five-year plans, in the late 1930's ". . . In fifteen short years (1925–40) Tadzhikistan was transformed from the poor and backward land it was earlier into a flowering socialist republic, and the Tadzhik people were consolidated into a socialist nation." [26]

The Russian proletariat and the Russian Communist Party were the vital element and the absolutely essential catalyst, respectively, in this transformation. "The Communist Party of the Soviet Union created the necessary prerequisites" for the formation of "the Tadzhik socialist nation," economically, by building the socialist economic basis; politically, in the struggle of the Soviet system against the national bourgeoisie; and theoretically, through the triumph of Marxist-Leninist ideology and a successful cultural revolution.[27]

It was only "under the leadership and with the assistance of the All-Union Communist Party" that "gigantic steps" were made toward "socialist transformation." The steps included the liquidation of the emirate, the defeat of the Basmachi, the formation of the Tadzhic autonomous (later union) republic, industrialization and collectivization, the cultural revolution, the liquidation of the exploiters, and the victory over the enemies of the people. The Russian Communist Party's influence was an integral part of the two prerequisites of nationhood: an economic base and a new psychological outlook (*psykhicheskii sklad*). The Tadzhik economy was developed as an integral part of the Central Asian and All-Union economies; the new psychological outlook resulted from the interaction of the elements of the old Tadzhik culture such as national epics, art, literature, habits, and tradition with new "in-

[25] Bogoutdinov, "Formirovanie i razvitie," September 8, 1954, p. 2.
[26] *Ibid.*, September 9, 1954, p. 2.
[27] Khamrakulov, "Rukovodiaschaia rol'," p. 2.

ternational factors" such as the Marxist-Leninist ideology, friendship of and cooperation with other peoples, and new Communist
attitudes. "Proletarian internationalism," "socialist patriotism,"
and "friendship of the people" were to be its basic characteristics.

> The psychological outlook of the Tadzhik socialist nation . . . has
> been formed on the basis of socialist relations of production, under
> the direct leadership of the Communist Party, and in the decisive
> battle with the overthrown exploiting classes and bourgeois nation-
> alists. The beneficial influence of the other peoples and particularly
> the great Russian people has placed the most important imprint on
> the Tadzhik psychological outlook.[28]

There is little doubt that the Soviet theory of the formation of
the Tadzhik nationhood is well based in reality insofar as it relates
to the absence of an articulate and well-defined sense of national
consciousness among the prerevolutionary Tadzhiks, and to the
special role played by the Russians, the Communist Party, and the
Soviet government in the building of the new nation. There is
actually no evidence that the Tadzhiks thought of themselves as a
separate national group, though they did share an Iranian heritage.
The three distinct subgroups into which they were divided had
little contact with one another. Only the cultivated upper classes
of the Plains Tadziks spoke Farsi, the literary Tadzhik which, by
administrative fiat, became the language of Soviet Tadzhikistan.
As the only educated group they should have been the bearers of
the Tadzhik national consciousness, and yet they conceived of
themselves in Pan-Islamic and Pan-Turkic terms, just as their
Uzbek-speaking co-religionists did. Other Tadzhik groups spoke a
variety of related Iranian dialects, were illiterate, and thought of
themselves in strictly regional or even immediately local terms.
Stalin's apparent ignorance of the Tadzhiks as a group distinct
from the Uzbeks at the Twelfth Congress may obviously be excused; when, at the time of the formation of the Tadzhik SSR, the
population of the Khodzhent region was asked to declare its
nationality, many people were confused, and some Iranian speakers called themselves Uzbeks, only to be reclassified later as Tadzhiks. In this connection it is interesting to note the discrepancy in
the 1929 ethnic composition figures of the Tadzhik Party, as given

[28] Khamrakulov, "O nekotorykh osobennostiiakh," p. 540.

in 1929 and 1965 sources. The total percentage of Uzbeks and Tadzhiks in the membership is the same in both sources, as is the percentage of the Europeans, but within the native group the 1929 source gives the Uzbeks a much higher actual number than does the 1965 source.[29]

The Turkic refugees from Soviet Central Asia do not recognize the separate national status of the Tadzhiks. The late Mustafa Chokai-Oglu, the head of the short-lived Kokand government and a leader of Turkestani emigrés in Western Europe, recognized the existence of the ethnically and linguistically Iranian Tadzhiks among the dominant Turkish majority of Kazakhs, Uzbeks, and other groups who spoke one Turkish language, but he believed that culturally Tadzhiks merged with the Uzbeks and that they regarded themselves as members of the same political body.[30] Apart from the emigrés' obvious political motivation to preserve the image of one Turkestan, their insistence on the lack of cultural differentiation between the Uzbeks and the Tadzhiks had a basis in fact.

An assumption has been made here that the awakening of a dormant national potential in the Tadzhiks was caused by the desire of the Russian Communists to extend their power and influence into neighboring Asia. The awakening was made easier by a fortuitous combination of circumstances which gave the Tadzhiks a unique and, for Communist purposes, useful historical and cultural heritage. In the four decades of Soviet power, the Party succeeded only too well in awakening the potential, it seems. A Tadzhik national consciousness undoubtedly exists now, but, as will be seen later, it does not necessarily serve the nationality policy as Moscow would wish.

The one flaw in the theory of the formation of the Tadzhik nation is the discrepancy between the leading role played by the Tadzhiks in the past and their dismal backwardness and lack of a sense of identity at the turn of the century, which only the Russian Communists could improve.

The emphasis on the leading role of the Russians in Tadzhiki-

---

[29] From a 1929 source (Briskin, *Strana Tadzhikov,* p. 56): Tadzhiks, 40.7 per cent; Uzbeks, 26.9 per cent; Europeans, 29.5 per cent; and others, 2.9 per cent. A 1965 source (*KPT v dokumentakh,* p. 37) listed: Tadzhiks, 48 per cent; Uzbeks, 18 per cent; Europeans, 29 per cent; and others, 5 per cent.

[30] Mustafa Chokai-Oglu, "Turkistan," *Türkeli,* no. 1 (September, 1951), 10.

stan was an irritant when seen in the context of the revival of past Tadzhik glories. Although Tadzhik youth was taught to think of its forebears as the political and cultural leaders, it was also told that it owed its very nationhood to the Russians, and was to be subordinated to the Russians in the republic's everyday life.

Reinterpretations of the Russian historical role in Central Asia make interesting reading. In the 1920's Soviet historiography was dominated by the Pokrovskii school, which equated the colonial policies of imperial Russia with those of any other imperialist power such as France or Britain. Accordingly, it labeled the Russian conquest of the borderlands, including Central Asia, an "absolute evil" (*absoliutnoe zlo*). The school regarded tsarist Russia as "the prison of the people," and consequently condemned the imposition of Russian rule on non-Russian nationalities.

The first doubts about the blanket condemnation of Russian imperial conquests began to appear in the 1930's when it was pointed out by Party historians that Russian administration of the borderlands had brought benefits which otherwise would not have been available to the people there. By 1937 the Russian conquest had come to be regarded as a "lesser evil" (*naimen'sheie zlo*).

The appeal to Russian patriotism and nationalism was especially necessary in World War II in view of the defection to the enemy of members of some ethnic groups.[31] In 1945, in Stalin's famous toast of May 24, the Russians were referred to as the "leading Soviet nationality," "the elder brothers," and "the most prominent nation among all nations which constitute the Soviet Union."[32] The new emphasis on the Russian leading role was immediately reflected in the mass media and in scholarly works. The Russian people, their culture, and their historic "leading role" became the subject of Marxist-Leninist study, interpretation, and obligatory adulation after Stalin's signal. In history, the Russian people proved themselves to be a progressive influence in relations with their more backward neighbors; and at the turn of the last century it was the Russian proletariat that took on the leading

---

[31] Ukrainian nationalist elements collaborated with the Germans (as in World War I), and defectors from the Asian nationalities formed the backbone of the "Vlasov Division," which fought at the side of the Germans on the Eastern front.

[32] "Russkii narod—rukovodiashchaia sila sredi narodov nashei strany," *Bol'shevik*, no. 10 (May, 1945), 3.

progressive role in contacts with other nationalities of the Russian empire.

Mistakes in the teaching of history of the various nationalities were criticized by authoritative Party organs: one such mistake was to ignore the leading role played by the Russian proletariat in the national movements of the borderlands; another was the non-recognition of the progressive influence that Russian culture had had on subject peoples before the revolution.[33]

The "lesser evil" interpretation of the Russian conquest was further developed in the famous 1951–52 discussion that followed a letter by M. V. Nechkina to *Voprosy Istorii* of April, 1951. It was said that while the conquered people suffered under tsarist oppression, the conquest gave them an opportunity of contact with the Russian people (equally suffering from the tsarist oppression) and their more advanced culture and revolutionary movement. It also introduced capitalism into feudal areas and thus was historically progressive. Without the conquest there would have been no revolution in the borderlands and no advancement to socialism. Ultimately, therefore, despite the accompanying hardships, the conquest was a progressive phenomenon, objectively a "good" thing. The Russian conquest had saved Central Asia from a "fate worse than death"—a conquest by the British.[34] It was at this stage of the discussion that the word "conquest" (*zavoevanie*) disappeared and the word "incorporation" (*prisoedinenie*) was adopted to describe the annexation of the borderlands by the defunct tsarist empire.

This reinterpretation of the Russian conquest also led to a re-evaluation of native actions and attitudes toward incorporation. Whereas previously all national movements that opposed tsarist Russia had been regarded as "good," the re-evaluation carefully began to distinguish between movements that were "progressive" (directed by the lower classes against their rulers) and those that

[33] N. Iakovlev "O prepodavanii otechestvennoi istorii," *Bol'shevik*, no. 22 (November 30, 1947), 28–29.

[34] Based on "Central Asia and the Russian People," *Central Asian Review*, no. 3 (1953), pp. 1–8; and Konstantin F. Shteppa, "The 'Lesser Evil' Formula," pp. 107–20, in C. E. Black, ed., *Rewriting Russian History: Soviet Interpretation of Russia's Past*, 2d ed., rev. (New York: Vintage Books, 1962). See also Frederick C. Barghoorn, *Soviet Russian Nationalism* (New York: Oxford University Press, 1956).

were "reactionary" (directed by local national rulers against the Russians).[35]

The new theory presented to the Tadzhiks differed little from the one being circulated elsewhere in the Soviet Union; but one of its major spokesmen was Gafurov, a historian, and also the First Secretary of the Tadzhik Party. In a 1955 revision of his book on Tadzhik history, Gafurov listed five major reasons why the Russian conquest of Central Asia was a historically progressive phenomenon. First, Central Asia was a backward and isolated area where a patriarchal feudal social structure was still dominant, while Russia was already a capitalist society. The conquest stimulated the change in Central Asia from feudalism to capitalism and thus was historically progressive.[36] In the 1949 version of his book Gafurov maintained that capitalism would have developed in Central Asia even without contact with the Russians—a mistake for which he was criticized,[37] and one which he duly recanted.

Gafurov's second important point was that after its incorporation, Central Asia began to participate in world trade and to develop industrially. With industrialization came the beginnings of a native working class, which in turn led to contact with the "other Russia"—not the Russia of the tsars and the officials but that of Belinskii and Chernyshevskii. The third factor in favor of the conquest was that the people of Central Asia were given an opportunity to benefit from Russian culture and from the revolutionary enthusiasm of the Russian proletariat. Had they been conquered by England instead, there would have been no revolution because the English workers had already lost their revolutionary drive. The fourth and fifth arguments stressed the benefits of law and order imposed by the Russians on unruly Turkestan: the end of internecine wars and the abolition of slavery. Amid all these benefits Gafurov also listed one drawback, the double oppression suffered by the people when tsarist officials joined native leaders in their exploitation after the conquest. This too had its "progressive"

[35] See Chap. 7.

[36] Gafurov, *Istoriia*, pp. 423–26.

[37] "O nekotorykh voprosakh istorii narodov Srednei Azii," editorial in *Voprosy Istorii*, no. 4 (1951), 8.

side, however, because it had led to an alliance between the Russian and the native proletariats.[38]

In general, Gafurov de-emphasized the oppressive and colonial aspects of Russian rule before the revolution and made a careful distinction between the "objectively progressive internal historical significance of the incorporation into Russia" and the "colonizatory way in which this incorporation was effected, and the reactionary policy of Tsarism." The incorporation introduced Central Asia to capitalism, but feudal survivals were not and could not have been liquidated under tsarism; final victory over feudalism came only after the successful socialist revolution.[39]

The emphasis on the beneficial influence of Russia in Turkestan led Soviet historians to study the seventeenth century and earlier periods. They found that Central Asia had emerged from centuries of "cultural and economic stagnation" only because of early contacts and trade with Russia. The incorporation, they said, was a long process during which the progressive change in economic and cultural life in Turkestan had responded to the growth of contacts with Russia. The new interpreters also discovered that historically the Central Asian people had felt a strong gravitational pull toward Russia, and that incorporation was achieved not only by military conquest but also by the voluntary adherence of many tribes attracted to Russian rule by the promise of protection against the khans. They strongly emphasized the political and economic fragmentation of Turkestan preceding the incorporation, and they criticized the previous historical assumptions that it had been Nasrullah Khan of Bokhara who unified parts of Turkestan and that economic revival there had begun before the Russian-imposed peace. The unity the Russians brought to Turkestan had been necessary for the direct contact between the Russian and Central Asian people and for all progress there.[40] Discussing mili-

---

[38] Gafurov, *Istoriia,* pp. 423–26.

[39] I. S. Braginskii, S. Radzhabov, and V. A. Romodin, "K voprosu o znachenii prisoedineniia Srednei Azii k Rossii," *Voprosy Istorii,* no. 8 (August, 1953), 40.

[40] *Ibid.,* pp. 28–40, and S. P. Tolstov, "Rol' arkheologischeskikh i etnograficheskikh materialov v razrabotke spornykh voprosov istorii Srednei Azii nakanune prisoedineniia ee k Rossii," *Kratkie Soobshcheniia* (Akademiia Nauk SSSR, Institut Etnografii) no. 26 (1957), 34–35.

tary conquests in Central Asia, Gafurov used the neutral term "army" when referring to Russian troops but always the term "occupants" (*zakhvatchiki*) in relation to the British troops.

The cultural impact of Russian progressive elements was said to have resulted in the formation of the new native intelligentsia, among whom were the famous Tadzhiks, Ahmadi Donish, an educator, and Sadriddin Aini, a poet and a writer. The Russian printed word (in the newspapers *Samarkand, Rabochii,* and *Russkii Turkestan*) was said to have had a great impact on the revolutionary awakening of the native masses; the strength of this influence is doubtful, however, in view of the masses' ignorance of the Russian language and their overwhelming illiteracy. It is significant that the new interpretation described the Russian cultural role in terms of a "civilizing mission":

> Because of the much faster socioeconomic development of Russia, in the contacts (between Russia and Central Asia) the civilizing role played by Russia in relations with the peoples of Central Asia appears all the more clearly.[41]

The revolutionary Russian proletariat was credited with having fomented unrest in 1904–5 and in 1916–17:

> The Russian revolutionary social democrats played the most important role in organizing the toilers of Central Asia for the struggle with exploiters, and in preparing the toilers for the decisive fight with tsarism, the capitalists, landlords, bais, clergy, emirs, and khans.[42]

It was alleged that the unrest of 1905 in the cities and among railroad workers had prepared the Moslem masses to follow the Russian proletariat in the attack against their own bourgeoisie. The influence of Russian workers as teachers and leaders in the struggle against autocracy and the bourgeoisie was said to have increased after 1905 and to have contributed to the "hundreds" of "registered national revolts" in Turkestan in the first three years of World War I.[43]

[41] Braginskii, Radzhabov, and Romodin, "K voprosu," p. 22.
[42] *Ibid.,* p. 36.
[43] *Ibid.,* pp. 37–40, and Dzhabar Rasulov, *40 Let Kommunisticheskoi Partii Tadzhikistana* (Dushanbe, Izd. "Irfon," 1964), pp. 11–12; Braginskii, Radzhabov, and Romodin, "K voprosu," quote the following figures for the "registered" national revolts (*vystupleniia narodnykh mass*): 1914, 216; 1915, 246; 1916, 268; 1917 until the October revolution, 547 (p. 38). No source for the data is given.

There is little historical evidence to support these claims. The native masses' blind devotion to Islam renders any claim that they joined with alien "unbelievers" against their own upper classes, appointed by Allah, questionable, and it is a matter of record that Russian workers in Turkestan were contemptuous of the natives and chauvinistic in the extreme. It is also known that there was little contact between Russians and natives in Turkestan, principally as a result of the self-imposed isolation of the Moslem community. The exactness of the data on "national revolts" is difficult to check, but there was no widespread native revolutionary movement in Turkestan, only cases of sporadic and localized violence, predominantly anti-Russian in character, directed primarily against forcible conscription. Gafurov discussed peasant unrest among the Tadzhiks, including cases of stoning Russian officials and raids on Russian officials and bai. He concluded that "under the influence of the Russian revolution . . . the leading part of the Tadzhik working people . . . awakened to an active political role." [44] One marvels at the sophistication of the Tadzhik peasants who were able to distinguish between the Russian "class enemy," the officials, and the Russian "brothers," the workers.

The Russian role in making and consolidating the revolution in Turkestan was decisive, and the debt was freely and fervently acknowledged. In Tadzhikistan the Red Army had played a vital role in crushing the resistance of the native "exploiters" and in establishing Soviet rule:

> The absence of a working class and a Communist Party denied the people of Eastern Bokhara the opportunity to carry on an independent successful struggle for the final liquidation of the power of the exploiters. This task was completed only with the assistance of the Red Army.[45]

The account of the subsequent development of Soviet Tadzhikistan and of Russian assistance assumes the proportions of a fairy tale about Big Bad Wolves (the Emir and the British) and Fairy Godmothers (the Russians). The Tadzhik toilers rose against the *Emir* (narrates an article in a 1945 issue of *Kommunist Ta-*

---

[44] Gafurov, *Istoriia*, p. 470.

[45] B. Iskandarov, "Iz istorii bor'by za ustanovlenie sovetskoi vlasti v Tadzhikistane, *KT*, August 26, 1954, p. 2. See also AN TSSR, *Istoriia*, III, Book 1, *passim*.

dzhikistana) [46] but, because of the foreign imperialists' help, he was too strong for them, and thus they called in the Red Army. The Red Army chased the Emir and the imperialists out, and in the struggle Red soldiers and Tadzhik fighters "mingled their blood together," which is how their "eternal friendship" began. But the Emir would not give up. With the help of the imperialists, he fostered the civil war and terrorized the people in the mountains, and again the Red Army came to help. The people all hated the Basmachi and welcomed the Red Army with open arms. Together they won a final victory, after which the Tadzhiks got their own autonomous republic. However, the new Tadzhik ASSR faced many difficulties because of its economic and cultural backwardness. Who rushed in with assistance then? The "great Russian people"! They came with financial help, machinery, equipment, and specialists; they helped the Tadzhiks to collectivize agriculture, to irrigate the land and grow a rich cotton crop, and to industrialize. All this changed the economic face of the land. As for art and culture: with the assistance of the great Russian people, and under the leadership of the great Party of Lenin and Stalin, the ancient Tadzhik culture was revived. Enriched with socialist content, it was presented to the toilers and became their inspiration. The new Soviet Tadzhik intelligentsia was educated in the new network of schools.

> In all the difficult periods of the struggle for their liberation and in the building and strengthening of the power of the toilers, the great Russian people had invariably rendered assistance to the Tadzhiks.[47]

All of the great achievements in Tadzhikistan, said the Tadzhik First Secretary in 1945, resulted from the fact that "in the total effort to raise the level of their economy and culture, the Tadzhiks found support in the assistance of all the people of the USSR, and mainly in the assistance of the great Russian people." [48] He was echoed in 1946 by the Chairman of the Tadzhik Council of People's Commissars: "The toilers of Tadzhikistan will never forget the great help which the great Russian people have shown

[46] T. Granik, "Tadzhikistan v seme narodov SSSR. V pomoshch agitatoru," *ibid.*, December 28, 1945, p. 3.
[47] *Ibid.*
[48] *Ibid.*, July 15, 1945, p. 2.

them, the great Russian people who are the first among the peoples of the Soviet Union and the elder brothers of them all. This help shows clearly in all the sectors of socialist construction in the republic." [49]

The lyrical ecstasy on the subject of the "great Russian people" reached considerable heights. In a 1949 article on the Russian "elder brother and friend of the Tadzhiks," the qualities ascribed to the Russians read like a description of a legendary hero: "courage, bravery, fiery love for the motherland and hatred for its enemies; persistence in gaining the desired aim; love of work; and creative dynamism." Russians were "the leaders in culture, agriculture, crafts, education, law, and architecture"; they were "fighters for civilization and progress" (here followed a string of names from Radishchev to Herzen); and they gave to the world Lenin and Plekhanov, Pushkin and Tolstoy, musicians, writers, painters, and generals. The great Russian people gave birth to "the most progressive, the most revolutionary working class"; they "created the most powerful and the wisest Party in the world—the Party of the Bolsheviks"; they helped all other Soviet people to "develop economy and culture." Russian "engineers, teachers, doctors, agronomists, architects, and others made their way into the new republic (Tadzhikistan) to help in socialist construction and in educating the new intelligentsia; Russian artists taught Tadzhik artists; Russian doctors put an end to village charlatans; Russian intellectuals and scientists, engineers and agronomists worked in the republic; Russian architects made Stalinabad out of Dushambe"; and "in the Great Patriotic War the Russians led other nationalities to victory." [50]

Oriental imagery decorates poems dedicated to the Russians or to Moscow—the symbol of Russia—by the two major Tadzhik poets, Stalin-laureates Mirzo Tursun-Zade and Mirsaid Mirshakar. In his poem "To the Russian People," Mirzo Tursun-Zade compares the Russians to an eagle, and the other nationalities to eaglets:

[49] *Ibid.*, January 13, 1946, p. 3. The speaker, M. Kurbanov, was dismissed shortly thereafter as the head of the government. It was later revealed that he was guilty of trying to "set the government above the party." See Chap. 5.

[50] S. Mulladzhanov, "Starshii brat i drug Tadzhiskogo naroda," *ibid.*, November 18, 1949, p. 2.

An eagle rules the hatch of his eaglets—he
Supports first one then another of the eaglets
On the wing
He teaches them how to glide, to soar upwards,
To drop down, and to look far and near!
When the eagle-hero sees
That each little one gained experience
And can fly freely and lightly
Far and wide,
Then, proudly flying ahead
He leads them on the blue highway . . .
The great heroic Russian people
are the Eagle-people; their flight soars so high!
You gave us the wings, you gave us the strength,
You brought up in us the eagle-like pride . . .
Of all the world people not one
Is your equal, oh Russian giant!
And my Tadzhik people are now forever
joined with you. . . .[51]

Mirshakar's ode to Moscow begins:

Like scarlet silk of banners
Was the silk of heavens
When I entered the city of joy
The capital of happiness, glory and victories,
Moscow,
The like of which there is none in the world.[52]

The above quotations represent only an infinitesimal fraction of the deluge of pro-Russian propaganda to which Tadzhiks were daily subjected at work and at play, in the press, in books, and on the radio, at meetings and in theaters, in pictures and in song.

A doctrine of the "friendship of the people" (*druzhba narodov*), served to incorporate the theme of Russian leadership into the body of Marxism-Leninism. Grown as a result of the socialist transformation that the Soviet nationalities have undergone, druzhba

---

[51] Mirzo Tursun-Zade, "Russkomu Narodu," *ibid.*, January 1, 1946, p. 1.
[52] Mirsaid Mirshakar, "Rodnaia Mat'—liubimaia Moskva," *ibid.*, July 20, 1947, p. 3.

narodov rests on three necessary conditions, according to a 1952 formulation in the *Kommunist:* a political system based on popularly elected Soviets under a constitution which presupposes equality of all nations and is international in character; an economic basis of industrialization and socialist agriculture; and a cultural basis which is national in form for all component nations, but uniformly socialist in content.[53]

In Tadzhikistan the concept of druzhba narodov received special attention in 1954 on the occasion of the tricentennial of the unification of Russia and the Ukraine; the press was full of articles and poems praising and discussing it. All articles concerning druzhba narodov combined an enumeration of political, economic, and cultural achievements in Tadzhikistan gained under the Soviet power with unflattering comparisons to neighboring countries. The conclusion inevitably included the statement that only the leadership of the Communist Party and the selfless assistance and beneficial influence of the great Russian people had made all this progress possible.

Zarif Radzhabov, Doctor of Historical Sciences and Rektor of the Tadzhik State University in the 1950's, seems to have specialized in the theory of druzhba narodov. In 1954 he wrote a book on the subject [54] and also contributed articles to *Kommunist Tadzhikistana.*[55] In all his works Radzhabov stressed the beneficial Russian influence in Tadzhikistan going back to antiquity (he maintained that Firdousi had been influenced by contacts with Kievan Russia), and he discussed the gains derived from the incorporation. By 1954 the Russian conquest was no longer referred to as the "lesser evil" but as "the most important event in the history of the peoples of Central Asia." [56] The great achievements of Soviet rule in Tadzhikistan under the Russian leadership, and the Tadzhik Soviet culture and the debt it owed to Russian models such as Gorkii and Maiakovskii were points of special emphasis.

The crudeness of this approach was moderated somewhat in the

[53] Kim, *Torzhestvo ideologii,* pp. 57–61.

[54] Ia. Nal'skii, review of "K voprosu ob istoricheskikh korniakh druzhby narodov Srednei Azii z velikim russkim narodom," by Z. Radzhabov, *KT,* January 8, 1955, p. 3.

[55] *Ibid.,* January 14, 1954, p. 2, and November 13, 1954, p. 3, and *passim.*

[56] *Ibid.,* January 14, 1954, p. 2.

direction of the old "lesser evil" interpretation after the death of Stalin. It was admitted, for example, that some spontaneous progress had taken place in Turkestan under feudalism and without the Russian catalyst, and the drawbacks of the tsarist rule were again discussed.[57] In 1961 a historical meeting of the USSR Academy of Sciences condemned the error of "glossing over the reality":

> Some historians, on the grounds that Russia's annexations of a number of non-Russian peoples had certain progressive consequences for the development of the economy and culture of these peoples, tended to paint the annexation itself in idyllic terms, thereby unwittingly absolving tsarism and the tsarist satraps.[58]

In Tadzhikistan, however, the new moderation did not seem to affect the interpretation of the Russian role. In 1964 the First Secretary of the Tadzhik Party, Dzhabar Rasulov, had this to say about the incorporation of Central Asia into the Russian empire:

> Notwithstanding the reactionary aims pursued by the Tsarist autocracy, the incorporation of Central Asia into Russia had great progressive significance. Like all the people of Central Asia the Tadzhik people forever joined their fate to the fate of the great Russian people and to Russian history, the history of Belinskii and Herzen, of Chernyshevskii and Dobroliubov; to Russia, the motherland of Leninism, the country which became the center of international revolutionary movement.[59]

While the interpretation in the late 1950's and the early 1960's attempted to minimize the more jarring irritants in the relations between the Russians and the local people, a new element introduced into the nationality policy aimed at undermining the very existence of separate national structures, and at their gradual merger into a unified Soviet state. In theory, the new trend was to be expressed by a gradual, ever closer, cooperation (*sblizhenie*) between the Soviet nationalities which would eventually lead to their merger (*sliianie*). As formulated in the 1961 Party program, the new formula read: "Full-scale Communist construction signifies a new stage in the development of national relations in the

[57] "Nationalism and Progress," *Central Asian Review*, V, no. 1 (1957), 1–5.

[58] *Vestnik* Akademii Nauk SSSR, no. 1 (January, 1962), quoted in *Current Digest of Soviet Press*, XIV, no. 15, 2.

[59] Dzhabar Rasulov, *40 let*, p. 10. For similar interpretation see also Khamrakulov, "O nekotorykh osobennostiakh."

USSR in which the nations will draw still closer together and their complete unity will be achieved." [60]

The new line meant an ever stronger emphasis on the factors common to all the Soviet nationalities, "the Soviet content" of administration, culture, social relations and economy, and a de-emphasis of particular factors such as national heritage, requirements, and peculiarities. In general terms, while Khrushchev's economic and administrative reforms decentralized the state structure, giving greater powers to the republics, the power of economic management rested in the newly created economic regions. These sometimes did and sometimes did not coincide territorially with the republics, especially after the consolidation of the regions in the early 1960's.[61] The tendency to minimize the role of republican organizations was visible in the Party administration. In Central Asia, the new Central Asian Bureau of the Central Committee of the Communist Party of the Soviet Union (CPSU) and the Central Asian Economic Region rendered the position of the republican state and Party hierarchies tenuous. Although the region as a whole obtained a greater degree of autonomy than it had had under the old centralized system, the Uzbeks were the nationality that actually benefited most under the new arrangement.

On the constitutional side, the new line was reflected in the discussion of the planned transformation of Soviet federalism. It was said that while the state forms that reflected objective realities in the early period of the existence of the Soviet state were being modified, the growing, new, common, "international" Soviet foundation would come to dominate. The new objective reality would have to be reflected, therefore, in a new constitutional structure in the forthcoming period of the "building of communism." The disappearance of the republics was never explicitly acknowledged but the implications of the new theory were made

[60] The Program of the Communist Party of the Soviet Union, quoted in Charlotte Saikowski and Leo Gruliov, eds., *Current Soviet Policies IV* (New York: Columbia University Press, 1962), p. 26.

[61] Tsentral'noe Statisticheskoe Upravlenie pri Sovete Ministrov SSSR, *Narodnoe Khoziaistvo SSSR v 1964 г. Statisticheskii Ezhegodnik* (Moscow: "Statistika," 1965), p. 12, lists the following economic regions: the Baltic (including the three Baltic republics and Kaliningrad oblast), the Caucasian (three Caucasian republics), the Central Asian (four Central Asian republics), and the Kazakh and Belorussian (each coincident with the respective republics); it divides the Ukraine SSR into three and the RSFSR into ten regions.

clear, implications which were strengthened by frequent references to the boundaries of constituent republics "increasingly losing their former significance." [62]

With the ouster of Khrushchev, his administrative and management reforms were reversed, and the new gains of regional autonomy were lost. At the same time an attempt was made to conciliate the widespread dissatisfaction of the various national elites by a theoretical retreat in the matter of the "obsolete" character of the republics. While the new leaders continued to stress the trend toward closer cooperation between the Soviet nationalities and the building of the common economic and cultural bases at the Twenty-third Party Congress in 1966, as well as in other programmatic statements, they failed to mention a merger as the next logical step. The above pronouncements were also tempered by references to the "safeguarding of the interests and national peculiarities (*osobennosti*) of each nationality," [63] the "respect for each nationality's rights to run its own house (*gospodinstvo*)," [64] and considerations for the "interests of the individual socialist nations." [65]

These theoretical "concessions" did not affect either the Moscow centered decision-making process or the emphasis on the development of the new Soviet base and the Russian role inherent in it.[66] The Tadzhik leaders continued faithfully to follow the Russian star. In a *Pravda* article commemorating the Great October, Mirzo Tursun-Zade referred to Moscow as the Mecca of a new Great Pilgrimage for the Soviet and other nationalities, and concluded with a reference to his fellow Tadzhiks: "My people have em-

[62] M. Kh. Khakimov, "O nekotorykh voprosakh razvitiia natsional'noi sovetskoi gosudarstvennosti v sovremennyi period," *Obshchestvennye Nauki v Uzbekistane*, no. 6, 1964, quoted in *Central Asian Review*, XII, no. 4, 1964, 254–56, and the Party Program, as quoted in Saikowski and Gruliow, *Current Soviet Policies IV*, p. 26.

[63] Leonid Brezhnev, Report to the Twenty-third Congress of the CPSU, March 29, 1966, *XXIII S'ezd Kommunisticheskoi Partii Sovetskogo Soiuza, 29 Marta–8 Aprelia 1966 goda. Stenograficheskii Otchet.* I (Moscow: Gospolitizdat, 1966), p. 104.

[64] Iu. I. Paletskis, "50 let sovetskogo mnogonatsional'nogo gosudarstva," *Sovetskoe Gosudarstvo i Pravo*, no. 11 (November, 1967), 20.

[65] Leonid Brezhnev at the celebration of the fiftieth anniversary of Soviet rule in the Ukraine, *Pravda*, December 24, 1967, p. 1.

[66] For a more detailed analysis of the recent developments in the Soviet nationality policy and federalism, see my chapter "The Dilemma of Nationalism in the USSR" in John W. Strong, ed., *The Soviet Union under Brezhnev and Kosygin*, to be published in 1970 by D. Van Nostrand Co.

barked on the Great Pilgrimage; they followed October, they followed Lenin." [67]

In retrospect, the role played by the Russians in Central Asia was not an agreeable one and did not endear them to the local population. It would be naive to suppose that they are liked there, in spite of all the progress the area has made under Soviet rule. In the eyes of the natives, the Russians have become identified with hardship and oppression at every stage of development since the revolution, and for all the emphasis on druzhba narodov and socialist brotherhood, they still represent an alien rule and a privileged minority.

[67] Mirzo Tursun-Zade, "Pokhod k Vershine," *Pravda*, October 25, 1967, p. 3.

THE POWER STRUCTURE AND SOCIETY:
THE ETHNIC PATTERN [1]

FOR POLITICAL AND DEMOGRAPHIC REASONS, the Tadzhiks as a national group were of negligible importance at the All-Union scene. The population of the Tadzhik SSR amounted to no more than approximately 1 per cent of the total in the postwar period; the percentage of the Tadzhik ethnic group was even smaller. The Tadzhik Party has never counted for more than 0.5 per cent of the total membership of the Communist Party of the Soviet Union (CPSU), and the proportion of ethnic Tadzhiks to all the other nationalities in the membership was even lower. The first 2 Tadzhiks joined the Party in 1917; in 1920 there were 88 of them, and in 1927, at 1,370, they constituted 0.1 per cent of all members.[2] Even in 1965, when the Tadzhik contingent in the Party had increased to almost 42,000, their proportion in the membership was not higher than 0.4 per cent of the total,[3] and not all Tadzhik Com-

---

[1] The methodology used here is based on an examination of names which appeared in the republican press in connection with daily Party and government activities. Persian and Turkic names can easily be differentiated from Slavic names, but it was not possible to distinguish the specific nationality within each group, unless it was given. Bearers of Asian names are here classified as "Local"; bearers of Slavic names as "Russian." A few of the Caucasian, Jewish, and other European names are included in the "Russian" category. The Russian custom of using a patronymic was helpful in the identification of doubtful names. Although a margin of error exists, the consequent deviation does not significantly affect the findings.

[2] *VKP(b) Perepis'1927 goda.* no. 7, Part I, 13, 148–49.

[3] "KPSS v tsifrakh," *Partiinaia Zhizn'*, no. 1 (January, 1962) 49; and "KPSS v tsifrakh," *Partiinaia Zhizn'*, no. 10 (May, 1965), 12.

munists were living within the boundaries of the Tadzhik republic.[4]

Qualitatively, also, the Tadzhiks had little importance in the All-Union hierarchy. Not one Tadzhik was ever included in the Politbureau (the old Presidium), the nerve center of the CPSU and the governing body of the USSR. The Tadzhik Party's First Secretary was usually included in the All-Union Central Committee, an *ex officio* privilege accorded to republican secretaries, but there he was one among many. As far as is known, no Tadzhiks were ever included in the membership of the highest executive agencies of the All-Union government. A substantial representation, given to Tadzhikistan because it was a republic with an autonomous oblast in the Council of Nationalities of the USSR Supreme Soviet, was of little political significance, even though it provided the only tangible benefit that their autonomous status gave Tadzhiks at the federal level. As a result of the centralized hierarchy of the Party and its monopoly of political power, and the centralized character of Soviet public administration (especially in the last decade of Stalin's rule), the Tadzhiks had no effective voice at all in the All-Union decision-making process which vitally affected the total picture of life in the republic.

Union republics have virtually no power to influence their own destinies, as their authority is limited to implementation of policies conceived and formulated in Moscow. Nevertheless, the republican authorities have some discretionary powers which are required for effective implementation of All-Union tasks. These are vested primarily in the republican Party apparatus, which, in turn, supervises the state bureaucracy. From the time of the establishment of Soviet power in Tadzhikistan, as in other Central Asian republics, the Party and state hierarchies were heavily infiltrated and controlled by the Russians, and the purges of the 1930's resulted in the creation of a pattern of direct Russian ascendancy, with top positions in republican and oblast administration occupied by representatives of the All-Union Party and state agencies, most of whom were either Russians or other Slavs. With the end of the war a new pattern in the placement of local and Russian cadres began to ap-

[4] In 1961 over 9,000 ethnic Tadzhik Party members lived outside the Tadzhik SSR (See "KPSS v tsifrakh," 1962, p. 49).

pear, however, which signified a change in the All-Union policy in the direction of greater emphasis on the formal autonomy of the union republics within the federal soviet structure. The new pattern provided for a "representative aspect," which satisfied the requirements of nominal sovereignty of the minority nationalities, and a "control aspect," which safeguarded the central political control of Moscow. In Central Asia, including Tadzhikistan, the pattern was introduced in 1944–45. Local nationals were required to occupy the highest hierarchical positions and all posts of representative character. Invariably, however, a local leader was either seconded by a Russian or backed by a Russian or Russians close to him in the hierarchy. The local leader satisfied the representative aspect of the pattern, and his Russian deputy provided the necessary control aspect. The lower executives were almost always Russian, especially in the central Party and state agencies. While not in the public eye, they actually formed the backbone of the republican bureaucracy.

In a subtle refinement of the usual Soviet practice, two men, instead of one, headed each power cluster within the Party and the government hierarchies—a device that undoubtedly proved useful in checking the power ambitions of both. One was a local Communist, offering visible proof to the Tadzhiks that one of their own people could attain honor, power, and prestige within the Soviet system. The other was a Russian; alien to the country and to its people, history, needs, and aspirations, he served as the "eyes and ears" of the Central Committee of the CPSU.

There is little doubt that the Russian generally had more authority than the Asian in the relationship, because he had behind him all the power of the All-Union apparatus. Nevertheless, the respective power of the two men at each level was strongly influenced by their individual standing in the Party and by their personal "pull" with the higher authorities. At least one of the Tadzhik first secretaries of the KPT Central Committee had strong enough support in Moscow to challenge his Russian counterpart.[5] Much depended on the controls exercised by each Asian leader over his own apparatus and on his ability to build and maintain a personal power machine. Some were quite successful, for a time,

[5] See Chap. 5.

in avoiding Russian interference. On the whole, however, the pattern of the distribution of the Russian cadres, and especially the customary supervision by the Russians of personnel placement at each administrative level, prevented the exercise of any meaningful local autonomy.

The system assured direct political control from Moscow, and it also maintained the fiction of national sovereignty which was important on the domestic scene and for foreign propaganda. The Asian republics, Tadzhikistan among them, were designed to attract their Asian neighbors into the Soviet orbit. The system also provided the Soviet-educated native intelligentsia with an outlet for their ambitions and aspirations. Those who were willing to toe the Moscow line were given a position in the power structure, sometimes a prominent one.

The pattern applied at the republican level, and also in the larger cities and the provinces. At the raion level, Asians predominated in the power structure, despite a continuous pressure to increase the number of Russian officials there. In general, local nationals were encouraged to enter rank-and-file Party and government positions, but key posts—in term of actual power—were reserved for the Russians. The pattern was flexible and allowed for considerable variation, as long as there was at least one Russian within each power cluster.

The Russian (European) ascendancy in the key positions was not exclusive to Tadzhikistan but applied throughout Soviet Central Asia in Uzbekistan, Kirgizia, and Turkmenia, and in the southern oblasts of Kazakhstan, which are geographically a part of the area. In fact, it is interesting to note that among the Central Asian republics the pattern was least clearly defined in Tadzhikistan. The ratio of local nationals to Russians in the Party and elective government bodies was higher there than in any of the other republics, and there were fewer Russians who were second in command in the Party oblast committees and the oblast soviet executive committees.[6]

[6] See *Soviet Central Asia;* Subcontractor's Monograph, HRAF-49 American University, 1, 3 vols. (New Haven: Human Relations Area Files, Inc., 1956), III, my chapters, "Structure of Government," and "Political Dynamics," 726–831. In the 1948–56 period the first secretaries of the central committees of the Soviet Central Asian republics (excluding Kazakhstan) were all "Local"; the second secretaries

Various explanations offer themselves. There were relatively few Russians in Tadzhikistan, despite the heavy influx after 1929, not enough to fill secondary posts in the hierarchy below the republican level. There may also have been no need to keep Russian deputies in areas that were thinly populated and economically poor and that were already controlled by Russian military border units. Another theory, offered here as speculation, concerns the role played by Bobodzhan Gafurovich Gafurov, the First Secretary of the Tadzhik Party from 1946 to 1956. Unlike his counterparts in the other republics, he held the post for a decade. It seems that he had support in Moscow and consequently more real local power, and it is possible that his influence was responsible for the "loopholes" in the pattern in Tadzhikistan.

One could argue that the placement of Russian Communist cadres within the Central Asian power structure was not a deliberate policy and that the pattern of alternate distribution of Asian and European cadres was simply a matter of filling jobs with the best available people in conditions of acute shortage of qualified native personnel. But the pattern appears to be much more than just a coincidence. In the war years Russians held top positions; their departure and replacement by native cadres began simultaneously, and the changeover was carried out, completed, and subsequently maintained in the same manner in all the republics of Central Asia. Another factor that argues against the coincidence theory is the Russian concentration in the parts of the power structure with the greatest power capacity: the more powerful a

were all "Russian." By 1952, the same pattern was formed in Party committees of all the oblasts of Uzbekistan and Kirgizia, in all but one oblast of Turkmenia, and in all nine southern oblasts of Kazakhstan. The same pattern existed in the councils of ministers and presidiums of the Supreme Soviets of the five republics, and in the executive committees of the oblast soviets; security agencies and armed services, on the other hand, were staffed predominantly by the Russians. See also H. Carrère-d'Encausse et A. Benningsen, "Pouvoir apparent et pouvoir réel dans les républiques musulmanes de l'URSS," *Problèmes Soviétiques,* no. 1 (April, 1958), 57–73; Michael Rywkin, *Russia in Central Asia* (New York: Collier Books, 1963), Olaf Caroe, *Soviet Empire: The Turks of Central Asia and Stalinism* (London: Macmillan, 1953), and Abdurakhman Avtorkhanov, "Denationalization of the Soviet Ethnic Minorities," *Studies on the Soviet Union,* new ser. IV, no. 1 (1964): 74–99. The pattern continued unchanged into the sixties. In 1962 all the Party first secretaries in the five republics were Asians, and all the second secretaries were Europeans; all the chairmen of the councils of ministers were Asians, and all the first deputy chairmen were Europeans. *Current Digest,* XIV (1962): no. 11, *passim.*

given unit in the Party or state hierarchy, the higher the proportion of Russians among its members. There were virtually no Asians among the directing personnel of the security agencies charged with safeguarding the political status quo, and of the armed service units stationed in the area. The Russian infiltration of the power structure in Central Asia assured political conformity and efficient implementation of All-Union policies. A specific aim was served in the policy of penetration of each of the several social and political strata of the Tadzhik society. The requirements of centralized decision-making were met by the penetration by the Party of the whole political, social, and economic structure, and by the placement of Russians within the Party apparatus itself. Deterrents to political opposition and unrest were provided by the police and the army, the membership of which was made immune to local influences. Administration and managerial needs of the society were served by emigrants from European Russia who brought with them the specialized knowledge necessary for modernization.

THE TADZHIK COMMUNIST PARTY

The Russians constituted 13 per cent of the Tadzhik population in 1959 (as compared to 9 per cent in 1939), and the European contingent (if the deported Germans are excluded) as a whole did not exceed 15 per cent. The Europeans in the Tadzhik Communist Party, on the other hand, made up almost 40 per cent of the membership in the late 1950's and the early 1960's, with ethnic Russians alone accounting for one-fourth of the total. Tadzhiks and Uzbeks combined in the membership did not make up more than 60 per cent, even though they constituted three-fourths of the population of the republic in 1959 (Tables 2-1 and 4-1).

The distribution and changes in the ethnic pattern of the Party membership can best be gauged by comparing ethnic proportions through the years of the Party's development; data on the Party's ethnic composition were not available in years of Stalin's rule, but a complete documentation was published in Tadzhikistan in 1965. Asians dominated the membership quantitatively before the great purges of the 1930's, even though the European share, one-fourth of the total, gave the latter a disproportionately large representa-

Table 4-1. Tadzhik Communist Party Membership

It is interesting to note the discrepancies between the series of membership figures below and the figures disclosed in reports of the Party's First Secretaries to Party Congresses: the latter were much higher. For example, the 1948 figure given at the Eighth Congress was 34,254 (*KT*, September 20, 1952, p. 2), the 1952 and 1954 figures given at the Ninth Congress were 37,801 and 38,096, respectively (*KT*, January 24, 1954, p. 2); the 1958 figure given at the Eleventh Congress was the same. (T. Ul'dzhabaev, *Otchetnyi doklad Tsentral'nogo Komiteta Kommunisticheskoi Partii Tadzhikistana XI S'ezdu Kompartii Tadzhikistana* (Stalinabad: Tadzhikgosizdat, 1958). Later figures were again higher: the 1961 figure (Fourteenth Congress) was 57,209 (*KT*, September 23, 1961, p. 4) and the 1963 figure (Fifteenth Congress) was 62,211 (*KT*, December 26, 1963, p. 3).

| | | Total Women | | Ethnic Composition | | | | | | | |
| | Total Member-ship | | | Tadzhiks | | Uzbeks | | Russians | | Other | |
Date[a]		No.	%	No.	%	No.	%	No.	%	No.	%
1925	435	14	3	234	54	64	15	64[b]	15[b]	73[c]	16[c]
1929	1,479	69	4	710	48	269	18	432[b]	29[b]	68[c]	5[c]
1932	12,671	1,016	8	6,005	49	2,748	21	2,704[b]	21[b]	1,214[c]	9[c]
1933	14,329		9	7,575	53	3,177	22	2,480	17	1,097	8
1935[d]	4,791		13	2,229	47	986	20	939	19	637	14
1936	5,153		13	2,418	47	981	19	1,192	23	562	11
1937	4,603		14	2,116	46	824	18	992	22	671	14
1938	4,715	700	15	1,971	42	776	16	1,197	25	771	17
1941	14,500	2,270	15	6,214	43	2,440	17	3,712	26	2,134	14

Year		%		%		%		%		%
1942	13,513	2,659	20	5,704	41	2,190	16	3,156	23	2,463	20
1945	16,890	4,783	28	7,104	42	2,423	14	4,121	24	3,242	20
1946	19,645	4,551	23	8,765	45	3,159	16	4,661	24	3,060	15
1947	26,721	5,398	20	11,193	42	4,225	16	7,143	27	4,160	15
1948	31,301	5,986	19	12,496	40	4,761	15	8,994	29	5,050	16
1949	31,832	5,982	19	12,671	40	4,702	15	9,267	29	5,192	16
1950	31,234	5,970	18	12,401	40	4,658	15	9,173	29	5,002	16
1951	32,428	6,245	19	12,721	39	4,724	15	9,783	30	5,200	16
1952	33,506	6,546	19	13,272	39	4,941	15	9,925	30	5,368	16
1953	34,844	6,841	20	13,871	39	5,118	15	10,415	30	5,440	16
1954	32,355	6,341	19	13,931	43	5,244	17	8,376	26	4,804	14
1955	33,082	6,382	19	14,491	44	5,247	16	8,431	25	4,913	15
1956	35,124	6,417	18	15,389	44	5,622	16	8,998	26	5,115	14
1957	39,052	7,467	19	16,942	43	5,968	15	10,324	27	5,818	15
1958	41,588	7,826	18	18,196	44	6,410	15	10,839	26	6,143	15
1959	44,788	8,547	19	19,949	45	6,966	16	11,388	25	6,485	14
1960	47,920	9,024	19	21,579	45	7,560	16	11,927	25	6,854	14
1961	52,014	9,651	19	23,423	45	8,345	16	12,769	25	7,477	14
1962	58,493	10,976	19	26,619	45	9,533	16	14,168	25	8,173	14

Source: *Kommunisticheskaia partiia Tadzhikistana v dokumentakh i tsifrakh (1924–1963 gg.) Sbornik dokumentov i materialov o roste i regulirovanii sostava partiinoi organizatsii* (Dushanbe: Izd-vo "Irfon," 1965), pp. 37, 62, 81–82, 98, 120, 121, 156–57, 214–15.

[a] As of January 1, except that data for 1933 are given for various periods during the year and data for 1962 are given as of December 10.
[b] Russians and other Europeans.
[c] Other Asians.
[d] Data were not available for six raions.

tion in comparison with their meager strength in the population. After the purges, the strength of the Asian contingent declined from three-fourths to roughly two-thirds of the total, while that of the Europeans increased to one-third. The proportion remained generally unchanged through the war years, even though a slight increase in favor of the European group was noticeable. The lowest point in the Asian participation, and, proportionately, the highest in that of the Russians, was reached in the last years of Stalin's rule, especially in the 1951–53 period: the Tadzhiks then constituted 39 per cent and the Russians 30 per cent of the total TSSR Party membership. The situation changed after 1953; there was somewhat greater Asian participation, and the proportion of Tadzhiks to Russians in the membership stabilized at 9 to 5. In this connection it is interesting to note that Stalin's death must have been followed by an exodus of Russians from Tadzhikistan: between 1953 and 1954 there was a sharp decline in the numbers of the Russian members of the Communist Party of Tadzhikistan (KPT) (a loss of approximately 2,000), but there was no corresponding decline in the Asian group (see Table 4-1). It is impossible to judge whether Russian functionaries and officials had been recalled to Moscow or whether they had pulled strings to get back to the capital in anticipation of changes and better assignments.

The quantitative strength of the Russians in the Party membership was further augmented by their qualitative distribution in the governing bodies of the Party, the Central Committee, its Bureau and Secretariat, and the regional Party committees: province committees (*obkom*) in the provinces (*oblast*), city committees (*gorkom*) in the cities(*gorod*), and district committees (*raikom*) in the districts (*raion*).

In the 1945–56 period the Russian strength in the Central Committee was comparable to that among the Party's rank and file; it also reflected the fluctuations of the period after Stalin's death. The Russian share of the membership varied from 37 per cent of the total in 1948 to 26 per cent in 1956, with a low of 21 per cent in 1954 (see Table 4-2).[7] The last figure indicates that many of the

[7] The ratio did not change in the sixties. At the Fourteenth Congress of the KPT in 1961, Europeans constituted 24 per cent of the newly elected Central Committee. A similar ratio existed at the Fifteenth Congress in 1963 (*KT*, September 24, 1961, p. 1, and December 27, 1963, p. 1).

Table 4-2. Central Committee of the KPT and Auditing Commission: Nationality and Sex[a]

Congress	Russians				Locals				Women		
	M	W	Total	GT	M	W	Total	GT	Total	GT	GT
				%				%		%	
Seventh, 1948											
CC members	26	1	27	35	41	9	50	65	10	14	77
CC candidates	15		15	43	15	5	20	57	5	14	35
CC total	41	1	42	37	56	14	70	63	15	13	112
Auditing											
commission	6	1	7	33	14		14	67	1	4	21
Eighth, 1952											
CC members	22	1	23	28	50	8	58	72	9	11	81
CC candidates	12	1	12	29	22	7	29	71	7	17	41
CC total	34	1	35	29	72	15	87	71	16	13	122
Auditing											
commission	7		7	21	24	2	26	79	2	6	33
Ninth, 1954											
CC members	19	1	20	24	54	11	65	76	12	14	85
CC candidates	5		5	14	26	4	30	86	4	11	35
CC total	24	1	25	21	80	15	95	79	16	13	120
Auditing											
commission	10		10	32	21		21	68			31
Tenth, 1956											
CC members	26	1	27	28	60	10	70	72	11	11	97
CC candidates	12		12	22	38	5	43	78	5	10	55
CC total	38	1	39	26	98	15	113	74	16	11	152
Auditing											
commission	11		11	27	28	2	30	73	2	5	41
Seventh–Tenth											
CC total average				28				72			

Sources: Compiled on the basis of lists of names in *KT,* December 24, 1948, p. 1; September 24, 1952, p. 1; January 21, 1954, p. 1; January 31, 1956, p. 1.

[a] M, men; W, women; GT, grand total.

Russians who left the republic after Stalin's death must have been high officials and members of the Central Committee. The Russian ratio was higher among members than among candidate members of the Central Committee, except in 1948, the last year in which the membership still included a few of the wartime Russian officials who had gradually been leaving the republic. Local nationals, including some ethnic Asians from outside the republic, made up the balance of the membership and averaged 72 per cent of the total. The average Russian-Asian ratio in the Central Committee for the postwar decade was 1 to 2.6 (see Table 4-2). On the whole the proportion of Russians (Europeans) in the Central Committee was almost, but not quite, double that in the population.

It is important to keep in mind that, as in the other Soviet republics, the Party Central Committee included the cream of the political leadership. In the period under review, the Tadzhik Central Committee included all of its secretaries and most of its department chiefs, all first secretaries of obkoms, and, after the abolition of four out of the six oblasts, about 70 per cent of all first secretaries of the raikoms. These included all first secretaries of raions directly under republican jurisdiction. In contrast, only the first secretary and, at most, three other secretaries of the Central Committee of the Young Communist League (Komsomol) were included. Chiefs of other important mass and professional organizations were also Central Committee members: the Chairman of the Central Council of Trade Unions, the Chairman of the paramilitary civilian defense agency called DOSARM (later DOSAAF), and a chairman, a secretary, and one other member of the Tadzhik Union of Soviet Writers (an organization of great importance in view of the Soviet cultural policies in the republic).

In the government hierarchy, the Chairman of the Council of Ministers, the Deputy Chairmen, and more than a half of the ministers and heads of agencies were included in the Central Committee, as were the Chairman and Deputy Chairman of the Presidium of the Supreme Soviet. Chairmen of the executive committees of the oblast soviets were also included, but not the chairmen of the raion soviets' executive committees (with a few exceptions). The Procurator General of the republic was a member, but none of the members of the Supreme Court were. The committee also included a token representation of "toilers," and many persons with Russian names whose official status could not be determined; doubtless the new functionaries sent from Moscow to guide the republic in its period of transition from the era of Stalin to that of Khrushchev.

The Central Committee was too large and met too infrequently (an average of 3 or 4 times a year in 1946–56), to exercise day-to-day political leadership. In conformity with the usual Soviet pattern, actual power rested with the Central Committee's Bureau

THE POWER STRUCTURE AND SOCIETY

and the secretaries; under the Stalinist system of "one-man rule" (*edinonachalie*), the post of first secretary was a key one, but in Tadzhikistan, as in other republics of Central Asia, power was actually shared between an Asian first secretary and a Russian second secretary. The third secretary was usually an Asian. Local first and third secretaries and Russian second secretaries continued to be combined throughout the period. Between 1945 and 1948 the ratio of Russian to local secretaries in the Central Committee was 5 to 4 in 1945 and 4 to 4 in 1946–48. In 1952–54 there were only 3 secretaries; of the 5 secretaries in 1956, 3 were local and two were Russian (see Chart 4-1).

The Bureau of the Central Committee included, *ex officio,* all of the CC's secretaries and some of its other leaders. In the period under review, its ethnic content was about evenly divided; there was a Russian majority in 1948 and a local majority in 1956. The ratio of Russians to locals was 8 to 6 in 1948, 7 to 7 in 1952, 6 to 6 in 1954, and 5 to 8 in 1956 (Chart 4-1).[8]

An analysis of the ethnic composition of the Secretariat of the Central Committee indicated a substantial Russian majority among its functionaries. The data, unfortunately, were not complete. The most complete series of the names of chiefs and deputy chiefs of the departments of the Secretariat available for 1946 indicated that there were twice as many Russians as there were local nationals. Only the names of department chiefs were available for later years, and among them there was an even balance between Russian and local functionaries (see Chart 4-2). An examination of scattered information appearing in the Tadzhik press seemed to confirm the impression that there was a large Russian majority, including many women, in the Central Committee apparatus.

A death notice of an organizer in the Organization and Instruc-

---

[8] The 1956 trend, the decrease in the number of Russians in the bureau, continued into the sixties. In 1958–60 the bureau was composed of 4 Russians and 10 Locals; in 1961 the ratio was 4 to 7; and in 1963 it was 3 to 9 in the Presidium (formerly the bureau). In 1963, however, three new bodies were added to the central Party organs, in line with the All-Union changes of the period, and the Russian contingent increased again; the Bureau for Industry (4 Russians, 2 Locals), Bureau for Agriculture (4 Russians, 3 Locals), and the Party-State Control Committee (6 Russians, 5 Locals). *Ezhegodnik Bol'shoi Sovetskoi Entsiklopedii* (hereafter referred to as *Ezhegodnik BSE*) (Moscow: "Sovetskaia Entsiklopediia," 1959), p. 164; *ibid.,* 1960, p. 158; *KT,* September 24, 1961, p. 1, December 27, 1963, p. 1.

tion Department of the Secretariat in 1945 was signed by 21 persons, 15 of whom were Russian.[9] Among the functionaries of the apparatus of the Party and the Komsomol Central Committees who received awards in December, 1945, for directing agricultural work, there were 21 Russians and 8 locals.[10] A high proportion of Russians was revealed by a perusal of three enormous lists of awards bestowed at the occasion of the twentieth anniversary of the Tadzhik SSR in 1949, and on the occasion of the Tadzhik thirty-year jubilee (the anniversary of the establishment of the Tadzhik ASSR) in 1954. To judge by the lists, the number of Russians in the apparatus of the Central Committee actually increased between 1949 and 1954. The Russian to local ratio in 1949 was 1 to 1, while in 1954 it was 2 to 1 (see Table 4-3).

Table 4-3. CENTRAL COMMITTEE SECRETARIAT: NATIONALITY AND SEX OF FUNCTIONARIES BELOW THE LEVEL OF DEPARTMENT AND DEPUTY CHIEF

The positions held by the Central Committee functionaries were frequently specified when their names were included in the lists of awards. The positions included Assistant to the First Secretary, Technical Secretary, Manager (*upravliaiushchii delami*), chiefs of sections within the departments, responsible organizers, lecturers, and instructors.

Nationality and Sex	1945–1946	1949	1954
Russians			
Men	10	38	21
Women	2	21	44
Total	12	59	65
Locals			
Men	1	49	27
Women		7	4
Total	1	56	31

Sources: *KT*, 1945–46 *passim* and December 31, 1945, pp. 1–3; December 18–31, 1949; October 24–29, 1954; November 17, 1954; and November 18, 1954.

It is interesting to note that the special section (*osobyi sektor*) of the Secretariat, commonly considered to be a secret police nucleus within the Party apparatus, was headed by a Russian woman in the period under review (see Chart 4-2). In 1954 there were five, or

[9] *KT*, March 13, 1945, p. 2.
[10] *Ibid.*, December 31, 1945, pp. 1–3.

possibly more, assistants to the First Secretary, all of whom were Russian. Russians also outnumbered the locals among lecturers, instructors, and clerical personnel of the Secretariat of the Central Committee: of the total of 70 decorated in 1954, 47 were Russians, most of them women (Table 4-3). To generalize, Russians appeared to have dominated the Cadres Department and the various administrative, technical, and economic departments, whereas local nationals were prominent in departments that required direct contact with the population and knowledge of local languages, such as the Department of Agitation and Propaganda and the various cultural departments. The head of the Department for Work with Women was always a local woman, as were many of its instructors, but the deputy chief of the department was a Russian woman. On the whole, Russians constituted from one-half to three-fourths of the functionaries of the Secretariat at all levels; their control of the placement of cadres throughout the republic was maintained through their control of the Cadres Department.

Russian concentration in the obkom apparatus was less heavy than in the Central Committee, as revealed by scattered information available in the Tadzhik press. There the Russian-Asian ratio was approximately 1 to 1; nevertheless, it was officially admitted that Tadzhiks were in the minority in the provincial Party administration. At a 1947 meeting to discuss party cadres, Kul'kov, then the Central Committee Secretary for Cadres, divulged that only 40 per cent of the obkom apparatus functionaries were Tadzhiks. He did not specify the nationalities of the remaining 60 per cent but presumably most of them were Russians. Speaking of individual obkoms, he said that in the Garm obkom the majority of raikom secretaries and department chiefs were of local origin. In the Stalinabad obkom, of the 66 people placed in leading positions in the five months of 1947, only 31 had been Tadzhiks and Uzbeks.[11] The 1949 award list included 71 names of obkom functionaries, of whom 37 were Russians and 34 locals.[12]

No complete data on obkom secretaries were available. An ethnic breakdown of the known names fails to indicate the clear "local-Russian-local" pattern characteristic of the obkoms of other

[11] *Ibid.*, June 28, 1947, p. 2.
[12] *Ibid.*, December 18–31, 1949.

Central Asian republics in comparable periods. In most cases, however, there were at least 1 or 2 Russians among the 5 secretaries of each obkom (see Table 4-4).

Table 4-4. OBKOM SECRETARIES: ETHNIC PRESENTATION[a]

Area	Year	First Secretary	Second Secretary	Secretary	Secretary for Cadres	Secretary for Agitprop
Stalinabad oblast	1948	L[b]	R	R	LW	L
	1950	L	R		LW	
Leninabad oblast	1948	R	L		L	L
	1950	R	L	R		
	1954	L	L	LW		
Gorno-Badakhshan	1948	L	R	L	R	
autonomous oblast	1952	L	R	L		
	1954	L	R	L		
Kulyab oblast	1946	R	L		L	R
	1952	L	L	L		
Garm oblast	1948	L	L	L		
	1952	L	R	L		
Kurgan-Tyube oblast	1946	L	R		R	R
Ura-Tyube oblast	1946	L	R		L	L
Leninabad city	1948	R	L	R		
	1953	L	R	LW		

Source: Based on scattered information in the issues of *Kommunist Tadzhikistana* for the appropriate years. Data include Leninabad city for the appropriate years.

[a] R, Russian; L, local; W, woman.
[b] Gafurov, B. G., thus the Second Secretary (Obnosov in 1948, Kuznetsov in 1950) was the *de facto* secretary.

More information was available on the Stalinabad obkom and gorkom. Of the 5 secretaries of the Stalinabad obkom in March, 1948, 3 were locals (first, cadres, and propaganda secretaries) and 2 were Russians (second and third secretaries), as was the deputy secretary for industry and transport. Gafurov, First Secretary of the Central Committee, was also nominally the First Secretary of the Stalinabad obkom, and thus the functions of first secretary there must actually have been carried out by the Russian second secretary. Bureau and department chiefs were evenly divided; there were 7 Russians and 7 locals, and 4 Russians and 4 locals, respec-

Table 4-5. STALINABAD GORKOM: ETHNIC PRESENTATION[a]

	1946	1947	1948	1951	1952	1953	1954	1956
Positions								
First Secretary	L	L	R	RW	RW	RW	L	L
Second Secretary	R	R	L	L	L	L	R	R
Secretary	L	L	RW	RW	R	R	R	R
Secretary for Cadres	L	L	L					
Secretary for Propaganda	R	R	RW					
Secretaries		2L		L				
Deputy Secretaries		2R, 1LW	2R, L					
Bureau members	5R, 4L	8R, 5L	7R, 5L	3R, 5L	5R, 4L	5R, 4L	4R, 5L	5R, 4L
Departments								
Cadres[b]		R	R		R		R	R
Agitation and Propaganda		LW	RW		R		R	R
Organization and Instruction		R	R/L					
Planning, Finance, Trade[c]					L		L	L
Industry and Transportation					R		R	R
City Economy					L			
Women			LW		LW		LW	LW
Military		R	R					
Gorkom members					31R, 39L	31R, 46L	43R, 38L	40R, 42L
Auditing Commission					4R, 3L			

Sources: *KT*, August 28, 1946, p. 1; December 27–28, 1947, March 11, 1947; March 21, 1948, p. 2; December 14, 1948, p. 1; April 10, 1951 and April 11, 1951, p. 1; September 17, 1952, p. 1; October 6, 1953, p. 1; December 1, 1954, p. 1; January 25, 1956, p. 2.

[a] R, Russian; L, local; W, woman.

[b] This was named the Department of Party, Trade Unions, and Komsomol Organs in 1952, Department of Party Organizations in 1954.

[c] In 1953, this was called the Administration, Planning, Finance, and Trade Department.

tively. The membership of the obkom itself consisted of 33 Russians and 47 locals.[13] The presence of a strong Russian contingent in the Stalinabad gorkom was fully justified by the high Russian share in the city's population (see Table 4-5). The uneven distribution of population and industry was reflected in the uneven regional strength of the KPT. The Tadzhik Party was dominated by Leninabad oblast and Stalinabad city Party organizations, which

[13] *Ibid.*, March 23, 1948, p. 2.

together accounted for close to 60 per cent of the total KPT membership.[14]

The raikom apparatus appears to have been staffed predominantly by local cadres. In 1944 and 1945 there were some Russian raikom first secretaries. Of the 59 raikom first secretaries included in a list of awards of February, 1945, 40 per cent were Russian. Many were listed as ex-secretaries, however.[15] Another list of awards, of December, 1945, listed 15 Russians (48 per cent) among the 31 raikom first secretaries who were decorated.[16] Four years later, however, a massive list of awards (about 2,500 names) given on the occasion of Tadzhikistan's twentieth anniversary, gave the ratio of Russians to locals in the raikom apparatus as 1 to 2.8. Of 135 raikom functionaries listed, 37 were Russians and 98 were locals.[17] An equally long list in 1954 indicated a further decline in the number of Russians. This time the Russian to local ratio was 1 to 4.6; only 27 out of 151 decorated raikom functionaries were Russian.[18]

The 1954 list included the names of 55 raikom first secretaries, of whom only 5 were Russians.[19] It is reasonable to suppose that the 5 included at least 2 and probably all 3 first secretaries of Stalinabad's urban raions, which means that almost all rural raikoms were headed by local people. The balance of raikom functionaries in the 1954 list—96 names, of which 22 were Russian—were listed as raikom secretaries.[20] Counting 56 raions in Tadzhikistan in 1954, and assuming that most Russian raion secretaries were included in the awards and that they were evenly distributed throughout the apparatus, it appears that there was a Russian secretary in only every second or third raikom in Tadzhikistan at that time.

---

[14] The regional strength of the two organizations is estimated on the basis of the number of delegates sent by each to Party congresses. In 1954 Leninabad oblast had 39 per cent and Stalinabad city 24 per cent of the membership (total, 63 per cent), *ibid.*, January 24, 1954, p. 2; in 1961, 34 per cent and 24 per cent, respectively (total, 58 per cent), *ibid.*, September 23, 1961, p. 5. In 1963 Stalinabad city had 27 per cent of Party members in the republic, *ibid.*, December 27, 1963, p. 3.

[15] *Ibid.*, February 13, 1945, pp. 1–2.

[16] *Ibid.*, December 31, 1945, pp. 1–3.

[17] *Ibid.*, December 18–31, 1949.

[18] *Ibid.*, October 24–29, 1954.

[19] *Ibid.*

[20] *Ibid.*

Apparently this was not considered enough. Two oblasts were abolished in 1955 in order "to strengthen the raion Party organization" by transferring oblast cadres into raion work.[21] Judged by other available information, the organizationally weakest raions most in need of "strengthening" were those in the high mountains. A campaign to transfer members of "inflated staffs" directly into "production" began in the government and economic apparatus at about the same time, if one is to judge by news stories about those who were "happily" transplanted. Many of them were Russians. No information on the ethnic breakdown of the raion cadres after 1954 was available.

No systematic data were available on the ethnic composition of urban Party organizations. Scattered information indicated that larger cities conformed to the obkom pattern, while Party organizations in small cities resembled Party organizations in rural raions.

In general, it seems that there was a decline in the number of Russians among professional Party functionaries in the fifties compared with the forties; in 1956, however, there were signs of a new Russian influx into the Party apparatus which continued into the sixties.

THE TADZHIK GOVERNMENT

Russians were deployed in the government on the same principle as in the Party; their strength was proportional to the political importance of a given agency. Their placement in the governmental structure was also affected by the local shortage of specialists and trained bureaucrats.

The primary political role of the soviets in the Soviet political system is representative. Consequently, the Tadzhik soviets reflected the ethnic composition of the population, with a slight bias in favor of the Tadzhiks as the titular nationality. In the Supreme Soviet of the TSSR, Russians were slightly over-represented in 1947 and 1951 but returned to their exact quota in 1955; the Uzbeks were generally under-represented; and the Tadzhiks had a 60 per cent plus majority, which was more than they had in the population at large.[22] There was no information on the national

[21] *Ibid.,* January 27, 1956, p. 2.
[22] See Table 2-1. The percentage breakdown of the membership of the Supreme Soviet of the TSSR in 1951 was: 20 per cent Russians, 60 per cent Tadzhiks, 12 per

composition of the lower soviets, except in Stalinabad city, but it
seemed fairly certain that they were Tadzhik-dominated.

Lists of deputies to the Stalinabad city soviets for 1948 and 1955
revealed high percentages of Russians—60 per cent and 43 per
cent, respectively.[23] The decline in percentage can be explained in
one of two ways: either the Russian share was first inflated and was
reduced to reflect the actual population distribution, or a special
effort was made to give more representation to local nationals in
their capital city. The latter explanation seems more probable. To
fulfill its "representative" function, the Stalinabad city soviet
should have had a Tadzhik rather than a Russian majority. It is
highly unlikely that the decline in the number of Russian deputies
reflected any actual decline in the Russian population in Stalinabad. By all indications, the steady influx of the Russians into the
city continued in the 1950's.

The Presidium of the Supreme Soviet of the TSSR was formally
the highest organ of government but in fact exercised little independent power. The importance of the body lay in its representative role; the chairman of the Supreme Soviet was thus the formal
head of the republic and a symbol of its statehood. After 1945 the
post was always occupied by a Tadzhik: Munavar Shagadaev
(1945–50), Nazarsho Dodkhudoev (1950–56), and Mirzo Rakhmatov after 1956. Between 1945 and 1954 the first deputy chairman was a Russian, Vladimir Semenovich Dvornikov; but with the
appointment of Saida Khalikova, a local woman, to this position in
1955, the ethnic pattern was no longer maintained. The other
deputy chairman and the secretary of the Presidium were of local
nationality, and there was only a token Russian representation
among members of the Presidium.[24]

Members of the Supreme Soviet Presidium were Party members
of high standing and membership was considered a high honor. It

---

cent Uzbeks, and 8 per cent "others"; in 1955, 14 per cent Russians, 66 per cent
Tadzhiks, 14 per cent Uzbeks, and 6 per cent "others." *Ibid.*, April 20, 1951, p. 1,
March 6, p. 1, March 31, p. 1, 1955.

[23] *Ibid.*, December 27 and 28, 1947; February 11 and 12, 1953.

[24] *Ibid.*, April 27, 1947, p. 2; April 25, 1951, p. 1; April 1, 1955, p. 1. In the late
fifties and the early sixties the chairman and deputy chairmen of the Presidium of
the Supreme Soviet of the TSSR were also Locals, and there were only a few Russians among the membership. See also *Ezhegodnik BSE* 1962 M, p. 167; *ibid.*, 1965,
no. 9, 166.

overlapped with the highest offices of the Party and the Council of Ministers and was also bestowed on such deserving "toilers" as Sadriddin Aini, one of the few surviving Young Bukharans and Old Bolsheviks and the founder of Tadzhik soviet literature.

The Council of Ministers of the Tadzhik SSR was politically the most important governmental body; its chairman and deputy chairmen were members of the Bureau of the Central Committee of the KPT (see Chart 4-1). Ethnically the Council was divided evenly between Russians and local nationals. Here again "the pattern" clearly emerged (see Table 4-6). The chairman (a position equivalent to that of prime minister) was always of local nationality (a Tadzhik rather than an Uzbek), while the first deputy chairman, through the period under review, was a Russian. The latter position was occupied by the same person throughout the 1945–56 period. Among other deputy chairmen, some were Russians and some were of local origin.[25]

Ministers and heads of independent agencies attached to the Council of Ministers were primarily locals; reading a list of the members of the Council of Ministers, one has the impression that it was a truly national body. The significant exceptions were the Ministers of Internal Affairs and of State Security, who were always Russians, except once in 1954 (see p. 120). The few other Russians headed ministries of Irrigation and of Communications and two of the agencies attached to the Council of Ministers, the Main Administration of Construction Materials Industry, and the Main Roads Administration (Table 4-6). Two ministries were of special interest, those of Foreign Affairs and of Defense. Established in each Soviet Union republic under the 1944 amendments to the USSR constitution for the purpose of creating an impression of independent statehood, the two Tadzhik ministries were left vacant after 1946. The Chairman of the Council of Ministers customarily assumed the title of Minister of Foreign Affairs; but despite an apparently strong military garrison in Tadzhikistan there was no minister of defense and, as far as can be determined, no actual ministry at all after 1946 (see p. 122).

[25] The pattern continued into the 1960's; a Local, A. Kakharov, was the chairman of the Council of Ministers, and two Russians were the first and second deputy chairmen, Mirzoiants and Novichkov, respectively (*Ezhegodnik BSE*, 1962 M, p. 167; *ibid.*, 1965, no. 9, p. 166).

Table 4-6. Council of Ministers of the TSSR: Ethnic Presentation[a]

	1945–46	1948–49	1951–52	1954–55
Chairman	L Kurbanov, M.	L Rasulov, Dzh.	L Rasulov, Dzh.	L Rasulov, Dzh.
First Deputy Chairman	R Mazaev, A. V.	R Mazaev, A. V.	R Mazaev, A. V.	R Mazaev, A. V.
Deputy Chairman	R Dvornikov, V.	L Imamov, A. N.	R Obnosov, P. S.	L Iskandarov, D.
Deputy Chairman	R Sviridenko	L Madzhutov	L Imamov, A. N.	L Rakhmatov, M.
Deputy Chairman		L Salomatshaev	R Kuznetsov, I. A.	R Saiko, V. A.
Deputy Chairman		R Saiko, V. A.	R Saiko, V. A.	
Deputy Chairman			L Salomatshaev	

Ministries	1945–46 Minister	1945–46 Deputy	1948–49 Minister	1948–49 Deputy	1951–52 Minister	1951–52 Deputy	1954–55 Minister	1954–55 Deputy
Finance	R	L	L/L	L/R	L	R	L	R
Justice	L		L	R	R	L	L	R
Health	R	RW	R	R/L	L		L	R
Trade	LW	R	L	R	L	R	L	R
State Control	L		L	R	L	R	L	R
Foreign Affairs	L			L		L		
Defense (War)	R	R						
MVD (Internal Affairs)	R	R	R	2R	R	R	L	R
MGB (KGB)	R/R	R	R	2R,2L	R		R	2L,R
Culture							LW	L
Food Industry[b]	L		L	L		R	L	L
Meat/Dairy Industry[c]	L	R	L/L	R		R	L	R
Light Industry[d]	L	R	L	2R	L	R/R	L	L
Textile Industry	L	R/L/L		2L	LW		L	
Agriculture	L	R	L	3R	L	2L,R	L	3L,2R
Cotton Cultivation	L	R						
Forestry				L		R	L	
Auto Transportation/Roads			L	R	L	R		

	Chief	Deputy	Chief	Deputy	Chief	Deputy	Chief	Deputy
Communications	R/R	L/R	R		R	R	R/LW	R
Housing/(Urban/Rural Construction)	R/L	R	L	R	L/L	R	R	R/R
Irrigation	L		L		L		L	
Municipal Economy				R			R	L
Local Industry			L	R	LW		LW	
Social Insurance		R		R		R		
Education	L		L		L		L	L
Agencies Attached to the Council of Ministers[e]	Chief	Deputy	Chief	Deputy	Chief	Deputy	Chief	Deputy
Planning Commission	L	3R	L	2R	L	R	L	R
Craft Coops Administration	L		L		L		L	
Main Roads Administration	R		R					
Sports, Physical Education	R		L					
Administration of Architecture		R						
Culture and Education Commission	L		L		L		L	
Administration of Construction Materials Industry	R/R			R		R	R	
Art Affairs Administration	L/L		L		L/L		L	
Narrow-gauge Railroad Administration	L							
Labor Reserves Administration		R	LW		LW		LW	

Sources: *KT*, February 13, 1945, pp. 1–2; April 29, 1947, p. 1; April 25, 1951, p. 1; April 1, 1955, p. 1; lists of awards in December 18–31, 1949; October 24–29, 1954; November 17, 1954, p. 1; and November 17–18, 1954, p. 1; also *passim*, 1945–55.

[a] R, Russian; L, local, W, woman.
[b] Later Ministry of Food Products.
[c] Later Industry of Meat and Milk Products Ministry.
[d] Later Ministry of Consumers' Goods Industry.
[e] Not a complete list—the Committee on State Security (KGB) is included in the list of ministries.

A consideration of the list of deputy ministers, almost all of whom were Russians, strongly modifies the superficial impression that the cabinet was primarily Asian in its composition, and reveals the existence of the ethnic pattern there also (see Table 4-6). Evidence provided by numerous press items indicates that even fewer Asians were to be found at the lower levels of the central government in administrative, managerial, or clerical positions. Apparently the personnel of industrial and technical ministries was overwhelmingly Russian, and the percentage of Russians in other ministries was also very high. In 1947 the Central Committee's Secretary for Cadres said that there were only 2 Tadzhik officials in the Planning Commission and only 1 Tadzhik in the Ministry of Light Industry.[26] The press was full of complaints that there were too few persons of local origin in the government apparatus. The long list of awards of December, 1949, gave 251 names of officials employed by the various ministries and independent agencies below the rank of deputy ministers; 74 per cent of them were Russian.[27] A 1953 list of awards to the workers of the finance-credit system in Tadzhikistan included 49 names, of which 78 per cent were Russian,[28] while a similar list of awards to the leading workers and senior and middle ranks of the Ministry of Communications of TSSR in 1954 included 212 names, 97 per cent of which were Russian.[29]

The procurators general of the Republic were Russian throughout the period under review (A. Ia. Romanov from 1945 to 1947 and N. V. Zhogin from 1948 to 1956), but their staffs included many local nationals. In 1947 all oblast procurators were reported to have been Tadzhiks, while all 73 raion procurators were Tadzhiks or Uzbeks.[30] Many of their subordinates, however, were apparently Russians. In a 1945 list of awards to the workers of the procuracy, 8 out of 21 were Russians; the Russians were either employed in the Procurator General's office or served as heads of departments in regional offices.[31] A 1947 award list to officials of the

[26] KT, June 28, 1947, p. 2.
[27] Ibid., December 18–31, 1949.
[28] Ibid., November 18, 1953, p. 1.
[29] Ibid., May 29, 1954, p. 1.
[30] Ibid., May 28, 1947, p. 3.
[31] Ibid., August 9, 1945, p. 1.

procuracy and investigators included 42 names, 32 per cent of which were Russian. These included a deputy procurator for special affairs, a military procurator of an MVD camp, a military procurator of an army corps, and chiefs of the procuracy's departments of civil cases, court system, militia, and prisons. Local nationals headed departments of criminal cases, complaints, and investigation. All oblast procurators and all but one of the raion procurators included were also local nationals. A 1945 list of awards to the employees of the Ministry of Justice listed 9 persons (most of them judges), 3 of whom were Russian.[32]

The judges of the Supreme Court of the Tadzhik SSR included 4 Russians and 6 local nationals in 1947 and 4 Russians and 12 local nationals in 1952. In both cases the chairman was a local national and the first deputy chairman was a Russian. In 1947 there were 104 people's assessors serving as members of the Supreme Court: 34 of them (33 per cent of the total) had Russian names.[33]

In the local government hierarchy in the period under review, all chairmen of the oblast soviet executive committees were of local origin and, with one exception, all the known first deputy chairmen were Russians (Table 4-7). Similarly, all chairmen of city and raion soviet executive committees were of local nationality. The 1954 all-inclusive list of awards gave the names of the 12 chairmen of the executive committees of the city soviets and the 53 chairmen of the executive committees of rural raion soviets. All of them were of local nationality. The 1945 and 1949 lists of awards gave 58 and 54 names of chairmen of raion executive committees, respectively; again, all of them were local.[34]

As far as can be determined there were few, if any, Russians in second positions in raion executive committees, but the local soviet apparatus had a relatively high percentage of Russian officials, nevertheless. It was higher at the oblast than at the raion level. Most of these officials were specialists. Of the names of officials in the apparatus of the oblast soviets given in the 1949 awards list, 34 per cent were Russian; among officials of the raion

[32] *Ibid.*, May 31, 1947, p. 1; May 22, 1945, p. 1.
[33] *Ibid.*, April 29, 1947, p. 1; April 25, 1952, p. 2.
[34] *Ibid.*, October 24–29, 1954; February 13, 1945, p. 2; December 18–31, 1949.

Table 4-7. Oblast Executive Committees: Ethnic Presentation[a]

Oblast	Year	Chairman	First Deputy Chairman	Deputy Chairman	Secretary
Stalinabad city	1948	L	R	L	
	1951	L	R	L	L
	1953	L	R	R,L	R
Stalinabad oblast	1948	L	R	R,L,L	L
	1951	L	R	R	L
Kulyab oblast	1946	L	R	L	L
	1951	L	R		L
Garm oblast	1948	L			
	1951	L			
Gorno-Badakhshan autonomous oblast	1948	L	R		
	1954	L			
Leninabad oblast	1948	L	L		
	1955	L	L		
Leninabad city	1951	L	R	L	L

Sources: *KT*, February 6, 1948, p. 3; February 11, 1948, p. 3; February 14, 1948, p. 4;
February 26, 1948, p. 1; January 14, 1951, p. 3; January 19, 1951, p. 3;
January 22, 1951, p. 4; March 21, 1953, p. 1; March 20, 1955, p. 3.

[a] R, Russian; L, local. Data includes Stalinabad and Leninabad cities.

soviets, 28 per cent were Russian.[35] There was no comparable information available for later years, but because the number of local
people who are receiving specialized education has increased, the
number of Russians in the local government apparatus has probably decreased.

SECURITY SERVICES

A border republic with a recent history of resistance to Soviet
rule, with difficult topography, and with a substantial number of
deportees and politically unreliable elements, as well as forced
labor camps,[36] requires a high concentration of security services.

[35] *Ibid.*, December 18–31, 1949.

[36] An item in the award list indicated that there was a forced labor camp or
camps in Tadzhikistan (*KT*, October 24–29, 1954). From a refugee source it is known
that a forced labor camp has existed in Kurgan-Tyube since 1931. Its early inmates,
kulaks from Siberia and the Caucasus, were used to build the Vakhsh Valley irri-

Harrison Salisbury of the *New York Times,* who visited Stalinabad in 1954, returned with a feeling of the omnipresence of security agents. He reported that: "Almost every place I had gone to, from remote villages on the route of Genghis Khan to modern Stalinabad, bore the unmistakable mark of that pervasive force which obviously had ruled so much of Central Asia before Stalin's death and which, so far as I could determine, was still ruling with undiminished force. I mean, of course, the MVD." [37]

A few items in the press indicated that perhaps there were still cases of individual resistance in Tadzhikistan. In the 1945–56 period, *Kommunist Tadzhikistana* reported several cases of officials having "tragically lost their lives in pursuit of their official duties." Accidents, perhaps; or sporadic acts of violence.[38]

The secret police in Tadzhikistan enjoyed special powers. Protopopov, First Secretary of the Tadzhik Communist Party from 1937 to 1946, had been a member of the Cheka (OGPU, NKVD) since 1917 and had specialized in purges throughout his professional career. (See Chart 5-1.) Many other Russians in the republic also had once been in the secret police. The MVD (Internal Affairs) and MGB (State Security) ministers were members of the Bureau of the Central Committee of the KPT, the only ministers to be so honored (see Chart 4-1).[39] They were Russian. The only other Russians among the ministers were probably also secret police agents, because they headed agencies that used forced labor (the Ministry of Irrigation and the Administrations of Roads and

---

gation system. Three parties, each of 10,000 people, were sent at the beginning of the construction. All of them died because of the lack of the most elementary facilities (no housing) and an epidemic of typhoid. Boris Iakovlev, *Kontsentratsionnye lageri SSSR.* Institut po Izucheniiu Istorii i Kul'tury SSSR, Issledovaniia i Materialy, ser. 1, no. 23 (Munich: Institut po Izucheniiu Istorii i Kul'tury SSSR, 1955), pp. 140–41.

[37] Harrison E. Salisbury, *American in Russia* (New York: Harper and Brothers, 1955), p. 213.

[38] *KT*, October 18, 1946, p. 4; September 13, 1949, p. 4; May 20, 1949, p. 4; February 11, 1954, p. 2.

[39] The practice (membership in the Bureau) was temporarily discontinued after the execution of Beria in 1954, when the secret police hierarchy was downgraded in relation to the Party, but was restored again in the late 1950's and in the 1960's. S. K. Tsvigun, a Russian, KGB Chairman, was a member of the Bureau of the Central Committee of the KPT from 1958 to 1963, when he was replaced by M. M. Miliutin, also a Russian *Ezhegodnik BSE*, 1959, p. 164; *ibid.*, 1960, p. 158; *KT,* September 24, 1961, p. 1; December 27, 1963, p. 1; December 29, 1963, p. 4.

of the Construction Materials Industry) (see Table 4-6). Most of the MVD-MGB deputy ministers were also Russians.

Numerous sources indicate that the secret police in Central Asia, including Tadzhikistan, was staffed exclusively by non-local people.[40] An OGPU member in the 1920's related that officials of the secret police had little confidence in oriental Communists as they were susceptible to the religious influence of Islam: ". . . most of our leaders have been wont to manifest . . . mistrust, whenever the question came up of admitting oriental communists into the OGPU machine."[41]   The efficiency of a terror apparatus in a police state depends on its members being free from local ties, prejudices, and preferences.

No direct information is given on the security agencies in the Soviet sources. However, an examination of names scattered in the Tadzhik press revealed that most secret police personnel were Russian but that there were some Asians. Until 1947, only Russian names were mentioned in connection with MVD-MGB activities. A list of awards to the MVD militia in 1947 included 2 (out of 10) local names; the 1949 list of awards cited 9 MVD officials (4 of whom had local names) and 20 MGB officials.[42] The 2 persons of local nationality among the latter were deputy ministers. By and large there were a few more local nationals in internal affairs than in state security. Only isolated items of information were available thereafter; these indicated that the few Asians among the police agents were generally heads of regional offices.

The decline in the powers of the secret police in Tadzhikistan after 1954 when MGB and MVD ministers lost their seats on the Bureau of the Central Committee reflected the downgrading of the two agencies at the All-Union level in the aftermath of the fall of Lavrenti Beria. 1954 was the first year in which an Asian (Bobo Makhkamov) became a minister of the MVD, but the Committee of State Security (KGB) was still headed by a Russian (Kochetov).

[40] A. Gokdepe, "Natsional'naia Politika Moskvy," *Türkeli*, 2–3 (October-November, 1951), 43; Kolarz, *Russia and Her Colonies*, pp. 261–62. See also Carrère-d'Encausse and Benningsen, "Pouvoir apparent . . .," Rywkin, *Russia in Central Asia*, Geoffrey Wheeler, *Racial Problems in Soviet Muslim Asia* (London: Oxford University Press, 1960), and Geoffrey Wheeler, *Modern History*.
[41] Agabekov, *OGPU . . .*, pp. 18–19.
[42] *KT*, June 27, 1947, p. 1; December 18–31, 1949.

The MVD Border Guards, an elite corps charged specifically with safeguarding Soviet frontiers, were a separate unit of the All-Union MVD. Very little information is available on the composition of the corps in Tadzhikistan, except an occasional name inserted in the list of awards and an occasional laudatory story with all meaningful content carefully expurgated. The few data available, however, seem to support the general assumption that there were no local nationals among the troops, or at least among the officers.

In his memoirs of a trip to Tadzhikistan in 1930, Boris Pil'nyak discusses the border guards and their work in trying to stop the Basmachi from crossing the border and in catching refugees and smugglers. Pil'nyak said that the border guards were ethnic Russians.[43] In *Kommunist Tadzhikistana* most information dates back to 1945 and 1946 when many postwar awards were made to the border guards. From 1945 to 1948 the commander-in-chief of the border guards in the Tadzhik district (*okrug*) was a Russian (General S. M. Kotenko): his chief for political work was also a Russian (Colonel I. V. Rumiantsev), as was his chief of staff (Colonel S. A. Sukharev). It is interesting that Rumiantsev was the member of the Central Committee of the KPT in 1948, while Kotenko was not. In a 1946 list of awards, 24 officers of the border guards (from captain to lieutenant-colonel) were decorated; all of them were Russians. In 1954 a new commander, General G. F. Shcherbina, was designated as the Chief of Administration of MVD Border Guards of the Central Asian District.[44] Shcherbina, a Slav, was a member of the KPT Central Committee in 1956.

Decorations were bestowed on 174 members of the border guards in February, 1945, but only 10 of them were mentioned by name; all were Russians. The troops were apparently divided administratively into sectors which corresponded to Tadzhik territorial oblasts. The chiefs of political departments for the GBAO and the Kurgan-Tyube sectors were mentioned in March, 1945; both were Russians. In September of that year a riding competition for the border guards was held in Tadzhikistan, including long-range marches across high mountain trails and equestrian competitions

[43] Pil'nyak, *Tadzhikistan*, pp. 70–96.
[44] *KT*, February 21, 1945, p. 1; February 27, 1946, p. 4; October 28, 1954, pp. 1–3.

in Stalinabad and Koktash. Six of the competing officers were mentioned by name; 5 of them were Russians and 1 had an Asian name. A 1945 story praising the war record of the border guards gave the names of those who were decorated and those who were killed in the war; among 14 names only 1 was Asian. In a report of a meeting on political education of the border guards in the Tadzhik district, 21 speakers were mentioned (most of them political officers), all of whom were Russians.[45]

From 1946 to 1956 there was virtually no mention of the border guards in the press, except for one story connected with the renewal of the "vigilance" campaign. It dealt with the interception of three American spies (equipped with a new radio transmitter) who attempted to flee to Afghanistan. The heroes of the story were a Russian corporal, a Tadzhik private, and a trained dog.[46] It is not clear whether the story related was an actual case or a fictional account.

ARMED FORCES

Regular troops stationed in Tadzhikistan received even less publicity than security services. It seems that the Commissariat of Defense (*Voenkomat*), apparently still functioning in 1945 and 1946, was primarily concerned with demobilization; its network of local offices was staffed by Russian personnel and a few local officials.[47] P. A. Khrustalev, a Russian, was then the Military Commissar (*Voenkom*) of the TSSR; he was also a member of the Central Committee of the KPT. The Commissariat and its local network was apparently disbanded later, because after 1946 there was never any mention of a defense official, and the post of Minister of Defense remained vacant.

Individuals serving in the Stalinabad military garrison were mentioned in the press on the occasion of every anniversary parade; some were included in the general lists of awards. Garrison personnel, or at least its officer corps, was composed entirely of Russians. Commanders-in-chief in the 1945–56 period (N. N. Niki-

---

[45] *Ibid.*, February 21, 1945, p. 1; March 14, 1945, p. 2; March 20, 1945, p. 2; September 30, 1945, p. 4; October 20, 1945, p. 2; November 28, 1945, p. 2.

[46] *Ibid.*, October 23, 1955, p. 3.

[47] *Ibid.*, February 21, 1947, pp. 1–2; 1945–46, *passim*. Of the 26 names of central, oblast, and raion officials of Voenkomat, 20 were Russian and 6 were Local.

shin; M. I. Kucheriavenko, and A. F. Chudesov) were always Russian general officers; the deputy commander for political affairs from 1952 to 1956 was also Russian (M. M. Bronnikov). While serving in Tadzhikistan all of the above were members of the Central Committee KPT. A Russian (V. A. Iazynin) commanded an aviation division in 1950; and the names of 4 generals and 6 colonels attached to the Stalinabad garrison mentioned at various times in the 1946–48 period indicated that they were all Russian.

A 1947 death notice of a Don Cossack colonel who served in the Stalinabad garrison was signed by 26 men, most of them presumably his colleagues; 21 names were Russian. A list of awards bestowed on the officer corps of the Stalinabad garrison in 1948 gave a total of 23 names, all of which were Russian; the lowest rank among them was that of major.[48]

Among the rank and file soldiers some must have been of local nationality. An analysis of the membership of the Tadzhik Komsomol in 1952 reveals that the sum of kolkhoz, factory, and school primary organizations, as given, accounted for only 58 per cent of the total number of primary organizations; as soldiers make up a large portion of the Soviet Komsomol membership, most of the unspecified 42 per cent of primary organizations must have been in the armed services. As it is known that 70 per cent of the Tadzhik Komsomol members in 1949 were of local nationality, some at least among those who served in the army must have been Tadzhiks and Uzbeks.[49]

MASS ORGANIZATIONS

Security services and the armed services serve as deterrents to potential disloyalty; thus the presence of many local nationals in their ranks would adversely affect their effectiveness. Mass organizations, on the other hand, which have the task of socializing the people and mobilizing them for active political participation,

[48] *Ibid.*, November 25, 1947, p. 4; February 24, 1948, p. 1.

[49] In 1952, 27 per cent of the primary organizations were located in kolkhozes, 27 per cent in schools, 4 per cent in industrial enterprises, and 42 per cent were not specified (*ibid.*, March 16, 1952, p. 2). Three years before, in 1949, 71 per cent of the Komsomol members were reported to have been of local origin (*ibid.*, January 20, 1949, p. 2). Komsomol membership increased by over 30,000 between 1949 and 1952 (*ibid.*).

require a broad local base. In Tadzhikistan the rank and file of mass organizations was dominated by Asians; its Russian members were found primarily in key positions in executive bodies.

The Komsomol is the Party's auxiliary for the mobilization of youth and for the education of future Party members. In Tadzhikistan its role was particularly important because of the need to win young people away from local traditions and to educate a new Soviet elite, professionally specialized and politically loyal. Many of the young Tadzhik leaders in the postwar period were Komsomol graduates. The Tadzhik Komsomol membership was generally more than double that of the Party in the comparable period, and unlike that of the Party, it presented an uninterrupted growth curve, except in the war period, when the Komsomol's losses presumably resulted from the war (see Chapter 2). Membership increased from nearly 3,000 in 1927 to 65,000 in 1940, and from 70,000 in 1949 to 155,000 in 1965.[50] The ratio of local nationals in the total membership was given only for the late forties, when it amounted to 70 per cent of the total.[51] Membership in the Komsomol Central Committee revealed a similar, if not higher, proportion of Asians: 80 per cent of the total in 1946 and 77 per cent in 1952. Nevertheless, an ethnic placement pattern similar to the one that characterized Party agencies appeared in the ruling bodies of the Komsomol: the Secretariat and its departments, and the Bureau of the Central Committee. The combination of a local first secretary and a Russian second secretary was maintained through the postwar decade, except for a short period in the late 1940's; other secretaries were also Russians at that time. The Tadzhik Komsomol apparently performed poorly in its three major responsibilities: socialization of youth (especially rural youth); mobilization of young people for an exemplary performance in political and economic activities; and recruitment of future Party members. The organization's troubles in the period under review were indicated by the constant turnover in the positions of secretaries of the Komsomol Central Committee and lesser functionaries and by the serious criticism of its performance heard at Party

[50] AN TSSR, *Istoriia*, III, Book 1, 183; *KT*, December 25, 1946, p. 2; January 20, 1949, p. 2; *Ezhegodnik BSE*, 1965, p. 167.
[51] There were 76 per cent in 1946 (*KT*, December 25, 1946, p. 2) and 71 per cent in 1949 (*ibid.*, January 20, 1949, p. 2).

and Komsomol congresses. The problems, as well as the turnover, continued to exist in the sixties.[52]

Very little information was available on the membership or the composition of other mass organizations. Because of the relatively small industrial sector, trade unions were of lesser importance in Tadzhikistan than elsewhere in the Soviet Union. Much of their membership was undoubtedly Russian, as a result of the high percentage of Russians among industrial workers in the TSSR. In 1948 the unions were reorganized from a branch to a territorial basis, and the first republican Central Council of Trade Unions was elected. The Council was composed of 13 Russians and 17 local nationals; [53] its Presidium was made up of 5 Russians and 4 locals. Manzar Sharipov, a Tadzhik whose past included service in the militia and a distinguished Party career, including the post of Third Secretary of the Central Committee (1945–48), was elected Chairman of the Council (a demotion). A Russian, A. V. Lychagin, was chosen as the Council's secretary.[54] Both were still in their posts in the middle 1950's.

Paramilitary organizations in the republic were also headed by a local-Russian combination. The chairman and vice-chairman of *Osoaviakhim* (Society for the Advancement of Defense, Aviation, and Chemical Warfare) in 1945 and 1946 were a local and a Russian, respectively. In the fifties the chairman of the republican committee of DOSAAF was a local national, while the deputy chairman was a Russian.[55]

THE SOCIETY

The Tadzhik social structure also revealed a distinct ethnic pattern, because the requirements of modernization and economic development favored newcomers from European Russia in the

[52] *Ibid.*, 1945–56, *passim*. Komsomol membership in schools and factories (comprising 27 per cent and 4 per cent of primary organizations, respectively, in 1952) was considered inadequate (*ibid.*, March 16, 1952, p. 2), but the membership situation in kolkhozes (*ibid.*, 27 per cent of primary organizations in 1952), discussed in 1951, was referred to by the Cadres Secretary of the KPT as "catastrophic" (*ibid.*, November 18, 1951, p. 2). For membership data in the sixties see *Ezhegodnik BSE*.

[53] *KT*, October 16, 1948, p. 1.

[54] *Ibid.*, October 17, 1948, p. 1.

[55] *Ibid.*, January 21, 1954, p. 1; December 2, 1953, p. 2; January 31, 1956, p. 1; and *passim*.

socioeconomic structure just as much as the requirements of political control did in the power structure. Few Tadzhiks possessed the skills necessary to a modernizing society, and the Tadzhik and Uzbek rural masses were not eager to abandon their traditional homes in order to go to school or settle in a town. Their attitude was in part the result of the distrust of Soviet ways and the fear of alienation from the traditional culture. It was also due to the relatively inadequate primary and secondary school training and the inability of many of the Asians to meet the Russian language requirements that were mandatory in all but a few of the specialized and higher educational institutions of the republic.

European emigrants settled primarily in urban and industrial areas, a trend attested to by Western travelers. After a trip through Central Asia the U.S. Supreme Court Justice William O. Douglas recorded his impression that Russians formed a majority of the inhabitants of the Central Asian capital cities: "One has only to walk the streets, visit the shops, or go to the Parks of Culture and Rest at night to know that the Russians are close to being a majority in these Central Asian capitals. . . ." [56]

There is little doubt that the newcomers constituted the economic elite of the republic. European specialists coming to work in Central Asia received preferential treatment, including salaries that were higher by a 30 per cent "hardship" allowance.[57] It would be interesting to know whether the differentiation in the scales of remuneration also applied in the political hierarchy, but no data are available. This typically colonial preferential treatment of Europeans in Central Asia was necessary in view of the almost total lack of other incentives to settlement. Even within the republic, Russians were most unwilling to leave urban centers to "rough it," in the Pamirs, for instance. Information in the press and other sources indicates that the standards of living in the urban areas, bad as they were, were considerably higher than those in the native-inhabited countryside.

As in the case of public administration, economic management

[56] William O. Douglas, *Russian Journey* (New York: Doubleday and Company, Inc., 1956), p. 218.
[57] Every Russian who goes to Central Asia to work—whether as doctor, teacher, engineer or manager—gets 30 per cent more salary than the same job pays the Asian. *Ibid.*, pp. 217–18; also in *Regional Economic Policy*, p. 67.

was primarily in Russian hands; Russians also ran the transportation network and provided most of the skilled labor and technical workers of the republic.

At the time that Soviet power was established in Tadzhikistan, no genuine Tadzhik proletarians existed. The formation of the native working class was considered a matter of first priority. The reasons were spelled out in a resolution adopted by the First Congress of the KPT in 1930:

> The establishment of proletarian cadres of the local core nationalities is the most important condition of success in the solution of problems of the socialist reconstruction of the Tadzhik national economy; (it is also essential for) the task of socialist transformation and the collectivization of peasant holdings, and for the strengthening of the proletarian influence in the soviet and economic apparatus.[58]

Native labor was initally recruited from among the landless peasants and by way of agreements made with the kolkhozes and municipal authorities, but in the early 1930's, Russians and other Europeans who arrived individually or through an "organized recruitment of the labor force" constituted a great majority of the 10,000 industrial workers in Tadzhikistan. In addition to manning the newly established Tadzhik industry, European workers were also expected to train the natives in industrial skills.[59]

Official publications intent on showing the progress made by Soviet Tadzhikistan described the growth of "national cadres" in the economic life. According to them one-half of the 16,000 industrial workers in 1937 were of local origin,[60] and among them were 3,700 Tadzhik and Uzbek women.[61] The proportion of native workers decreased with industrial development, however; by 1953, they constituted only one-third of the industrial labor force, probably not more than some 20,000 people.[62] Tadzhik and Uzbek women then constituted only 13 per cent of all the women in in-

---

[58] AN TSSR, *Istoriia*, III, Book 1, 229.

[59] *Ibid.*, pp. 229–30, 292.

[60] Aliev, *Uspekhi razvitiia*, p. 12. As of June 1, 1936, Tadzhiks constituted 46.3 per cent of the total number of industrial workers (AN TSSR, *Istoriia*, III, Book 1, 293).

[61] *BSE, 1st ed., LIII*, p. 438.

[62] Approximate calculation, based on *TSSR. Nar. Khoz. 1957*, p. 211, and KPSS, *Tadzhikskaia SSR*, p. 18.

dustrial employment. In actual figures there were about 4,000 women,[63] which represented little change since 1937. Even the textile industry in Tadzhikistan was manned largely by immigrant women. This shortage of Moslem women had its basis in the continued strength of the traditional Moslem rule forbidding woman's employment outside the home.

There was a general shortage of engineers, technicians, economists, and other specialists in Tadzhikistan in the 1930's; among those available (about 1,000 in 1932 and 3,000 in 1937) [64] few individuals were of local origin. The education of local specialists began during the second Five-Year Plan, and the first native graduates of higher educational institutions began to join the labor force in the late thirties. The number of native engineers and technicians increased from 262 in 1939 to more than 4,000 in 1956.[65]

Modest as the above figures are, considering the Asian-European ratio in the population, there are indications that they were inflated. Award listings supported the official data, but these awards were somewhat slanted in favor of the "representative" aspect by including more Asians than Russians in proportion to their actual percentage in any given employment or institution. Statements of local leaders, on the other hand, indicated that there was an extreme shortage of native cadres in economic employment, much greater than that admitted to in official publications.

An over-all impression is that there were relatively more native workers in light industry than in heavy industry and that most of them were unskilled. There were some Asian factory managers, but the middle echelons of technical and administrative personnel and posts of political control seem to have been almost exclusively in Russian hands. Justice Douglas's impressions confirm the evidence of the Tadzhik press. He relates that at the time of his visit to Central Asia the Russians "occupied the strategic positions in practically every factory I visited." [66]

The acute shortage of native cadres in specialized occupations

[63] Aliev, *Uspekhi razvitiia*, p. 12. The absolute figure is an approximate calculation. According to data available in *TSSR. Nar. Khoz. 1957*, p. 211, the number of women workers in industry and transportation in 1956 was 34,000.

[64] AN TSSR, *Istoriia*, III, Book 1, 231, 293.

[65] TsK KPT, *Tadzhikskaia SSR za 25 let*, p. 97; Aliev, *Uspekhi razvitiia*, p. 31.

[66] Douglas, *Russian Journey*, p. 217.

and in the industrial labor force as a whole was a subject of concern to the Tadzhik leaders. In 1947 First Secretary Gafurov complained of the absence of local nationals among engineers, agronomists, doctors, and teachers; he criticized local Party organizations for failing to encourage Tadzhiks and Uzbeks to train for specialized employment. Apparently many natives came to work in industry during the war; however, unskilled workers displayed a lack of interest in securing permanent positions and drifted back to the countryside. The trained graduates of craft and factory schools felt insecure and did not establish themselves permanently because of the failure of local Party and trade union organizations to provide for their "special cultural living needs." [67] Gafurov's remarks emphasize the great cultural gap between the Russians and the Asians.

K. G. Kul'kov, Secretary for Cadres in the Central Committee, also disclosed in 1947 that there were few workers of local nationality in industry. He reprimanded the Ministry of Food and Light Industry for dismissing primarily Uzbeks and Tadzhiks in a recent reduction in force. It can be deduced from Kul'kov's remarks, however, that these Uzbeks and Tadzhiks had been among the least qualified workers.[68]

Russian personnel predominated among factory managers, trade union organizers, and secretaries of factory Party organizations, to judge by the published results of socialist competition in 1945 and 1946.[69] These were no longer published after that date. In the long list of awards of December, 1949, there were approximately twice as many Russian factory managers as native managers (29 and 16), but workers of local origin were more numerous than Russians (93 and 77). There were only 2 local names among the 29 factory administrative and technical personnel, and none among the 14 managers, officials, and technicians of hydroelectric power stations.[70]

---

[67] B. G. Gafurov, "Nekotorye voprosy vospitaniia natsional'nykh kadrov," *Partiinaia Zhizn'*, no. 15 (August, 1947), 18–19.

[68] *KT*, June 28, 1947, p. 2.

[69] The results of socialist competition in industry in 1945 listed 19 Russians and 10 Locals (*ibid.*, October 24, 1945, p. 1); a similar list in 1946 in industry and transport in 1946 included 28 Russians and 9 Locals (*ibid.*, March 20, 1946, p. 4).

[70] The total number of awards was 2,482 (*ibid.*, December 18–31, 1949).

The problem of the shortage of native workers in light industry (which comprised 80 per cent of Tadzhik industry) was discussed in the press in 1947 and 1948. According to a 1947 report there was an increase in the recruitment and training of native labor in Stalinabad city, but the task was not considered easy because it was difficult to train people "straight from the fields." The report admitted that because of the necessity to train workers from scratch, factory managers actually *"did not want to hire people of local nationality."* Native workers constituted only 3.5 per cent of the labor force in a Stalinabad shoe factory in 1947, and the ratio was comparable in other factories.[71]

The problem of local cadres in Stalinabad was brought up again in 1948. Apparently there were only 9 workers of local nationality in a printing plant and only 37 local workers in a silk textile mill. A silk-spinning plant, however, adopted a new policy whereby its native workers were placed in charge of native recruitment; the plant increased its native contingent threefold in one year.[72] There is no information about whether or not other plants adopted the method or if workers so recruited stayed on the job. Lists of awards in light industry subsequently indicated a native majority among workers ranging from 60 per cent in textile mills in 1947 [73] to 80 per cent of the officials and engineering-technical staff of the Leninabad silk combine in 1953.[74] The ratio in general, especially the latter figure, is questionable in view of a statement made exactly one year later by a Leninabad gorkom secretary who said that there was not a single engineer of local origin in all of the city's industrial enterprises.[75] The apparent discrepancy between data disclosed at Party meetings by local leaders and information obtained from the analysis of the lists of awards is probably the result of the requirements of self-criticism on the one hand and the operation of the representative bias on the other. The truth probably lay between the two.

The small Tadzhik heavy industry and transportation networks

---

[71] *Ibid.*, June 2, 1947, p. 2 (italics mine).

[72] From a report at the meeting of the Stalinabad gorkom (*ibid.*, January 18, 1948, p. 2).

[73] There were 15 Russians and 26 Locals (*ibid.*, July 12, 1947, p. 1).

[74] There were 10 Russians and 40 Locals (*ibid.*, January 9, 1953, p. 1).

[75] *Ibid.*, January 22, 1954, p. 3.

were under direct All-Union management in the period under review. Their managerial and technical personnel was primarily Russian; their labor forces included few natives. There was not 1 local name among the 8 members of the Shurab Coal Trust administration who participated in a Shurab raion Party conference in 1945; of the 11 Stakhanovite miners praised in 1946 only 3 had local names.[76] The Shurab coal mines apparently suffered from a labor turnover in the period following the war; many of the workers who left the mines were of local origin.[77]

Central Asian railroads were traditionally manned by Russian workers, a practice which was continued in the Soviet period. Europeans constituted from 70 to 80 per cent of the personnel of the Ashkhabad and Tashkent railroads and narrow gauge lines in Tadzhikistan who received state awards between 1947 and 1953.[78] A similar, or probably higher, proportion existed among the personnel of the State Air Fleet (*Gosudarstvennyi Vozdushnyi Flot, GVF*); the names of GVF personnel mentioned in the press were invariably Russian.[79]

In contrast, the agricultural population was predominantly of local origin. Russian exceptions were to be found only in two raions of the newly irrigated Vakhsh Valley, Molotovabad and Oktiabr', where cotton kolkhozes had been established by Russian colonists; among agrotechnical personnel; and in sovkhozes and Machine Tractor Stations (MTS). The picture clearly emerged after an examination of numerous lists of awards to agricultural personnel. Among some 300 names of kolkhozniks in a 1945 list of awards, only 5 (from kolkhozes in the Oktiabr' and Molotovabad raions) were Russian. The same list included the names of 90 agronomists and technicians in various sovkhozes and MTS, two-thirds of whom were Russian.[80]

---

[76] *Ibid.*, March 14, 1945, p. 2; March 1, 1946, p. 2.

[77] In 1947 one-third of the 1,000 miners who left the mine were of local origin (*ibid.*, March 15, 1947, p. 2).

[78] The percentages of Europeans in the total number of railroad personnel who received awards were as follows: 68 per cent of 22 in 1947 (*ibid.*, August 10, 1947, p. 1); 73 per cent of 15 in 1949 (*ibid.*, July 31, 1949, p. 1); 80 per cent of 161 in 1953 (*ibid.*, October 15, 1953, p. 1); and 74 per cent of 46 in a 1949 list of awards to railroad and GVF personnel (*ibid.*, December 18–31, 1949).

[79] *Ibid.*, December 18–31, 1949; February 21, 1945, p. 1; June 20, 1954, p. 2.

[80] *Ibid.*, December 31, 1945, pp. 1–3.

A 1948 list of awards to cotton growers included only 7 Russians out of the total of 145: of the 7, 2 were raion Party secretaries, 1 was an agronomist, 1 was an MTS brigade leader, and 3 were kolkhozniks from the Oktiabr' and Molotovabad raions. Another list of awards to kolkhoz members in 1948 listed 781 names; of these, 42 were Russian. The Russians were all members of 11 kolkhozes in the Oktiabr' and Molotovabad raions. This information indicated the ethnic homogeneity of the new kolkhozes, which must have been the result of a deliberate policy or possibly a concession to ethnic preferences which resulted in the creation of European enclaves among the natives. In 1945, awards to agrotechnical and MTS personnel of the two raions listed 36 names, all of them Russian.[81]

The 1949 general list of awards given on the twentieth anniversary of the republic also included kolkhozniks and other agricultural personnel; of 769 kolkhoz members listed only 2 were Russians, both of them kolkhoz chairmen. Of a total of 83 directors and staffs of sovkhozes and MTS, only one-third were Russians,[82] a reversal of the ratio found among technical agricultural personnel in 1945. According to official data the number of agricultural specialists of native origin in Tadzhikistan increased from 674 in 1939 to more than 3,000 in 1956.[83]

Tadzhiks, Uzbeks, and Kirgiz may have found it easier to specialize in the more familiar agricultural pursuits requiring rural residence than to accept urbanization in industrial or professional occupations. Not all agricultural specialists, however, found the traditional atmosphere congenial, to judge by the criticism many of the "new aristocrats" were subjected to when they refused to leave the cities in 1954 after a September, 1953, Party directive ordered specialists en masse into "production." [84] Both Russians and natives were criticized.

[81] *Ibid.*, March 3, 1948, pp. 1–3; March 11–12, 1948; April 24, 1945, p. 1.

[82] *Ibid.*, December 18–31, 1949.

[83] TsK KPT, *Tadzhikskaia SSR za 25 let*, p. 97; Aliev, *Uspekhi razvitiia*, p. 31.

[84] *KT*, January 6, 1954, p. 3, and following issues. Discussing cadres in cotton campaigns, Gafurov complained that there were many Party functionaries who tried to escape difficult assignments; he gave an example of a backward raion where conditions were so bad that many people refused the job of Party secretary there. B. G. Gafurov, "Vospityvat' kadry na preodolenii trudnostei," *Kommunist*, XXXII (December, 1955), 68.

A Soviet ethnographic study throws an interesting sidelight on the traditional ethnic-occupational preferences and prejudices in rural areas. The subject of the study was the Chkalovsk kishlak in the Leninabad raion. The predominantly Tadzhik population (10,178 out of 10,953 in 1939) engaged in cotton growing; of the remainder, the Russians, Uzbeks, and Tatars were primarily employed in government offices and economic enterprises, and the Kirgiz were herders. Traditionally, the Tadzhiks of the Fergana Valley would have nothing to do with pastoral pursuits, and no Tadzhik woman was allowed to take care of livestock. The official kolkhoz herders were the Kirgiz, and a few Uzbeks and Tatars.[85]

Relatively few Asians were found among the educated and cultural elite of the republic, in spite of the determined efforts made by the authorities to improve the existing educational opportunities and to encourage the Asians to take advantage of them, but their participation in cultural life was more extensive than in economic life. Despite the backwardness of the area and the psychological restraints imposed by the traditional attitudes, official efforts to educate a new cultural Tadzhik elite began to bear fruit in the postwar decade. Data available on the percentage of students of local origin in the secondary and higher schools promised further increases, even though the Tadzhik educational system was plagued by numerous problems and shortcomings.

The scientific elite of the republic was still predominantly Russian, although there were Asians among the social scientists, many of them immigrant Uzbeks educated in Tashkent. The Tadzhik State University was opened in 1948; a research center of the Academy of Sciences of the USSR, first established in Tadzhikistan in 1932, was transformed into an autonomous branch (Tadzhikskii Filial Akademii Nauk—TFAN) in 1941 and into the Academy of Sciences (Akademiia Nauk) of the Tadzhik SSR (AN TSSR) in 1951. The scientific research personnel of both these centers was primarily European, and the debt to the Russian scientists who developed the centers and continued to work there has been freely and fervently acknowledged. As educated Asians entered the centers of learning, the leading posts were the first to be filled.

The first two presidents (*rektor*) of the Tadzhik State University

[85] Kisliakov, *Kul'tura i byt,* pp. 12, 64, 92.

were Tadzhiks (Zarif Radzhabov and Ibadullo Kasymovich Narzikulov); E. N. Pavlovskii, the first chairman of TFAN, was replaced in 1946 by the writer Sadriddin Aini, the leader of the
Tadzhik Soviet culture. When Aini died in 1954 his replacement
was a physicist and mathematician, S. U. Umarov, brought in from
Tashkent. His appointment was apparently bitterly resented by the
local members of the Academy.[86]

The emphasis placed by the Party on the study, development,
and utilization of the Tadzhik culture found its reflection in the
establishment of appropriate institutes of the AN TSSR and the
University; these were staffed and headed by local nationals, most
of whom had close ties with the agitation and propaganda and
culture departments of the Secretariat of the Central Committee
of the KPT. Institutes of natural and applied sciences, on the other
hand, seem to have been staffed predominantly by Europeans.[87]
When it was first appointed in April, 1951, the membership of the
Academy of Sciences was almost equally divided between Asians
and Europeans: of the 11 members, 5 were Russians and 6 were of
local origin (including such notables as Aini, First Secretary
Gafurov, and the poet Mirzo Tursun-Zade), and of the 14 corresponding members, 7 were Russians and 7 were of local origin.[88]

The shortage of Asians among the specialists and the scientific-
educational elite was a subject of the Party's continuous concern.
As reported at the Seventh Party Congress in 1948, the specialists

[86] First Secretary Ul'dzhabaev strongly criticized members of the Academy of Sciences of the TSSR for their resentment of Umarov at the Eleventh Congress of the
KPT. According to Ul'dzhabaev, the Central Committee "noticed shortcomings" in
the work of the Academy after Aini's death, and sent Umarov, Narzikulov (an ex-
deputy chairman of the Council of Ministers), and two others to it to "improve the
situation." "As the new Presidium took over, some comrades who were used to
peaceful life resented the intrusion . . . and attacked Umarov. . . ." Ul'dzhabaev
expressed strong support for Umarov on behalf of the Central Committee, and
reprimanded his detractors. T. Ul'dzhabaev, *Otchetnyi doklad Tsentral'nogo Komiteta Kommunisticheskoi Partii Tadzhikistana XI S'ezdu Kompartii Tadzhikistana*
(Stalinabad: Tadzhikgosizdat, 1958), pp. 62–63 (See also Chap. 7).

[87] *KT, passim.* For example: awards to 5 professors in the Medical Institute, all
Russians (*ibid.,* March 4, 1945, p. 1); awards to 5 scientists of the Tadzhik Agricultural Institute, all Russians (*ibid.,* November 11, 1953, p. 1); awards to science personnel in the republic, 77 Russians (16 women), 22 Locals (1 woman) (*ibid.,* December 18–31, 1949).

[88] *Ibid.,* April 15, 1951, p. 1 (the Decree of the Council of Ministers of the TSSR
dated April 14).

of local nationality in the republic in 1947 numbered 7,600, but among them only 1,000 had received higher education; the others were graduates of technikums and various specialized schools. Secretary Gafurov said that there were only three doctors of science and 27 candidates of sciences of local origin in the republic, but 72 Tadzhiks were candidates for the *aspirantura* and the doctorate in the institutes of Moscow and Leningrad. A representative of the TFAN complained that the organization had only 17 Tadzhik staff members, and that there were no more than about 50 Tadzhiks among research workers in the republic and only 30 Tadzhiks among the 53 candidates for the TFAN aspirantura.[89] The latter figure (58.5 per cent of the total), however, strikes an observer rather favorably.

There was apparently little increase in the number of specialists of local nationality between 1947 and 1951, and the ratio of Tadzhiks in the aspirantura of TFAN in 1951 also remained substantially the same (60 per cent of the total).[90] It declined, however, in 1953, when only 42 per cent of the candidates were of local origin.[91] It was also disclosed in 1953 that only 17 per cent of the scientific staff of the AN TSSR were Tadzhiks (35 out of 206), and that Uzbeks and Tadzhiks generally failed to take advantage of the opportunities for higher education available to them outside the republic. In 1956 it was reported that out of 1,272 research personnel in Tadzhikistan only 359 (28 per cent) were Tadzhik.[92]

Not surprisingly, as a result of the long and specialized training required, there were almost no Asian doctors in Tadzhikistan. Doctors, dentists, veterinarians, and specialized medical personnel were almost exclusively European immigrants; most doctors were women. There were also few Asians among the so-called lower medical personnel (feldshers, nurses, midwives, and medical technicians), even though their number was increasing. According to

[89] *Ibid.*, December 22, 1948, p. 2; December 23, 1948, p. 3; Gafurov, "Nekotorye voyprosy," pp. 17–22. In this context is it not entirely clear whether the designation "Tadzhiks" meant ethnic Tadzhiks only or whether it also included members of other local nationalities.

[90] The ratio was 46 to 32 (*KT*, April 14, 1951, p. 1).

[91] The ratio was 49 to 66 (*ibid.*, December 29, 1953, p. 2).

[92] *Ibid.;* "The Population of Central Asia and Kazakhstan," *Central Asian Review*, V, no. 2, 125.

official sources the national medical personnel in Tadzhikistan
("our national intelligentsia") had increased from 2,105 in 1939 to
about 5,500 in 1956.[93] On the basis of statistical data on the Tadzhik health and educational systems and the proportion revealed
by the award lists, the above figures seem to be much inflated and
are unbelievable unless they are taken to include total medical personnel in the republic, rather than its native component only.

The various lists of awards to doctors and medical workers gave
a clear picture of the shortage of local cadres, the representative
bias notwithstanding. The ratio of Asian names in award lists
varied from 4 to 30 per cent of the total, an average of approximately 15 per cent. Lists of awards to doctors in 1945 gave 1 Asian
name out of 15, 2 out of 11 in 1946, and 2 out of 10 in 1952.[94] The
ratio of Asian names was low even when the lists included lower
medical personnel in addition to doctors and when samples were
larger: in 1949 Asian names amounted to 31 per cent, in 1953 to 32
per cent, and in 1954 to 10 per cent of the total.[95]

The need for the growth of local cadres among doctors and
medical technicians was frequently discussed in the press, and
much was done in the postwar decade to increase the educational
facilities locally available for medical training. This in itself, however, proved no solution for the shortage of Asians. As reported in
1945, there had been only 15 Uzbeks and Tadzhiks among the 264
specialists who graduated from the Stalinabad Medical Institute
in two years,[96] and the picture improved little in the following
years. One apparent reason for the small number of native appli-
cants to medical schools was their poor educational preparation,
and especially their poor command of the Russian language; in
1947 the Tadzhik Ministry of Health opened a special preparatory
school in Leninabad to overcome this educational handicap.[97] The

[93] TsK KPT, *Tadzhikskaia SSR za 25 let*, p. 97; Aliev, *Uspekhi razvitiia*, p. 31.

[94] *KT*, March 4, 1945, p. 1; April 4, 1945, p. 1; April 7, 1945, p. 1; March 3, 1946,
p. 1; July 3, 1952, p. 1.

[95] In 1949, there were 13 Locals and 29 Russians (*ibid.*, December 18–31, 1949);
in 1953, there were 41 Locals and 87 Russians in the medical personnel included in
the list (*ibid.*, October 10, 1953, p. 1); in 1954 there were 7 Locals and 66 Russians
(*ibid.*, April 4, 1954, p. 1).

[96] *Ibid.*, March 23, 1945, p. 2.

[97] *Ibid.*, April 12, 1947, p. 2.

poor supply of medical facilities outside urban centers was not solved automatically by the increase in medical graduates, because many of them were unwilling to leave the urban centers. Two Russian graduates of the Stalinabad Medical Institute who remained in Stalinabad instead of allowing themselves to be shipped off to remote villages were severely criticized in 1953; this was not an isolated incident.[98]

Few data were available on the ethnic origin of the members of the "free" professions such as lawyers, trade employees, journalists, and the like, except within the general framework of state employment discussed in the preceding chapter. There were no data on lawyers, except those employed by the Ministry of Justice and the Procuracy, where there seems to have been a mixture of native and Russian employees. An occasional press mention of court cases indicated that some judges and attorneys were Russians and others were of native origin. It was also difficult to judge the ethnic origin of employees of the trade network, except on the basis of data available for government employees as a whole. Occasionally trade employees would be brought to trial for theft and bribery; defendants' names in Stalinabad were almost exclusively Russian, but groups of local names appeared, especially if the transgressions took place in a small town or a rural raion.

Members of the journalistic professions were about equally divided on the basis of the language of the publication they worked for. In Uzbek and Tadzhik publications, some members of the technical staff were undoubtedly of non-local origin. A 1945 list of awards to the staff of the publishing industry showed 62 per cent with Russian names, but a similar list of awards to newspaper personnel of the oblasts and raions had more than 90 per cent local names. Newspapermen decorated at the twentieth anniversary of the republic (1949) were divided almost evenly between Russians and members of local nationalities.[99]

[98] *Ibid.*, March 5, 1953, p. 3. An article about the placement of graduates of the higher educational institutions indicated that some graduates refused to go to rural areas, and "wouldn't budge from Stalinabad" (*ibid.*, June 9, 1955, p. 3).
[99] There were 13 Russians and 8 Locals (*ibid.*, July 1, 1945, p. 1); 13 Locals and 1 Russian (*ibid.*, June 9, 1945, p. 1); and 14 Russians and 12 Locals (*ibid.*, December 18–31, 1949), respectively.

One would expect the pattern of European domination to have been less pronounced in the cultural life of Tadzhikistan, if for no other reason than the need for proficiency in the native media of cultural expression. However, the European cultural hegemony was still very prominent, with one exception; the literary scene was pre-empted by ethnic Tadzhiks.

The development of the Tadzhik-language literature in the spirit of the new "socialist realism" constituted one of the major aims of the Party's cultural policy, and consequently the training of and artistic activity by Tadzhik poets and writers was encouraged. Few, if any, Russians were capable of literary activity in the Tadzhik language. Members of the Council of the Union of Soviet Writers of the TSSR were almost all Tadzhik; Uzbek and Russian writers, writing in their own languages, constituted a small minority.[100]

Most of the "Tadzhik" painters were of European origin. Among the 18 "Tadzhiks" whose paintings were displayed at the Inter-Republican Show of the Artists of Central Asia and Kazakhstan in 1955, only 5 had local names. Of the latter, 1 specialized in traditional Persian miniatures and 2 were young men just beginning to show their works. The 7 representatives of the graphic arts were all Russians, as were 2 of the 3 sculptors.[101] The artistic education of local nationals made progress slowly, while the turnover of Russian artists in Tadzhikistan was high, since few were willing to settle there permanently.

A similar situation existed among the "Tadzhik" musicians. Of the 2 major composers in the republic 1 had an Armenian name (Balasanian), and the other was a Russian (Lenskii); only among the young musicians were there a few local names. It was the Russians who began to collect Tadzhik musical folklore, to record Tadzhik music, and to utilize folk motifs in new compositions. A

[100] As of August, 1954 (after the elections at the Third Congress), the Council of the Union of Soviet Writers of Tadzhikistan had 15 members, of whom only 1 was a European, V. Kirillov, a poet who specialized in translating Tadzhik poets into Russian (*ibid.*, August 22, 1954, p. 1).

[101] N. A. Belinskaia and V. A. Meshkeris, "Mezhrespublikanskaia Vystavka Khudozhnikov Srednei Azii i Kazakhstana, 1955 g.," *Sbornik statei posviashchenykh isskustvu Tadzhikskogo naroda*, AN Tadzhikskoi SSR, Institut Istorii Arkheologii i Etnografii, Works, XLII (Stalinabad: AN Tadzhikskoi SSR, 1956), 49–85.

standard complaint against Tadzhik musicians was their alleged unwillingness to accept polyphonic music.[102]

Among the performing arts, theater and ballet played an important role: there were Russian-language theaters as well as Tadzhik- and Uzbek-language ones. The personnel of the former was European; that of the latter was mixed. Directors and managerial personnel were generally Europeans, while artists were of local origin. A similar dichotomy existed among the movie-making personnel of the republic. The representative bias in the awards lists was clearly discernible in the mammoth list of awards of 1949. One hundred one awards were bestowed on writers, musicians, actors, dancers, and theater and movie personnel; only 22 recipients were Europeans.[103]

CONCLUDING REMARKS

On the evidence presented, an Asian-European ethnic pattern is clearly visible in Tadzhik society. In the power structure the pattern facilitates the transmission of directives from the center and the achievement of instant response to them, and keeps open channels of control between Moscow and the provincial national capital. It also serves to prevent the formation of local power centers in national minority areas and to counter and neutralize the apparently strong pressure for greater political autonomy on the part of major national groups in the border regions.

In practical application, variations in the pattern responded to functional needs. Because the central government was also concerned with the socialization and mobilization of the elite, the Party included in its membership a large representative sample of Tadzhiks and other major nationalities, but kept the key control posts and the bulk of its managerial responsibilities in European hands. A similar pattern, with greater emphasis placed on Tadzhik representation, existed in other mass organizations.

In the government apparatus, the major concern was to maintain the façade of local participation and at the same time to maxi-

[102] O. Dansker, "Sobiranie i izuchenie Tadzhikskoi narodnoi pesni," in *ibid.*, pp. 87–105. See also Chap. 7.
[103] *Ibid.*, December 18–31, 1949.

mize efficiency of performance. This meant that the management of affairs rested primarily in the hands of Europeans while representative posts were reserved for the Asians, who also, it seems, were deliberately excluded from participation in the police and defense apparatus.

Tadzhik society in the late forties and early fifties closely resembled the colonial societies of Asia and Africa during the period of transition from dependence and economic backwardness to limited self-government and a developing economy. The colonizing Europeans in Tadzhikistan were in firm control of the power structure and occupied a privileged position in the social, economic, and cultural life of the republic. They clustered in urban and industrial areas, while Asians continued to dominate the countryside. The Asians, who formed a substantial majority of the population, provided unskilled manpower for the economy and especially for the growing of cotton, the major product of the republic. A small but rapidly growing European-educated native elite joined the European upper classes, but in so doing paid the price of cultural alienation. "Displayed" prominently in "representative" positions, they still remained under European tutelage. The actual management of the society was in the hands of the middle class of administrators, technicians, and specialists; it is in this class that the absence of Asians was the most glaring and, from the viewpoint of the colonial characteristics of the regime, the most significant.

The special role played by Europeans in Soviet Central Asia is not officially recognized by the Soviet Union. Instead, much emphasis is placed on the participation of local national cadres in the political processes of the union republics, which, superficially, is undeniably very impressive. The emphasis may be summarized by Khrushchev's mocking remarks made at the Conference of Agricultural Workers of Central Asia in 1961 on the subject of alleged British suspicions of Russian "colonialism" in Central Asia. *Pravda* reported his speech:

> Once a Minister in England asked me: '. . . where do you get the cadres for the Central Asian Republics?' I looked at him in astonishment and asked what cadres he meant. 'Well,' he said, 'you need

cadres for those places.' I answered that they are already there—that they are born there; they study and grow up there, and they run their own republics.[104]

Khrushchev's answer is true enough but, unfortunately, it tells only part of the story.

[104] *Pravda*, November 19, 1961, pp. 1–3.

Chart 4-1. CENTRAL COMMITTEE OF THE TADZHIK COMMUNIST PARTY: SECRETARIES AND BUREAU, BY NATIONALITY, SEX, AND FUNCTION

	1945	December 31, 1946	February 11, 1948	December, 1948, Seventh Congress	September, 1952, Eighth Congress	January, 1954, Ninth Congress	January, 1956, Tenth Congress[a]
First Secretary	R Protopopov	L Gafurov	L Gafurov	L Gafurov	L Gafurov	L Gafurov	L Gafurov[b]
Second Secretary	L Isaev/Gafurov	R Shil'kin	R Shil'kin	R Shil'kin	R Obnosov	R Obnosov	R Obnosov
Third Secretary	L Sharipov	L Sharipov	L Sharipov	LW Khalikova	LW Khalikova	L Ul'dzhabaev	L Imamov
Secretary							R Nosenkov
Secretary							L Rakhmatov
Secretary—Cadres	R Shil'kin	R Kul'kov	R Kul'kov	R Kul'kov			
Secretary—Propaganda	L Gafurov/Pulatov	L Pulatov	L Pulatov	L Pulatov			
Secretary—Industry	R Kul'kov	R Obnosov	R Obnosov				
Deputy Secretaries							
Livestock	R Obnosov						
Trade and Communal Feeding	L Kasymov/Kabilov	L Kabilov	L Kabilov				
Industry and Transportation	R Saiko	R Saiko	R Mikhailov				
Bureau of the CC Members				L Gafurov R Shil'kin LW Khalikova R Kul'kov L Pulatov L Rasulov (PM)	L Gafurov R Obnosov LW Khalikova L Dodkhudoev (Pres. SS) R Mazaev (1st Dep. PM)	L Gafurov R Obnosov L Ul'dzhabaev L Dodkhudoev (Pres. SS) R Mazaev (1st Dep. PM)	L Gafurov R Obnosov L Imamov R Nosenkov L Rakhmatov L Dodkhudoev (Pres. SS)

R Mazaev (1st Dep. PM)	R Saiko (Dep. PM)	R Saiko (Dep. PM)	R Mazaev (1st Dep. PM)
R Saiko (Dep. PM)	R Vishnevskii (MGB)	R Vishnevskii (MGB-MVD)	L Ul'dzhabaev (PM)
R Vishnevskii (MGB)	R Kul'kov (Dept. CC)	LW Khalikova (Dep. Pres. SS)	L Khasanov (?)
R Kharchenko (MVD)	L Narzibekov (1st Secy. Koms)	L Rasulov (PM)	
	L Pulatov (Dept. CC)		
	L Rasulov (PM)		

Candidate Members

R Presnov (CC Dept.)	R Presnov (?)	R Presnov (CC)	R Saiko (Dep. PM)
R Obnosov[c] (Stal. Obk.)	R Zakharov (Dept. CC)	R Zakharov (Dept. CC)	R Zakharov
L Iskandarov (Stal. Gork.)	L Iskandarov (Dep. PM)	L Iskandarov (Dep. PM)	L Iskandarov (Dept. CC)
L Radzhabov[d] (1st Secy. Koms)			L Khalikova (Dep. PM)
			LW Khalikova (Dep. Pres. SS)

Sources: *KT*, 1945–46, *passim*; December 31, 1946, p. 1; February 11, 1948, p. 1; December 25, 1948, p. 1; September 24, 1952, p. 1; January 21, 1954, p. 1; and January 31, 1956, p. 1.

[a] The ethnic pattern of Central Committee secretaries remained unchanged in the late fifties and early sixties. They were, in the order of importance, in 1958 and 1960: Ul'dzhabaev (L), Obnosov (R), Rasulov (R), Koval (L), Zaripova (LW); in 1961: Rasulov (R), Koval (L), Zaripova (LW), Ergashev (L); in 1963: Rasulov (L); Koval (R), Aliev (L), Asimov (L), Zaripova (L), Ergashev (L). *Ezhegodnik BSE* 1959, p. 164; 1960, p. 158; *KT*, September 24, 1961, p. 1; and December 27, 1963, p. 1.

[b] In May, 1956, Gafurov was replaced as First Secretary of the Central Committee by Ul'dzhabaev Tursunbai.

[c] Obnosov was formally the Second Secretary of Stalinabad obkom. Gafurov, First Secretary of the Central Committee, was nominally also the First Secretary of Stalinabad obkom.

[d] Dropped as candidate member in April 1951.

Chart 4-2. Departments of the Secretariat of

1946			1948[c]		
Departments	Personnel		Departments	Personnel	
Cadres			Party, Trade Unions		
Secy for Cadres	R	Kul'kov, K. G.	and Komsomol		
Deputy Chief	R	Kormilin, N. A.	Chief	R	Presnov, S. A.
Deputy Chief	L	Rakhmatov, N.	Propaganda and Agitation		
Propaganda and Agitation			Chief	L	Pachadzhanov, N
Secy for Propaganda	L	Pulatov, T.	Agriculture		
Deputy Chief	R	Granik, T. V.	Chief	R	Stotskii, V. N.
Deputy Chief	L	Irkaev, M.			
Organization and Instruction			Administrative		
Chief	R	Presnov, S. A.	Chief	R	Lukin, A. A.
Deputy Chief	R	Zakharov, P. I.	Planning/Finance/Trade		
Agriculture			Chief	L	Kabilov, A.
Chief	R	Stotskii, V. N.	Industry		
Deputy Chief	R	Pavliuchenko, A. A.	Chief	R	Zakharov, P. I.
Deputy Chief	R	Karamov, A. M.[b]			
Deputy Chief	R	Matiakin, I. Ia.	Transport		
			Chief	L	Iskandarov, D.
Livestock					
Deputy Secy for Livestock	R	Obnosov, P. S.	Work with Women		
Deputy Chief	L	Iakubov, Khola	Chief	LW	Gafarova, M. K.
Industry and Transportation					
Deputy Secy for Industry	R	Saiko, V. A.			
Deputy Chief	L	Akhmedov, L.			
Work with Women					
Chief	LW	Kasymova, M.			
Deputy Chief	RW	Spitsina, A.			
Schools					
Chief	L	Imamov, A. N.			
Military					
Chief	R	Palii, N. A.			
Deputy Chief	R	Lukin, A. A.			
	L	Kurbanov, Kh.			
Special Section					
Chief	RW	Kaplan, S. G.			

Sources: *KT*, December 31, 1946, p. 1 and 1946 *passim;* December 25, 1948, p. 1;
September 21, 1952, p. 3 and September 24, 1952, p. 1; 1954 and 1955
passim.

[a] In his report to the Eleventh Congress of the KPT in December, 1958, First Secretary Ul'dzhabaev said that after the Party reorganization following the twentieth Congress of the CPSU the number of departments of the Central Committee of the KPT was reduced from eleven to five.

[b] Anton Mikhailovich.

[c] A list of awards in *KT*, December 18–31, 1949, gave several names of chiefs and deputy chiefs of departments of the Central Committee without naming the departments; these included four Russian chiefs and four Russian deputy chiefs, four local chiefs and three local deputy chiefs.

[d] Similarly, a list of awards in *KT*, October 28, 1954, and October 29, 1954, gave several names of department deputy chiefs. In the total of 12 names, four were Russian, eight local.

1952			1954–55[d]		
Departments		Personnel	Departments		Personnel
Party, Trade Unions and Komsomol			Party Organizations		
Chief	R	Zakharov, P. I.	Chief	R	Shabardin, P. Z.
			Deputy Chief	L	Burkhanov, I.
Propagation and Agitation			Propaganda and Agitation		
Chief	L	Pulatov, T.	Chief	L	Khakim-Zade, K.
			Deputy Chief	L	Sharipov, V.
Agriculture			Deputy Chief	L	Samadov, A.
Chief	R	Stotskii, V. N.			
			Agriculture		
Administrative			Chief	R	Stotskii, V. N.
Chief	R	Lukin, A. A.			
Planning/Finance/Trade			Administration, Trade and Finance Organizations		
Chief	L	Kabilov, A.	Chief	R	Kozlov, N. I.
Industry			Industry		
Chief	R	Kul'kov, K. G.	Chief	RW	Fadeicheva, O.P.
Deputy Chief	R	Shtatnov, V. D.			
Transport			Transport and Communications		
Chief	R	Kozlov, N. I.	Chief	L	Panoev, A.
Work with Women			Work with Women		
Chief	LW	Tairova, Kh. Z.	Chief	LW	Zaripova, N.
Science and VUZy			Science and Culture		
Chief	L	Imamov, A. N.	Chief	L	Islamov, N. A.
Literature and Art			Schools		
Chief	L	Radzhabov, M.	Chief	L	Rakhmet-Zade, U. K.
Schools			Special Section		
Chief	L	Rakhmet-Zade, U. K.		RW	Pankratova, V. A.

5

❀

THE POLITICAL ELITE

CAREER PATTERN AND COMPOSITION

LEADING PARTY AND GOVERNMENT OFFICIALS constituted the political elite of Tadzhikistan; its membership was synonymous for all practical purposes with the membership of the Central Committee of the Tadzhik Communist Party. The elite increased from 100 to approximately 150 people in the postwar decade. Although the information collected in the press on the background of the elite was fragmentary, conclusions reached on the basis of available data indicated that it differed little from other elites throughout the Soviet Union, except in such features as were imposed by local conditions and the requirements of the nationality policy.

The career sequence of the Europeans differed from that of the Asians. As members of the All-Union service most Europeans were sent to the republic for a tour of duty; after its completion they went to other parts of the Soviet Union. The Asians, on the other hand, were for the most part permanent members of republican hierarchies, remaining within the boundaries of Tadzhikistan; some were exchanged with neighboring republics. Some Uzbeks, for example, worked in Tadzhikistan, in line with the policy of a more "advanced" republic helping a "backward" one.

The Russians were prominent in positions near the top, and they also dominated middle bureaucratic echelons. They were either professional Party (or security) functionaries (*apparatchiki*) or technical and professional specialists in state and economic management. The Secretariat of the KPT Central Committee provided a reservoir of Russian functionaries who could be directed, according to need, into the Soviet and Party central or territorial administration. The careers of these functionaries progressed downward and laterally; there was relatively little upward mobility and relatively low turnover. In contrast, the upward mobility of the Asian cadres was high, as was their turnover. Generally the prerequisites for an Asian's upward movement included a period of training in Party schools outside the republic, a relatively sound formal education and professional specialization, and a period of experience in the work of the Party (less frequently, the state) apparatus. Members of the European group were on the average older than those of the Asian group, and their Party seniority was higher. In addition to the apparatchiki, the European group included prominent bureaucrats posted temporarily in Tadzhikistan, and also some elderly functionaries domiciled in the republic who worked at routine jobs, received little recognition, and apparently had known better days. In addition to the rapidly advancing young leaders there were also some "has-beens" among the Asians.

In conformity with the general Soviet practice, executive positions in the Party and soviet hierarchy were interchangeable and were all occupied by Party members. There was a bias, however, in the direction of exchange. Many state leaders were recruited from the Party apparatus, but the reverse was rarely true. This pattern was clear in local territorial administration and was also noticeable in central Party and state agencies, notwithstanding the career of some officials who, in moving upward, combined experience by working in both hierarchies. Most officials worked in only one hierarchy, however. This was true of the "perennial" raikom secretaries shifted from one raion to another, the functionaries of specialized departments of Party obkoms and the Central Committee, and the public administration specialists who worked in the offices of territorial soviets and republican ministries. As far as could be determined there was absolutely no exchange of personnel between the armed services administration (including the

MVD Border Guards) and the Tadzhik state and Party apparatus. Security agencies also constituted a relatively closed service, even though some Party and state functionaries, especially among the Russians, had had some security background, and some members of the MVD apparatus were known to have served as Party functionaries.[1] Within hierarchy, careers frequently developed laterally through an exchange of approximately equal jobs.

Certain posts gave the incumbent an advantage in launching a career. Komsomol and Party work promised most rapid promotion; cadres and propaganda activities were the best starting point. Experience in economic and state work also constituted a good base for political promotion, as did work in important areas such as the capital or the Leninabad oblast. It was considered a demotion to be posted to the mountain territories, or to be shifted from Party work to state work at the same level. As is usual in the Soviet Union, Party posts were considered to be more prestigious and ranked higher than state posts.

Only tentative conclusions could be reached on career patterns of the functionaries of the territorial Party and state apparatus in the 1945–56 period. Among the 20 secretaries of oblast and city Party committees (12 Asians and 8 Europeans) fewer than half were recruited from the obkom-gorkom apparatus; more than one-fourth (mostly Europeans) came from the Central Committee apparatus, and one-fourth from raikom positions. Among the 34 raikom first secretaries (23 Asians and 11 Russians), 80 per cent belonged to the category of perennials who had been transferred from raion to raion for the better part of ten years. Some could be classified as "trouble-shooters"; others were mostly failures who managed to get themselves transferred after each unsuccessful tour of duty because they had personal "pull" in Party headquarters. Of the remaining 20 per cent, one-half had been recruited from the obkom-gorkom apparatus, and the rest had come to the raikoms

---

[1] For example, Ivan Grigor'evich Fedoseev, Deputy Minister of the MVD in October, 1954, was previously mentioned in the press as Secretary of the Kulyab obkom (December, 1949), and as Second Secretary of the Garm obkom (January, 1951) (*KT, passim.*) A death notice of a Russian official in the Ministry of State Control indicated that before coming to Tadzhikistan he had been an official of the Cheka (1920–27). Since his arrival in the republic he had occupied only economic and state posts (*ibid.*, January 29, 1954, p. 4).

from the Central Committee and other backgrounds (the Komsomol and the soviets).[2]

A small sample of officials in the local soviet hierarchy (15 chairmen of local soviet executive committees, all Asians) revealed that one-third had been recruited within the Soviet structure and two-thirds had been transferred from Party posts. The evidence available suggested that many chairmen of local soviets were locals who had "made good" and been rewarded with representative posts in their home area.

Samples were larger and the data were somewhat less fragmentary in the case of functionaries of the central state and Party agencies. In the 1945–56 period some 50 Party functionaries were named in the Tadzhik press as heads and deputy heads of the departments of the Secretariat of Central Committees; their number was divided almost equally between Asians and Europeans.[3] An examination of the sample clearly indicated that most members of the group were professional apparatchiki who had risen through the ranks and had had little, if any, experience except Party work; they came to their posts either from within the apparatus of the Central Committee or from lower Party committees. A few had been recruited from the soviets or the Komsomol hierarchy. Among the Russians within the group, most came from Central Committee apparatus; some were old Bolsheviks.[4] The turnover among Central Committee department heads was extremely high; it was unusual for a man to remain in the post longer than from one Party Congress to another.[5] Nothing can be said about careers of other functionaries of the Secretariat, as there was not biographical information available for employees below the rank of department head.

[2] Information in these and the following paragraphs is based on biographical information cards compiled on the basis of data extracted from *KT*, 1945 through 1956.

[3] The total number of persons who held the posts of chiefs and deputy chiefs of the Central Committee departments in 1945–56 was 53, of whom 26 were Asians and 27 European (see Chart 4-2 for a partial list).

[4] The three most prominent were Semen Andreevich Presnov (b. 1892, a Party member since 1918), Aleksei Alekseievich Lukin (b. 1897, a member since 1918), both heads of Central Committee departments, and Sergei Andreevich Khandkarov (b. 1895, a member since 1917), an obkom secretary (*KT, passim*).

[5] See Chart 4-2. Only 6 department heads (4 of them Russians) lasted through more than one Congress.

Some data existed on a sample of 57 leading officials of the central government,[6] some 60 per cent of whom were Asians. A substantial majority among them were career government officials who kept their rank through the decade under review. Their changes of assignments were caused more by reorganization than by other factors, such as alleged poor performance or misconduct. Many were technical specialists recruited from the ministerial apparatus; most of the Russians among them belonged to this category. It is interesting that practically none of the ministers was recruited from the lower soviets. A significant, if much smaller, group among the ministers consisted of ex-Party functionaries who had previously been in Central Committee work. Some of them, such as the 2 ministers of culture in 1953–56 and their deputy,[7] had had experience in agitation and propaganda (*agitprop*) activities; others had worked in industrial or administrative control work.[8] Chiefs and deputy chiefs of MGB-MVD in Tadzhikistan formed a separate category and were not included in the above sample. Of the 18 names of MVD personnel gathered in the reading of ten years of *Kommunist Tadzhikistana,* most were those of Russians or Ukrainian career Chekists.

THE LEADERSHIP CORE AND MAJOR PERSONALITIES

Not more than a maximum of 15 people were found at any one time at the apex of political power in Tadzhikistan; in the 1945–56 period the total was 36 people, with a ratio of Asians to Europeans in the group of approximately 3 to 2 (22 Asians and 14 west-

[6] These included ministers, deputy ministers, heads of independent agencies and deputy chairmen of the Presidium of the Supreme Soviet of the TSSR.

[7] Musa Radzhabov, 1953–55 (dismissed for "feudal-bai" attitudes), had previously been the Central Committee's Chief of the Department of Literature and Art; Kasym Khakim-Zade (1955–56) had previously been in charge of Agitprop in a raikom, a Deputy Minister of Education, head of two government agencies on art and cultural affairs, and a head of the Central Committee's Department of Agitation and Propaganda. The latter post was also held at one time by his deputy minister, N. P. Abdullaev. The careers of other ministers such as Pulatov and Imamov followed a similar pattern.

[8] P. A. Palii, Deputy Minister of State Control (1949–56), had previously been an obkom secretary and a head of the Central Committee's Military Department; a Tadzhik woman engineer, Khamro Zairovna Tairova, Minister of the City and Rural Construction in the mid-1950's, had previously been in charge of three of the Central Committee's departments. Kurbansho Gadaliev, Minister of Local Industry (1953–56), had been one of the Central Committee's secretaries.

ern Slavs). The formal leadership group included all men who held secretarial posts in the Central Committee of the KPT, and chairmen and deputy chairmen of the Council of Ministers and Presidium of the Supreme Soviet of the Tadzhik SSR. To gain an accurate picture of the hierarchy of power, however, the formal list above had to be compared with the composition of the Bureau of the KPT Central Committee in comparable periods. The group analyzed below includes all Bureau members and candidates, as well as the few members of the formal hierarchy who were not included in the Bureau (see Chart 5-1).

A clue to the relative importance of any individual was provided by his ranking order in appearance at the state and Party holidays and anniversaries. In the 1945–56 period the ranking order within the Tadzhik leadership group varied widely (Chart 5-2), though the First Secretary of the KPT always led the list. The variations affected the relative placement of Party and state functionaries which, if the representative bias is discounted, presumably reflected their relative power positions. By the early 1950's, the pattern stabilized, with the second position occupied by the head of the government, and the third by the head of state, followed by Central Committee secretaries. The rise and fall in the careers of certain individuals, Ul'dzhabaev for example, are well illustrated by the variations in their ranking order over the years.

The Asian group among the leaders consisted of relatively young men in their thirties and forties. Most of them were ethnic Tadzhiks of peasant origin, many coming from the Fergana Valley (both Gafurov and Ul'dzhabaev were born near Leninabad); fewer came from the mountains of Garm and the Pamirs. Some had started life as hired laborers; others had been able to gain a formal education. Most had been trained in special Party schools in the republic and in Moscow or Leningrad and had the combined experience of local Party and soviet work. There were two distinct groups among the Asian leaders. The larger, an in group, was composed of younger men in the top positions or on their way up. It included Gafurov, Ul'dzhabaev, Imamov, Narzikulov, Rakhmatov, Dodkhudoev, Rasulov, Narzibekov, Khasanov, and 3 women, Khalikova, Kasymova, and Rakhimova. Their political careers had begun after the purges of the 1930's, in wartime, or even after the war, and had no direct connection with the bourgeois nationalists who were purged. Only a few of the Asian leaders who had become prominent after the purges remained in the postwar leadership, and the careers of those who did were in decline. Men such as Shagadaev, Kurbanov, Ashurov, Iskandarov, and Sharipov were older (in their forties in 1945) and constituted the second and smaller group in the leadership, the "out" group.

The "in" group was better educated. Gafurov had studied at the Moscow Institute of Journalism and later gained the degree of candidate of historical sciences; Ul'dzhabaev had graduated from a pedagogical institute; Rasulov was a graduate agronomist. Narzikulov, who held high posts in the Tadzhik Academy of Sciences and became rektor of the Tadzhik State University, must have had an appropriate higher education. Little information was available on the schooling of the others; nonetheless, it seemed certain that they must have had secondary education at least, as all had studied in higher Party schools.

In contrast, the members of the "out" group had little, if any, formal education. Some were self-taught (Iskandarov) or had had incomplete primary education (Isaev); others had attended factory schools (*rabfak*) (Shagadaev and Kurbanov), or occupational schools (Ashurov and Sharipov). They too had been trained in Party schools, but at lower levels.

Most members of the younger group had started their careers as teachers, Komsomol leaders, or propaganda workers, and served apprenticeships in educational and propaganda work, mostly within the Komsomol and Party apparatus (Gafurov, Ul'dzhabaev, Imamov, Rakhmatov, Narzibekov, and the 3 women members). The members of the older group had begun as farm laborers or workers and seem to have performed their apprenticeships in soviet and economic work (Kurbanov, Shagadaev). Some of the younger men had also risen through the soviet rather than the Party hierarchy (Narzikulov, Dodkhudoev, Rasulov). Only one member among the whole group had participated in the "establishment of the Soviet power in Tadzhikistan"; Sharipov had been a member of the Red Sticks from 1924 to 1927 and was a member of the militia until 1940. As in the case of other Tadzhik old Bolsheviks, his career was definitely on the downgrade in the 1950's.

The length of Party membership was not an index of a successful career. None among the ins had joined the Party before 1930, and most had joined it in the late thirties or even the forties. The outs had become Communists in the 1920's or 1930–31.

Some members of the Asian power elite did not quite belong to either of the two groups. Pulatov, for instance, shared career decline, but no other characteristic, with the out group. As Central Committee Secretary for Agitation and Propaganda from 1945 through 1952, he had been ranked fifth from the top among Tadzhik leaders, but in 1952 when his work was criticized he was demoted to the post of Chief of the Agitation and Propaganda Department of the Central Committee. He was further demoted in 1954 when he became the Minister of Education, at which time he also lost his seat on the Central Committee Bureau. Iskandarov, on the other hand, shared all the characteristics of the out group and yet remained a candidate member in the Bureau throughout the postwar decade, and later.

Some young Asian leaders appeared to be well on their way toward membership in the in group. Khasanov, about whom relatively little is known, rose from the apparatus of the Central Committee to the position of the Stalinabad gorkom's First Secretary and at the age of thirty-six became a full member of the Bureau. There were others who did not quite succeed, such as Narzibekov, who was demoted from the First Secretary of the Komsomol to deputy chief of a Central Committee department. The task of being leader of the youth organization was among the most difficult ones in the republic, and must have been dreaded by ambitious young leaders. Three men were removed as Komsomol first secretaries in the postwar decade under a barrage of criticism: Narzibekov; Ul'dzhabaev, whose career was temporarily eclipsed as a consequence; and Radzhabov, who subsequently disappeared from the political scene. The incumbent in 1956 was a young woman, Ibodat Rakhimova, who had risen through the ranks of territorial Komsomol organizations. Komsomol leadership also proved to be detrimental to the careers of numerous Russians.

A word should be said here about the three women in the political elite. All were young and, in addition to their official duties, served as examples of the emancipation of women under Soviet rule. Although they were included in the top political leadership, none could aspire to a share in real power. This was the result of the attitude prevalent not only among the tradition-bound Tadzhik society but also among the supposedly modernized male Tadzhik leaders, and even among their Russian mentors. The three Tadzhik women were the symbol of an attractive theoretical slogan, not proof of universal practical achievement in female emancipation, and their political elevation had all the earmarks of tokenism.

Khalikova, as Third Secretary of the Central Committee from 1948 to 1954, ranked highest among the women. Demoted in 1954 to the post of Deputy Chairman of the Presidium of the Supreme Soviet, she lost full membership in the Central Committee Bureau. She remained a candidate member, however, and was the only woman to be found at the hub of political power. Kasymova was moved from the Party to the state apparatus, and Rakhimova's prospects were uncertain in view of her involvement with the problems of Komsomol.[9]

The division between the ins and the outs indicated that postwar developments had brought new requirements for the Asian leadership. Despite their proven loyalty and impeccable proletarian background, older leaders, uneducated and clearly identified as Russian "stooges," were unable to implement new policies and were being replaced by a new elite, the younger "Soviet product." Sharing in the changing characteristics of the Party membership as a whole in the postwar period, the younger people were well educated and well trained politically in the Komsomol-Party apparatus. The first Asian leaders to be true members of the new Soviet generation, they were better suited to carry out the complex tasks of a modernizing society than their older colleagues. Specialization and efficiency in professional performance and political loyalty were the primary criteria for advancement among the Tadzhik new elite in the 1940's and 1950's. To judge by the in group, the most valuable background was provided by training in cotton technology and in cultural-propaganda work.

Little information was available on the background of the 14 Russians who were members of the Tadzhik political leadership in

[9] She was no longer in the Komsomol hierarchy in the 1960's.

the 1945–56 period, but their known characteristics classified them as members of the Stalinist generation of Party functionaries and economic managers. Dmitri Zakharovich Protopopov, the outgoing First Secretary in 1946, typified the wartime Party policy in the borderlands. A Russian from Voronezh who participated in the civil war as a Chekist, he specialized in supervising purges (including one in a borough of the city of Moscow) in his subsequent Party career. He was in charge of the Tadzhik 1937–38 purge, first as a representative of the CPSU Central Committee and later as the First Secretary of the KPT.[10] He was recalled as a result of the change of policy in 1946 and was replaced as First Secretary by Gafurov, a Tadzhik.

Two Russians served as second secretaries of the Central Committee of the KPT in the postwar decade, Mikhail Sergeevich Shil'kin (1946–52) and Petr Stepanovich Obnosov (1952–61). Before becoming Second Secretary Shil'kin had been the Central Committee Secretary for Cadres. Obnosov's previous career had been more varied: he had served as the Central Committee's Secretary for Livestock, as an obkom secretary, and as a deputy chairman of the Council of Ministers. Shil'kin and Konstantin Grigor'evich Kul'kov, who replaced him as Secretary for Cadres in 1946, were both demoted and eventually removed in 1952 in an apparent conflict with First Secretary Gafurov over policy concerning cadres. Obnosov, who then moved into the position of Second Secretary, apparently proved more willing to cooperate with his Tadzhik colleagues. His remarkable continuity of career (nine years in one post) was matched by only a few among the Tadzhik leaders, but among the Russians there were some equally "long-lived." Aleksandr Vasilevich Mazaev remained in the position of First Deputy Chairman of the Council of Ministers (Council of People's Commissars before 1946) throughout the period; Vladimir Semenovich Dvornikov was a deputy chairman of this body from 1945 to 1947, and subsequently served as Deputy Chairman of the Presidium of the Supreme Soviet; his replacement in the Council of Ministers, Viktor Antonovich Saiko (previously a department head in the Central Committee), remained in this post through

[10] *KT*, January 12, 1946, p. 3.

the 1950's.[11] Another of the Russian deputy chairmen of the Council of Ministers in the period under review, Ivan Andreevich Kuznetsov, served in this capacity for only a short period between tours of duty as obkom and gorkom secretary and as a minister.

Only selected members of the Secretariat were also members of the Central Committee's Bureau: these included functionaries heading cadres and Party organization departments. The 2 Russian incumbents, Petr Ivanovich Zakharov and Semen Andreevich Presnov, were both professional apparatchiki, whose careers centered around posts within the Secretariat of the Central Committee.

Heads of the republic's security agencies were included in the top leadership group until the downgrading caused by Beria's downfall in late 1953. In all, 3 security agents were members of the Tadzhik political leadership from 1945 through 1953, 2 Russians and 1 Ukrainian. Major General Dimitri Stepanovich Tokarev headed the state security organization from 1945 until 1948, when he left the republic. He was replaced by Dimitri Konstantinovich Vishnevskii, who after the 1953 reorganization, headed the combined Ministry of Internal Affairs–State Security. In 1954 he also departed. The Ukrainian, Andrei Vladimirovich Kharchenko, was Minister of Internal Affairs until 1951, when he too left Tadzhikistan. Tokarev's background included some twenty years of service in the security organs, first in the border guards and later in the NKVD territorial apparatus. Kharchenko spent most of his prewar years in Komsomol and Party political work in rural areas and joined the NKVD in 1939, at which time he was sent to Tadzhikistan. Vishnevskii's background is not given in available sources; he was a member of the state security apparatus in the republic in 1945.

Nothing is known about one other Russian who was included in the leadership group because of his official status. A. V. Nosenkov appeared on the Tadzhik political scene only in 1955, as a secretary of the Central Committee (listed fourth).

The postwar decade in Tadzhikistan was seemingly completely

---

[11] Saiko and Mazaev were still in Tadzhikistan in the early 1960's. Both were listed as members of the Central Committee of the KPT at the Fourteenth Congress (*KT*, September 24, 1961, p. 1).

dominated by Bobodzhan Gafurovich Gafurov, the Central Committee's Tadzhik First Secretary and the highest ranking Communist in the republic. Soviet-educated and a member of the Komsomol since early youth, he began his career as a newspaperman.
He was at school in Moscow at the time of the first great Tadzhik
purge and returned to the republic in 1935 as an editor of the
central Party newspaper and a member of the Central Committee's propaganda apparatus. He is reported then to have "fought
the bourgeois-nationalist and Trotskyite-Bukharinite deviations."
He was allowed to pursue graduate work in history in Moscow in
1940 and 1941, and was summoned home at the outbreak of World
War II to become the Central Committee's Secretary for Agitation
and Propaganda. He became Second Secretary in 1945 and First
Secretary in 1946. Gafurov was, in a sense, the connecting link
between the old and the new leaders. As First Secretary, he continued his research in the history of Central Asia—a sideline
unique among professional apparatchiki—and became the spokesman for the new Soviet Tadzhik historiography and an authority
on the interpretation of the Tadzhik past.[12]

Because of the lack of available information, it is somewhat useless to speculate here on the extent of Gafurov's real power in the
republic. Like all other Central Asian first secretaries he undoubtedly shared power with his Russian alter ego, the second
secretary, and was hemmed in by all the Russian assistants in the
Central Committee from the Secretary for Cadres to the various
"assistants to the First Secretary." There were, nevertheless, certain
unique features of his incumbency which lead one to suspect that
his grip on the republican power structure may have been stronger
than was customary for someone of local origin in Soviet Central
Asia.

The pattern of Russian infiltration of the Tadzhik hierarchy in
the 1945–56 period was less complete than in any of the other Central Asian republics, and it is possible that a Moscow "connection"
of the first secretary might have been a contributing factor.
Gafurov alone among the Central Asian first secretaries retained
his post throughout the postwar decade. He successfully carried out

---

[12] *Ibid.,* January 15, 1946, p. 2, and *passim.* See also Chap. 7.

the purge of the leaders of the Central Committee of the KPT in 1952. It is significant that two of the victims were powerful Russian secretaries who controlled personnel policies and had probable security links: Shil'kin was in charge of cadres under Protopopov, and Kul'kov in charge of industry. Shil'kin, who had become Second Secretary when Gafurov moved to the top, disappeared from the Tadzhik scene in 1952. The position of Kul'kov, who succeeded Shil'kin in direct management of the *"nomenklatura"* [13] in 1946, was also seriously damaged in 1952; he also vanished within two years. Thereafter it was Gafurov (rather than the new Second Secretary) who acted as the Party's spokesman in personnel matters. The third important secretary who suffered in 1952 was Pulatov, an Asian in charge of agitation and propaganda work. Agitprop work, it should be remembered, was Gafurov's specialty, and in this field he also assumed major responsibilities. On the basis of the foregoing evidence it appears that an internal power struggle was resolved at the time in favor of the First Secretary. Obnosov, the new Second Secretary apparently was no match for the power of the First Secretary, which situation, on the basis of later evidence, continued under Gafurov's successor, Tursunbai Ul'dzhabaev.

It is probable that the September 1952 changes in the Tadzhik political leadership were connected with the Beria-Khrushchev confrontation in the Kremlin which preceded, and followed, Stalin's death. If that was the case, the timing was unusual. The changes in favor of nationality elements in the union republics which are associated with Beria's initiative took place in the Ukraine and some other republic some ten months later (June, 1953), and were reversed after Beria's arrest and liquidation. While Gafurov appears to have represented the nationalist element, he

---

[13] Nomenklatura—a pool of all important executive positions (Party, state, economic, cultural, etc.) within a given Party committee's territorial jurisdiction. Functionaries in charge of cadres appoint and/or recommend or approve every appointment, dismissal, transfer, and promotion in nomenklatura posts within their jurisdiction. Customarily a committee's Second Secretary is in charge of nomenklatura. When a special secretary for cadres is appointed, he generally functions under the supervision of the second secretary. For a discussion of the nomenklatura see Fainsod, *How Russia is Ruled*, p. 224; Merle Fainsod, *Smolensk under Soviet Rule* (Cambridge, Mass.: Harvard University Press, 1958), Chaps. III and IV; Jerry F. Hough, "Technical Elite vs. the Party: A First Hand Report," *Problems of Communism*, VIII, no. 5, 56–59; A. Avtorkhanov, *The Communist Party Apparatus* (Chicago: H. Regnery Co., 1966).

was not affected by the usual repercussions: he survived Beria's downfall and Khrushchev's ascendancy until 1956; and his removal as the Tadzhik First Secretary did not curtail his activities in other fields. At the same time Gafurov must have been a Stalinist of good standing to have survived the trials and tribulations of the last years of Stalin's rule. After Stalin's death, the Tadzhik newspapers continued to carry laudatory articles about the late dictator on the anniversaries of his birth and death until the very eve of the CPSU Twentieth Congress.[14] Gafurov himself wrote an article in *Kommunist* of April, 1955, praising Stalin as Lenin's faithful disciple and "most loyal co-worker." [15] Gafurov's close identification with the Stalinist period and policies was undoubtedly a major factor in his dismissal.[16]

On the other hand, there is evidence that Khrushchev was not directly hostile toward Gafurov. During a visit to Tadzhikistan in November, 1954, Khrushchev showed great interest in the republic's cotton cultivation,[17] and at a meeting of Party and soviet officials and cotton specialists of all the cotton-growing republics, he conspicuously applauded Gafurov when the Tadzhik Secretary attacked Niiazov, First Secretary of the Uzbek Party, because of disagreements in cotton-growing techniques between the two republics.[18] Khrushchev again took Gafurov's part against the Uzbeks (this time against the Uzbek Chairman of the Council of Ministers, Iusupov) at a plenum of the Central Committee of the

[14] The items included: Stalin's picture and an article, "The Great Follower of Lenin" (*ibid.*, March 5, 1954, pp. 1–2); a picture and two articles (*ibid.*, December 21, 1954, pp. 1–3); a picture of Lenin and Stalin on a background of red banners, at the occasion of elections (*ibid.*, February 27, 1955, p. 1); an article praising Stalin (*ibid.*, March 5, 1955, p. 2); and a picture and article (*ibid.*, December 21, 1955, pp. 1, 2–3).

[15] Gafurov, "V. I. Lenin i pobeda," p. 78.

[16] The Second Plenum of the Central Committee of the KPT of May 24, 1956, which relieved Gafurov of his duties as First Secretary in connection with his transfer to "other work," was attended by E. I. Gromov, chief of the Department of Party Organizations in the Union Republics of the Central Committee of the CPSU (*KT*, May 25, 1956, p. 1).

[17] *KT*, November 19, 1954, p. 1.

[18] Gafurov attacked Niiazov when the latter said that Tadzhiks had not increased the area under cotton cultivation. Gafurov pointed out that Tadzhikistan did not have an area comparable to that of Uzbekistan in which to expand, but that nevertheless the Tadzhiks had shown higher indices in the percentages of acreage growth than the Uzbeks in the postwar period, and that their yields were higher. Gafurov's speech was interrupted by Khrushchev's applause and favorable comments (*ibid.*, November 25, 1954, p. 3).

CPSU in January, 1955. He then commented on the "long-standing feud" between the two leaders on the subject of best methods of growing cotton and praised Gafurov for his willingness to try "new methods." [19]

Iusupov and Niiazov had both been removed from their posts by January, 1956; Gafurov survived them in office by only a few months. The significant difference was, however, that whereas the Uzbeks were severely criticized and disappeared from the political scene, Gafurov was allowed to continue his career as historian and propagandist on the All-Union scene. In August, 1957, he was named director of the Institute of Oriental Studies of the Academy of Sciences of the USSR. He also retained his seat as a member of the CPSU Central Committee *after his dismissal* and was still listed as such at the Twenty-first Congress of the CPSU in 1959—a rather unusual situation.[20] He was dropped from the Central Committee in 1961, but remained a spokesman for Soviet Asians in contacts with the newly independent African and Asian states. In the 1960's he was also the editor-in-chief of the Academy of Sciences' popular magazine, *Asia and Africa Today (Aziia i Afrika segodnia)*.

Tursunbai Ul'dzhabaev, the "stormy petrel" of Tadzhik politics, replaced Gafurov as First Secretary. Younger than Gafurov, he had grown up politically in the Komsomol hierarchy. A member of the Komsomol Central Committee at the age of twenty-one, he became its Secretary at twenty-three, and First Secretary, the post in which he served during the war, at twenty-seven.[21] In 1946 Ul'dzhabaev (and his Russian Second Secretary Burlin) came under attack by the Central Committee of the All-Union Komsomol for "suppressing criticism" within the Komsomol hierarchy.[22] He was charged with "amoral behavior," non-Communist personnel policies, and *semeistvennost'* (the formation of "family groups"), all of which led to an "intolerable situation of servility and toadyism" (*podkhalimstvo*). Ul'dzhabaev went through the ritual of self-criticism

[19] *Ibid.,* February 5, 1955, p. 3.
[20] Leo Gruliow, ed., *Current Soviet Policies III: The Documentary Record of the Extraordinary 21st Communist Party Congress* (New York: Columbia University Press, 1960), p. 217.
[21] *KT,* January 9, 1946, p. 2.
[22] *Ibid.,* October 8, 1946, p. 1.

at a subsequent Komsomol plenum, and was retained as the First Secretary at the Komsomol's seventh Congress in December, 1946, while all other Komsomol secretaries were removed.[23] Dismissed eventually from his Komsomol position in September, 1947,[24] Ul'dzhabaev was sent to study at the Moscow Higher Party School, a move which was a reward rather than a punishment. One cannot escape the conclusion, especially in view of his subsequent career, that he must have had a powerful protector; it is entirely possible that it was Gafurov himself who favored the bright young man from his home district. While in Moscow Ul'dzhabaev undoubtedly made contacts which proved valuable later.

After his return in 1950, Ul'dzhabaev's career was meteoric. First named a secretary of the Stalinabad obkom, he then became Chief of the Central Committee's Agitation and Propaganda Department, but after eight months he was shifted to the Kulyab obkom as First Secretary. He was praised by Gafurov at the Eighth Congress of the KPT in 1952 for his success there in "consolidating the local party leadership" and "improving production indices." As chief trouble-shooter, he was then posted as First Secretary to the Leninabad obkom [25]—his home base—where he remained for a year and a half. This time was apparently sufficient for him to establish a strong power base in that most important oblast of Tadzhikistan. Rising steadily in the ranks of power, he became the Third Secretary of the Tadzhik Central Committee in January, 1954, the Chairman of the Council of Ministers in 1955, and the First Secretary of the Tadzhik Central Committee in May, 1956.

Ul'dzhabaev's career ended disastrously in five years, however. At the Seventh Plenum of the Central Committee of the KPT in April, 1961 (attended by Frol Kozlov), it was suddenly revealed that top leaders in Tadzhikistan were guilty of "hoodwinking and direct deception," "gross distortion of Leninist principles of leadership," "incorrect practices in selection and assignment of personnel," and "padding of report figures on cotton procurement." [26] Ul'dzhabaev was the major culprit, but removed with him for direct complicity were Dodkhudoev, Chairman of the Council of

[23] *Ibid.*, October 15, 1946, p. 2; October 30, 1946, p. 3; December 28, 1946, p. 1.
[24] *Ibid.*, September 12, 1947, p. 2.
[25] *Ibid.*, September 20, 1952, p. 2.
[26] *Pravda*, April 16, 1961, p. 4.

Ministers since May, 1956,[27] some other officials of the central government, and a group of Party-soviet functionaries from the Leninabad oblast. Major culprits were not only discharged from their posts but also expelled from the Party. Ul'dzhabaev pulled down with him the Russian Second Secretary Obnosov, removed "for lack of political principles and for a time-serving attitude," who obviously failed in his "watch dog" duties and proved too accommodating.[28]

As a footnote to the Ul'dzhabaev scandal, it is worth noting that his successor as First Secretary was none other than Dhabar Rasulov, who had served as Chairman of the Council of Ministers while Gafurov was First Secretary and had been eclipsed, together with Gafurov, by the rise of Ul'dzhabaev.[29]

The careers of Gafurov and Ul'dzhabaev underscored the importance of contacts in Moscow as well as the need for a local power base and local protectors in an upward political climb in Central Asia. The Ul'dzhabaev scandal also threw light on the manipulation of cadres and positions practiced by Asian leaders for personal aggrandizement and to frustrate political controls from Moscow and accommodate local requirements.

The "representative" posts of the Central Committee's First Secretary and the Chairman of the Council of Ministers are linked by common characteristics and by a shared responsibility, and a change in one post implies the change in the other, as in the cases of Gafurov and Rasulov in 1955–56, and Ul'dzhabaev and Dodkhudoev in 1961.[30] The careers of Russian seconds-in-command, on the other hand, do not seem to be affected by the fate of their

[27] It should be noted that before the scandal, Dodkhudoev was among the few Asian leaders who had not been affected by the changes of the fifties. See Chart 5-1.

[28] *Pravda*, April 16, 1961, p. 4; *KT*, April 14, 1961, pp. 1–2. The new Second Secretary appointed in the aftermath of the scandal, I. G. Koval, was a Ukrainian, new in Tadzhikistan. He was an agricultural specialist. His biography appeared in SSSR. Verkhovnyi Sovet, *Deputaty Verkhovnogo Soveta SSSR*. 6th session. (Moscow: Izd. "Izvestiia Sovetov Deputatov Trudiashchikhsia SSSR," 1962).

[29] Dzhabar Rasulov, a Tadzhik, who was born in 1913 and was a trained agronomist, didn't join the Communist Party until 1939, but served as minister or deputy minister in agricultural ministries from 1934 to 1946. From 1946 to 1955 he was Chairman of the Council of Ministers. An eclipse of two years was followed by the post of secretary of the KPT Central Committee (1958–60); in 1961 he replaced Ul'dzhabaev as First Secretary. He was still in this post in 1967.

[30] In 1946 also, the Chairman of the Council of Ministers, Kurbanov, was dismissed after the recall of First Secretary Protopopov.

Asian superiors, except, as in the case of Obnosov, in conditions of clear complicity.

RECRUITMENT, DISTRIBUTION, AND TURNOVER OF CADRES

The Asian members of the political elite discussed above were the first "full-fashioned" product of much care and effort. Well-trained and effectively socialized administrators are the touch-stone of success in any political system; in Tadzhikistan, as else-where in Soviet Central Asia, the recruitment and training of cadres and their effective placement and performance were at the center of the Party's concern and interest. Designed to attract and maintain indigenous personnel, the cadres policy of the Party attempted at the same time to introduce western standards of performance and to minimize the influence of traditional behavior, to meet the demands of the "representative-control pattern," and to assure successful implementation of the All-Union tasks. Of the numerous problems which beset the cadres policy, some were familiar to secretaries for cadres throughout the Soviet Union. Others were caused by cultural traits dysfunctional to Soviet re-quirements, and by the stresses of rapid modernization, compli-cated by the existence of national tensions between the Asians and the Europeans and between the various nationalities within the Asian group itself. An excessive and virtually endemic turnover of personnel was one of the manifestations of the complexity of the problem; others were found in the operation of the Party and state machinery, where shortcomings existed in the technical aspects of public administration and economic management and also in the failure to involve the masses sufficiently in required activities.

The general shortage of trained cadres in Tadzhikistan was alleviated only in part by the influx of personnel from other parts of the Soviet Union. Among the Asians available, many were poorly trained in the skills required and poorly prepared for the tasks of leadership in Soviet society. In the postwar period Party and state criticism centered on the problem of shortages of local personnel in the governing apparatus, and especially on the shortage of re-cruits from special "target" groups: youth, women, workers, and peasants.

Complaints were voiced at every congress of the KPT; numerous

meetings were called to discuss solutions to the problem. On becoming First Secretary in 1946, Gafurov urged an increase in the
size of trained manpower in the republic, especially in the number of specialists of local origin. The need was restated in his
speech at the Seventh Congress (1948), when he also expressed
concern over the Party's admission policies and the high turnover
of the cadres. Much of the discussion at the Eighth Congress in
1952 was centered on the distribution, composition, and turnover
of the cadres; it was then that Kul'kov, Secretary for Cadres, came
under attack before his dismissal. At the Ninth Congress (1954),
Gafurov again admitted the existence of serious shortcomings
(*krupnye nedostatki*) in the management of the cadres, and complained of "a gap between the growth of the economy and culture
and the level of national cadres" (*razryv mezhdu rostom khoziaistva i kul'tury i urovnem natsional'nykh kadrov*). Although
the speakers stressed that there had been qualitative improvement
in the cadres, similar complaints were repeated at the two subsequent Party congresses in 1956 and 1957.[31]

Admissions to the Party were the subject of special concern. Designed to preserve the balance between the elite character of the
Party and the need for adequate staffing of key positions, the admissions were also expected to emphasize the recruitment of local
cadres, and to maintain the required "social composition" of the
ranks.

Mass recruitment of new members in the war period was followed by a retrenchment and a purge of "unreliable elements."
Speaking at the Seventh Congress of the KPT in December, 1948,
Gafurov criticized the wartime admission of "all-comers" and its
lack of proper selectivity,[32] a complaint which culminated two
years of criticism. Kulyab oblast reported admissions of "thieves"
or "alien" elements (such as a certain Aliev, who boasted five
wives),[33] and Stalinabad city raikoms were criticized for mass ad-

---

[31] *KT*, June 8, 1946, p. 2; December 22, 1948, p. 2; September 20–24, 1952; January
19, 1954, p. 1; January 27, 1956, p. 3; Ul'dzhabaev, *Otchetnyi doklad XI s'ezdu*, p. 58.

[32] *KT*, December 22, 1948, p. 2.

[33] The designation of "thieves" here referred to people who stole "socialist" or
"communal" (kolkhoz) property. The stealing of kolkhoz property (livestock, imple-
ments, and land) was one of the major problems in Tadzhik agriculture after the
war (*ibid.*, September 27, 1946, p. 2).

missions of "unworthy" elements.[34] A 1948 *Pravda* article, which castigated such practice in one of the Tadzhik raikoms, extended its criticism to the Tadzhik Party's organization as a whole.[35] The subsequent purge, while it removed many of the culturally un-assimilated Asians, only aggravated the standing complaint of the shortage of native cadres in the Party organization.[36]

The shortage of local women was considered particularly de-plorable; many of the women who substituted for men in various political and economic posts in wartime were returning to domestic seclusion, and there were few women among new Party recruits.[37] Only 10 per cent of the women admitted to the Party in Stalinabad city in 1944 were Tadzhik or Uzbek; similar proportions were found in the Stalinabad, Kulyab, and Kurgan-Tyube oblasts in 1946 and 1947, and in GBAO in 1946 and 1952.[38] Although com-plaints abated in the following period, it is doubtful that the situation had substantially improved, because there was a notice-able reluctance to admit Tadzhik and Uzbek women into the Party and to promote them.

Another major problem in admissions was the failure to attract a sufficient number of persons from "production"—technicians, workers, and peasants—a common grievance in the CPSU as a whole. The social composition of the KPT, divided almost equally among peasants, workers, and officials in the late 1920's, came to be dominated by officials after the war, when some 70 per cent of the membership belonged to this category. The bias in favor of officials was also illustrated by the social breakdown of postwar ad-mission figures. The available regional data uniformly indicated that only a small percentage of new members were either workers or members of kolkhozes; in predominantly rural areas this meant

---

[34] *Ibid.,* July 30, 1947, p. 2.

[35] *Ibid.,* January 18, 1948, p. 2.

[36] At the Eighth Congress of the KPT Gafurov said: "It is important to bring forth locally born people (to positions in local administration), and it is also important to have representatives of the various regions in the local apparatus" (*Ibid.,* Septem-ber 20, 1952, p. 3).

[37] *Ibid.,* November 13, 1945, p. 2.

[38] *Ibid.,* October 26, 1946, p. 2; September 27, 1946, p. 2; October 22, 1946, p. 2; December 14, 1946, p. 3; March 4, 1947, p. 5; June 7, 1947, p. 2; April 30, 1952, p. 2; and *passim.*

that Party organizations were failing to grow.[39] The scarcity of workers among the Party membership was especially embarrassing in Stalinabad city and the Leninabad oblast, the two industrial centers of the republic; the workers' share in admissions varied from 9 to 16 per cent of the total.[40]

The growth of the Party organization was also hampered by another feature characteristic of the postwar period, the failure to raise candidate members to full membership within the statutory time limit. Data available indicated that many persons remained candidates for a number of years.[41] Candidates of five years' standing were not uncommon,[42] and there were some who continued to be candidates for ten years, or even in some cases (the Leninabad oblast) for close to fifteen years.[43] Many were not advanced because of their general and political illiteracy, even though a large proportion among them could be classified as "leading economic workers." [44] The result primarily of neglect shown by appropriate Party organizations, the situation also indicated a remarkable lack of incentive on the part of the candidates themselves.

An exceedingly high turnover rate of officials in the Party and state administration and economic management was a matter of record. This became a major problem in postwar Tadzhikistan. Highest in the late forties, the turnover rate continued to be elevated in the fifties and sixties. The effective operation of the territorial Party apparatus in the 1940's was seriously hampered by the constant changes of raikom and obkom secretaries and other functionaries of Party committees. Complaints at a joint meeting of the Stalinabad obkom and gorkom revealed that the turnover in the obkom nomenklatura in 1945 and 1946 stood at 40 per cent of the total, while the turnover in the apparatus of some raikoms

[39] *KT*, November 13, 1945, p. 2; September 17, 1946, p. 2; September 27, 1946, p. 2; June 7, 1947, p. 2; April 30, 1952, p. 2; and *passim*.

[40] *Ibid.*, November 13, 1945, p. 2; August 20, 1946, p. 2; October 20, 1946, p. 3; March 11, 1947, p. 2; and *passim*.

[41] *Ibid.*, August 28, 1946, p. 2; March 4, 1947, p. 5; June 7, 1947, p. 2; April 8, 1951, p. 2; April 10, 1951, p. 2; September 21, 1952, p. 2; October 6, 1953, p. 2; and *passim*.

[42] *Ibid.*, April 7, 1951, p. 1; May 6, 1953, p. 2.

[43] *Ibid.*, April 30, 1952, p. 2; May 6, 1953, p. 2; November 13, 1945, p. 2.

[44] *Ibid.*, March 4, 1947, p. 5; April 4, 1947, p. 1; and *passim*.

reached a high of 70 per cent of the total personnel.[45] The situation had not improved in 1947, when it was reported that 80 per cent of the recently elected raikom members and candidate members (376 out of 439) were new,[46] a staggering proportion which undoubtedly reflected the results of the postwar purge. An exceptionally high turnover in raikom secretaries was also reported in the Leninabad oblast in 1947, and in the Kulyab oblast in 1948, when approximately one-half of all raikom personnel changed jobs in one year.[47]

A similar situation existed in the state apparatus. The turnover rate of executive officials in the soviet and kolkhoz managerial cadres was so high that their work was seriously affected. Documents were lost and the work of the local soviets was disrupted in 1946 because of constant changes in the positions of secretaries of soviet executive committees; kishlak soviets could barely operate because of the constant replacement of chairmen.[48] Managerial personnel of the kolkhozes was also constantly shifting.

The high turnover of the leading cadres continued into the 1950's, even though there was an improvement in comparison with the preceding period. Raikom secretaries were still transferred three or four times a year, and the rotation of kolkhoz chairmen and other kolkhoz officials was detrimental to agricultural performance.[49] Even Stalinabad city did not escape the problem. Fadeicheva, First Secretary of the gorkom, criticized the frequency of changes in the positions of secretaries of primary Party organizations, the Komsomol, and trade union organizations, and reported that in 1953 alone, 30 per cent of all persons within the gorkom nomenklatura had changed jobs.[50] In January, 1956, Gafurov again complained of the continued high turnover of the Party and soviet cadres, which he attributed to appointments "made un-

---

[45] The raikoms in question were Gissar, Rokhatin, and Zheleznodorozhnyi (*ibid.*, December 14, 1946, p. 3).

[46] *Ibid.*, April 4, 1947, p. 2.

[47] *Ibid.*, June 28, 1947, p. 2; December 12, 1948, p. 2.

[48] *Ibid.*, March 23, 1946, p. 1.

[49] This was the case in the Kulyab oblast (*ibid.*, March 27, 1953, p. 2); and the Garm oblast (*ibid.*, July 15, 1953, p. 2).

[50] *Ibid.*, January 8, 1954, p. 2.

critically and without proper screening." [51] The high figure in the mid-1950's undoubtedly also reflected the mass transfer of staff people into "production," ordered by the September, 1953, Plenum of the CPSU Central Committee. In Tadzhikistan it meant that some 82 members of the central and oblast apparatus were sent to raikoms, while more than 1,000 Party and soviet officials and specialists were assigned to work in kolkhozes, sovkhozes, and MTS.[52]

The change in leadership of 1956 did not affect the turnover. Reporting in 1958 to the Eleventh Congress of the KPT, Ul'dzhabaev, the new First Secretary, gave a complete set of turnover data: the 1956–58 average turnover in the raikom nomenklatura had varied between 25 and 37 per cent of the total, while the turnover in the nomenklatura of obkoms and gorkoms had continued to be high. The rate was relatively lower in the Central Committee nomenklatura: the changes affected 19 per cent of the total in 1956 and 13 per cent of the total in 1957.[53] Ul'dzhabaev also disclosed that there continued to be a high turnover in the apparatus of the local soviets, and in the agricultural administration: one-half of the MTS directors had been replaced during a period of two years, while more than 100 kolkhoz chairmen (approximately 20 per cent of the total) had been changed in one year.

Data for the whole period indicate that the turnover in general, though uniformly high, was more prevalent at lower administrative levels than it was in the central republican administration. The high turnover among Party personnel was also confirmed by a comparison of data on the voting delegates to Party congresses, which indicated substantial changes in composition from congress to congress. The high turnover continued into the 1960's; it was disclosed in 1961 that about one-half of the staffs of Party committees in primary, raion, and city organizations had been changed between the Thirteenth (February, 1961) and Fourteenth (Sep-

[51] *Ibid.,* January 27, 1956, p. 3.

[52] *Ibid.*

[53] The figures disclosed by Ul'dzhabaev allow the calculation of the approximate total number of positions under the nomenklatura of the KPT Central Committee. In 1956, when 19 per cent equaled 350 people, the total must have been 1,842; in 1957, when 13 per cent equaled 178, the total must have been 1,370. There is no ready explantation for the decrease (Ul'dzhabaev, *Otchetnyi doklad XI s'ezdu,* p. 58).

tember, 1961) Party Congresses [54] as a result of the Ul'dzhabaev
purge.

The constant movement of the Party, state, and economic cadres
was reflected in the composition of the political elite. The membership of the Central Committee of the KPT changed radically
in the postwar decade. Only a hard core of 39 people retained their
membership between 1948 and 1956; they constituted 35 per cent
of the 1948 total and 25 per cent of the 1956 total. The changes in
membership from congress to congress were higher among candidates than among members. In 1952, 44 per cent of the members
and 88 per cent of the candidates were elected for the first time: the
comparable figures in 1954 were, respectively, 29 and 71 per cent,
and in 1956, 38 and 73 per cent of the total.[55] The turnover in
the Bureau of the Central Committee was comparable; a hard core
of approximately one-half (6 of the 14 in 1948 and of the 13 in
1956) retained their membership through the postwar decade. Of
the 6, 3 were Russians and 3 were Tadzhiks; of the latter only 1,
Gafurov, held a post of primary importance.[56] This relative stability, however, disappeared in the subsequent period. Gafurov was
removed within three months of the Tenth Congress, which reduced the hard core to 5 people. Four of these were removed or
reduced in rank in the aftermath of the Ul'dzhabaev affair; by
1963 the membership of the Presidium of the Central Committee
of the KPT (as the Bureau was renamed) was totally new.[57]

The high over-all cadres turnover reflected a steady pattern of
lateral shifts and frequent demotions, promotions, and dismissals,
many of them caused by incompetence and abuse of power by
affected officials, or by the changing political winds. A transfer, in
fact, seems to have been regarded as the best remedy for all manner
of ills. Territorial Party committees and their cadres sections were
the agencies blamed for the high volume of turnover, because of

[54] *KT*, September 23, 1961, p. 4.

[55] The percentages were calculated on the basis of membership lists published at
the conclusion of each Party congress (*ibid.*, December 24, 1948, p. 1; September 24,
1952, p. 1; January 21, 1954, p. 1; January 31, 1956, p. 1).

[56] The 6 were: Gafurov, Khalikova, and Iskandarov (locals), and Obnosov, Mazaev,
and Saiko (Russians).

[57] The one exception was Iskandarov, who was listed as a candidate member of
the Bureau in 1961 but not in 1963 (*KT*, September 24, 1961, p. 5; December 27,
1963, p. 1).

their control of the nomenklatura.[58] Abuses in the personnel policy
in Tadzhikistan in the postwar period made this controlling role
of the Party, normally concealed by formal elections (in Party and
soviet agencies) or appointments (in state and economic administration), exceptionally clear.

A 1946 editorial in the press revealed, for example, that raion
Party committees were busily engaged in the appointment and
removal of chairmen of kishlak soviets (formally elective positions)
and "did not even bother to inform the appropriate soviets" of the
changes made. Another item criticized the practice of administrative appointment and removal of kolkhoz chairmen; the chairmen
were being removed "by practically everybody, even the militia."
Still another story told of a kolkhoz chairman who was removed
by a raikom secretary for "polygamy." In 1952 the Chairman of the
Presidium of the Supreme Soviet admitted that many of the chairmen, deputy chairmen, and secretaries of raion and kishlak soviets
were not even the elected deputies of the soviets that they led. The
Leninabad gorkom was criticized in 1953 for "moving the people
around, nothwithstanding their abilities or the needs of the appropriate government agencies." [59]

Rakhimov, the Minister of the Food Industry, answering charges
of bad personnel management in his ministry at the Eighth Congress of the KPT in 1952, referred to the Central Committee's
Secretary for Cadres, Kul'kov, as the man who "selects the leading
cadres"; by implication, someone who not only knows all the personnel shortcomings in the state apparatus but also is, in fact,
responsible for them.[60] The need to improve daily control by
higher Party officials over the hiring and firing of personnel in the
government and economic establishments, and in the selection
of secretaries of primary Party organizations in kolkhozes, sovkhozes, and MTS, was strongly emphasized at the Eighth Plenum of
the Central Committee of the KPT in 1953.[61] An irate Minister of
Education, reporting to the Tadzhik Supreme Soviet in 1948,
complained of local interference (presumably by Party committees)

[58] See footnote 13, above.
[59] *KT*, March 23, 1946, p. 1; April 3, 1946, p. 3; July 23, 1946, p. 3; September 23,
1952, p. 2; March 5, 1953, p 2.
[60] *Ibid.*, September 24, 1952, p. 2.
[61] *Ibid.*, December 2, 1953, p. 1.

in the appointments and transfer of education officials. The shifts were made ". . . locally, irresponsibly, and arbitrarily, following narrow departmental requirements. [They] hire, transfer and fire not only the primary school teachers and heads of children homes and nurseries, but also officials within the nomenklatura of the ministry itself. . . ." [62]

The staff of a raikom cadres department is expected to know personally all the people included in the raikom's nomenklatura, and to keep up-to-date files on all the leading officials in the raion. This was revealed by an article criticizing cadres practices of a certain raikom in which people were approved in a purely "formal" fashion and candidates were approved for positions within raikom nomenklatura without investigation and a personal interview. Positions so listed included Party, Komsomol, and kolkhoz posts (among them the formally elective positions of kolkhoz chairmen and secretaries of kolkhoz primary Party organizations).[63]

BEHAVIOR PATTERNS

Much of the instability of the Tadzhik managerial, bureaucratic, and political elite was blamed on routine causes such as a general shortage of politically reliable men, a "closed circle of people on whom the Party could depend," a shortage of specialists, and a continuous influx and departure of Russian cadres. The lack of specialized knowledge among the native official contingent, their inability to cope with complex economic tasks and the new technology, and simple mismanagement were other contributory factors. All of these tended to diminish with the development of the educational system and the increase in the numbers of well-trained new local cadres; yet there was no corresponding decrease in the high rate of personnel turnover.

The answer to this apparent discrepancy lies in the pursuit of certain behavioral patterns by the officials, who combined a deeply rooted desire for self-preservation and personal gain with traditional cultural and political attitudes; this led to abuses, which, in turn, caused much of the high personnel turnover. Leaders of local power clusters at all levels (starting with kolkhozes and kish-

[62] *Ibid.*, June 1, 1948, p. 2.
[63] *Ibid.*, July 3, 1946, p. 2.

laks and ending with the Party's Central Committee) based their selection, distribution, and transfer of personnel on traditional familial, friendly, religious, and cultural obligations, and on the need to secure followers. They concealed the various transgressions of their friends and subordinates, and attempted to create "family groups" for the mutual advantage of all local elements concerned. These groups maintained a united front, intended to frustrate the efforts of a higher authority to impose controls and to atomize local structures. In the tug-of-war between the local and the central authority, family groups appeared and were solidified and then destroyed in a continuing cycle. The appointment and removal of a kingpin and his associates formed the center of a drama, played out at every level of the administrative hierarchy, which significantly affected the effectiveness of political control exercised from the center and the quality of economic performance in the republic. The continuous high turnover of the Party, state, and economic cadres reflected the difficulties in maintenance of central control in the borderlands.

The "anti-Party" and "anti-Leninist" criteria that governed the placement of cadres were criticized constantly in the press as the sources of abuse and turnover. "Localism," emphasized by certain local leaders in the selection of cadres, was criticized by Gafurov in 1947, and again in 1948, when he deplored "localism and friendship ties" (*mestnichestvo i znakomstvo*) which led to the selection of ignorant, inexperienced people who lacked "political faith" and thus had to be dismissed later. In 1952 he again castigated some leading functionaries for promoting their "countrymen," [64] though it is doubtful that he himself practiced what he preached. Accusations that friendship, personal devotion, common place of origin, and family ties provided the key motivations in the placement of cadres were repeated by many speakers at the Eighth (1952) Congress of the KPT. In 1953 two editorials in the Party press pointed out that appointments made through criteria of friendship, family, and locality favored family groups and smothered criticism "from below." [65]

---

[64] Gafurov, "Nekotorye voprosy," p. 18; *KT*, December 22, 1948, p. 2; September 20, 1952, p. 31.

[65] An editorial discussed the question of cadres in the light of the Eighth Congress (*ibid.*, October 21, 1952, p. 1). See also *ibid.*, February 27, 1953, p. 1; December 2, 1953, p. 1.

The culturally conditioned behavior of many native leaders was also a target for criticism. This applied to such phenomena as "nepotism, toadyism, and fawning" (*semeistvennost', podkhalimstvo, i ugodnichestvo*) and "political myopia, indifference, and loafing" (*politischeskaia blizorukost', bezpechnost', i rotozeistvo*), which violated Party ethics and encouraged tolerance of abuses.[66] Because it was not considered polite to criticize a man directly to his face, Party officials, guilty of what Gafurov called "eastern gallantry" (*vostochnaia vezhlivost'*), looked the other way when their comrades committed irregularities. A general talk about shortcomings was considered an adequate substitute for condemnation. As a result of this procedure, many officials continued to carry on their "incorrect practices" unchecked.[67]

The traditional attitudes toward work and people appeared to be commonly held. One example was provided by the many kolkhoz chairmen who still "strongly held to the old and feared the new and progressive";[68] another example was the persistence of the traditional attitude toward women of even the highest officials. The officials' unwillingness to recruit and promote women, the survival of polygamy, and child marriages indicated that women continued to be regarded as inferior creatures.[69] The promotion of women, especially Tadzhik women, in the Party and state hierarchy was still considered a major problem in the 1950's,[70] because of the "survival in the minds of many leaders" (such as the Minister of Culture, Musa Radzhabov) of feudal-bai attitudes.[71]

Strong familial, regional, and friendly ties were particularly important in the practice of shielding a protégé from the consequences of his irregularities by transferring him to a comparable post elsewhere. The practice was widespread, not only at lower administrative levels but also among the highest oblast and republican officials, and criticism of such practices did not spare those

[66] *Ibid.*, August 20, 1946, p. 2; August 28, 1946, p. 2 (Stalinabad oblast and city); March 5, 1953, p. 2 (Leninabad oblast).

[67] Among them was the ex-Minister of Health, Bobokhodzhaev. B. G. Gafurov, "O proverke ispolneniia," *Kommunist*, XXX, no. 12 (August, 1953), 76.

[68] *KT*, October 21, 1952, p. 1.

[69] Gafurov, "Nekotorye voprosy," p. 18.

[70] *KT*, December 2, 1953, p. 1.

[71] The quote is taken from a speech by Olga Fadeicheva, First Secretary of the Stalinabad gorkom, reporting to her Party organization (*ibid.*, January 8, 1954, p. 2). See also footnote 83, below.

at the highest level of the Tadzhik power hierarchy. Extant, but apparently tacitly accepted in the 1940's, the practice received a barrage of criticism in 1952 at the Eighth Congress of the KPT, where it served as a weapon to remove the two Russians who were *ex officio* in charge of the cadres policy.

Gafurov and Obnosov, the new Second Secretary-designate, were major spokesmen "for the prosecution"; their major theme was that people responsible for cadres appointment indulged in the practice of "shifting the cadres around," so that functionaries who did badly in one position were placed in another one of equal importance. Examples given included the case of the ex-Minister of Local Industry, Malla Rakhimov, who took bribes and was guilty of other criminal acts; the First Secretary of the Obi-Garm raion whose incompetence caused its economy to suffer; the Deputy Chairman of the Council of Ministers, Z. R. Salomatshaev, who was discharged for "non-Party activities"; and two department heads in the Central Committee (a Russian and a Tadzhik) who were shifted from one department to another despite the fact that they had no special knowledge of the areas they were to supervise and that their performance was poor.[72] Other cases of covering up by transfer were quoted in personal attacks on Kul'kov. The Minister of Food Industry, Rakhimov, defended his ministry by counteraccusations:

> Comrade Kul'kov said cadres' selection and promotion in the Ministry are poorly managed. This is well known to comrade Kul'kov, who himself selects the leading cadres. At the same time they (the Central Committee) often send us people who failed in other work. For example, they could not use Tadzhibaev in the apparatus of the Procuracy, so they placed him in a leading position in Khlebmel'trest [a trust administered by the Ministry]. . . . Also, Iakubov was relieved as chairman of the Gissar raion Soviet executive committee, and now he has been placed with us.[73]

Further abuses revealed in 1952 and 1953 affected economic management as well as the Party and state administration. Cases of frequently transferred economic managers who engaged in steal-

[72] *Ibid.,* September 20, 1952, p. 3; September 23, 1952, p. 3; September 24, 1952, p. 2 (speeches by Gafurov, Obnosov, and Pulatov, respectively).

[73] Kurban Rakhimov's speech at the congress (*ibid.,* September 24, 1952, p. 2).

ing in each place of employment, and were able nonetheless to continue unchecked, were quoted as being by no means unique phenomena.[74] Two cases of transfer which served as rewards for wrongdoings were even described by a *Pravda* correspondent in Tadzhikistan: a trade official, removed for irregularities, was made an instructor in the industrial department of the Stalinabad gorkom by his friend the gorkom's secretary; and a leading official who failed in one raion was moved to another, failed again, and was finally "rewarded" by a post in the Kulyab obkom apparatus.[75]

Revelations in the Ul'dzhabaev case of 1961 neatly summarized the various practices in the manipulation of cadres engaged in by the Tadzhik political elite in the 1950's; these practices were designed to favor regional and personal interests and short-circuit Moscow's lines of political control:

Executive personnel were appointed right and left because they came from the same towns as officials, were their relatives, or were personally loyal to them. This gave rise to nepotism and mutual protection and led to the infiltration of alien ways into some Party and Soviet agencies and to crude suppression of criticism. In this situation there flourished violations of Soviet legality and of the constitutional rights of citizens, and a feudal-bai and essentially mocking attitude toward women. Some leading officials gave outright backing to thieves, adventurers, and plunderers of state and collective farm property.[76]

In many cases officials who had compromised themselves, yes-men and toadies, held executive positions for a long time. They had obviously failed in the work, but being personally loyal to Comrade Ul'dzhabaev [First Secretary of the Central Committee of the KPT at that time] they were protected in every way, saved from being criticized, and transferred from one executive position to another. It was not for working or political qualities but on the basis of personal loyalties that executive posts were given. . . .[77]

[74] *Ibid.*, October 21, 1952, p. 1; December 2, 1953, p. 1; March 5, 1953, p. 2.
[75] *Pravda*, July 8, 1953, quoted in *KT*, July 10, 1953, p. 2. In still another case, a Ukrainian secretary of the Stalinabad gorkom, Vasilli Danilovich Shtatnov, was criticized strongly for poor performance and was not re-elected (*ibid.*, August 28, 1946, p. 2). He reappeared as Deputy Secretary for Industry of the Stalinabad obkom (*ibid.*, 1947 *passim*), and later became the Deputy Chief of the Industrial Department of the Central Committee of the KPT (*ibid.*, September 21, 1952, p. 1; October 29, 1954, p. 1).
[76] *Pravda*, April 16, 1961, quoted in *Current Digest*, XIII (1961), no. 15, 10.
[77] *KT*, April 14, 1961, pp. 1–2, quoted in *Current Digest*, XIII (1961), no. 15, 11.

The removal of Ul'dzhabaev does not seem to have affected the Tadzhik officials' *modus operandi,* as instances of corruption and abuses of power in the republic continued to be the subject of frequent criticism in the 1960's. Speaking at the Fifteenth Congress of the KPT in 1963, First Secretary Rasulov again condemned frequent violations of "Leninist principles" in Party work and quoted, in support of his criticism, a recent scandal in the GBAO which had caused the dismissal of the First Secretary and all other secretaries of the oblast Party committee.[78]

ETHNIC TENSIONS

A glimpse of the informal dynamics of power was given occasionally by the momentary appearance of the tensions that were usually well hidden in the limited Soviet source material available. In the relations between the members of the power elite, tensions were caused by a combination of several factors, some universal, others strictly local. The usual personality conflicts were prompted by an individual's perception of his political role and its requirements, but this perception was molded by factors inherent in the Soviet political system, each man's position within the hierarchy of power, and his position *vis-à-vis* the very sensitive area of delimitation and overlap of Party and state powers and jurisdictions.[79] In the borderlands (Tadzhikistan, inclusive), there was also the individual's position in the vortex of the various national subgroups. In relations with peers, inferiors, and superiors, the behavior of every member of the Tadzhik political elite was conditioned by a combination of abilities and personality, ethnic origin and cultural heritage, and position within the Party-state power hierarchy. All these factors were also decisive in the determination of his actual, as opposed to formal, political status and prestige.

Little imagination is required to realize that much tension existed between Asians and Russians in high positions, and much

---

[78] *KT,* December 26, 1963, p. 3.

[79] The conflict of jurisdictions, for example, is apparent in the case of Kurbanov (see below), and may be gleaned from the speech of the Minister of Education quoted above.

effort was expended by Asians to undercut the Russians' position and thereby consolidate their own power, as illustrated by the manipulation of cadres described above. Sometimes one Russian was played off against another, and sometimes, as demonstrated in the case of Obnosov, accommodations were made between Russians and local leaders. The Russian presence in key positions did not always suffice to keep the direct control lines to Moscow open. *De jure* there was no division of authority along ethnic lines and although the reins of power were entrusted to the Russians, lines of authority at the top were blurred sufficiently to give a local Communist opportunity to neutralize the "pattern" temporarily, given a good power base at home and influence in Moscow.

The career of Gafurov, especially his apparent victory over Shil'kin and Kul'kov in 1952, lends itself to this kind of interpretation. It is interesting that in his criticism of the cadres policy before and during the Eighth Congress, that is, in his indirect criticism of both men, Gafurov was using their weapon, the control of the cadres, to his own advantage when he harped on the theme that "not enough functionaries of local nationality were advanced through the ranks." [80] The career of Ul'dzhabaev also supports the theory that it is entirely possible for an Asian leader to gain temporary ascendancy in the political hierarchy. It provides additional evidence for the existence of an Asian-Russian rivalry in the republic's governing bodies. Manifestations of a similar rivalry were also seen at the level of local government.

An attempt by the Tadzhik head of the government in 1946 to assert the authority of the state hierarchy over the Party was revealed by a marginal remark made by Obnosov (then Second Secretary of the Stalinabad obkom) at the Seventh Congress in 1948. Mamadali Kurbanov, Chairman of the Tadzhik Council of People's Commissars since the 1937 purges, had been abruptly removed in July, 1946; [81] no reasons were given. The reasons were supplied by Obnosov. Criticizing two Asian ex-chairmen of raion soviet executive committees, he made the following remark:

[80] *KT*, September 20, 1952, p. 3.
[81] *Ibid.*, July 22, 1946, p. 1. Kurbanov, born in 1905 and a Party member since 1930, was a genuine proletarian, a miner and later mine director, and the Commissar of Local Industry and Agriculture (*ibid.*, January 13, 1946, p. 2).

It is necessary to eradicate the attitude which pits the soviet organs against the Party organs, the attitude cultivated in his time by Kurbanov, the ex-Chairman of the Council of People's Commissars.[82]

Kurbanov's attempt to minimize the prerogatives of the Party indicated the desire for greater autonomy of more than one Tadzhik state official; the problem did not end with his dismissal. Under the federal system the Party, much more than the state, represented the rule of Moscow, and the challenge to it present in the attitudes of many Asian officials was undoubtedly one of the reasons for the high turnover in the cadres. The numerous complaints of "local" motivations in the appointment and promotion of cadres discussed above also provided ample evidence of the existence of nationalist feelings in the republic.

An incident at the Eighth Congress which involved a clash between a female First Secretary of the Stalinabad gorkom, Olga Fadeicheva, and Kul'kov, then Secretary for Cadres, throws an interesting light on the relative standing of government and Party officials and the relative powers of Party bodies. Since criticism of the powerful Secretary for Cadres was permitted, Fadeicheva took the opportunity to air a grievance against Kul'kov that she had acquired when he reprimanded her for rudeness to a Tadzhik head of a Central Committee department who was also the Chairman of the Tadzhik Supreme Soviet. When the Chairman, Musa Radzhabov, then head of the Department of Literature and Art in the Central Committee,[83] was summoned by Fadeicheva to a meeting in the gorkom, but failed to appear, she demanded an explanation of his absence. To quote Fadeicheva:

> When I attempted to find out the reason from comrade Radzhabov, he took offense that he, worker of the Central Committee, was asked to come to the Party gorkom, and he reported it to comrade Kul'kov.

[82] *Ibid.*, December 23, 1948, p. 2.

[83] Musa Radzhabov was Second Secretary of the Stalinabad gorkom (1948–51) and Chairman of the TSSR Supreme Soviet (he was relieved as such at the third session in 1953), and the first Tadzhik Minister of Culture (April, 1953–March, 1955). Dismissed for "poor leadership," he was criticized twice for his feudal-bai attitude toward women (*ibid.*, January 8, 1954, p. 2). The second criticism was made by Fadeicheva (see footnote 71, above), who apparently tried to damage Radzhabov's reputation. For Radzhabov the results of criticism were delayed (he was dismissed in 1955), while Fadeicheva herself was demoted sooner (in 1954) to the post of department head in the Central Committee (*ibid., passim*).

Comrade Kul'kov read me the riot act, saying that I should not treat comrade Radzhabov in this manner, and that we have no right to summon him because he is not only in charge of a department but is also the Chairman of the Supreme Soviet.[84]

The quotation reveals several things. It emphasizes the importance of the Secretary for Cadres and also that of the secretary of the capital city's Party committee. Fadeicheva's right to summon department chiefs of the Central Committee was implicitly admitted in Kul'kov's reprimand; his complaint was concerned primarily with Fadeicheva's tactlessness in disregarding the niceties of the ethnic pattern. The case also shows how negligible the Supreme Soviet really was in the power hierarchy. It is an open question whether Fadeicheva would have behaved in similarly arbitrary fashion to a fellow Russian. A personal factor also must have entered the case; the antagonism between Radzhabov and Fadeicheva had probably started when they were both secretaries of the Stalinabad gorkom.

The relationship between the Tadzhiks and the Uzbeks provided another source of tension. Their mutual dislike is rooted in Tadzhik history and the master status of the Uzbeks in the Bukhara emirate. The testimony of both Soviet and emigré sources indicates that Uzbeks have retained a degree of contempt for the minorities they used to rule and that they were hostile to the Soviet policy of giving the Tadzhiks independent status. The traditional dislike was further strengthened by the Uzbeks' position as a more advanced nationality in the early days of the Tadzhik ASSR, when the Uzbeks had more than their just share in the Tadzhik Party and power hierarchy. After 1945 the balance shifted in favor of the Tadzhiks and the percentages of Uzbeks in the Party declined below that in the population. Nevertheless, Uzbeks were still sometimes placed in important positions in Tadzhikistan. The Soviet policy aiming at the development of the new Tadzhik historiography also contributed to the growing Tadzhik consciousness of cultural identity separate from and superior to that of the Uzbeks. The dislike was also aggravated by the fact that the ancient centers of Tadzhik culture, Bukhara and Samarkand,

[84] *Ibid.*, September 21, 1952, p. 2.

were within the Uzbek SSR. Modern manifestations of the traditional dislike were, *inter alia*, the long-standing feud between the
Tadzhik and Uzbek leaders in the field of cotton technology re-
fered to by Khrushchev in 1955 and the pressures for recognition
of national interests within the Central Asian Economic Region,
the formation of which restored some of the traditional hegemony
to the Uzbeks in 1963.[85]

The CPSU spokesman for Central Asia in the sixties, the Uzbek
Party's First Secretary Sharif Rashidov, complained in 1963 of
"survivals of nationalism" which hampered the economic and
cultural integration of the region:

> . . . vestiges of [nationalism] are still tenacious among a certain seg-
> ment of politically immature people. . . . [They manifest them-
> selves] . . . either in a desire to idealize the past and to gloss over
> the social contradictions in the history of peoples . . . or in attempts
> to preserve archaic and obsolete forms of national culture under a
> flag of national originality, or in denying that a national culture is
> enriched precisely through the mutual influence of the cultures of
> fraternal peoples.[86]

The abolition of the system of national economic councils and
of the Central Asian Economic Region [87] that followed Khrushchev's downfall deprived the regional authorities of their newly
won powers, but at the same time, in Central Asia, it restored a
degree of independence to the Tadzhik and other republics, *vis-
à-vis* the Uzbeks. Discussing the decisions of the September, 1965,
Plenum of the CPSU Central Committee on economic reorganization, *Kommunist* emphasized that the reform had "created favorable opportunities for the development of the economy of the
entire country and of each soviet republic separately . . ." but it
also warned against the "exaggeration of national characteristics
and localism":

> Especially intolerable is localism, which expresses itself in the op-
> posing of falsely understood interests of "one's own" republic to the
> interests of the entire state. The necessity for genuinely scientific
> leadership of the national economy, free from both local and depart-

---

[85] See also Chap. 7.

[86] *Pravda*, May 23, 1963, quoted in *Current Digest*, XV (1963), no. 21, 28–29.

[87] *Pravda*, December 23, 1964, quoted in *Current Digest*, XVI (1964), no. 51, 25.

mental influence, was pointed out at the September plenary session of the CPSU Central Committee. The Party also stresses the inadmissibility of any *manifestations of national exclusiveness in the upbringing and utilization of personnel of various nationalities in the Soviet republics.*[88]

ADMINISTRATIVE PERFORMANCE

The efficiency of the Tadzhik Party and state apparatus was measured by the effectiveness with which it carried out central policy decisions; data available indicated that in most cases the implementation left much to be desired. Some of the problems have been discussed in the preceding sections; in addition, a major complaint has been the failure of the higher authorities to supervise local activities effectively. The communications breakdown between the higher and the lower Party and state organizations was the characteristic feature of the Tadzhik public administration. The lower organizations did not bother to report, and the higher ones showed little concern with what was going on as long as periodic written reports were forthcoming. Many contacts within the hierarchy consisted of an exchange of memos based on "make-believe" data which bore little relation to reality.[89] The duty of the network of primary Party organizations was to oversee its parent organization on behalf of the Party, but the network was weakly developed in Tadzhikistan, especially in the rural areas. Although the Tadzhik Party's program postulated a primary organization in every institution, enterprise, and kolkhoz in the republic, the network in kolkhozes before 1940 was virtually nonexistent, and in 1949 only one in every three kolkhozes had a Party organization. Kolkhoz consolidation in the early fifties was designed to remedy the situation, and was successful in forming Party units in 80 per cent of the new kolkhozes,[90] but this was the result of bringing scattered members together and not of any significant increase in the rural membership as a whole. In general,

[88] "Druzhba Narodov, Stroiashchikh Kommunism," *Kommunist,* no. 16 (November, 1965), pp. 11–12. Italics mine.

[89] One of the complaints in the Ul'dzhabaev case was that the All-Union authorities had been "hoodwinked by direct deception" in preparation of reports and by "padding of report figures on cotton procurement" (*Pravda,* April 16, 1961, quoted in *Current Digest,* XIII (1961), no. 15, 10).

[90] Gafurov's report to the Eighth Congress (*KT,* September 20, 1952, p. 2).

the size of primary Party organizations in Tadzhikistan was small; in 1957 only 44 per cent of the total had sufficient members to form bureaus, and their total number barely exceeded 2,000.[91]

The improvement in quantity did not mean an improvement in quality, and press criticism clearly indicated that few of the Tadzhik primary organizations fulfilled their tasks well. Most of their members were described as politically "idle"; few meetings were held and few people were recruited. Almost none of the primary organizations systematically reported on its work to territorial raikoms, and few raikoms conducted systematic educational and supervisory work with primary organizations in their jurisdiction.[92]

A 1955 case of "collusion" between a raikom and its kolkhozes' primary organizations will serve as an example. The raikom produced ready-made forms for the reports to be submitted to it by secretaries of the raion primary Party organizations. All a secretary needed to do was to fill in appropriate names, in phrases such as: "most Communists in the kolkhoz studied well in the political school; only two (names to be supplied) were often absent or unprepared." [93] Obviously, there was no connection between the report and the actual political work being done in a given kolkhoz. Each raikom had cadres of inspectors charged with checking on the activity of subordinate units; their numbers and their role as a direct link between the raikom and rural Party units were enhanced after the abolition of MTS in the summer of 1957, and the resulting transfer of personnel. Each instructor was placed in charge of 5 or 6 primary units, instead of 25 to 50 units.[94]

Raikoms were the most important link in the day-to-day administrative work of the republic. They were charged with the supervision of the fulfillment of economic plans—a task of overriding importance in cotton-growing raions—and with the super-

[91] Bureaus existed in 947 out of 2,159 primary Party organizations (Ul'dzhabaev, *Otchetnyi doklad XI S'ezdu*, p. 52). According to the 1956 Party statutes, bureaus were formed only in primary Party organizations of 15 or more members (Gruliow and Saikowski, *Current Soviet Policies* IV, p. 38).

[92] *KT*, August 28, 1946, p. 1; February 25, 1947, p. 3; March 5, 1947, p. 2; April 14, 1947, p. 2; February 25, 1951, p. 2; March 7, 1951, p. 1; September 20, 1952, p. 2; January 27, 1956, pp. 2–3.

[93] *Ibid.*, October 5, 1955, p. 2.

[94] Ul'dzhabaev, *Otchetnyi doklad XI S'ezdu*, pp. 53–55.

vision (frequently the actual administration) of educational work among the masses. Neither task seems to have been carried out to the satisfaction of higher authorities, to judge by the recurrent criticism. Because raikom secretaries were ultimately responsible for their raion's successful implementation of economic and political tasks, many of them were removed as a result of failure, especially in cotton production. Secretaries were accused of "formal" attitudes toward work (reliance on paper work rather than on active supervision), suppression of criticism, and failure to hold meetings and conferences as scheduled.[95] Abuses reflecting the survival of old attitudes were especially numerous in the Leninabad oblast. Special difficulties were also faced by the staffs of high mountain raions isolated in the winter months, where the percentage of illiterate functionaries was the highest, the shortage of specialists was most acute, and survivals of traditions were strongest.[96] Criticism of obkom work reflected problems similar to those in the raions, but with the gradual abolition of oblasts (by 1956 only two, Leninabad and GBAO, remained), the raions took over most of the administrative burden. Their staffs were reinforced by transferred obkom functionaries.

The shortcomings in local work were inevitably reflected in the criticism directed at the Secretariat of the Central Committee at Party congresses and plenums. Much of this took the form of self-criticism, generated by pressure emanating from Moscow. The point of departure for criticism in 1945–46, for example, was a resolution of the Central Committee of the CPSU, "On the work of the Central Committee of the KPT," of December 14, 1944.[97] At the Eighth Congress of the KPT (1952), every speaker found something to criticize in the work of the Central Committee as a whole, and in its secretaries, Bureau, and departments; not a single department chief escaped criticism, and many were replaced.[98]

[95] *KT*, August 28, 1946, pp. 1–2; October 20, 1946, p. 3; March 15, 1947, p. 1; April 4, 1947, p. 2; January 25, 1948, p. 1; December 22, 1948, p. 2; September 20, 1952, p. 2; January 19, 1954, p. 1; January 27, 1956, pp. 2–3; and *passim*. Also Gafurov, "O proverke ispolneniia," pp. 73–75.

[96] Gafurov discussed the problem at a meeting with secretaries of the mountain raions (*KT*, September 19, 1947, p. 2). At the Ninth Congress he again touched on the situation (*ibid.*, January 19, 1954, p. 1).

[97] *Ibid.*, March 14, 1945, p. 1.

[98] *Ibid.*, September 20–23, 1952.

Whereas in 1952 complaints centered on internal Party matters (organizational and cadre policies), in 1954 (Ninth Congress) the emphasis was on economic shortcomings and the criticism centered on the work of the departments of agriculture, industry, and transport.[99] Economic, political, and cultural departments, appropriate government ministries, and the Bureau itself were again strongly criticized in 1956 (Tenth Congress), in a prelude, presumably, to the ouster of First Secretary Gafurov three months later.[100]

Central ministries and the soviet hierarchy, which actually carried out economic, social, and cultural activities under the Party's supervision, were the target of even stronger criticism than the Party apparatus. Like Party committees, the soviet executive committees were guilty of not holding regular sessions and of failing to call periodic meetings of the elected soviet deputies; higher soviets took little interest in the work of lower soviets, and there was an almost total failure to check on the implementation of decisions.[101] In one case, the executive committee of the Leninabad oblast soviet checked on the execution of only 12 out of the 482 decisions it had made, and the oblast's raion executive committees followed up the implementation of 60 directives out of the total of 2,505 they had previously adopted. Kishlak soviets, which should have served as an important link in the fulfillment of cotton-growing plans, were bypassed by raion authorities working directly with kolkhozes.[102] The inactivity of the soviets was lamented not only as the cause of economic and administrative shortcomings, but also because of the loss of the participation by members of the soviets (approximately 12,000 deputies between 1948 and 1955) in the tasks of political mobilization of the republic's population. As Gafurov put it in 1948, "With the help of his army of soviet activists we can do tremendous things!" [103] The consolidation of administrative-territorial units in Tadzhikistan in the early 1950's was designed to improve the over-all performance of the

[99] *Ibid.*, January 19–24, 1954.
[100] *Ibid.*, January 28, 1956, pp. 2–3.
[101] *KT*, April 27, 1946, p. 2; May 16, 1947, p. 3; September 20, 1952, p. 2; January 27, 1956, p. 3.
[102] *Ibid.*, April 27, 1946, p. 2; March 23, 1946, p. 1.
[103] *KT*, December 22, 1948, p. 3.

soviets, but in 1956 they were declared to be too large and inefficient.[104]

The problems of breakdowns in administrative controls and possible remedies for them were discussed at length by First Secretary
Gafurov in a 1953 issue of the CPSU theoretical journal, *Kommunist*. He complained about the "hoodwinking" (*ochkovtiratel'-
stvo*) practiced by many officials to cover up their shortcomings
and about their failure to act on decisions from above. He emphasized the importance of the institutional features which facilitated
implementation and control: the plenary meetings of Party committees, attended by all the functionaries concerned (including the
lower officials within a given unit or area), and the meetings of activists, helpful in effective fulfillment of a given directive or decision and investigation of the results. Apparently neither of these
devices was successfully utilized in Tadzhikistan. Gafurov also
stressed the importance of the grassroots network of strong primary
Party organizations, and posed an ideal for which the KPT should
strive: "to activate every Party member." He deplored the hostility
toward criticism shown by most Tadzhik officials, who either did
not allow any criticism, or seemingly accepted it only to take re-
venge later.[105]

Gafurov also discussed methods of control over the implementation of Party policies. These included the practice of the Tadzhik
Central Committee of sending inspection brigades to raikoms and
obkoms. Their reports to the Central Committee were always accompanied by reports on the Party committee inspected. The problem was that reports customarily put all the blame on lower officials, and that, once inspected, a committee usually lapsed back
into its old errors, secure in the knowledge of having already been
investigated. Another method was for the Central Committee to
follow up a specific directive by sending a group of propagandists,
instructors, and specialists who assisted in its implementation. By
1950, brigades of agricultural specialists were used in the supervision of checking on fulfillment of cotton plans, because a single
specialist (*upelnomochennyi*) tended to usurp the powers of
raikom secretaries and other permanent officials. Yields were also

---

[104] *Ibid.*, January 27, 1956, p. 3.
[105] "Gafurov, "O proverke ispolneniia," pp. 72–77.

improved through a new practice of mutual checks (*vzaimop-roverka*) between brigades within a kolkhoz, kolkhozes within a raion, competing raions, or even competing republics. Gafurov deplored the fact that the method, which proved to be valuable in agriculture, was not used more in other sectors, notably industry.[106] Khrushchev's example in the mid-fifties also spurred frequent visits by republican notables to factories and kolkhozes, even in the remote mountain raions, though the theme "no one ever goes to GBAO" (or other mountain raions) was a recurrent leitmotiv of criticism at Party meetings.

The methods described by Gafurov must have been quite successful, to judge by the improvement which took place in the economic indices in Tadzhikistan in the period under review, though they added to the tensions already existing in relations between local notables and central republican agencies. In the final analysis the performance of Tadzhik administrators suffered from all the familiar shortcomings generated by the conflicting requirements for control and efficiency inherent in the Soviet system. The specific problems caused by ethnic diversity, the tenacity of traditional attitudes, and rapid modernization were also reflected in political and economic performance.

[106] *Ibid.*, pp. 66–72.

Chart 5-1. POLITICAL LEADERS OF TADZHIKISTAN, 1945–56

ASIANS

Ashurov, Nigmat, b. 1904, Kanibadam, CP—1926. Raikom, obkom work (1930–38), Secretary, CC (1938–42); obkom work (1945–49); minister (1949——); member, CC (1945——).

Dodkhudoev, Nazarsho, b. 1915, GBAO. Soviet work (1949); Chairman, Presidium SS (1950–56); Chairman, Council of Ministers (1956–61); member, CC (1948——); member, Bureau (1952——); removed with Ul'dzhabaev.

Gafurov, Bobodzhan Gafurovich, b. 1908, Leninabad raion; CP—1934. Komsomol, then journalist work (1928–31, 1935–40); study in Moscow (1931–35, 1940–41); CC Secretary for Agitprop (1941–45); Second Secretary (1945–46); First Secretary (1946–56); member, CC and Bureau (1945–56); propaganda work in Moscow (1956——).

Imamov, Alikula, b. 1910. CC apparatus (1945–46); Deputy Chairman, Council of Ministers; head Administration of Art (1946–50); department head, then secretary, CC (1950——); member, CC (1948——); member, Bureau (1954——).

Isaev, Tadzhitdin, b. 1904, Shul'mak raion; CP—1931. Worker, economic and soviet work (1922–37); minister (1937); CC Secretary (1937–41); Second Secretary (1941–45) (did not appear after 1946); member, CC, Bureau (——1946).

Iskandarov, Dzhurabek, b. 1902, Kanibadam raion, CP—1927. Soviet and party work (1923–37); Second Secretary (1937); economic work (1937–40); party work and CC department head (1940–51); Deputy Chairman, Council of Ministers (1951——); member, CC and Bureau (1946——).

Kasymova, Munavar, b. 1914. Party work in CC apparatus (1945–50); Minister, and Secretary Presidium SS (1950——); member, CC (1952——).

Khalikova, Saida, b. 1911. Raikom Secretary (1948); Third Secretary, CC (1948–54); Deputy Chairman, Presidium SS (1954——); member, CC (1948——); member, Bureau (1948–56); candidate member (1956——).

Khasanov, Abduvakhid, b. 1920. Gorkom and CC apparatus (1950–54); First Secretary, Stalinabad gorkom (1954——); candidate member, CC (1952–54); member, CC (1954——); member, Bureau (1956——).

Kurbanov, Mamadali, b. 1905, CP—1930. Miner, mine director (1924–36); Minister (1936–37); Chairman, Council of Ministers (1937–46); disappeared.

Narzibekov, Makhmudbek, b. 1919, CP—1945. Party work (——1951); First Secretary, Komsomol (1951–54) ; CC apparatus (1954——); member, CC (1952–54); member, Bureau (1952–54).

Narzikulov, Ibadullo Kasymovich, b. 1909. Study (1946–50); Deputy Chairman, Presidium TFAN, later Secretary, Academy of Sciences of TSSR (1950–54); Rektor, Tadzhik State University (1954——), Deputy Chairman, Council of Ministers (1956——); candidate member CC (1952–54).

Pulatov, Tair Pirmukhamedovich, b. 1906. Secretary for Agitprop and Department Chief, CC (1945–54); Minister of Education (1954——); member, CC (1948——); member, Bureau (1948–54).

Radzhabov, Solidzhan Nasreddinovich. Komsomol work; First Secretary, Komsomol (1947–52); member, CC (1948–52); candidate member, Bureau (1948–51); disappeared.

Rakhimova, Ibodat, b. 1922, CP—1944. Komsomol background; Secretary, Komsomol (1951–54); First Secretary, Komsomol (1954——); member, CC (1952——).

Rakhmatov, Mirzo, b. 1914 (Tadzhik), CP—1940. Komsomol, Party and Soviet work (——1948); CC apparatus (1948–51); Deputy Chairman, Council of Ministers (1951–56); Chairman, Presidium SS (1956——); member, CC (1952——); candidate member, Bureau (1954–56); member, Bureau (1956——).

Rakhmet-Zade, Usman Kurbanovich, b. 1906. CP—1929. Party work; Deputy Chairman, Council of Ministers (1947–48); obkom work and CC apparatus (1948——); member, CC (1952——).

Rasulov, Dzhabar, b. 1913 (Tadzhik), CP—1939. Graduate, Central Asia Cotton Institute, Tashkent; Deputy Minister and Minister (1934–46); Chairman, Council of Ministers (1946–55); member, CC and Bureau (1946–55); into oblivion (1955); reappeared as Secretary, CC (1958–60); dropped for one year; returned 1961 as First Secretary, CC.

Salomatshaev, Zarif Rakhimovich, b. 1909, CP—1938. Minister and Deputy Chairman Council of Ministers (1946–52); criticized, but reappeared as Deputy Minister, 1954; member, CC (1948–52).

Shagadaev, Minovar, b. 1898, Garm oblast, CP—1925. Industrial worker 1930; Party and soviet work (1930–37); Chairman, Presidium SS (1937–50); member, CC and Bureau (1948–50); disappeared.

Sharipov, Manzar, b. 1903, Garm oblast. Farm laborer, member, Red Sticks (1924–27); militia work (1927–40); Party work (1940–45); Third Secretary, CC (1945–48); Chairman, Presidium, Tadzhik Council of Trade Unions (1948——); member, CC (1942——); member, Bureau (1945–48).

Ul'dzhabaev, Tursunbai, b. 1916, Leninabad raion. Teacher, Komsomol work (1932–39); CC apparatus (1939–43); First Secretary, Komsomol (1943–47); study in Moscow; Party work, obkom and CC apparatus (1950–54); Third Secretary, CC (1954–55); Chairman, Council of Ministers (1955–56); First Secretary, CC (1956–61); removed from his posts and from the Party for abuses of power, 1961.

RUSSIANS

Dvornikov, Vladimir Semenovich, b. 1901, CP—1927. Deputy Chairman, Council of Ministers (——1947), First Deputy Chairman, Presidium SS (1947——); member, CC (1952——).

Kharchenko, Andrei Vladimirovich, b. 1907, Nikolaev oblast, CP—1929. Komsomol and Soviet work until 1930; Red Army (political work), (1930–34); Party work (1934–39); 1939, sent to Tadzhikistan; NKVD work; Minister of Internal Affairs (1946–51); member, CC and Bureau (1948–51); left Tadzhikistan.

Kotenko, Stepan Mikhailovich,* Major General, b. 1902, Don Cossack. Worker and soldier of Red Army in the Civil War; Tadzhik Border Guards (1927–34); service in the Far East, returned to Tadzhikistan as commander of the Border Guards (1944–46?).

Kul'kov, Konstantin Grigor'evich, b. 1907. Secretary for Industry, then for cadres, CC (——1952); Chief, Department of Industry, CC (1952——?); disappeared; member, CC and Bureau (1948–52).

Kuznetsov, Ivan Andreevich, b. 1903, CP—1922. Obkom and gorkom work (1946–52); Deputy Chairman, Council of Ministers (1952——); Minister (1955——); member, CC, KPT (1948——).

Mazaev, Aleksandr Vasilevich, b. 1904. First Deputy Chairman, Council of Ministers (1945——); member, CC and Bureau (1946——).

Nosenkov, A. V., Secretary, CC (1955——); member, CC and Bureau (1955——).

Obnosov, Petr Stepanovich, b. 1905. CC apparatus (1945); Deputy Chairman, SS (1945–48); Obkom Secretary (1948–50); Deputy Chairman, Council of Ministers (1950–52); Secretary, then Second Secretary, CC (1952–61); removed with Ul'dzhabaev.

Presnov, Semen Andreevich, b. 1892, CP—1918. CC apparatus (——1954); left Tadzhikistan; member, CC, and candidate member, Bureau (——1954).

Protopopov, Dmitri Zakharovich, b. 1897, Voronezh oblast, CP—1917. Cheka work (1917–21); Party and "political work" in Voronezh, Tambov, Moscow (1921–37); CC CPSU representative in Tadzhikistan (1937); First Secretary, CC (1937–46); left Tadzhikistan 1946; member, CC and Bureau (——1946).

Saiko, Viktor Antonovich, b. 1905. CC apparatus (1945–47); Deputy Chairman, Council of Ministers (1947——); member, CC (1946——); member, Bureau (1948–56); candidate member, Bureau (1956——).

Shil'kin, Mikhail Sergeevich. Secretary for Cadres (1945); Second Secretary, CC (1946–52); disappeared; member CC and Bureau (——1952).

Tokarev, Dmitrii Stepanovich, Major General, b. 1902, Chkalov oblast. Soviet work 1917–24; Border Guards (1924–38); Internal Security Chief, Kalinin Oblast (1938–45); Minister of State Security, Tadzhikistan (1945–48); left Tadzhikistan; member, CC and Bureau (1945–48).

Vishnevskii, Dmitrii Konstantinovich, b. 1905. Deputy Minister and Minister of State Security (——1953); Minister of Internal Affairs (1953–54); sent to "other work"; member, CC and Bureau (——1954).

Zakharov, Petr Ivanovich, b. 1904. CC apparatus (department chief) (1945——); member, CC, and candidate member, Bureau (1945——).

Source: *KT*, 1945–56, *passim*.

* Not a member of the leadership group proper.

CHART 5-2. RANKING ORDER OF THE TADZHIK POLITICAL LEADERSHIP AT THE MAY–NOVEMBER CELEBRATIONS, 1945–56

Year	First	Second	Third	Fourth	Fifth	Sixth	Seventh	Eighth	Ninth
1945 Nov.	Protopopov 1st Secy CC	Gafurov 2nd Secy CC	Pulatov Secy for Agitprop	Kul'kov Secy for Industry	Kurbanov Ch. C. of M.	Shagadaev Ch. Pres. SS	Ul'dzhabaev 1st Secy Komsomol		
May	Gafurov 1st Secy CC	Kurbanov Ch. C. of M.	Shagadaev Ch. Pres. SS	Kharitonov[a]	Ul'dzhabaev 1st Secy Komsomol[b]				
1946 ——— Nov.	Shil'kin[c] 2nd Secy CC	Rasulov Ch. C. of M.	Shagadaev Ch. Pres. SS	Sharipov 3rd Secy CC	Kul'kov Secy for Cadres	Pulatov Secy for Agitprop	Kharitonov[a]		
1947 May	Gafurov 1st Secy CC	Shil'kin 2nd Secy CC	Sharipov 3rd Secy CC	Pulatov Secy for Agitprop	Kul'kov Secy for Cadres	Shagadaev Ch. Pres. SS			
1948 Nov.	Gafurov 1st Secy CC	Rasulov Ch. C. of M.	Shagadaev Ch. Pres. SS	Shil'kin 2nd Secy CC	Pulatov Secy for Agitprop				
1949 May	Gafurov 1st Secy CC	Rasulov Ch. C. of M.	Shagadaev Ch. Pres. SS	Khalikova 3rd Secy CC	Pulatov Secy for Agitprop	Kul'kov Secy for Cadres	Mazaev 1st Dep. Ch. C. of M.	Saiko Dep. Ch. C. of M.	Salomatshaev Dep. Ch. C. of M.
Nov.	Gafurov 1st Secy CC	Rasulov Ch. C. of M.	Shil'kin 2nd Secy CC	Pulatov Secy for Agitprop	Khalikova 3rd Secy CC	Kul'kov Secy for Cadres	Mazaev 1st Dep. Ch. C. of M.	Imamov Dep. Ch. C. of M.	Saiko Dep. Ch. C. of M.
May	Gafurov 1st Secy CC	Rasulov Ch. C. of M.	Shagadaev Ch. Pres. SS	Khalikova 3rd Secy CC	Pulatov Secy for Agitprop				

Nov.	Gafurov 1st Secy CC	Rasulov Ch. C. of M.		Pulatov Secy for Agitprop	Kul'kov Secy for Cadres	Dvornikov 1st Dep. Ch. Pres. SS
May	Gafurov 1st Secy CC	Rasulov Ch. C. of M.	Dodkhudoev Ch. Pres. SS	Khalikova 3rd Secy CC	Pulatov Secy for Agitprop	
1951						
Nov.	Gafurov 1st Secy CC	Rasulov Ch. C. of M.	Dodkhudoev Ch. Pres. SS	Pulatov Secy for Agitprop	Kul'kov Secy for Cadres	
1952 May	Gafurov 1st Secy CC	Rasulov Ch. C. of M.	Dodkhudoev Ch. Pres. SS	Pulatov Secy for Agitprop	Kul'kov Secy for Cadres	Khalikova 3rd Secy CC
1953 Nov.	Gafurov 1st Secy CC	Rasulov Ch. C. of M.	Dodkhudoev Ch. Pres. SS	Obnosov 2nd Secy CC	Khalikova 3rd Secy CC	
1954 May	Gafurov 1st Secy CC	Rasulov Ch. C. of M.	Dodkhudoev Ch. Pres. SS	Obnosov 2nd Secy CC	Ul'dzhabaev[b] 3rd Secy CC	
May	Gafurov[c] 1st Secy CC	Ul'dzhabaev[d] Ch. C. of M. designate	Dodkhudoev Ch. Pres. SS	Obnosov 2nd Secy CC	Imamov 3rd Secy CC	Asrorov[e] Ch. Stalinabad Gorispolkom
1955						
Nov.	Gafurov 1st Secy CC	Dodkhudoev Ch. Pres. SS	Ul'dzhabaev Ch. C. of M.	Imamov 3rd Secy CC	Nosenkov Secy CC	
1956 May	Ul'dzhabaev[d] 1st Secy CC	Dodkhudoev Ch. C. of M.	Obnosov 2nd Secy CC	Imamov 3rd Secy CC		Rakhmatov Ch. Pres. SS

Source: KT, 1945–56, passim.

[a] In 1946 Anatolii Aleksandrovich Kharitonov was a plenipotentiary of the CPSU Party Control Commission for Tadzhikistan. He was subsequently listed as Secretary of the Central Committee of the KPT (February, 1951) and a member of the Presidium of the Supreme Soviet TSSR (April, 1951). He was released from the latter job in September, 1953 and left the republic.

[b] Ul'dzhabaev was dismissed as First Secretary of the Komsomol under strong criticism and sent out "to study"; he returned in 1950.

[c] Gafurov was absent at the time.

[d] Although appearing at the second place in 1955 and first place in 1956, Ul'dzhabaev was not formally appointed as Chairman of the Council of Ministers and First Secretary, respectively, until after the celebration.

[e] Asrorov appeared in the line-up as the chief Soviet official in Stalinabad.

6

POLITICAL SOCIALIZATION

POLITICAL SOCIALIZATION was the major concern of the Party in Central Asia. It presented a formidable task, because the establishment of new Soviet values and patterns of behavior required that the old, traditional ones be discredited. The clash between a modern political culture and a traditional one that was typical of the whole range of colonial and ex-colonial societies was especially severe in Central Asia because each culture formed a closed and exclusive system, an orthodoxy which required total commitment on the part of its believers.

In its socialization efforts in Tadzhikistan the Party differentiated between two major targets, the elite and the mass of the people. The Asian elite was assumed to have a basic commitment to the system; their political indoctrination was designed to maintain and maximize this commitment, and to build support for specific Party policies as they were transmitted to the borderlands from Moscow. The loyalty of local leaders and their identification with each policy were of vital importance for the success of the policy's implementation and for the effectiveness of the system as a whole. The leaders' attitudes toward Party goals directly affected the attitudes of the people and, as they were fed back to Moscow, were also a factor in formulating central policy. The indoctrination of the elite was carried out through the Party system of political education, designed primarily to impart Marxist-Leninist philosophy, to substitute the Marxist-Leninist *Weltanschauung* for the Islamic one, and to develop a sense of organic unity between Russia and the borderlands. In practical terms the program of political education was also designed to teach the mechanics of rule and to train pupils in executive and managerial skills.

No assumption of prior political commitment of the Asian masses could be made, however. Emphasis was thus placed on resocialization, with the aim of engendering political loyalty to the new system in its Tadzhik representative guise and of mobilizing manpower for the necessary participation in the economy. The political education aspect of the assignment included introducing the masses to the Marxist-Leninist outlook, but the sights were set much lower than in the indoctrination of the elite. In political terms, the aim of mass propaganda was to cause a breach in the traditional pattern of loyalties and attitudes, especially in the matter of religious beliefs and practices, and to replace them with the new Soviet value system. In economic terms, the aim was to paint a favorable picture of the benefits to be gained from economic effort on behalf of the state in the tangible form of material rewards and the intangible form of prestige and prominence.

POLITICAL EDUCATION OF THE ELITE

The political education of the ruling elite—the leading Party state and economic officials and cultural leaders—was considered the primary task of the Tadzhik Party's organization. It was important not only because of the usual requirements imposed by the pursuit of a currently correct Party line and planned economic tasks but also because of the need to breed voluntary solidarity with the Party and to reinforce basic political loyalties to the system.

The magnitude of the task and the problems inherent in it cannot be appreciated unless one remembers the Tadzhik setting: the history of recent resistance to Soviet rule, the cultural background, and the general conditions of backwardness and illiteracy. It was necessary to understand (in the words of the Party's Secretary for Propaganda) that without the political education of the leading cadres there could be no political education of the masses and no achievement of economic and political goals.[1] The implied, if not

[1] Pulatov, *KT,* September 30, 1945, p. 2.

stated, consequence of a failure in the political indoctrination of the elite was the eventual failure of the system itself.

The need to indoctrinate the elite was especially great in the postwar period, because many members were relative newcomers who were "politically illiterate." As much as 75 per cent of the republican Party organization in the middle-1940's was composed of members admitted during or after the war. Most of the incumbents in the leading positions were also newly appointed and politically poorly trained.[2] It was repeatedly emphasized by Party spokesmen that it was absolutely essential to make a major effort to educate the new cadres politically.[3]

The political loyalty of the new national intelligentsia could not be taken for granted in the period following the war because, as a 1947 editorial put it: ". . . the most backward among them fail to understand the advantages of our system and greatness of our tasks; they genuflect before the reactionary bourgeois culture and show servility and toadyism toward foreign things." [4]

Seven years of sustained effort to indoctrinate the intelligentsia did not bring the expected results. In 1954, the Central Committee Secretary for Propaganda, Imamov, again raised the problem of the survival of the "capitalist attitudes in the thinking of some of our people." He blamed it on the capitalist encirclement and on the delay which intervened between the transformation of the economic base and the formation of new attitudes. Imamov enumerated some of the offending attitudes: "non-socialist attitude toward work and socialist property," "drinking and hooliganism," "nationalist and religious superstitions," "kowtowing to the bourgeois culture," and "cosmopolitanism." The "most stubborn" among the surviving attitudes was "bourgeois nationalism," Imamov pointed out. He added that no attitude would disappear by itself, and that all would have to be exorcised by continuous indoctrination in the Marxist-Leninist ideology and by special em-

[2] This complaint was made in an editorial on the political education of the new Party cadres (ibid., April 4, 1947, p. 1) and in Gafurov's report to the Seventh Party Congress (ibid., December 22, 1948, p. 2). See also Chap. 5.

[3] Ibid., October 1, 1946, p. 2; October 26, 1947, p. 1; and passim.

[4] Ibid., September 28, 1947, p. 1.

phasis on the themes of "brotherly friendship of the peoples" and "the Great Russian people's assistance to the Tadzhiks." [5]

Tadzhikistan's border location made its people more vulnerable to capitalist influences and the danger of capitalist encirclement more real; the elite were warned by Gafurov to cultivate their own and the masses' "revolutionary vigilance":

> Our cadres' mastery of Marxism-Leninism takes on an even greater importance in conditions existing in the republic. We live at the border of the colonial East and, in this respect, we, the Bolsheviks of Tadzhikistan, carry a great responsibility. Thus, when we conduct educational work with the cadres, we should pay special attention to the increase of revolutionary vigilance of our workers.[6]

The mastery by the political elite of Moscow's latest version of the theory of Marxism-Leninism was considered absolutely essential, and the failure to grasp the ideological tenets was alleged to be the source of a whole range of "theoretical and practical mistakes." [7] "Those who lead the masses," exhorted Gafurov, "should study Marxism-Leninism three times as hard as anybody else" in order to overcome "the inherited handicap of cultural backwardness"; "they should not presume that their lack of theoretical preparation will be excused because of the general shortage of qualified cadres." [8]

The knowledge of Russian, the "powerful medium for the mastery of the heights of knowledge and culture," was indispensable for learning Marxism-Leninism. This was so not only because otherwise one could not "become a truly cultured person," but also because there was a shortage of Tadzhik translations of Marxist-Leninist classics.[9]

A vexing problem in the system of Communist political education was that it had to cope with teaching not only Marxism-Leninism but also the three R's to the numerous illiterate and

[5] A. N. Imamov, "Nekotorye problemy ideologicheskoi raboty partiinykh organizatsii v respublike," *ibid.*, August 18, 1954, p. 2.

[6] Gafurov at the Seventh Congress (*ibid.*, December 22, 1948, p. 2).

[7] As used in the editorial, the phrase "theoretical mistakes" referred to such deviations as bourgeois nationalism; "practical mistakes" meant violations of "socialist property laws" (state and kolkhoz property) (*ibid.*, October 1, 1946, p. 1).

[8] Gafurov, "Nekotorye voprosy," p. 20.

[9] *Ibid.*, p. 21. See also Chap. 7.

semi-literate Party and soviet activists. Gafurov admitted in 1947 that many members of the leading cadres had not received a secondary education and some had attended only two or three grades of primary school.[10] There were other references to the illiteracy of Party members in the press. The relative cultural backgrounds of the European and Asian Party cadres made it clear that the complaints referred primarily to the Asians. To cope with the situation in the 1940's the Central Committee Bureau established general education groups for Party activists. The groups were attached to secondary schools in cities and raion centers and offered an accelerated course of study; they continued to function in the 1950's.[11]

Differences in the educational background of students made effective instruction in the Party's educational network extremely difficult, and forced the establishment of separate facilities for backward and advanced pupils; the local cadres usually were included in the first category. This resulted in the establishment of a *de facto* segregation system with separate classes for Tadzhiks (or Uzbeks) and for Russians. As pointed out by the Central Committee's Deputy Chief of the Agitprop Department, separate facilities were necessary "because the semi-literate Tadzhiks and Uzbeks could not compete with other members of study circles who had middle and higher education." [12]

The problem of differences in the educational preparation of the students tended to reappear when, as was sometimes the case, separate classes had to be combined because of prevalent low attendance. Reading the various reports by Russian functionaries in Tadzhikistan, one cannot escape the impression that the Russian cadres cultivated a lively sense of cultural superiority and felt condescension and impatience toward the backward local cadres.

[10] *Ibid.*

[11] An item on education of Party cadres in Tadzhikistan in "Partiinaia Khronika," (*Partiinaia Zhizn'*, no. 13 [July 1947], 71); *KT, passim.*

[12] T. V. Granik at a republican meeting of propaganda workers (*KT*, November 3, 1946, p. 2). An MTS political school in the Ordzhonikidzeabad raion included 6 Russians, 2 Uzbeks, 2 Tadzhiks, and 1 Ossetin. Lectures were given in Russian, but "all the non-Russians were semi-literate and could not follow the lectures." It was further reported that similar situations existed throughout the raion (*ibid.*, November 12, 1946, p. 2). The existence of bilingual groups was frequently reported in the forties (*ibid.*, September 30, 1945, p. 2; March 13, 1945; January 3, 1945; January 27, 1948, p. 3; July 26, 1946, p. 2; and *passim*).

The basic source of Marxist-Leninist theory in the postwar decade was the *History of the VKP(b), Short Course,* then the primer of Soviet political education. Published in at least two Tadzhik and Uzbek editions, the *Short History* was the first book studied in Party schools, study circles, and individual study programs. The collected works of Stalin and Lenin (which were gradually translated and published in the native languages) were the other major doctrinal source. The Party line was taught on the basis of the current pronouncements of Stalin and other leaders, and the resolutions and directives of the Central Committee of the CPSU and of the All-Union Council of Ministers. The curriculum also included themes of local significance such as atheistic propaganda and criticism of feudal-bai survivals, practical instruction in organizational and administrative matters, historical themes, and topics of current interest in domestic and international affairs. The beneficial role of Russian culture and the Russians in Tadzhikistan also figured prominently. The higher the educational level of the audience, the more sophisticated the offerings were.[13]

The need to inculcate the leading cadres with a Marxist-Leninist outlook was constantly emphasized in Communist policies in

[13] The following are some specific examples. (1) In a Stalinabad city raion, topics of seminars for secretaries of primary Party organizations included the role and the meaning of Party meetings and how to conduct them, and the organizational principles of Bolshevism (*ibid.,* October 27, 1945, p. 2). (2) Lectures organized by the Stalinabad gorkom in August, 1945, for the "intelligentsia" (in Russian) had the following titles: *The San Francisco Conference: Lomonosov; Lenin's April Theses; The Results of the British Elections; Pushkin; Imperialism, the Highest Stage of Capitalism; The Youth in the Great Fatherland War;* and *The Great Russian People (ibid.,* August 1, 1945, p. 4). (3) The plan of study prepared by the Central Committee of the CPSU for raion evening Party schools included a total of 160 class hours in the period of 8 to 10 months, divided as follows: *The History of the VKP(b), Short Course* (80 hours); geography of the USSR and foreign countries (42 hours); the Five-Year Plan (14 hours); and problems in Party and government work (24 hours) (*ibid.,* October 22, 1946, p. 2). (4) Gafurov described the content of political education in Tadzhikistan, stressing four major themes: friendship of the peoples; Soviet patriotism; national pride; and gratitude to the Great Russian people for liberation from oppression by local feudalism and by tsarism and also for assistance (Gafurov, *Nekotorye voprosy,* pp. 17–27). (5) The following lectures were heard by a republican seminar for Party lecturers of the Central Committee, obkoms, and gorkoms: the Five-Year Plan; Lenin on materialism and empiriocriticism; Russian classical philosophy of the nineteenth century; international reaction and the plans for a new war; man as an instrument for earth transformation; and the classical Tadzhik literature (*KT,* May 28, 1946, p. 3). (6) The following lectures were heard at a 10-day seminar for propaganda workers in Leninabad obkom: tasks to combat feudal-bai survivals; Tadzhik history and geography; and the international situation (*ibid.,* April 25, 1948, p. 2).

the postwar decade in Tadzhikistan, but despite much talk of
growth and improvement, progress was not spectacular, and shortcomings in the system of political education continued to be criticized by the CPSU. Even official statistics failed to support the
claim to improvement. Although the total number of students in
the network more than doubled between 1945 and 1955, most of
the growth was due to the number of pupils in individual study
and correspondence courses; the size of the graduating classes of
the top-level school actually decreased. The paucity of data released also indicated that political education remained a problem
(see Table 6-1).

At the apex of the Party's educational hierarchy were the advanced schools. The Republican Party School at the Central Committee of the KPT served Party members; the educated elite attended evening universities of Marxism-Leninism. The course of
study in the Republican Party School (it admitted only Party and
soviet activists with secondary education) was divided into soviet
and Party departments; the latter was subdivided into organization, propaganda, and Komsomol sections. Most of the students
appeared to be of local ethnic origin; after graduation they were
directed into raion Party work, but a few of the best were sent to
Moscow for further study.[14] Students in the three universities of
Marxism-Leninism were divided almost equally between Party,
government, and economic functionaries and the intelligentsia;
many were not members of the Party. More than one-half of the
students in the Stalinabad evening university had had higher education,[15] and many of them were undoubtedly Europeans. The
high dropout rate and low attendance were major problems in the
higher schools.[16]

At a lower level, the network included raion Party schools and
evening schools, political schools attached to primary Party organizations (mostly in rural areas), study circles, correspondence

[14] *KT*, August 19, 1945, p. 2; August 27, 1946, p. 2; September 17, 1946, p. 1;
August 2, 1949, p. 2; August 12, 1951, p. 2; August 14, 1952, p. 2; and *passim*. See
also Table 6-1.

[15] *Ibid.*, January 11, 1952, p. 2; and July 23, 1953, p. 2.

[16] *Ibid.*, August 19, 1945, p. 2; August 27, 1946, p. 2; September 17, 1946, p. 1;
August 2, 1949, p. 2; August 7, 1951, p. 2; August 12, 1951, p. 2; August 14, 1952,
p. 2; and *passim*.

Table 6-1. TSSR: The Political Education Network

Schools and Students	1945	1946	1948–49	1952	1954–55
Republican Party School at the CC KPT: graduates	94[a]	134	110[b]		87
Evening universities of Marxism–Leninism					
No.	2	3			
Students	300[c]				
Raion Party schools					
No.	72	80	57		
Groups	118				
Students	2,500				
Political schools					
No.	570	500+	805		
Students	11,000				
Study circles					
No.	256				
History VKP(b)					
No.			473		
Students				45,000[c]	
Stalin/Lenin biographies					
No.			636		
General education schools and groups for Party members			286		
Correspondence course students	40[c]				7,000[c]
Individual study students		2,764	4,983	6,390	7,543
Students in all schools and circles					14,700
Students in the total network		19,500[c]		51,000	

Sources: *KT*, August 19, 1945, p. 2; September 30, 1945, p. 2; October 1, 1946, p. 2; August 27, 1946, p. 2; December 22, 1948, p. 2; August 10, 1949, p. 2; November 14, 1952, p. 2; September 20, 1952, p. 2; November 23, 1955, p. 3; August 10, 1954, p. 2; August 12, 1955, p. 2.

[a] Of these, 21 were women.   [b] Of these, 97 were Asians.   [c] This figure is approximate.

courses, and programs of study for individual activists. Most circles studied Party history, but there were also groups for the study of the biography of Lenin and Stalin, and more advanced ones for the study of political economy and historical and dialectical materialism. Instructors, lecturers, and consultants in the Party's educational network were all professional propagandists, trained in special courses, summer courses, and seminars organized by the Central Committee, obkoms, and raikoms for the staffs of the agitprop, education, and communications departments in their jurisdiction. The Central Committee also organized periodic republican conferences in propaganda and ideological work which were attended by all the Party and state officials concerned.[17]

Outwardly, the system presented a formidable organizational façade. It would seem that the Party's sustained worry about its effectiveness was unnecessary, but constant complaints and criticism, supported by detailed evidence in the press, indicated that the system functioned primarily on paper. Two kinds of reports were published. One gave a series of statistical data which showed the growth of educational facilities and students and hailed the achievements of a particular propaganda sector. These were usually written by the men in charge of a given sector. The other reports were written by the same men in a fervor of self-criticism or by the various inspectors sent by higher party bodies to investigate local conditions. Reports of the latter type generally shattered the make-believe world of supposed achievement. Political schools and circles were formed but rarely convened; students enrolled but did not attend; the dropout rate in Party schools was staggering; individuals engaged in individual study hardly ever progressed beyond the first few chapters of the *Short History;* propagandists met and adopted resolutions they later failed to implement; and Party and soviet officials displayed shocking ignorance of the basic Marxist-Leninist concepts.

The level of political sophistication of the leading cadres is illustrated by the following story. An official in a state control agency was asked to explain the difference between Lenin's and Martov's concepts of Party membership. Martov, he answered, re-

[17] *Ibid.,* February 24, 1945, p. 2; October 30, 1945, p. 2; May 28, 1946, p. 2; November 3, 1946, p. 2; March 25, 1947, p. 2; September 28, 1947, p. 1; June 16, 1951, p. 2; November 14, 1952, p. 2; December 26, 1952; November 23, 1955, p. 3.

quired a member "to work (*rabotat'*) in one of the Party organizations," while Lenin wanted him "to fulfill Party obligations" (*vypolniat' partiinye nagruzki*). Another leading state official had this to say about the turn-of-the-century Populists: "They tried to achieve freedom and will by the use of various terrors and various strikes, while Lenin thought that power should be seized, and opposed various strikes. . . ." [18]

The situation improved little in the following years. In 1948, the KPT Secretary for Propaganda complained again that "the leading Communist cadres are extremely poorly armed with Marxism-Leninism." The Seventh Congress revealed that the political education system was ideologically poor and failed to meet the Party needs, and that the importance of general education for Communists was grossly underestimated. Some improvement, but also the continuation of basic shortcomings was indicated at the Eighth Congress in 1952 and the Tenth Congress in 1956. At the latter congress Gafurov admitted that despite quantitative progress, the system of political education still suffered from interrupted course work, low quality of instruction, and the students' failure to work. He also stigmatized propagandists for their "failure to connect with reality," "dogmatism and pedantry," and their "parrot-like repetition of formulas." [19]

The most frequent complaint concerned the failure of numerous political schools and circles to work regularly, to complete their programs, and to secure full attendance. In 1945 in the Garm oblast only 3 out of the 10 formally existing raion Party schools were really in operation, and none of the formally listed 88 rural political schools and those which met intermittently in 1947 had no textbooks. Schools in the Stalinabad oblast existed only on paper in 1946; [20] the same was true of the GBAO schools in 1947, and out of 800 circles and political schools in Stalinabad city, not one was operating regularly.[21] Political schools in the Leninabad oblast in 1951 were active only at the beginning and at the end of

[18] "Oni stremilis' raznymi terrorami, raznymi stachkami dobivatsia svobody, voli, a Lenin schital chto nado brat' vlast' a ne raznymi stachkami. . . ." (as quoted by a lecturer of the Stalinabad gorkom, *ibid.*, October 3, 1945, p. 2).

[19] *Ibid.*, December 26, 1948, p. 2; January 9, 1949, p. 1; September 20, 1952, p. 2; August 18, 1954, p. 2; January 27, 1956, p. 3.

[20] *Ibid.*, September 5, 1945, p. 2; October 10, 1947, p. 2; June 26, 1946, p. 2.

[21] *Ibid.*, October 26, 1947, p. 1; March 4, 1947, p. 5.

the academic year, and the Kulyab oblast schools in 1955 existed only on paper.[22] Many political schools failed to complete their study program. In 1947 only 2 out of 401 students in Stalinabad's 42 political schools were able to complete a one-year program in the time specified; in the Kulyab oblast only 11 out of 69 schools covered the required program of study.[23] In 1949 Pachadzhanov, Chief of the Propaganda Department of the Central Committee, reported that 63 per cent of all the political schools in the republic failed to complete the study program.[24]

Attendance data indicated the complete indifference—not to mention resistance—of the students to "being armed" with Marxism-Leninism. In 1946–47 no more than 10 to 20 per cent of registered students attended classes in the Kulyab city school and a raion Party school in Stalinabad. In Leninabad in 1948 attendance at the evening Marxist-Leninist University was good (70 per cent of the registered students), but in a general education school for Party members only 16 per cent of students enrolled appeared at their classes.[25]

Political education in rural areas was frequently interrupted by the need for all hands to participate in field work such as cotton picking.[26] Local Party functionaries were frequently trapped between the need to fulfill an economic plan at all costs and the need to keep up their work of political indoctrination. During cotton campaigns it was indoctrination that usually suffered. Individual study was most popular among the various kinds of political education. A student registered the fact that he was studying Marxist-Leninist classics on his own with a Party committee, and was periodically "examined." In fact, individual study was the most difficult to supervise, which was probably the secret of its popularity. Complaints were common that individual study was a farce because there was no control over students' work, that many students were registered for years but never completed the program or even

---

[22] *Ibid.*, July 26, 1951, p. 2; February 9, 1955, p. 2.

[23] *Ibid.*, July 30, 1947, p. 2; October 26, 1947, p. 1.

[24] *Ibid.*, September 3, 1949, p. 2.

[25] *Ibid.*, May 24, 1946, p. 2 (Kulyab—15 out of 70 students); March 4, 1947, p. 5 (Stalinabad—10 out of 80 students); March 9, 1948, p. 2 (Leninabad).

[26] *Ibid.*, September 30, 1945, p. 2; October 26, 1947, p. 1; April 29, 1951, p. 2; and *passim*.

progressed beyond the first chapter of the *Short History,* and that many of them did nothing at all.[27]

A typical case of individual study was reported in the Kulyab gorkom in 1946. Among those registered for individual study some did nothing, some read only newspapers, and some never managed to progress beyond the third chapter of the *Short History.* Colonel Muradov, of the oblast MVD, for instance, studied the first three chapters for more than a year, but could not give the date of the founding of the Party; comrade Khodzhaev, chief of the political department of the oblast MVD, had not studied at all for "lack of time," and a secretary of a primary Party organization did not know when *Iskra* had been established or when the Second Party Congress had met.[28] The report is rather revealing of the low degree of "sophistication" in Marxism-Leninism required of local party functionaries, as shown by the type of questions asked, and the almost complete lack of knowledge of dogma evident from the answers. One cannot help sympathizing with Irkaev, the Obkom Secretary for Propaganda, who was faced with the choice of antagonizing local MVD officials by checking on their study or of failing in his appointed propaganda task. The choice he actually made in this case (to do nothing) was characteristic of propaganda work in Tadzhikistan.

Troubles in political education were in large part the result of the shortage of propagandists and their poor political training, or even illiteracy. In 1945 propagandists were described who were not only illiterate politically but also in general. "Feeling their illiteracy, they were afraid to start propaganda work among the people." [29] Propagandists of this kind must have found it rather difficult to explain the Party line to their audience and to parry questions, and one cannot help wondering how well they knew their Marxist-Leninist classics. The training and literacy of propa-

[27] *Ibid.,* October 1, 1946, pp. 1–2; September 28, 1947, p. 1; September 3, 1949, p. 2; January 13, 1952, p. 3; January 29, 1952, p. 2; November 14, 1952, p. 4; August 12, 1955, p. 2; January 29, 1956, p. 2; and *passim.* In 1953 Gafurov disclosed that thousands of Party members who were supposed to study Marxism-Leninism by themselves did no work at all, that many Party republican functionaries had failed to study Marxism-Leninism for years, and that the "political illiteracy" of the lower functionaries was notorious (Gafurov, "O proverke ispolneniia," p. 75).

[28] *KT,* May 24, 1946, p. 2.

[29] *Ibid.,* February 24, 1945, p. 2.

204 POLITICAL SOCIALIZATION

gandists gradually improved, but the quality of their performance was still being criticized during the fifties.[30]

Complaints continued to be heard in the sixties at the Fourteenth (1961) and Fifteenth (1963) Congresses of the KPT: the teaching of Marxism-Leninism suffered from a "statistical attitude" and Party committees did not do a good job of political education. An improvement in ideological work was noted at the Sixteenth Congress in 1966, but significant shortcomings were still reported to exist, especially in work with the Tadzhik youth.[31]

The general impression created by the system of political education in Tadzhikistan was that to most members of the elite, propagandists included, the constant emphasis on political indoctrination was a nuisance. The Tadzhiks did not care about the minor differences in the interpretation of dogma by the splinter groups of Russian Social Democracy before 1917; they probably would have preferred to forget some of the subsequent chapters of Party history such as the liquidation of the bourgeois nationalists.

Much of the instruction and emphasis in the postwar decade, when economic effort was stressed, must have seemed irrelevant to many "good" Communists in Tadzhikistan, especially the Party and soviet activists who were actively engaged in accomplishing economic tasks.[32] Even when the system of political education was actually working (and there was an undeniable improvement in the postwar decade), it appears that little was learned and even less was retained. The new political creed and ethics had little effect on the traditional modes of behavior and attitudes of minor functionaries and also of some members of the elite, as proved by the Ul'-dzhabaev scandal and other similar cases.

Reaching the point of diminishing returns as a result of the constant repetition of political slogans is a familiar phenomenon in the Soviet system of political education and is not limited to

[30] *Ibid.*, August 16, 1949, p. 1; September 3, 1949, p. 2; August 18, 1954, p. 2; August 12, 1955, p. 2; and *passim.*

[31] *Ibid.*, September 23, 1961, p. 5; the report of First Secretary Rasulov at the Fourteenth Congress (*ibid.*, December 26, 1963, pp. 3–4), and the Sixteenth Congress (*Pravda*, March 9, 1966, p. 2).

[32] In the sixties the Party added a new economic emphasis to political education, and introduced economic training as part of the curriculum of political education (*KT*, December 26, 1963, p. 3).

Tadzhikistan. The problem, however, seemed greater there because of the two factors already emphasized: the cultural background that made Tadzhiks hostile to any orthodoxy other than
Islam, and the antagonism between the ruling Europeans and the
subordinate Asian groups which was aggravated by enforced Rus-
sian-inspired socialization.

INDOCTRINATION OF THE MASSES

The shortcomings of the political education of the elite were
inevitably reflected in the quality and effectiveness of the political
indoctrination of the masses. It was important to breed loyalty
to the Soviet system among the local Tadzhik population, or at
least to obtain a degree of popular support for the participation in
the whole range of necessary political and economic activities.
Much effort was expended on mass agitation and cultural-educational work and on the build-up and improvement of mass communications media; paper and print and Party time were used up
in evaluation and criticism of the work. In the customary Soviet
pattern, the broad spectrum of political socialization activities
ranged from political meetings to theatrical performances and from
newspaper reading, listening to the radio, and attending lectures
to performing in folk art groups, participating in discussions,
marching in parades, and voting in elections.

Objective conditions confronted a propagandist agitator with a
staggering set of problems. It was relatively easy to move about in
the valleys (notwithstanding the extreme transport difficulties),
but traveling on foot, sometimes on dangerous, narrow trails, was
still the only way to reach most of the mountain settlements, many
of which were cut off in winter months. An agitator had to put up
with primitive conditions and was forced to use extreme ingenuity
in improvising needed props and technical equipment. Communications media such as radio and the telephone were poorly developed and mail distribution was often curtailed; the network of the
so-called cultural-educational establishments (clubs, teahouses,
libraries, movies) was developed poorly and unevenly.

The propagandist faced a population steeped in local traditions
and distrustful of change, especially when the change was fostered
by outsiders and was designed to subvert traditions. Although the

situation in this respect was immeasurably better in the forties and fifties than it had been in the twenties or thirties, when an agitator's life was often in danger, there was still much passive resistance to the new socialization.

The task of mass agitation was further complicated by linguistic difficulties and the still extant, if much reduced, illiteracy and semi-literacy of the population. At least three major languages had to be used in mass propaganda work: Tadzhik, Uzbek, and Russian. Furthermore, there were still other minority groups such as the Turkmen or Kirgiz who had to be addressed in their own language. Mountain Tadzhiks spoke separate dialects and found the literary Tadzhik hard to understand. In this multilingual situation, most agitators and propagandists had to be recruited from among the local people (except in the largely Russian-speaking cities). A native agitator could communicate with the people, but being a product of the traditional culture himself, he frequently failed as a salesman of the new creed. The agitators' inadequate training was an important contributory factor to the ineffectiveness of mass propaganda work.

The gap between traditional amusements and the new ones sponsored by the regime as indoctrination vehicles did much to render cultural indoctrination ineffective. In routine propaganda and even in special campaigns, propaganda workers generated little enthusiasm. An occasional glimpse provided by the press into popular preferences indicated a lack of response to Soviet themes; attendance at propaganda functions was notoriously low and readership of newspapers and propaganda materials was limited. The postwar emphasis on the urgency of economic tasks placed mass propaganda work on a secondary priority level (*de facto* if not *de jure*); Party and government activists were too busy to give more than perfunctory attention to political work and undoubtedly resented the encroachment on their time that it entailed. Bureaucrats, workers, and peasants also seemed to resent the time spent participating in propaganda activities after a hard day of work or when their leisure and amusements were used to point up a political object lesson.

Mass propaganda was pitched at a different intellectual level than the political training of the elite, and the order of priorities reflected a utilitarian approach. Although concern with the inculcation of new values was always present, the masses were still considered too bound by tradition to change their values quickly, and major emphasis was placed on the short-range fulfillment of economic tasks and formal political requirements. From the Marxist point of view, participation in the new collectivist economy would enable workers to acquire the socialist consciousness. A 1946 newspaper editorial called for improvement in mass educational work in rural areas in order to improve performance in cotton-picking, because "cotton is the main treasure of Tadzhikistan." It illustrated the order of priorities clearly:

> All the mass political work should be carried out . . . in order to mobilize the toilers for new labor efforts, to educate them in the spirit of state interests, and to raise their consciousness and political and productive activity.[33]

Mass indoctrination in Tadzhikistan was so badly neglected in 1945 that it merited special attention of the Central Committee of the CPSU. In 1944, the Committee charged, "mass political work among the population of the republic [had been] stagnant"; mountain and border areas were targets of special criticism.[34] A flurry of activity in the Tadzhik Central Committee and its subordinate agencies followed. It was revealed that little attention had been paid to mass educational work, especially for women and youth, and to cultural-educational work in general. No systematic mass political work had been conducted by agitprop departments of local Party committees, and agitators themselves needed political training.

The emphasis on mass indoctrination started to pay dividends in the late 1940's and the early 1950's, when the quantitative propaganda indices, as well as over-all economic performance, in the republic began to improve, but the preoccupation with economic targets was criticized as one-sided. In 1948 Gafurov compared the progress in mass agitation work to that in technical and economic matters and criticized the failure to explain domestic and foreign policies and to educate workers "in the spirit of Soviet

---

[33] *Ibid.,* October 15, 1946, p. 1 (the resolution of the plenum of the CC of the CPSU of December 14, 1944).
[34] *Ibid.,* March 4, 1945, p. 1. See also Chap. 7.

patriotism and national pride." [35] Pulatov, the Secretary for Propaganda, criticized the practice of campaigning (*kampaneishchina*), which was punctuated by lapses into inactivity.[36] The resolutions of the Seventh Congress emphasized the need to select better agitators and to raise their ideological level and output.[37] A general improvement was reported in the fifties, but old weaknesses still existed, such as kampaneishchina, poor cultural-educational work, insufficient work with women and youth, and lack of success in atheistic propaganda.[38] In 1956 Gafurov was still bemoaning the same problems, complaining specifically of the failure to "unmask the survivals of the past and their bearers," [39] and the same story was repeated in the 1960's.[40]

SPECIAL CAMPAIGNS—ELECTIONS

The prevalent practice of kampaneishchina is illustrated by mass propaganda activities that preceded elections held in Tadzhikistan in the postwar decade to the Supreme Soviets of the USSR, and of the Tadzhik SSR, and to local soviets. Hardly a year passed without an election, yet each time the whole campaign had to be organized anew. This included setting up agitation points, organizing propagandists and agitators, and revamping the general system of transportation and communications, which habitually lapsed into ineffectiveness in the intervening periods.

Propaganda Secretary Pulatov gave a detailed outline of how a pre-election campaign should be run. Raikom secretaries were to exercise general supervision, but primary Party organizations were actually in charge in each locality and were to receive assistance from mass organizations and the soviets. An intensive use of all communications media was strongly recommended, as was the use of visual aids. The message was to be differentiated on the basis of

[35] *Ibid.*, December 22, 1948, p. 2.

[36] *Ibid.*, December 26, 1948, p. 2. Kampaneishchina described intense short spurts of activity in support of an economic or propaganda campaign, such as those for cotton planting or picking or for elections.

[37] *Ibid.*, January 9, 1949, p. 1.

[38] *Ibid.*, September 20, 1952, pp. 2–3; March 19, 1955, p. 1; September, 1955; *passim*.

[39] *Ibid.*, January 27, 1956, p. 3.

[40] *Ibid.*, September 23, 1961; December 26, 1963; *Pravda*, March 9, 1966.

the social groups to which it was addressed. Agitators were told to go directly to kishlaks, and to know their material well in order to be convincing. They were urged to learn biographies of candidates in order to be able to conduct a "personal" campaign. They were to concentrate on explaining the electoral process and the Soviet constitution, stressing its superiority over capitalist constitutions, and to explain Soviet domestic and foreign policies. They were also instructed to make a major effort to emphasize how much better life was in Soviet Tadzhikistan than it had been under the rule of the Emirs or across the border, reinforcing their argument by citing actual achievements and locally known examples.[41]

Press coverage yielded rich data on electoral campaigns between 1945 and 1955. Hundreds of agitation points were established; thousands of agitators gave talks and lectures and organized discussions, meetings with candidates, conferences of the voters, movies, shows by local artistic folk groups, youth evenings, literary discussions, and many other activities. According to Pulatov, in the 1947 election to the Supreme Soviet of the Tadzhik SSR, more than 23,000 agitators worked in the campaign; 8,883 groups were organized to study the USSR constitution; 19,244 lectures were given by Party officials; 522,000 copies of electoral pamphlets were distributed in the three major languages; special film shorts were shown at approximately 900 shows; candidates held 647 meetings with the voters; question-and-answer programs were carried on the radio in addition to 12 concerts and 158 literary and musical broadcasts; brigades of artists and writers performed in various electoral districts; the press carried electoral articles every day; and economic competitions in all fields were held in honor of the elections.[42]

This is a staggering recital, but on closer examination the figures are less formidable. Most of the campaign activities were centered in and around highly saturated oblast and raion centers, while rural areas were scarcely exposed to them.

Commenting on these activities, Pulatov himself complained that many raikoms played only a "formal" role in the campaign, many agitators did not work at all, others worked poorly, and

[41] *KT*, October 23, 1945, p. 2; December 15, 1946, p. 2.
[42] *Ibid.*, March 7, 1947, p. 2.

most failed to differentiate various target groups in their campaign.[43] Similar criticisms were also heard after other elections; the failure to establish direct contact with the masses was the one which recurred most frequently. An interesting sidelight on the character of political work in Tadzhikistan was provided by an item referring to a 1947 electoral campaign in Stalinabad city: of the 353 voters in an electoral quarter of one of the city's raions, all were Tadzhiks, but there was not a single agitator available who could speak the Tadzhik language.[44]

Electoral campaigns were generally accompanied by the publication of appropriate propaganda literature. In 1946, for example, the Central Committee's appeal to the voters was published in 150,000 copies in pamphlet form and in 100,000 copies in posters. Slogans taken from the appeal were published separately in 80,000 copies; all the literature was in the three major languages.[45] It was a drawback to many campaigns, however, that frequently such propaganda materials reached the voters too late or not at all.

Problems which clearly emerged from the survey of electoral campaigns were the difficulty of access to the mountain regions and the general inadequacy of the transportation and communications networks, especially in winter. The high mountains of the Garm, GBAO, and other raions were effectively isolated despite special arrangements made before each election for air delivery of the campaign literature, and for its local distribution by special relay messengers on skis or horseback. Much effort was spent on laying and maintaining telephone and telegraph lines and on radio communications between raion centers and mountain kishlaks, in order to prevent frequent breakdowns.[46]

[43] *Ibid.*

[44] *Ibid.*, February 7, 1947, p. 1. The item indicated that the Party apparatus in Stalinabad city was Russian-dominated, and also that the city was divided into native and European quarters.

[45] The elections were to the Supreme Soviet of the USSR; among the pamphlets, 75,000 copies were in Tadzhik, 50,000 in Uzbek, and 25,000 in Russian (*ibid.*, February 8, 1946, p. 3).

[46] *Ibid.*, October 28, 1945, p. 2; December 23, 1945, p. 2; February 1, 1946, p. 1; November 21, 1947, p. 2; November 22, 1947, p. 3; January 24, 1953, p. 2; January 25, 1953, p. 3; and *passim*. Telephone and telegraph communications were in a state of chronic breakdown, especially in the mountains, where telephone poles were stolen and local kolkhoz workers were unwilling to do any repairs. Mail was kept

Given the customary Soviet turnout of 99.99 per cent of eligible voters, the campaigns served their purpose, but it is doubtful that they significantly increased political socialization and popular support. The campaigns were superficial and inefficient, with peak activity concentrated in urban areas; they did teach the people, however, the habit of political participation. The campaign techniques described above were used in support of numerous other policies, among them the timely fulfillment of a particular economic task. Among non-economic campaigns, the Peace Campaigns of 1951 and 1955 should be briefly noted. Major cultural figures made speeches; republican conferences and a series of lectures, meetings, and rallies, all of which compared the peace-loving Soviet Union with the war-mongering West, particularly the United States, were organized with familiar results. Their impact on the Tadzhik population appears to have been minimal.

THE PRESS AND PUBLICATIONS

The press and the publishing industry play an extremely important role in Soviet mass socialization activities; in Tadzhikistan they have been seriously handicapped by linguistic difficulties, problems of literacy, and breakdowns in the distribution network. Changes in the alphabet have affected the volume of publications available and the literacy of the readers, and the shifts in the interpretation of history and the dogma have caused withdrawals of many books and the need to write and publish new ones. The problem is especially acute in the case of textbooks.

The first printing press in Tadzhikistan started in 1923, and the Tadzhik State Publishing House (*Tadzhikgosizdat*) was established in 1931.[47] There were only a few publications in the 1920's. The volume increased substantially in the 1930's, but it was considerably reduced during the war years. Only in 1950 did the volume of publications reach the prewar level, but the development has been steady since then (see Table 6-2). The total number of items pub-

---

in raion centers for days and weeks undelivered; telegrams were delayed for weeks (*ibid.*, October 28, 1945, p. 2). In 1946 only one-half of the rural soviets had telephones (240 out of 460) (*ibid.*, August 11, 1946, p. 3). Despite an improvement in the fifties, serious shortcomings were still reported in 1954 (*ibid.*, May 30, 1954, p. 2).

[47] AN TSSR, *Istoriia*, III, Book 1, pp. 152 and 271; *KT*, July 1, 1945, p. 1; May 5, 1955, p. 2.

Table 6-2. TSSR: Books, Magazines, and Newspapers, 1932–55

Publications	1932	1937	1940	1945	1946	1949	1950	1955
Books								
Titles, total			372		98		347	482
Titles in Tadzhik			285		61		269	333
Total no. of copies[a]			2,823		1,257		2,784	3,307
No. of copies in Tadzhik[a]			2,448		900		2,313	2,643
Magazines								
Titles, total	4[b]	6[c]	9[d]				14[d]	10[j] 29[d]
Titles in Tadzhik			4[d]				7[d]	13[d]
Annual circulation[a]			141[d]				1,030[d]	1,287[d]
Annual circulation in Tadzhik[a]			127[d]				873[d]	936[d]
Annual circulation of books and magazines[a]			3,000				3,100	4,600
Newspapers								
Titles	29[b]	65[c]	83	64[e]			75	67
Daily circulation[a]	85	176	282	188[f]	230[g]	260[i]	252	335
Annual circulation[a]			44,000				40,000	63,000
Republican newspapers				3[f]	6[g]	7[i]		7[j]
Oblast newspapers				10[f]	12[g,h]	8[i]		4[j]
City newspapers								6[j]
Raion newspapers				54[f]	50[g,h]	55[i]		42[j]

Sources: Unless otherwise specified, the source is *TSSR. Nar. Khoz. 1957*, pp. 290–91 and 325–26.

[a] In thousands.
[b] AN TSSR. *Istoriia*, III, Book 1, p. 271.
[c] *Ibid.*, p. 324.
[d] Including bulletins and other periodicals
[e] *KT*, February 11, 1945, p. 1.
[f] *Ibid.*, July 15, 1945, p. 2.
[g] *Ibid.*, May 5, 1946, p. 2.
[h] *Ibid.*, September 18, 1946, p. 2.
[i] *Ibid.*, May 5, 1949, p. 1.
[j] *Ibid.*, October 20, 1955, p. 1.

lished by Tadzhikgosizdat up to and including 1952 was 7,500 titles in 64,000,000 copies (see Table 6-3); these presumably included items written in Arabic and in the Latin alphabet. In 1955, 482 book titles were published in over 3,000,000 copies (see Table 6-2). A thematic breakdown of publications indicated that political literature constituted the largest single field, followed by textbooks, with belles-lettres in the third place. Many popular science and agrotechnical publications and posters were also produced (see Table 6-3). Out of the total volume of political literature pub-

Table 6-3. PUBLICATIONS OF THE TADZHIK STATE PUBLISHING HOUSE
(DESCRIPTION, TITLES, AND NUMBER OF COPIES)

Years	Publications	Titles	No. of Copies[a]
1928–45	Political literature	1,249	8,224
	Belles lettres	453	1,940
	Textbooks	920	16,560
	Popular science and agriculture	370	1,553
	Others		4,370
	Graphic posters, etc.	130	558
	Total (books and pamphlets)	4,830[b]	35,736[b]
Wartime			
1941–45	Total	1,387	4,460
1927–47	Political literature in Tadzhik	117	1,472
	Total	5,938[c]	47,000
1925(?)–48	Political literature in Tadzhik	125	1,592
	Total	6,183	49,709
1928	Total	56	281
1948	Total	356	2,862
1925–52	Total	7,500	64,000

Sources: *KT*, July 1, 1945, p. 1; July 15, 1945, p. 2; November 18, 1947, p. 2; May 5, 1948, p. 2; May 6, 1952, p. 2.

[a] In thousands.

[b] The total does not add up in the original source.

[c] Number of books published by Tadzhikgosizdat from the time of its establishment in 1927.

lished in Tadzhikistan, probably no more than 10 to 15 per cent of the titles were in the Tadzhik language (see Table 6-3). The official statistics quoted in Table 6-2 would indicate otherwise, but the evidence of the daily press made it abundantly clear that very few of the Marxist-Leninist classics appeared in the Tadzhik language.[48] The Tadzhik publishing industry suffered from a chronic shortage of qualified translators, and the absence of Tadzhik translations of the political classics constituted a major and recurrent point of criticism. Selected works of Lenin and Stalin were translated slowly; the appearance of each volume was hailed as a major achievement.

Literary works published included works by Tadzhik writers, translations from the Russian classics, and selected Western classics

[48] Pulatov revealed at the Seventh Congress of the KPT that as of December, 1948, only the following Marxist classics had been translated into Tadzhik: *The History of the VKP(b), Short Course; The Communist Manifesto;* Lenin's *What's to be Done, One Step Forward,* and *To the Village Poor;* and three volumes of Stalin's *Collected Works,* the third of which appeared on the day the speech was made (*KT,* December 26, 1948, p. 2).

(by Shakespeare, Molière, Lope de Vega, Hugo, Dickens, Mark Twain, and Jack London). Some of the Tadzhik-language works were contemporary (those of Sadriddin Aini, Mirzo Tursun-Zade, and others); others were expurgated versions of the Samanid classics. Translated Russian works included a broad selection of the nineteenth-century writers and the more prominent ones of the Soviet period. Criticism of items published in Tadzhik deplored the small number of original works, and, in the field of political and technical literature, the scarcity of items dealing with concrete local experience in public administration and agricultural management, the shortage of technical literature and textbooks, the poor ideological content, and the poor technical and artistic form of the publications. The publishing industry operated with antiquated equipment and suffered from high printing costs.[49] As a result of multilingualism, most works had to be published in two, or even three, languages.

The first Tadzhik-language newspaper appeared in 1925, and the first Russian-language one in 1929.[50] In 1955, 67 newspapers were published, with a daily circulation of 335,000 (an annual circulation of 63 million) and 10 magazines (29, if bulletins and other periodical publications are included), with an annual circulation of over one million (see Table 6-2). Both volume and circulation appear substantial for a republic of one million people, but the statistics are misleading: only a few of the newspapers were serious publications in general circulation, and these appeared in multilingual editions, each of which was counted as a separate paper.

Other newspapers for raions or cities were published with great irregularity and were constantly assailed for political and general inaccuracy. From 7 to 10 magazines were published for the whole republic in the middle 1950's; they included the organ of the Central Committee of the KPT, young people's, literary, school, and

---

[49] *KT,* July 1, 1945, p. 1; December 22, 1948, p. 2; May 6, 1953, p. 2; April 3, 1954, p. 2; *passim.* Literary works published in Tadzhikistan and available in the West belied some of the criticism. Although they were printed on poor quality paper with inferior print, their form was generally esthetically pleasing.

[50] AN TSSR, *Istoriia,* III, Book 1, p. 207; *KT,* May 5, 1955, p. 2. Another issue of *KT,* however, stated that the first Russian-language newspaper, *Sovietskii Tadzhikistan,* was first published in 1925 (*ibid.,* May 5, 1948, p. 2).

women's magazines, technical journals, and the basic agitator's text, *Bloknot Agitatora* (in three languages). A satirical journal, *Khorpushtak* (the hedgehog), published by the Tadzhik Union of Soviet Writers, was of special interest.

Criticism of the republican newspapers was usually relatively mild, despite a general sweeping criticism that appeared in *Pravda* in 1946.[51] Gafurov made general disparaging remarks at two of the Party congresses, pointing out that the press showed "little initiative and interest in basic economic and cultural problems," and that it did "not reflect the Party, Soviet and mass organization activities" and failed "to popularize achievements and socialist competition." [52] In 1953 the republican press was criticized by the CC Plenum on Agitprop Work for a lack of atheistic themes, a failure to condemn feudal-bai survivals, and a paucity of positive propaganda.[53]

The local press received much more criticism. Only 5 of the 51 raion newspapers in 1945 were judged satisfactory; these propagandized economic experience, criticized shortcomings, and mobilized toilers for the war effort. All the others were found to be unacceptable in content, form, and language.[54] Political and grammatical ignorance was prevalent among their editors and staffs, and the papers were a dismal failure as agents of agitation. Similar complaints appeared in 1946 and 1947.[55] The newspapers' failure to criticize shortcomings in the work of the Party and government agencies was frequently admonished. The fault was not entirely theirs, however; some Party and government functionaries suppressed press criticism. In the Garm oblast, for example, the circulation of issues of newspapers which criticized local notables (mostly for feudal-bai attitudes) was interrupted, and authors were penalized.[56] *Pravda's* 1946 criticism of the Tadzhik local press was

[51] *Pravda,* September 14, 1946, quoted in *KT,* September 18, 1946, p. 2.

[52] *KT,* December 22, 1948, p. 2; September 20, 1952, p. 2.

[53] *Ibid.,* August 18, 1953, p. 1.

[54] *Ibid.,* February 11, 1945, p. 1. Some of the cases quoted follow: only 10 numbers of the paper *Bol'sheviki Ramit* were published in 1944; only 20 numbers of the GBAO oblast newspaper, *Krasnyi Badakhshan,* appeared in 1944; the Obi-Garm raion newspaper was full of orthographic mistakes; and the newspaper of the Vanch raion was still published in the Latin alphabet.

[55] *Ibid.,* May 15, 1945, p. 2; November 30, 1945, p. 2; May 5, 1946, p. 2; October 25, 1946, p. 2; March 25, 1947, p. 2.

[56] *Ibid.,* October 14, 1947, p. 2.

scathing, pointing out the low ideological and cultural level and blaming the leaders of the Tadzhik Party for their "totally impossible attitude" toward the press. Oblast papers were condemned for being only obkom bulletins (Garm and Ura-Tyube); for making serious ideological mistakes—praising the bai—(Kulyab); and for appearing irregularly in an abbreviated form (GBAO).[57]

Criticism of the local papers was repeated in 1948, 1949, and the 1950's.[58] Although the picture improved in comparison with conditions in 1945, the usual complaints (irregular appearance, inadequate and ill-trained staffs, and failure to educate the people through criticism of abuses, publicity for achievements, and mobilization for productive efforts) were still being made. The image of the local press which emerges produces serious doubts about its effectiveness as an instrument of mass political socialization, especially in the light of the prevalent problems of linguistics and literacy.[59] The value of the printed word for mass indoctrination was further reduced by the problems of subscription, delivery, and distribution, factors which placed the official circulation figures (see Table 6-2) in doubt.

Kolkhoz members subscribed to newspapers; this was also true of most of the urban population, because the retail sales network was virtually non-existent in some localities. Annual subscription campaigns were advertised in the republican press; locally, subscriptions were solicited by mailmen and *kiosk* (newsstand) managers (a task which was regarded as "political work"), aided by raion organizers of the state press organization (*Soiuzpechat'*), whose duty it was to transmit the printed word to the masses. Subscriptions were accepted by local agencies of the All-Union Ministry of Communications which were also in charge of the actual distribution.[60] Republican newspapers and magazines were sent daily from Stalinabad to raion centers (by air, rail, or car) for local

[57] *Pravda*, September 14, 1946, quoted in *KT*, September 18, 1946, p. 2.

[58] *KT*, December 22, 1948, p. 2; October 12, 1949, p. 2; September 15, 1951, p. 1; January 29, 1952, p. 2; September 20, 1952, p. 2; and *passim*.

[59] An item in 1952, for example, reported that a newspaper in Dzhilikul' was published in the Uzbek language, though 60 per cent of the raion's inhabitants were Tadzhiks (*ibid.*, September 14, 1952, p. 2).

[60] *KT*, May 6, 1951, p. 2; November 1, 1951, p. 1; Kisliakov, *Kul'tura i byt*, p. 222.

distribution. In 1951 more than 80,000 copies were sent daily from Stalinabad.[61] Oblast and raion papers were distributed locally.

Numerous problems beset the distribution system. In the forties annual subscription campaigns were accompanied by complaints of non-fulfillment of subscription quotas. In the fifties the number of subscribers increased, but there were still few subscriptions to specialized journals and children's, agricultural, pedagogical, and other magazines.[62] The increase in subscriptions did not solve the problem of reaching the masses, because of the poor distribution system.

Delays and stoppages in the delivery of newspapers and magazines were a common complaint. Newspapers for kolkhoz subscribers were left in the mail rooms of raion centers for weeks or were delivered to kolkhoz or kishlak administrations rather than to individual subscribers. Failures in rural distribution were attributed directly to the inefficiency of general mail delivery, especially in high mountain raions; there was a virtual absence of regular delivery in 1946 in the Garm oblast and in GBAO, and sporadic failures were still occurring in other localities in 1955.[63] The fact that mail (including newspapers) was piling up in raion centers literally by tons was explained by the lack of available transportation, because kolkhozes and kishlaks which should have provided a horse to pick up their own mail frequently failed to do so.[64] Even in the best of circumstances newspapers arrived at their destination days, weeks, or even months late, which substantially reduced their effectiveness. Distribution problems existed also in the cities, as shown by cases reported in Stalinabad itself.[65]

Additional evidence suggests that even when they were available, newspapers were not read with great avidity. In many cases neither the subscriber nor the agitators read them; they were not

[61] The total daily circulation figure for newspapers in 1950 was 252,000 (see Table 6-2), which would indicate that oblast and raion papers accounted for as much as 50 to 60 per cent of the total (*KT*, May 6, 1951, p. 2).

[62] *Ibid.*, March 25, 1947, p. 2; October 31, 1953, p. 2; *passim*.

[63] *Ibid.*, April 28, 1946, p. 2; March 25, 1947, p. 2; May 18, 1947, p. 1; May 6, 1951, p. 2; November 1, 1951, p. 1; October 31, 1953, p. 2; May 30, 1954, p. 2; April 20, 1955, p. 3; and *passim*.

[64] *Ibid.*, October 15, 1947, p. 2; February 27, 1954, p. 3 and *passim*.

[65] *Ibid.*, April 18, 1952, p. 2.

even read aloud for purposes of mass agitation. An editorial comment was: "All these facts are frightening; they show that we still fail to use our periodical publications as a powerful means for the political education of the toilers."[66]

To the dedicated propagandist the press picture must have frequently assumed the proportions of a nightmare. Many papers left in distribution centers never reached the subscribers, and if they reached the subscriber they were usually late. Even if they were not late, often they were not read, but even if they were read their content was bare of required political message and thus worthless from the agitators' point of view.

Sales and distribution of books closely paralleled those of newspapers and magazines. There were too few sales outlets and in some localities books much in demand were not available in sufficient quantities; in other localities these same books accumulated in warehouses. Sometimes an Uzbek-speaking area received Tadzhik-language books and vice versa.[67] By all accounts, the distribution in rural areas was particularly poor, with few, if any, books reaching the hands of Tadzhik and Uzbek peasants.[68] Not enough books were published, especially in the native languages, and those available did not always find their way into the hands of the reader. It was also by no means sure that all the books purchased were read, understood, and absorbed.

RADIO BROADCASTING

As a result of the limitations imposed on the effectiveness of written propaganda, radio broadcasting was especially important. In this field, again, the authorities had to start from scratch building a new radio broadcasting and receiving network in extremely difficult mountain terrain, while they coped with perennial shortages and breakdowns in equipment. As elsewhere in the Soviet Union, initial emphasis was placed on the development of radio relay centers in raions and a system of outlets in villages and kolkhozes, served by loudspeakers or battery-operated receivers. The

---

[66] *Ibid.*, August 3, 1951, p. 1.

[67] *Ibid.*, April 15, 1949; June 15, 1952, p. 1; September 14, 1954, p. 3; May 21, 1955, p. 3.

[68] *Ibid.*, July 23, 1955, p. 1 and *passim*.

radio network in Tadzhikistan, extremely poor before and during the war, showed some development in the postwar decade, but it was still unsatisfactory. The number of radio relay centers increased from 4 in 1930 to 32 in 1933 and 71 in 1948,[69] while the number of radio outlets increased from about 7,000 in 1945 to more than 26,000 in 1949.[70] At the same time it was reported that only 10 per cent of the outlets were located directly in kolkhozes and sovkhozes, and ony 7 per cent of the kolkhozes were equipped with radio receivers.[71] As Gafurov said at the Seventh Congress, "There are still hundreds of kolkhozes in which there are neither radio receivers nor radio outlets." [72] No figures were reported for the period after 1949, though in 1956 it was said that the number of radio outlets in the past Five-Year Plan had increased 2.3 times.[73]

Complaints about radio broadcasting centered on the technical difficulties and the quality of programs. In 1945 there were many raions where there was no reception for months or the reception was marred by static. Relay centers failed to work for long periods of time because of breakdowns of equipment, shortages of trained personnel, and failures in the power received from local hydroelectric stations.[74]

The quality of the programs left much to be desired. Gafurov complained in 1948 that most republican programs were dull and failed to use news of achievements in factories and kolkhozes to the best advantage or to present cultural events attractively. He bemoaned the low quality of programs originating locally.[75] On some programs, newspapers were read aloud; on others, old records were played. Komsomol efforts to stimulate interest in radio listening by organizing a movement of "radio lovers" met with little success. The poor quality of local radio programs may be justified by the fact that in some cases the salaries of local radio personnel

[69] (Radiotranslationnye uzly), ibid., May 5, 1948, p. 2.
[70] (Radiotochki), ibid., November 6, 1945, p. 2; May 7, 1949, p. 1.
[71] Ibid., May 7, 1949, p. 3. Out of a total of 2,685 kolkhozes, 180 had radio receivers. The proportion is almost unbelievably small.
[72] Ibid., December 22, 1948, p. 2.
[73] Ibid., January 27, 1956, p. 2.
[74] Ibid., February 24, 1945, p. 2; March 25, 1947, p. 2; May 18, 1947, p. 1; May 7, 1952, p. 1. In the first quarter of 1954, relay centers worked only 16.5 per cent of the planned time (ibid., May 30, 1954, p. 3).
[75] Ibid., December 22, 1948, p. 2.

were in arrears for as long as five months, which meant that many had to hold another job; some radio workers were criticized for stealing radio receivers.[76]

In contrast to the generally dismal picture of the radio-receiving network in rural areas, large and prosperous cotton kolkhozes (in the Leninabad oblast) with more than one radio relay center, numerous outlets, and hundreds of kolkhozniks who owned private radio receivers were described in 1951.[77]

MASS CULTURAL-ENLIGHTENMENT ACTIVITIES

Political indoctrination through cultural activities constituted an important part of mass educational work. Neglected and ineffective in the war years, cultural-enlightenment work (*kulturno-prosvetitel'naia rabota, kultprosvet* for short) received special attention after 1945. Various cultural agencies were tried out in the 1940's; in 1953 mass cultural work came under the jurisdiction of the newly established Ministry of Culture. Under direct and constant supervision by the Party's Central Committee, the Ministry carried out kultprosvet work, which included sponsorship and management of movie and theater networks, museums, parks of culture and rest, local libraries, popular lectures, and local entertainment and amusements in Red Teahouses, local clubs, and houses of culture.

The great importance attached by the Party to cultural work was stressed at all the congresses; the shortcomings were considered a major problem. There was a steady growth in the network of kultprosvet establishments in the postwar decade, but the work did not bring the expected qualitative results because of poorly trained agitators, low-quality political content, technical shortages and breakdowns of equipment, and popular indifference.

At the Seventh Congress Gafurov complained that existing cultural possibilities had not been developed because of the lack of good Party leadership; [78] this criticism was frequently repeated in

[76] *Ibid.*, April 4, 1946, p. 3; May 18, 1947, p. 1; May 7, 1952, p. 1; November 15, 1953, p. 3.
[77] *Ibid.*, March 3, 1951, p. 2 (Kolkhoz im. Stalina, Leninabad raion); Kisliakov, *Kul'tura i byt*, p. 222.
[78] *KT*, December 22, 1948, p. 3.

the fifties. The situation was worst in the high mountain raions and rural areas in general; many kolkhozes had no cultural establishments of any kind and most of them never used all of the money assigned to them for mass cultural work.[79] The general failure of kultprosvet work in industry and the inactivity of trade unions in the sphere of culture were also severely criticized. The shortage, quality, and constant turnover of cultural cadres were the major drawbacks in kultprosvet work.[80] Criticism was directed not only at professional agitators but also at the intelligentsia, who failed "to pay their debt to society."[81] When an intensive atheistic propaganda effort was begun in the early 1950's, complaints were heard about its ineffectiveness and the continuing survival of feudal-bai attitudes and bourgeois nationalism. The Sixth Plenum of the Central Committee, called to deal with the problem in 1953, described the existing lecture program as quantitatively inadequate, "ideologically low," and full of "talmudism or even ideological deviations," and condemned the whole kultprosvet network for poor work and misuse of funds.[82]

Movies were an important medium of the political message. Permanent movie theaters existed in cities and towns, while rural areas were served by mobile units with projectors mounted on trucks. The service was far from satisfactory: equipment broke down, there was a shortage of good mechanics, equipment and trucks were frequently misappropriated by local authorities, and mobile units never reached the more remote kolkhozes.[83] Some permanent theaters had no seats or other equipment, and only a few mobile vans were in working order.[84] In 1947, 20 per cent of the republic's

[79] Ibid., August 18, 1951, p. 1; February 12, 1952, p. 1; March 12, 1952, p. 2; June 15, 1952, p. 1; November 14, 1953, p. 2; November 19, 1953, p. 1; February 24, 1954, p. 1; October 22, 1955, p. 2; passim.
[80] Ibid., August 26, 1947, p. 1; August 27, 1947, p. 3; May 18, 1947, p. 1; February 12, 1952, p. 1; November 19, 1953, p. 1; February 24, 1954, p. 1; July 26, 1955, p. 1; August 26, 1955, p. 1.
[81] Ibid., August 27, 1955, p. 1.
[82] Ibid., August 18, 1953, p. 1. The calling of the Plenum and its work were connected with the new cultural offensive.
[83] Ibid., March 4, 1945, p. 1; March 22, 1949, p. 2; January 6, 1951, p. 2; January 19, 1951, p. 3; August 18, 1951, p. 1; February 15, 1952, p. 2; February 23, 1953, p. 3; March 5, 1955, p. 2; and passim.
[84] Ibid., May 26, 1948, p. 2; March 22, 1949, p. 2; Gafurov's report at the Seventh Congress of the KPT (ibid., December 22, 1948, p. 3).

movie establishments were idle.[85] More units and shows were provided in the fifties, but movie units were still frequently idle, and in an average month films would be shown for three days for every twelve days spent on the road and fifteen days spent in storage. It was considered an achievement, as in the case of the Isfara raion, when each kolkhoz was shown a movie three times a month; many were still deprived of the pleasure of moviegoing.[86] Equipment continued to break down, and film-showing plans were underfulfilled.[87]

The political and educational influence of the movies was seriously undermined by the negative attitude of the administrators themselves and the indifference of the viewers to any movie which did not represent traditional artistic forms and themes (as some of the Uzbek-made movies did). At one point it was stated officially that the "indifference of the leading cadres" constituted the major part of the problem.[88]

Most programs consisted of reruns of old movies; [89] documentaries, popular scientific films, and new Russian movies dubbed or subtitled in local languages were rarely shown. A 1951 newspaper article revealed why operators were unwilling to show "new" movies. Van operators and theater managers "preferred to take to the kolkhozes the kind of movies which did not require conducting mass agitation work" (ideally a showing was to be accompanied by a political talk) "and from which they could gain extra income." [90] The article did not state whether they collected an admission price on the showing of popular movies or exacted bribes. Operators and managers clearly catered to popular preferences, which did not care for official propaganda fare and Russian cultural themes. In

[85] Ibid., March 25, 1947, p. 2. Out of 4 mobile units in Stalinabad oblast, 3 were out of order in 1947 (ibid., May 18, 1947, p. 1). Garm oblast had only 1 in 1948 (ibid., May 26, 1948, p. 2), and of its 8 units in 1949 each averaged 3 performances a month (ibid., March 22, 1949, p. 2).

[86] Ibid., February 23, 1953, p. 3.

[87] Ibid., December 2, 1953, p. 2; August 29, 1953, p. 1; November 26, 1954, p. 1; March 5, 1955, p. 2; October 22, 1955, p. 2; and passim.

[88] Ibid., April 15, 1952, p. 1. The statement was made in an editorial following the Eleventh Plenum of the Central Committee of the KPT.

[89] Indirect evidence suggests that the popular "old movies" which were shown were Uzbek-made movies on traditional themes, easily understood by the population. The sources indicated that many "new" films were returned unused (ibid., November 14, 1953, p. 3; December 2, 1953, p. 2; March 5, 1955, p. 2).

[90] Ibid., September 16, 1951, p. 2.

1955, it was reported that some culture departments of the raion soviets refused to show dubbed Russian films and agricultural and popular scientific films.[91]

Stage drama was another important medium of socialization. Stalinabad had a Theater of Opera and Ballet, a Philharmonic, and two drama theaters (one Russian and one Tadzhik); there was also a drama theater in Leninabad, in the two towns of the ex-Stalinabad oblast, and in Khorog.[92] Rural areas were generally served by amateur "folk art circles," formed under the auspices of raion culture departments and regarded as "an important medium for Communist education of the toilers." In 1947 some 5,000 people were reported to have participated in the activity of these circles.[93] Because many of the activities of the circles were presented in the traditional genre, they appeared to have had better success, relatively speaking, than other mass propaganda activities.

Lectures which provided personal contact between the agitator and the people were the major vehicle of propaganda, especially for the popularization of anti-traditional themes such as atheism and the emancipation of women. Lectures were organized by republican cultural agencies and their offices in the local soviet executive committees; the cadres of lecturers included Party and government officials and members of the intelligentsia, in addition to professional propagandists and agitators. The quantity of lectures fluctuated widely, depending on a particular campaign and the efficiency of a given unit. The 52 lecture bureaus of the Committee for Cultural-Educational Institutions gave 1,200 lectures in 1946, attended by some 100,000 people; the Committee's oblast, city, and raion departments gave over 4,000 lectures attended by 450,000 people, while in 1951 republican lecture bureaus gave 1,000 lectures and the oblast and raion bureaus—more than 13,500 lectures to the cotton-growing kolkhozes.[94] Lecturers' guidelines were charted by the Deputy Chief of the Administration of Cultural-Enlightenment Establishments in 1951.

---

[91] *Ibid.*, March 12, 1955, p. 2.
[92] *TSSR. Nar. Khoz. 1957*, p. 317; *KT, passim*.
[93] *KT*, October 26, 1947, p. 2.
[94] *Ibid.*, May 27, 1947, p. 2; January 30, 1952, p. 3.

> In the Soviet propaganda of scientific knowledge, bourgeois objec-
> tivism, non-politicism, and impartial instruction cannot be tolerated.
> The Bolshevik *partiinost'* [party spirit] has to be in the center of
> the work of any lecturer propagating scientific knowledge. The de-
> cisive aim of lecturer-propagandists is to bring up the people in the
> spirit of Marxist-Leninist materialistic world outlook; to overcome
> the survivals of capitalism in the people's conscience; and to struggle
> for deep ideological correctness (*ideinost'*) and scientific character in
> the lectures.[95]

As in other fields of mass educational activities, the actual effectiveness of political lectures lagged far behind the official statistics.
Mountain raions were left largely outside the lecture circuit. There
was little coordination of offerings by the various agencies, with
the result that representatives of the Ministry of Culture, the
Society for the Spread of Political and Scientific Knowledge, and
the obkom would all arrive in one locality at the same time with
the same lecture. Speaking in 1956, Gafurov enumerated the
"major shortcomings" in the field of lecture propaganda: limited
themes, poor ideological quality, lack of preparation for special
types of audiences and failure of local rural intelligentsia (teachers,
doctors, agronomists, zootechnicians, and others) to participate.[96]

The Society for the Spread of Political and Scientific Knowledge
was given the specialized and vital task of combating the survivals
of bourgeois nationalism, feudal-bai values, and religious beliefs
in the minds of the people. It mounted an impressive array of
activities, but with limited success. A 1951 article discussing the
struggle with religion and superstition concluded:

> The number of lectures and the quality of lectures given on scien-
> tific atheistic subjects are both extremely unsatisfactory. There are
> still many settlements in the republic where scientific lectures either
> are not heard at all or else only very rarely.[97]

The lectures were characterized as formal, boring, and full of
factual and scientific mistakes. Many of the lecturers (three-fourths
of the Society's total membership in 1951) did not bother to participate in lecture campaigns, and few of the lectures were directed

[95] *Ibid.*, July 14, 1951, p. 2.
[96] *Ibid.*, January 27, 1956, p. 3.
[97] *Ibid.*, July 14, 1951, p. 2.

against feudal-bai survivals and the "reactionary content of Islam." [98] The Society's work in the field of anti-religious propaganda was characterized as "extremely unsatisfactory" in 1954,[99] and *Kommunist Tadzhikistana* editorialized that anti-religious propaganda hardly reached many of the areas in the Leninabad and Kulyab oblasts, where the survivals were the strongest, and that it was completely absent in the high mountains of the Tavil-Dara, Kalai-Khumb, and Murgab raions.[100] Similar complaints were also expressed in 1955.[101]

The breach in the people's devotion to Islam was still negligible in the sixties, if one is to judge by the statement of the Tadzhik First Secretary, Rasulov, at the Fifteenth Congress of the KPT in 1963:

> We cannot peacefully accept the fact that a sizeable number of our people are still enthralled by religious superstitions, that they still allow incorrect attitudes toward women, and carry on a wrong mode of life, drinking and behaving like hooligans and parasites. The struggle with all the survivals of the past should be regarded as one of the most important tasks of the Party organizations in their effort to educate a new man.[102]

The day-to-day, face-to-face mass agitation work was the task of local Party activists and agitators in a network of cultural establishments such as libraries, teahouses, clubs, or houses of culture. Statistical data concerning the number of these establishments were highly unreliable and fluctuated widely. Some of the figures reported were probably arbitrary, others fictitious; fluctuations were also affected by the kolkhoz consolidation campaign.

The ideal postulated situation, a library in every kolkhoz, each run by a qualified librarian-propagandist, did not exist in Tadzhikistan.[103] The existing libraries frequently had fewer than 100 books and even fewer readers; many lacked catalogues and proper quarters and had librarians who were themselves barely literate.

[98] *Ibid.*, July 15, 1951, p. 1; November 27, 1951, p. 2; November 23, 1951, p. 3; December 30, 1953, p. 2 (a report by the Society's chairman, G. Aliev).
[99] *Ibid.*, January 23, 1954, p. 2.
[100] *Ibid.*, August 26, 1954, p. 1.
[101] *Ibid.*, August 20, 1955, p. 2; September 29, 1955, p. 1.
[102] *Ibid.*, December 26, 1963, p. 4.
[103] *KT*, July 29, 1949, p. 1; March 17, 1955, p. 1.

After the kolkhoz consolidation of the early 1950's, the kultpros-vet agencies lost track of kolkhoz libraries and gave no further data.[104]

An example of a "bad" library was the one in the Miskinabad kishlak of Obi-Garm raion. It served 1,000 households but had only 40 members. There were no newspapers or magazines, and few political books in it; the librarian's other job was that of a night watchman in the kishlak soviet.[105]

The largest of the Tadzhik libraries was the State Public Library im. Firdousi in Stalinabad, which, in 1954, had almost 8,000 volumes and 12,000 readers. Its collection included all the items published in Tadzhik since 1932 and more than 20,000 ancient manuscripts in eastern languages.[106] Although the management was made up of Party members, it was taken to task in 1951 for glaring political illiteracy: the library did not even have *Das Kapital*; it failed to cross-reference Stalin's works; worse that that, it had on a shelf, side by side ideologically correct and ideologically condemned books on the same subject, thus making reactionary, unscientific literature available to mass readers. It also had a complete collection of books on Yugoslavia in which the "renegade Tito" (in 1951) was depicted as a national hero.[107]

The teahouse (*chaikhana*) was a traditional local institution where men met, smoked, drank tea, exchanged news, and enjoyed the tales of passing travelers. In an effort to take advantage of traditional usages, the Soviet government attempted to transform teahouses into mass agitation points; this met with only partial

[104] The real ratio of libraries to kolkhozes was difficult to determine. Figures for 1940 indicated that there were 400 libraries and over 3,000 kolkhozes; for 1949, 1,022 libraries and 2,685 kolkhozes; for 1955, 823 libraries and 453 kolkhozes (after consolidation). (*Ibid.*, March 17, 1955, p. 1; May 18, 1947, p. 1; August 12, 1947, p. 2; August 27, 1947, p. 3; October 26, 1949, p. 3; February 26, 1949, p. 1; March 12, 1952, p. 2; June 15, 1952, p. 1; February 1, 1953, p. 1; February 9, 1954, p. 2; March 17, 1955, p. 1).

[105] *Ibid.*, August 20, 1955, p. 1.

[106] *Ibid.*, January 25, 1946, p. 3; May 27, 1954, p. 3.

[107] In biology, for example, a book by the Academy of Sciences of the USSR condemning the "reactionary" theories of Mendeleev and Morgan was placed next to a book by Morgan; in history, Bagirov's book on the "reactionary" character of Shamil's rising was placed next to a 1939 book praising Shamil as a great hero in the struggle for independence in the Caucasus (*ibid.*, October 13, 1951, p. 4). It is to be hoped that the library preserved some of the condemned books. Its Tito collection, for example, should now be again acceptable.

success. The statistics for teahouses were even less reliable than those for mass libraries. To serve the purposes of mass agitation, a chaikhana was supposed to be a place where a Tadzhik or an Uzbek could read, listen to the radio or a lecture, or watch a play. Few chaikhanas developed into such centers. Most of them, especially in rural areas, continued to serve traditional purposes.[108] Clubs and houses of culture were intended to serve as quarters for various cultural and political events, but only a few fulfilled their appointed tasks. Some had no cutural equipment, mass activists, or artistic circles; most opened on rare occasions in order to show movies, and at other times were used as storage places or soviet and court offices. Mass indoctrination work conducted through the clubs appears to have been minimal.[109]

An example cited in *Kommunist Tadzhikistana* of a prosperous kolkhoz in the Leninabad raion,[110] where people lived in European-style houses with gardens, and where there was a school, an active club, a library, a teahouse, and a nursery, appeared rather atypical, as did the kolkhoz described by Kisliakov in an exhaustive ethnographic study of 1954. The cultural centers of the latter kolkhoz included several permanent and seasonal teahouses, each decorated with propaganda posters and with a corner set aside for reading the press (*krasnyi ugolok*—red corner). In the evenings agitators read newspapers aloud or led discussions on current political themes. The nearby town of Chkalovsk had a club with a 600-seat auditorium and rooms for artistic activity, as well as a library with 3,000 volumes and 7,000 readers. Although some of the traditional winter pastimes such as *tugma* and *gap* (evenings shared by a group of men, which included talking, singing, dancing, and eating) were still preserved, the people took advantage more and more of the new Soviet entertainments such as movies, concerts, lectures, and meetings.[111]

Regional variations were visible in the effectiveness of the

[108] *Ibid.,* August 26, 1947, p. 1; May 18, 1947, p. 1; August 27, 1947, p. 3; March 12, 1952, p. 2.

[109] *Ibid.,* May 18, 1947; October 26, 1949, p. 3; August 18, 1951, p. 1; February 12, 1952, p. 1; March 12, 1952, p. 2; June 15, 1952, p. 1; and *passim.*

[110] *KT,* February 8, 1948, p. 1. Kolkhoz im. Stalina, in the Leninabad raion, was the same kolkhoz singled out for praise as a model of radiofication (see above).

[111] Kisliakov, *Kul'tura i byt,* pp. 208–9; 218–21. This kolkhoz near Leninabad was possibly the same as the one referred to above.

kultprosvet network. No other locality seemed to have kolkhozes where political indoctrination work was as well organized as it was in the Fergana Valley kolkhozes described above, though there were some complimentary descriptions of kolkhozes in the Stalinabad oblast.[112] On the whole, propaganda and cultural work in the rural areas of Stalinabad and Leninabad oblasts left much to be desired, but some agitation activity did take place, even if it was limited to loud reading of newspapers and a sporadic campaign.[113] A similar situation also existed in the GBAO.[114] The political education of workers in the cities was largely neglected. Both Leninabad and Stalinabad had numerous well-appointed teahouses, but most of them were used for the traditional pastime of tea-drinking, without political overtones.[115]

In the Garm and Kulyab oblasts mass educational work appeared to be virtually non-existent. Facilities were used for other purposes than those for which they were intended; lecture groups gave few lectures; and if the libraries had books they had few readers (the Garm raion library had 10,000 volumes but only 37 readers in 1947 and 124 in 1949). There were few teahouses, and some mountain raions did not see an agitator for months at a time.[116] Of the four teahouses in Kulyab city in 1946, one was closed. Of the other three, one served as a dining room and another as a traditional tea-drinking establishment; the sole political equipment of the third was a torn map hung upside down.[117]

The Tadzhiks seemed as much out of the reach of mass propaganda in the early 1960's as they had been in the 1950's. In 1963 the First Secretary again deplored the narrowness of the scope of

[112] *KT*, July 9, 1947, p. 3.

[113] *Ibid.*, February 6, 1949, p. 1; March 4, 1949, p. 2; June 14, 1949, p. 2; November 4, 1951, p. 1; November 23, 1951, p. 2; November 25, 1953, p. 3; and *passim*.

[114] *Ibid.*, April 13, 1946, p. 2; January 14, 1948, p. 2; June 19, 1949, p. 2; December 11, 1949, p. 3; August 26, 1953, p. 2; September 9, 1953, p. 2; September 1, 1954, p. 2.

[115] *Ibid.*, July 31, 1945, p. 3; March 25, 1947, p. 2; January 2, 1951, p. 2; November 23, 1951, p. 2; October 12, 1951, p. 2; August 13, 1952, p. 2.

[116] *Ibid.*, June 26, 1946, p. 2; June 6, 1947, p. 2; February 6, 1949, p. 1; March 29, 1949, p. 3; June 9, 1951, p. 2; November 23, 1951, p. 2; October 25, 1953, p. 2; January 22, 1954, p. 2; January 12, 1955, p. 2.

[117] *Ibid.*, March 22, 1946, p. 3, letter to the editor.

mass propaganda and concluded his remarks by saying: "We do not reach every person, and yet this is what the Party wants us to do." [118]

CONCLUDING REMARKS

After almost three decades of Soviet rule, the task of the political socialization of Tadzhikistan was far from completed. Its effectiveness, though by no means negligible (especially in the case of the elite), was nevertheless limited, and lagged behind general political needs.[119] The gap between the required and the actual commitment of both the elite and the masses to the Soviet value system was the largest obstacle in the path to successful sovietization. In part a result of the extreme ineptitude and inefficiency of the political education and mass agitation networks, the continuous existence of the gap was also due to lively traditional socialization conducted by family and informal social groups.

A general evaluation of the effectiveness of political socialization of particular groups must take into consideration a whole range of variables, such as the degree of exposure to and of dependence on traditional values, the content and intensity of propaganda campaigns and the extent to which they deny traditional concepts, the limitations imposed by objective conditions such as literacy, and the effects of the availability of technical equipment, economic factors, geography, and climate. In the case of the elite, their personal stake in the system should also be considered.

A survey of the postwar decade indicates that much of the indoctrination effort widely missed the mark. There has been little evidence so far that the Marxist-Leninist value system has been assimilated by the Asian political elite, or that it has made many inroads into the thinking and behavior of the people at large. The

[118] *Ibid.*, December 26, 1963, p. 4.

[119] At the Sixteenth Congress of the KPT, held in March, 1966, the familiar criticisms were heard again. Local agitation work was still poorly organized, especially in remote kishlaks and the mountains; the press, radio, television (a new addition), movies, and kultprosvet establishments were poorly utilized; and manifestations of bourgeois ideology, survivals of the past, feudal-bai attitudes toward women, abominable (*vrednye*) customs and traditions, and "localism" continued to appear (*Pravda*, March 9, 1966, p. 2).

degree of exposure among the people appears to have been rather limited, though they do perform their economic tasks better and participate in required activities.

It would be a mistake to discount the impact of Soviet political socialization in Tadzhikistan, especially in its long-range significance. A basic commitment to the system (a prerequisite to political participation) did exist among the political elite, despite the inadequacy of the system of political education, the strong pull of traditional values in personal and group behavior, and the lack of response to the finer philosophical points of Marxism-Leninism. The masses had barely been touched by the indoctrination and were very resistant to it, and the mass agitation network and communications media were woefully inadequate. However, in considering the impact one should realize that even though many people were still illiterate and few books and newspapers or broadcasts or movies, were available to them or taken advantage of, the very fact that such things existed marked an enormous progress from the Emir's times. However pitiful the educational and cultural network appeared by Western standards, it was vastly superior to anything available in the non-Communist East. Whatever the content of socialization, the progress made was bound to leave a lasting mark. From the point of view of Communist indoctrination, the mass impact on traditional values and customs was still small, but the process of change had begun. The opening made in the wall of the traditional outlook and values was being continuously enlarged. At the same time the foundations of the wall were being shaken by changes which had already occurred in the economy and the whole way of life.

7

THE TADZHIK SOVIET CULTURE

THE NEW TADZHIK SOVIET CULTURE which formed an integral part of the content of political socialization emphasized both aspects of Leninist nationality policy: national form and socialist content. Its successful development was regarded as vital to the transformation of Tadzhikistan into a Soviet society. In the process, the new Soviet content was grafted onto the "progressive" elements of the traditional culture, the "bourgeois nationalist" elements of which were rejected. Lenin and Stalin both had distinguished between the "progressive" and "reactionary" aspects of national cultures, the first regarded as an embodiment of the spiritual needs of the oppressed, the second as an expression of the interests of the ruling class. Stalin spoke of the national proletarian and the national bourgeois culture, and Lenin, more poetically, characterized the dichotomy as consisting of "two streams" (*dva potoka*) of cultural development. It was the "progressive" proletarian stream which the Party sought out to develop in the Soviet national republics. The policy served to break up the national unity of local cultures. It attempted to eliminate the dangerous nationalist element (characterized, by definition, as reactionary), at the same time permitting the use of national forms and symbols as vehicles for the new Soviet content. Anti-Russian national ambitions came to be identified with the heretical "one stream" (*odin potok*) approach, which accepted national heritage *in toto* and failed to recognize the principle of class struggle in national historical development.

Because it reflected the "common interest of all the Soviet

peoples" (as articulated by the Party), the content of the new cultures was to be the same throughout the Soviet Union: "socialist," "proletarian-internationalist," and "Soviet patriotic." At the same time, however, it did not substitute a Russian culture for a local one, but sought to blend local elements into a Russian-determined Soviet model. A particular local cultural heritage was revived (or sometimes created), developed, and adapted to the new tasks. History and language, epics and literature, folklore and traditional arts of each group were "discovered" anew, studied, developed, and transformed into the means of carrying the new message to the people and integrating them into the Soviet body politic. National proletarian cultures could not be developed without a socialist content, according to Soviet theoreticians. As Stalin expressed it:

> The proletarian culture, socialist in content, takes various forms and means of expression among the various peoples who participate in socialist construction, depending on their differences in language, mode of life, etc. . . . [It] does not change a national culture, but gives it content. And conversely, the national culture does not change the proletarian culture, but gives it form.[1]

The creation of proletarian cultures in Central Asia promoted national differentiation, thus contributing to the breakup of the Pan-Turkic and Pan-Islamic unity of Turkestan. The Tadzhik culture claimed a Persian heritage, separate and distinct from the Turkic heritage of the Uzbeks and the nomads of the steppes. The revival and adaptation of this heritage amounted, in fact, to the creation of a wholly new culture. Some of its aspects were artificial, such as the link that was said to exist between the culture of the Samanids and that of the Tadzhiks of Bukhara and the imposition of Farsi (Persian) on the Iranian speakers of the Pamirs. The Tadzhik texts of the 1940's and 1950's credited Stalin, the "great coryphaeus of science, teacher, and leader," with the discovery of the ancient character of the Tadzhik culture. It was he who had "showed that the Tadzhik people had an ancient culture of their own," [2] had given "high marks" to the ancient Tadzhik culture,[3] and had encouraged its further development.[4]

[1] "O sotsialisticheskom soderzhanii i natsional'nykh formakh sovetskoi kul'tury," *Bol'shevik*, no. 22 (November, 1946), p. 3.
[2] *KT*, January 3, 1953, p. 2.
[3] *Ibid.*, March 29, 1946, p. 2.
[4] *Ibid.*, May 30, 1948, p. 2.

The formation of the new Tadzhik culture was accompanied by certain important historical assertions. The Tadzhiks were declared to be the most ancient people of Central Asia, the Samanid empire to be the embodiment of their cultural and political leading role.[5] Modern Tadzhiks were therefore regarded as the heirs of the Samanids:

> We are the authentic heirs of our great classics and only we can evaluate their majesty and transform them to benefit the people. . . . The day will come when reactionary rule will end in Iran, and the Tadzhik people will return to the Persians the heritage of their poets. . . .[6]

The Tadzhik mission to restore the true meaning of the ancient heritage to those who had lost it in Iran and India, expressed by Mirzo Tursun-Zade above, formed an important political theme in the creation of the Tadzhik Soviet culture.[7]

Efforts to create a new culture centered on the development of a new Tadzhik historiography, the study of the classical Persian literature, the development and modernization of the Farsi language, and the promotion of a national literature and of the arts. Special care was taken to build on the "progressive" base of the Tadzhik past and on "the achievements of the fraternal Soviet peoples, and especially the great Russian people" in order to join the "world cultural heritage" (represented by the Russian culture) to the "cultural traditions of the Tadzhiks."[8]

The historical and classical themes selected for emphasis and development either complemented some of the basic aspects of Marxism-Leninism or served current policy requirements. These included such themes as popular resistance to foreign invaders, peoples' revolts against domestic oppressors, and materialistic and

---

[5] *Ibid.*, August 6, 1947, p. 2 (by Morochnik).

[6] Mirzo Tursun-Zade, "Protiv Kosmopolitizma i Paniranizma," *ibid.*, March 5, 1949, p. 2.

[7] *Ibid.*, April 24, 1949, p. 3 and *passim*. See also Alexander Fadeev, *ibid.*, January 9, 1949, p. 3; Vernon V. Aspaturian, *The Union Republics in Soviet Diplomacy: A Study of Soviet Federalism in the Service of Soviet Foreign Policy* (Geneva-Paris, Publications de l'Institut Universitaire des Hautes Études Internationales, no. 36, 1960). Compare with my thesis on the reasons for the establishment of the Tadzhik Republic in Chap. 3 of this volume.

[8] *Ibid.*, February 2, 1946, p. 3 (Gafurov on culture); *ibid.*, March 29, 1946, p. 2 (Pulatov's speech); *ibid.*, May 12, 1946, p. 2 (the Five-Year Plan in culture).

atheistic ideas of the medieval thinkers and philosophers, especially those that had been directed against Islamic orthodoxy and the aristocracy. Modern themes concentrated on the "building of communism," the "friendship of the peoples," and the struggle with the survivals of the past.

The building of the new culture was not without its difficulties, especially in its endeavors to eradicate the dysfunctional survivals of the past, and its attempts at Russification. Bourgeois nationalism and cosmopolitanism (the denial of the leading role of the Soviet culture and the adoption of western models) "infested" the thinking of many among the new intelligentsia and were reflected in mistakes and deviations discovered in their historical and literary works.

HISTORIOGRAPHY

The major purpose of the new Tadzhik historiography was to endow the Tadzhik republic with legitimacy in response to the refusal of neighbors in Soviet Asia, notably the Uzbeks, and Iranians across the border, to recognize the distinct cultural and political status of the Tadzhiks. The new interpretation attempted to validate a double claim *vis-à-vis* the Iranians: that the Tadzhiks were the originators of the classical Persian culture and its true heirs, and that they had inherited the leading political role of the Samanids. Another important aspect of the new historiography was the legitimization of the Russian conquest and of the continuing Russian presence and domination. The combination of the two themes necessitated a re-evaluation of the history of nationalist movements and of the value of local heroes and a new interpretation of philosophical thought and literary developments. Social and economic interpretations of human relations and political events provided a background. Responsive as the new historiography had to be to the current twists and turns of the Party line, it inevitably contained contradictions and "mistakes," none of which, however, significantly affected the major themes stated above.

In the western interpretation, shared by such Russian historians as Barthold and Bertel's, the Tadzhiks are a branch of the Persians,

their culture is a branch of Persian culture and their language is
a Persian dialect. This view was vigorously disputed by the spokesmen for the new Tadzhik historiography, among whom Gafurov
was the most prominent. In his major work on the Tadzhik history, he asserted that the Tadzhik culture and traditions were
unique and that they had predated, in their development, the
culture and traditions of the Persians. According to him, the eastern Iranians (ancestors of the Tadzhiks) and the western Iranians
(ancestors of the Persians) had been developing separately since
antiquity, notwithstanding some cultural exchange between them
and a common development from the ninth to the fifteenth century.[9] The claim to the ancient and unique cultural status of the
Tadzhiks was bolstered by the claim that their culture had influenced other cultures, in Central Asia and even farther afield:

> It was not Central Asia which was the periphery of the areas south
> of it but, conversely, the latter should in many instances be regarded
> as the periphery of ancient cultural centers of Central Asia. The cul-
> ture of the peoples of Central Asia in Arab times was developing on
> the basis of indigenous traditions and was incomparably higher than
> the culture of the Arab conquerors.[10]

Gafurov pointed out that other invaders had also benefited culturally from the conquered Central Asian peoples. According to
him many Central Asian elements had been found in the Greek
and Roman culture after Alexander's conquest of Bactria and
Sogd; Arab culture had also transmitted Central Asian influence
to Western Europe. Even the Chinese had been enriched by their
contacts with Central Asia; Buddhism had come to China through
contact with the Tokhari. The medieval Persian culture was in
fact the Tadzhik culture, developed at the time of the Samanid
empire, which spread into Iran and contributed to the development of western Iranian culture.[11]

[9] Gafurov, *Istoriia*, Chap. 2 and pp. 496–97. Russian historians criticized for the
false interpretation of the history of Central Asia included V. V. Barthold and
F. Rosenberg (*ibid.*, p. 497), and A. A. Semenov, Ye. E. Bertel's, and B. N. Zakharov
(*O nekotorykh voprosakh*, p. 4; *KT*, January 9, 1949, p. 3).

[10] "O nekotorykh voprosakh," pp. 4–5.

[11] Gafurov, *Istoriia*, Chaps. 4 and 6 and *passim; KT*, July 25, 1951, pp. 3–4. V. V.
Barthold, the great authority on Central Asia stated that "the cultural development
of Eastern Iranians was far inferior to that of Western Iranians," but recognized the
importance of the conquered Iranians in the development of Arab culture, and

The struggle with foreign invaders had formed a continuous theme in the history of Central Asia, according to the new interpretation. Outstanding examples of resistance to invaders based on popular support were the struggle of the Sogdian leader Spitamen against the Greeks in 329–27 B.C., the great revolt against the Arabs led by Mukanna (776–83), and the social revolt against local lords, vassals of the Mongols, led by Mahmud Tabari in 1238.[12]

The dangerous analogy between the struggle against earlier invaders and the struggle against the Russian conquest and rule in the nineteenth and twentieth centuries was outwardly avoided by the identification of resistance to alien rule with class struggle, and the insistence on the Leninist two-stream dichotomy in historical analysis. The Russian conquest and rule were proved to be historically progressive and beneficial to the people of Central Asia,[13] and thus, by definition, any resistance must have been led by a national bourgeoisie or aristocracy and have been *ipso facto* reactionary. Resistance movements under Russian rule had acquired progressive historical significance only when the struggle was based on an alliance of the local masses with the Russian proletariat, directed against local lords or tsarist officials. National liberation movements had been carried out under conditions of feudal and colonial oppression, and cross-pressure had contributed to their "localized" and "ideologically primitive" character. Not infrequently, a genuine mass protest had been adapted by the clergy and reactionaries to their own ends.[14]

---

the great cultural influence of immigrants from Western Iran (V. V. Barthold, *Four Studies on the History of Central Asia,* trans. from the Russian by V. and T. Minorsky [Leiden: E. J. Brill, 1956], vol. I, *A Short History of Turkestan: History of the Semirechy'e,* pp. 3, 12–15.) An over-all balanced view is offered by Professor Richard N. Frye of Harvard: "By 1,000 A.D., when I use the term Iranian, I mean that new combination which was developed in Transoxiana from the old east and west Iranian traditions plus Arab Islam. This was the rich fare of which the Turks partook when they became converted to Islam, and the Turks themselves contributed to the melting pot. The new amalgam was accomplished primarily in Central Asia where later a separation from the Iranian world took place." R. N. Frye, *Bukhara: The Medieval Achievement,* p. 192.

[12] Gafurov, *Istoriia,* Chaps. 4, 9, and 14.

[13] See Chap. 3.

[14] A. Zevelev and Sh. Abdullaev, "Diskussiia o kharaktere natsional'nykh dvizhenii v Srednei Azii i Kazakhstane v kolonial'nyi period," *Voprosy Istorii,* no. 9 (1951), 174.

In this new interpretation of history, the early approval of nationalist movements in Central Asia required an extensive re-evaluation.[15] In Tadzhikistan, for example, the mass revolt in Bol'dzhuan and Kulyab led by the peasant Vose (1885–88) was judged to have had a deeply revolutionary and progressive character, infused with the spirit of national liberation. The same interpretation was applied to the peasant revolts in the mountains of Kulyab, Bol'dzhuan, and Kurgan-Tyube in 1905–7 against the Emir of Bukhara.[16] On the other hand, the 1898 attack on the Russian garrison in Andizhan by the Sufi leader Dukchi Ishan, eulogized previously, was re-evaluated as "deeply feudal and bourgeois-nationalist" in character, because it was directed by the clergy and feudal lords, anxious to regain old privileges with the help of Turkish and British agents.[17] Numerous outbreaks in 1916 which had previously been regarded as progressive were re-evaluated also, and only those that had been directed against local oppressors and tsarist officials were found ideologically acceptable. The clergy (especially the Sufi) and local aristocrats, it was explained, had tried to use some of these outbreaks, with the assistance of Turkish and German agents, to separate from Russia in order to join Persia or Afghanistan.[18] Proletarian revolutions and peasant risings after 1917 had also acquired a reactionary character because they were taken over by the nationalist bourgeoisie.[19] Thus the Basmachi revolt had been profoundly feudal and reactionary in character. Led by the bai, the Moslem clergy, merchants, bourgeois nationalists, and officials of the Tsar and the Emir, it had

[15] This was a part of a massive re-evaluation of the Soviet historiography with respect to Central Asia, the Caucasus, and other areas. It involved the condemnation of such national movements as those of Shamil in the Caucasus and Kenesary Kasymov in Kazakhstan because of their alleged "reactionary" character.

[16] Gafurov, *Istoriia*, pp. 446–49; Chap. 22; *KT*, July 26, 1951, p. 3 (Gafurov on historiography).

[17] Gafurov, *Istoriia*, Chap. 22 (pp. 455 ff.); *KT*, July 26, 1951, p. 3; B. G. Gafurov, "Ob Andizhanskom 'Vosstanii' 1898 goda," *Voprosy Istorii*, no. 2 (1953), 50–61. The interpretation of the Andizhan revolt was a sore point with Gafurov, as he himself had described it as progressive in the 1949 edition of his history. It is interesting to notice the emphasis placed on the alleged participation by foreign agents, here and below.

[18] Gafurov, *Istoriia*, Chap. 23 (p. 479 ff.); *KT*, July 26, 1951, p. 3.

[19] Gafurov, *Istoriia*, Chap. 23 (p. 484 ff.).

served the interests of former oppressors and foreign intervention-
ists, this time the British and the Americans.[20]

The progressive-reactionary approach was also applied to the
analysis of philosophical and literary thought. Progressive philosophical thought was believed to have been linked to class struggle
at a given historical period. Mazdakizm, which lasted from the
sixth to the eighth century A.D., for example, was progressive because it was the ideology of Mukanna's national liberation struggle
against the Arabs. Other religious heresies of progressive character
had been directed against orthodox Islam's glorification of feudal
oppression and foreign rule. Despite the dominant feudal structure
which was reflected in reactionary aspects of their philosophy, the
great thinkers of the Samanid period had also developed progressive tendencies. Avicenna's thought was directed toward materialism and atheism and was characterized by a spirit of scientific in-
quiry; Nosir-i-Khisrou, the leader of the Ismailite heresy, had
defended the interests of the lower classes and doubted the existence of a just and omnipotent God, in view of the rampant oppression and injustice of the times; Omar Khayyam had pursued
many of the features of Avicenna's materialist philosophy. Materialistic and atheistic tendencies in philosophical thought had
continued to exist after the Mongol invasion and, with the beginning of the Russian contacts, had been strengthened and developed
by the impact of Russian revolutionary thought.[21]

Islam had been the major obstacle to the development of progressive sociopolitical thought; as its orthodoxy grew more rigid,
the suppression of free thinking received strong religious sanctions.
Sufism had started as a progressive anti-clerical and anti-feudal
movement in the ninth century, but later it became one of the
most reactionary manifestations of Islamic thought. Sufi leaders
had acquired great political power by insisting on the blind obedience of the people to the will of God, as explained by themselves,
and frequently dictated policies to the Timurides, and the Mangit
rulers of Bukhara. Despite Sufism's reactionary qualities, however,
some of its thinkers had been able to express progressive ideas. In

---

[20] Gafurov, "V. I. Lenin i pobeda," pp. 78–82; *KT*, June 18, 1949, p. 3.
[21] *KT*, August 6, 1947, p. 2 (by Morochnik); January 9, 1949, p. 3 (by Fadeev).

modern times Sufism was used by the feudal leaders and the bourgeoisie to turn the masses against the revolution and to make them
into tools of "British imperialists." [22]

Jadidism, the nationalist movement of the educated elite in
turn-of-the-century Turkestan,[23] was the most difficult ideology to
re-evaluate. Most of the early Central Asian Soviet leaders, such
as the members of the Young Bukhara group, including the Tadzhik Sadriddin Aini, had a Jadidist heritage. At the same time, the
movement had distinct nationalist overtones and a separatist and
autonomist character. Although in 1930 it was still being referred
to as "the movement which united all that was progressive in the
Bukhara khanate," [24] the terms used by Gafurov to describe it in
1955 were uncompromising: "Jadidism has never had a progressive
character and was never a national liberation movement. Jadidism
has always been an anti-national, bourgeois-nationalist, counter-
revolutionary movement in Central Asia. Awakening religious
fanaticism, pitting the toilers of one nation against the toilers of
another, the Jadidists brought enormous harm to the common
revolutionary struggle of these nations and the great Russian
people against social oppressors." [25] Gafurov and others also be-
littled the influence the movement had in Turkestan in the 1905–
17 period.[26]

Because of the difficulty involved in rescuing some of the "progressive" leaders from their Jadidist past, an effort was made to
portray them as "enlighteners" (*prosvetiteli*), thinkers who had
separated early from the main stream of reactionary Jadidism and
believed in "democratism" and "liberalism." [27] This view was condemned in 1953,[28] but was subsequently given new approval.[29]

---

[22] *Ibid.*, July 26, 1951, pp. 3–4 (Gafurov on historiography); B. G. Gafurov, "Ideologicheskaia rabota v partiinoi organizatsii Tadzhikistana," *Bol'shevik*, no. 2 (1952),
pp. 45–55.
[23] See Chap. 2.
[24] Briskin, *Strana Tadzhikov*, p. 31.
[25] Gafurov, *Istoriia*, p. 476.
[26] *Ibid.*, Chap. 23, *passim; KT*, January 9, 1953, p. 3 (by Mirzoev).
[27] *KT*, November 1, 1951, p. 3 (Bogoutdinov's book review).
[28] *Ibid.*, January 9, 1953, p. 3 (by Mirzoev).
[29] "Jadidism—A Current Soviet Assessment," *Central Asian Review*, no. 1 (1964),
30.

Ahmadi Donish and Adzhizi (Saiid Akhmat Khodzha Siddiki), the early protagonists of the movement, were counted among the prosvetiteli, even though the progressive character of the latter caused some controversy. Pan-Turkism, Pan-Islamism, and Pan-Iranianism were all uniformly condemned because they were regarded as counter-revolutionary movements and tools of the bourgeois nationalists and foreign imperialists who aimed at separating Central Asia from the Soviet Union.[30]

The official historiography assumes a history of friendship and cooperation not only between the Tadzhiks and the Russians but also between the Tadzhiks and other Soviet nationalities, including the Uzbeks, notwithstanding the emphasis on the "progressive revolts" of the Tadzhik peasants against their Uzbek overlords. There is evidence, however, that there was strong Uzbek resistance to the formation of a separate Tadzhik nation and to the recognition of an independent Tadzhik culture. It has been said that in the 1920's and 1930's "Pan-Turkic elements" expressed the view that Tadzhiks were not a nation, but a small Turkish group which adopted Iranian culture, and that they were unfit for self-government.[31] An Uzbek newspaper, *Turkestan*, of January 2, 1924, was quoted as having been violently opposed to the use of a separate Tadzhik language as "useless and superfluous" and recommending that the Tadzhiks immediately start using the Uzbek language.[32] In more recent times, a Tadzhik literary critic took strong exception to a book published in Uzbekistan which described a purported fifteenth-century feud between a Tadzhik poet (Kamodulin Binoi) and an Uzbek poet (Alisher Navoi) over which language should be used as the literary language; the Tadzhik was portrayed as an enemy of the Uzbek language and thus as an amoral, unprincipled man. This episode was not true, said the critic, and was based on "two questionable anecdotes." He concluded that "history does not know one shred of evidence of national, ethnic, or

[30] Gafurov, "V. I. Lenin i pobeda;" Iu. V. Bromlei and B. V. Lunin, "Nauchnaia sesia po istorii Srednei Azii i Kazakhstana v dooktiabr'skii period," *Voprosy Istorii*, no. 4 (1954), 172–78; *KT, passim*.

[31] I. S. Braginskii, *Ocherki po istorii Tadzhikskoi Literatury* (Stalinabad, AN Tadzhikskoi SSR, 1956), p. 36.

[32] Fanian, *K istorii sovetskogo stroitel'stva*, p. 16; I. S. Braginskii *et al.* eds., *Antologiia Tadzhikskoi poezii s drevnikh vremen do nashikh dnei* (Moscow, Izd. Khudozhestvennoi Literatury, 1951), p. 22; AN TSSR, *Istoriia*, III, Book 1, p. 268.

tribal hostility between the two peoples," the ancestors of both having fought side by side against "foreign invaders." [33]

This new historical interpretation of Tadzhik and Central Asian history was resisted by at least some of the Soviet Tadzhik historians, whose historical writings were critized for numerous "shortcomings." These included their failure to illuminate the process of the unification of Russia and Central Asia and the progressive role played by the Russians in the history of the region, and their apparent unwillingness to work in the recent period, especially the time between 1905 and 1917, the Revolution, and the Soviet era. Other shortcomings were an unwillingness to study relations between the "fraternal peoples," a lack of emphasis on the theme of the "struggle with foreign invaders," a lack of differentiation between the "progressive" and the "reactionary" streams of historical development, and a failure to show the reactionary character of bourgeois nationalism and of the bourgeois-nationalist movements of the past. Criticism based on "mistakes" committed in one or another of these broad spheres of interpretation was applied to almost all the new Tadzhik historians, including even Gafurov, then the incumbent First Secretary of the Tadzhik Party.

LINGUISTICS

The linguistic policy in Central Asia was designed to equip each new union or autonomous republic created by the national delimitation of 1924 with its own national language, an indispensable component of a republic's "national form." It was also aimed at breaking up the cultural unity of the area, as the Turkic languages differed little from one another and all used Arabic script. The Soviet policy was designed to magnify the differences. In the case of Iranian speakers, the effort to weld them into one nation was accompanied by the transformation into a modern language of Farsi, which had survived in Turkestan as a court and diplomatic language and as the spoken language of the Tadzhiks of the oases.

[33] *KT,* December 7, 1952, p. 2 (A. Mirzoev's review of a book, *Navoi,* by Aibek). Early bilingualism in Turkestan is confirmed by R. N. Frye, who states that Persian and Turkish languages existed side by side in Turkestan, and a majority of the people were bilingual. Poets were able to compose in both Turkish and Persian. R. N. Frye, *Bukhara: The Medieval Achievement,* p. 185.

The Soviet policy, though not always consistent, took three basic steps toward the development of modern Central Asian languages: "enrichment and completion," removal of foreign (Arabic and Persian) accretions, and introduction of Russian as the "second mother tongue." Enrichment-completion work included the modernization of the written language through the introduction and development of grammar, phonetics, and morphology (even the creation of new written forms for spoken dialects, if necessary) and the creation of a new literature in each language. Persian and Arabic accretions were systematically removed and replaced by Russian grammatical forms and loan words, which were also used to create a new technical vocabulary. The Russian language was introduced as the lingua franca of the area, the Cyrillic alphabet had been introduced into all the languages of the area in 1940, replacing the Latin alphabet used since 1929–30.[34] The use of Cyrillic made it easier for local people to learn Russian, and prevented them from reading foreign publications printed in Roman characters. The classics had already been denied to them, except in Soviet-approved versions, since the 1929 ban on Arabic script. The political purpose of the reforms clearly emerges from the following quote:

> It has been characteristic of bourgeois nationalists to attempt to orient the development of languages of the peoples of the USSR not upon Russian but upon foreign languages. Thus the nationalists of the eastern republics were oriented toward Persian, Turkic, and Arabic languages, etc. They sought in this manner to estrange the languages of the peoples of the USSR from the Russian language and from Soviet culture, and to strengthen the influence of foreign bourgeois culture.[35]

The instruction in local schools was given from the beginning in native languages, but there were also schools with Russian as the language of instruction, and the study of Russian in local schools was compulsory between 1938 and 1958 (no similar provisions existed for the study of native languages in Russian schools). The knowledge of Russian became a necessity for any Asian who wanted to progress up the political, economic, or cultural ladder.

[34] The decree on the latinization of the alphabet was adopted in April, 1928, and was carried out by 1930. AN TSSR, *Istoriia*, III, Book 1, 206.
[35] Quoted from *Voprosy Filosofii*, no. 3 (1950), by *Current Digest*, III, no. 10, 3.

There were chronological variations in the application of the linguistic policy in Central Asia. In the twenties and thirties the emphasis was placed on the differentiation among the various native languages; in the forties and fifties (especially after Stalin's famous dictum on linguistics in 1950),[36] it shifted in the direction of a more intensive Russification of grammar, syntax, and vocabulary. Under Khrushchev, in line with his policy of greater regional unity, an effort was made to minimize the differences between the Turkic languages, but this was played down after his removal.[37]

The development of the Tadzhik language and linguistics followed the general pattern described above, but in Tadzhikistan the language was not differentiated from other languages of the same family (as in the case of the Turkic languages); instead, the various Iranian dialects were forced into a common mold, the Farsi, or literary Tadzhik. The major preoccupation of the theory of Tadzhik linguistics was to prove that Tadzhik was not just a dialect of Persian, but a language in its own right, the formation of which had predated the Arab conquest and the creation of the Persian language. It was pointed out that the forefathers of the Tadzhiks had a written language as early as the fifth century B.C., that the process of the formation of the Tadzhik literary language had begun before the Arab conquest, that this language had been consolidated to form one of the chief tools of resistance in the struggle with the Arabs, and that it had flowered in the great Samanid literature, which was neither Arab nor Persian but Ta-

[36] Stalin contended that language was not a part of the superstructure because none of the four characteristics of the superstructure applied to it. 1) There is no basic change in the language accompanying the change in the economic base (vocabulary and grammar remained basically the same). 2) The language serves all classes impartially, not only the ruling class. 3) The language lives longer than any basis or superstructure. 4) The language is connected directly with productive activity and, unlike the superstructure, reflects changes in production directly and at once (*KT*, February 4, 1952, p. 2). Many of the Soviet languages were described by Stalin as being multi-dialect languages; the Tadzhik language was a case in point. In the process of creating a literary language, one dialect is taken as a base (in this case the literary Farsi) and others disappear; archaic forms of old literary languages are not intelligible to the people and should be removed. (A. Mordinov and G. Sanzheev, "Nekotorye voprosy razvitiia mladopis'mennykh iazykov narodov SSSR," *Bol'shevik*, no. 8 (1951), 45–46.)

[37] See Geoffrey Wheeler, *Modern History;* Geoffrey Wheeler, *Racial Problems in Soviet Muslim Asia* (London: Oxford University Press, 1960); and *Central Asian Review, passim,* for discussions of the Soviet linguistic policy in Central Asia.

dzhik.[38] A natural follow-up of this argument was the contention that the Tadzhik literary language has had great influence on the cultures of Iran, Afghanistan, Pakistan, and India.[39]

According to the 1956 edition of the *Great Soviet Encyclopedia*, the Tadzhik language belongs in the group of the southwestern Iranian languages; its literary norms evolved as a result of the influence of the eastern Iranians in the ninth and tenth centuries, and were used by the Tadzhiks and Persians until the fifteenth century. Later these norms were adopted in western Iran and in a number of other regions of the Middle East and Asia Minor. In the course of the centuries they had changed comparatively little and thus they formed the base for a rich literature created by Tadzhiks, Persians, and some other peoples.[40]

The argument of the greater antiquity and general influence of the Tadzhik language directly contradicted the findings of western scholars, as well as those of the early Soviet scholars, notably V. V. Barthold, whose interpretation was vigorously attacked by Tadzhik linguists and historians in the 1950's. Barthold's argument was that before the Persian and Arab conquests the people of present-day Tadzhikistan had spoken a Sogdian language, which had disappeared in the ninth and tenth centuries under the impact of Persian immigration and been replaced by the Tadzhik language, "which differs little from Persian"; old Sogdian had survived only in the Yagnob valley.[41] What Barthold was saying, in fact, was that the Tadzhik language is a dialect of the Persian language which was formed under the influence of the Persians who came to Central Asia.

---

[38] S. Mullodzhanov, "Torzhestvo mirnoi nauki v Tadzhikistane," *KT*, April 8, 1951, p. 3. In fact the Farsi language developed under the Samanids as the result of Arabicization of the original Persian, and was thus heavily infused with Arabic terms, many of them archaic. This amalgamation of Arabic and Persian continued until modern times. "Attempts to eliminate Arabic from Persian have been as futile as any elimination of Latin and French influences in English." R. N. Frye, *Bukhara: The Medieval Achievement*, pp. 172–4.

[39] *KT*, April 24, 1951, p. 3.

[40] *BSE*, 2d ed., XLI, p. 500. The 1946 edition (*BSE, 1st ed. LIII*, p. 451), on the other hand, generally followed Barthold's interpretation (see below).

[41] V. V. Barthold, *Four Studies, 1*, p. 15. Barthold adds further: "How small was the difference, in the tenth century, between the language spoken in Turkestan, at least among the educated classes, and that spoken in Persia, can be judged by the fact that poets, who were native of Turkestan, such as Rudaki, could achieve eminence in the Persian Parnassus." The distinction made here should be compared with the Soviet theory of Tadzhik literature, below.

Another difficult theoretical point was the need to reconcile the claims of Soviet linguists to the ancient character of the Tadzhik literary language with the absence of a Tadzhik nation on the eve of the Revolution, and with the catalytic role played by the Revolution and the Russian influence in the process of formation of the nation. The argument was made that under the Samanids the Tadzhik language had been that of a nationality, and had been fragmented subsequently into a multitude of dialects as a result of the territorial economic and political dispersion of the Tadzhik people. It had become a national language only after the Revolution, when its vocabulary and grammatical construction developed to form universal standards that subordinated the variety of dialects to united scientific-technical and sociopolitical vocabulary and the terms used in daily and professional life.[42]

This process of transformation and enrichment meant, in practice, the replacement of the Arabic sociopolitical vocabulary by that of the Marxist-Leninist, Russian, and international classics. The process has been described as an "ideological battle" between the bourgeois-nationalist intelligentsia which, under the influence of Pan-Islamic, Pan-Iranian ideology, fought for the "purity" of the language (for the retention of "Arabicisms and archaisms") and the Tadzhik Soviet scholars who struggled for the introduction into the language of the "Soviet-internationalist" vocabulary.[43] The major battle was fought at the linguistics conference in Stalinabad in February, 1938; it was won by the Soviet internationalists. Prominent among them was Sadriddin Aini, who is credited with the "democratization" of the Tadzhik language because of his research in the field of linguistics and his creative contribution to the new Tadzhik literature. Aini opposed the use of Arabicisms and archaic expressions in grammatical forms and vocabulary; he also resisted the introduction of Iranianisms borrowed from contemporary Persian (by those who felt that Tadzhik was a Persian dialect) and the use of dialecticisms and vernacular expressions not found in the literary language.[44]

The problems inherent in making the literary Farsi into the

[42] *KT*, September 8, 1954, p. 3 (Bogoutdinov on linguistics); Khamrakulov, "O nekotorykh osobennostiiakh," p. 541; Verkhovtsev and Maiatnikov, "O natsiiakh," p. 17.
[43] *KT*, June 17, 1954, p. 3 (Kalontarov on linguistics).
[44] *Ibid.,* April 25, 1953, p. 3 (Karimov and Arzumanov on Aini).

modern national language can be appreciated only when one considers that, in the words of one of the articles in the Tadzhik press: "Until the Revolution there was a great difference between the literary Tadzhik language and spoken Tadzhik." Even educated people used the latter in daily contact,[45] and mountain Tadzhiks spoke a variety of non-Persian, Iranian dialects. The Tadzhik press complained of the difficulties Tadzhik students had in learning the Tadzhik language and literature (the percentage of failures in the native language examinations were high), and the inability of the students and even teachers to write Tadzhik grammatically.[46]

The confusion in the standardization of usages seems to have been fairly widespread, as the various interpretations struggled for control of the new grammar and lexicography. After Stalin's dictum of 1950, the need arose to eradicate the "mistaken" linguistic theories of Marr, who saw the language as part of the superstructure and a product of dialectical progression. Marr's theory viewed the Tadzhik language as the synthesis of Arabic and Persian languages; this view was vigorously opposed. Instead, the binding interpretation in the 1950's was that the terms the language had assimiliated from Arabic, Mongol, Turkic, and modern Persian had enriched it but had not basically changed its character.[47] The Tadzhik linguists were thrown into feverish activity, standardizing the language according to the new line; major emphasis was placed on study of lexicography (its natural laws of development), standardization and modernization of grammar, and analysis of the various Tadzhik dialects. A new Institute of Language and Literature of the Academy of Sciences of the Tadzhik SSR was established in April, 1951. Publication of dictionaries and scientific monographs followed the new activity in the field of linguistics; as in other areas of cultural activity, Russian models and experience provided guidelines for the Tadzhiks.[48]

The study of the Russian language with the purpose of making

[45] *Ibid.*
[46] *Ibid.*, March 30, 1951, p. 3; and *passim.*
[47] *Ibid.*, April 8, 1954, p. 2 (Oranskii on linguistics).
[48] Based on: M. F. Fazylov, "O Tadzhikskoi Filologii," *ibid.*, June 22, 1951, p. 3; M. F. Fazylov, "Itogi perestroiki i ocherednye zadachi Instituta Iazyka i Literatury Akademii Nauk Tadzhikskoi SSR,"*Voprosy Iazykoznaniia*, no. 6 (1953); B. N. Niiazmukhammedov and A. S. Edel'man, "Razvitie Tadzhikskoi filologii za 25 let," AN TSSR, Otdelenie Obshchestvennykh Nauk, *Izvestiia*, no. 6 (1954), 11–26; *KT*, 1951–56, *passim.*

it the other mother tongue of the Tadzhiks played an important role in the linguistic policy. Although Russification has generally been connected with Stalin, Lenin was the first to emphasize the importance of the Russian language as the means of communication between the Soviet peoples.[49] In the borderlands Russian was from the beginning the *de facto* language of the government, for reasons best understood within a historical context, but an effort was made in the 1920's to promote local languages as the official ones, not only *de jure* but also *de facto*. In Tadzhikistan, a resolution of the Revolutionary Committee in late 1925 designated Tadzhik, Russian, and Uzbek as the three official languages of the ASSR, with the proviso that although central organs could use any of them, lower organs of government were to carry out their business exclusively in the language of the local population.[50] The decree met with Russian as well as Uzbek resistance (the latter insofar as the use of Tadzhik was concerned), and proved largely impracticable.

The study of the Russian language in non-Russian schools throughout the Soviet Union became compulsory in 1938. This step was said to be justified by the need to have a common language, to enable the non-Russian cadres to improve their scientific and technical knowledge, and to ensure a knowledge of Russian in Red Army conscripts.[51] (Military service has since proved to provide the best language school for Asian soldiers.) In Tadzhikistan the obligatory study of Russian in incomplete middle and middle schools had been introduced earlier, in the 1933–37 period; this had been met with resistance and sabotage by nationalist elements.[52]

Since that time, particularly in the forties and fifties, emphasis on the study and the use of the Russian language has been strong and constant.

[49] See John S. Reshetar, Jr., "Russian Ethnic Values," in Cyril E. Black, ed., *The Transformation of Russian Society* (Cambridge, Mass.: Harvard University Press, 1960), p. 58.

[50] Fanian, *K istorii sovestskogo stroitel'stva*, pp. 81–82; AN TSSR, *Istoriia*, III, Book 1, 163.

[51] The Decree of the Council of Peoples' Commissars of the USSR and the Central Committee of the All-Union Communist Party (Bolsheviks) of March 13, 1938, quoted by *KT*, March 16, 1951, p. 3.

[52] AN TSSR, *Istoriia*, III, Book 1, p. 315; *KT*, August 10, 1945, p. 2.

> One cannot overemphasize the importance of the Russian lan-
> guage. It belongs to the nation which has produced great revolution-
> aries and thinkers of genius; it has become one of the international
> languages of the world. Lenin wrote and spoke in this language,
> comrade Stalin writes and speaks in this language.[53]

The above newspaper editorial emphasized the utilitarian value
of knowing Russian, the language which offered "unlimited opportunity to join the most progressive human culture, and to gain
a deep and lasting knowledge in all the fields of science." The Russian language has been called the "key to the mastery of the riches
of the leading culture," the necessary means for the "formation of
national cadres in all the fields of science, culture, and national
economy," and a "powerful means of strengthening the friendship
of the peoples of the USSR." [54] Mirzo Tursun-Zade's poem "The
Language of Peace and Friendship," pointed out that all messages
of joy, progress, and culture had first been brought to Tadzhikistan and its sister nations by the Russian language.[55]

Teaching Russian in the the non-Russian schools in Tadzhikistan has proved to be an uphill struggle. Through the postwar
period and into the 1960's it has been the target of continuous
criticisms and complaints, centering on the shortage of teachers and
the poor qualifications of the available ones, the absence of com-
prehensive teaching programs and adequate methodology, the
shortage of adequate textbooks, the poor system of inspection, and
the absence of instruction available through extracurricular activities.[56] The Tadzhik teachers barely knew Russian, while Russians could not communicate in Tadzhik and, moreover, found
conditions of teaching in kishlaks unacceptable. Conditions were
worst in primary schools; in 1946 most of them were reported not
to have any Russian instruction.[57] Although it improved, the situation was still unsatisfactory in the fifties. In 1952 it was reported
that graduates of seven- and ten-year non-Russian schools studying

[53] *KT*, March 29, 1952, p. 1.
[54] *Ibid.*, August 30, 1946, p. 3; April 14, 1955, p. 3; Rasulov, *40 let*, p. 95.
[55] *KT*, March 29, 1952, p. 1.
[56] *Ibid.*, August 10, 1945, p. 2; August 30, 1946, p. 3; January 30, 1948, p. 3; March
16, 1951, p. 3; March 29, 1952, p. 1; August 8, 1952, p. 3; November 17, 1952, p. 2;
February 24, 1954, p. 2; October 8, 1954, p. 3; April 14, 1955, p. 3 and May 12, 1964;
"The Second Mother Tongue," *Central Asian Review*, no. 4 (1965), 310–22.
[57] *Ibid.*, September 24, 1946, p. 2; August 30, 1946, p. 3 (by Pulatov).

in technikums and higher schools had great difficulties with Russian.[58] *Kommunist Tadzhikistana* commented:

> Graduates of the seventh grade of Tadzhik schools mix vowels and consonants, are unable to use words in a sentence, and cannot use prepositions. They do not know orthography and punctuation; their accent is bad. They are not familiar with the theory of literature. . . .[59]

Poor instruction in the Russian language placed the Tadzhiks and the Uzbeks at a marked disadvantage in their pursuit of higher education, in daily contacts with the Russians, and in employment prospects. The knowledge of Russian was desirable even for a peasant; for an aspiring member of the elite it was absolutely essential. Most government, Party, and other business was conducted in Russian, because Russians and other Europeans very rarely knew any local language. The study of Tadzhik was not compulsory in the Russian schools in the republic, and the prevalent Russian attitude was that there was no need to learn.[60] For the convenience of the Russian settlers the Tadzhik constitution was changed to provide that court proceedings were to be conducted in the Russian language in raions in which the majority of the population was Russian,[61] and in 1956 the press reported that signs and advertisements in many parts of Tadzhikistan were

[58] This meant that Russian was the language of instruction in most technical and higher schools. *Ibid.*, March 29, 1952, p. 1.

[59] *Ibid.*, August 8, 1952, p. 3.

[60] The attitude was expressed to Kisch in his travels through Central Asia in 1930 (Kisch, *Changing Asia, passim*); it was also part of the impressions received by a recent traveler who reported: "I never met a Russian or an Ukrainian throughout my travels who admitted speaking Tadzhik, Kazakh, Kirgiz, or Uzbek. My question was invariably answered in the negative with a deprecating shrug, followed by 'Why?'" "Some Impressions of the Central Asian Republics" by a correspondent, *Central Asian Review*, no. 1 (1965), 12. A decree of the Ministry of Education of the Tadzhik SSR of April 29, 1954, provided for the following language examinations on graduation from tenth-grade (full middle), or seventh-grade (incomplete middle) schools: obligatory for Russian and non-Russian schools, a written examination and an essay in the Russian language, and an oral examination in Russian literature; obligatory for non-Russian schools, an additional essay in local language and literature *(KT,* May 5, 1954, p. 3). Thus, while students in all schools were required to pass a written and oral test in the Russian language on graduation, only Asian students were required to take an examination in the Asian language.

[61] Article 97 of the Tadzhik Constitution was changed. *KT,* April 24, 1951, p. 1.

written in Russian only, as were the announcements and notices in the Stalinabad Post Office.[62]

LITERATURE

Literature was the most important expression of the new Ta-dzhik culture; the bulk of the "national" heritage consisted of literary works and folklore which were adaptable to the development of the new political line. Soviet-educated Tadzhik intelligentsia found a new challenge in literary activity, and the growing, literate Tadzhik audience was more receptive to the Soviet message when conveyed through familiar media. As in other republics of Central Asia, in Tadzhikistan the Party considered a new national literature the single most important instrument of socialization. Like historiography and linguistics, the new literature was expected to employ traditional themes in support of the new Soviet content. Another important aspect in the development of the new Tadzhik literature was its potential influence on "the struggling people of the East . . . and especially the Persian speaking people to whom the language of the Tadzhik literature is close and understandable"; the task of influencing them was characterized as being of "outstanding international importance." [63]

The difficulties which beset the creation of a new literature had their source in the Islamic and nationalistic roots of the traditional literature, and in the unwillingness of the Tadzhik artists to develop modes of literary expression other than the traditionally sanctified poetry. The type of literary development needed in the struggle with bourgeois nationalism was described by Gafurov in 1945. It was necessary for writers to gain ". . . the mastery of the rich inheritance of the Tadzhik classical poetry in its essence rather than formally, while at the same time creatively to take over and perceive the best in the literature of the brotherly peoples of the Soviet Union, particularly in the literature of the great Russian people." [64] They should also enrich the Tadzhik literature with prose and dramatic works which would appeal to all Soviet

[62] *Ibid.*, December 9, 1956, as quoted in the *Central Asian Review*, no. 1 (1957), 100.

[63] Braginskii, *Ocherki*, p. 33; *KT*, September 24, 1952, p. 2 (by Mirshakar).

[64] *KT*, July 17, 1945, pp. 2–3 (by Gafurov).

peoples, not only to Tadzhiks, and make an effort to acquaint the Tadzhiks with the rich Russian literature and the Western classics. Like all Soviet writers, Tadzhik writers were considered to be "engineers of human soul"; their work was "one of the streams flowing into the general Soviet river," built on the basis of the "one creative method—socialist realism" and devoted to the common aim, "the building of Communism."

The three sources of the new Tadzhik literature were classical literature, oral poetic tradition (folklore), and Russian and Soviet literature.[65] The Tadzhik claim to the medieval Persian literature,[66] did not mean that all of its works were used uncritically; much in them was found to be ideologically unacceptable. Prominent poets and writers of the past were considered classic only if their works "reflected their whole historical epoch" and "served the interests of the masses." [67] Soviet scholarship required that the classics be used selectively and with caution, because all of them combined elements of the two streams of development, the progressive (ideologically acceptable) and the reactionary (to be rejected). The progressive (popular) elements of the classics included atheism, anti-despotism, humanism, praise of labor, and struggle with oppressors and invaders. These were said to be represented by realistic-expressionist writing, in contrast to reactionary symbolic iconography, and by the popular poetry and songs, in contrast to court panegyrics.[68]

Because of the feudal setting of the times, progressive and reactionary elements were said to have been intertwined in the poetry of the first classical period, the tenth through the fifteenth century,[69] but popular progressive elements were clearly discernible in

[65] Braginskii, *Ocherki,* pp. 9–10, 14.

[66] The claim embraces not only the poets who were born in the territory of the Samanid Empire or lived there (such as Rudaki or Firdousi) but also those who were born and lived in western or southern Persia (such as Sa'adi or Khafiz), because they also were "indissolubly connected with the development of the literature, and were organically intertwined with its history." The Tadzhiks were said to have "had the cultural priority" in the literature (Braginskii *et al., Antologia,* p. 6).

[67] *KT,* July 25, 1951, p. 4.

[68] Braginskii *et al., Antologia,* pp. 8–9; Braginskii, *Ocherki,* p. 20.

[69] No attempt is made here to discuss the classical Persian literature, or to evaluate its merits (many scholarly works exist on the subject), but only to show how it has been interpreted and used for political purposes in Soviet Tadzhikistan, and what relevance it had to the contemporary Soviet Tadzhik literature.

the writings of the great poets. Abulkhasan Rudaki (d. 941) was commended for his deep philosophical thought, belief in youth, and open-mindedness to new ideas. The great epic poem *Shakh Name* (the Book of Kings) of Abul'kosim Firdousi (Abu'l-Qasim Firdosi) (934–1025), which glorifies the mythical political unity of ancient Iran and is thus regarded as the Persian national epic, is important in Soviet Tadzhikistan not in its "class context," but in its "humanistic ideas." These include such themes as that of a popular revolt led by the legendary smith Kova (representing the Iranian people) against the dragon-tsar Zakhkhok (representing the Arabs), and of the struggle of good and evil (historically a portrayal of the struggle of Iranians against Turanians), the good represented by the popular hero, Rustem. Firdousi's other ideas regarded as progressive are those of a just tsar, defending the people from feudal oppression, of the courage, heroism, and wisdom of women, and of the brotherhood of people of various tribes and religions.[70] The real importance of Firdousi and his work, however, as attested by Western scholars,[71] lies in it being a symbol of Iranian nationalism. By claiming *Shakh Name* as their rightful heritage, the Tadzhiks place themselves at the head of the movement for Iranian unification to be carried out under the Soviet aegis, but at the same time they accept its nationalistic message, which may have dangerous connotations in the Soviet context.

Of the later poets Omar Khayyam (1040–1123) is represented as expressing a hidden protest against the feudal system and the "spirit of slavery" enforced by the clergy and Islam; his skepticism and hedonism are played down carefully in the Soviet versions of his quatrains, and their analyses. The works of Nosir-i-Khisrou (1003–88) are said to be filled with a strong protest against social injustice, as are the works of the Iranian poets who lived outside Tadzhikistan after the Mongol invasion, such as Muslikhiddin Sa'adi (1184–1292) and Shamsiddin Mukhammad Khafiz (d. 1389). The poetic revival of the fifteenth century is portrayed as the pe-

---

[70] Braginskii, *Ocherki*, pp. 14–16; Braginskii *et al.*, *Antologia*, pp. 10–11, 581.

[71] "The importance of Firdosi as the forger of a document of Iranian unity and nationalism cannot be minimized, and his work is fascinating because of this as well as its literary interest," R. N. Frye, *Bukhara: The Medieval Achievement*, p. 99. The term "forger" refers to the fact that, historically, Iranian unity did not exist in the pre-Islamic period.

riod of cooperation and exchange of ideas between the progressive Uzbek poets, such as Alisher Navoi, and the Tadzhik poets, such as Abdurrakhman Dzhami (1414–92); they were bilingual, but each wrote in his own language. The literary activities of the khanate of Bukhara from the fifteenth to the twentieth century are characterized as "reactionary," because of the development of a court poetry, with sharp social protest being expressed only by a few poets, such as the seventeenth-century weaver Saido Nasafi. By the nineteenth century, the contact with Russian culture is said to have inspired a "broad educational movement" characterized by pro-Russian cultural orientation, deep compassion for the misery of the peasants, and proposals for an educational program. Ahmadi Donish (1827–97) was typical of this trend.[72]

As in the classics, all of the feudal-bai "distortions" found in Tadzhik folklore were uncompromisingly rejected.[73] Ancient national epos played an important part in the adaptation of folklore. The revival included the word-of-mouth ancient Sogdian epos *Shakh Sugdiuch,* as well as the great epos *Gurguli,* which was known to the whole of Central Asia and the Middle East. In its Tadzhik version it described a mythical happy country of peasants, *Chambul Maston,* ruled by a just ex-shepherd, and its continuous struggle to defend itself from predatory invaders and greedy rich merchants and lords. One of the two popular heroes of the epos, Avas (the son of a butcher), who was instrumental in finally defeating the invaders, was a Tadzhik.[74] Other parts of the oral tradition included proverbs, folk songs, stories, and satirical anecdotes. The epos and songs were traditionally preserved by itinerant professional singers, *khafiz,* many of whom were great artists in their own right. In the Soviet period some of the khafiz continued to practice their art, but were careful to make their offerings ideologically acceptable.[75]

All "alien" themes in the new literature were firmly rejected, especially those which glorified the past, praised feudal rulers and Islam, and emphasized blind obedience to rulers and submission to

---

[72] Braginskii, *Ocherki,* pp. 16–17; Braginskii *et al., Antologia,* pp. 7–14, part IV.
[73] Braginskii, *Ocherki,* p. 23.
[74] I. S. Braginskii, "Zametki o Tadzhikskom epose 'Gurguli,'" AN SSSR, Institut Vostokovedeniia. *Kratkie Soobshcheniia,* no. 9 (1953), 48–57; *KT,* April 8, 1945.
[75] Braginskii, *Ocherki,* pp. 20–23; *KT,* April 27, 1952, p. 3.

the will of God or the forces of nature. Erotica, an important component of classical Persian poetry, was also firmly rejected. Passages in the classics, epos, stories, and songs which contained forbidden themes were simply excised and removed from works published in Central Asia. In justification of the practice, a local critic colorfully described unacceptable writings as "whole diseased organs" rather than "just blemishes on the healthy body," and advocated "cutting them out whole" as the only remedy.[76] Further justification for the practice was provided by the ever-present fear of bourgeois nationalism which was said to be hidden in the attitudes of Tadzhik writers. Those who grew up with a deep appreciation of the classics felt that "the Tadzhik culture [was] in itself beautiful and in no need of enrichment." [77] They thus rejected the need to learn from Russian and Soviet literary experience, which was officially regarded as the most important source of the new Tadzhik literature.

In literature, Russian influence was traced to the prerevolutionary period; the writer who first made it intelligible to the Tadzhiks was Sadriddin Aini (1878–1954). Russian influence was seen also in the ideological impact and the adoption of the new method of socialist-realism, and in the new literary forms. Maxim Gorkii was the most important model for the Tadzhik prose writers; Bednyi and Maiakovskii were the models for the new Tadzhik poetry. Russian literary language and style influenced the development of those of the Tadzhiks. Using Russian models, Tadzhik writers learned to apply the traditions of the Russian classics so that they "became part of their own inheritance," and also to adapt their own national inheritance to the new requirements.[78]

The development of Soviet Tadzhik literature did not really begin until the 1930's. The two major representatives in the 1920's were Sadriddin Aini and a Persian revolutionary, Abulkosim Lakhuti (1887–1957), who arrived in Tadzhikistan in 1922. Aini (who broke with the Jadidists only at the outbreak of the Revolution) was the first Tadzhik to write prose; his first two novels, describing prerevolutionary oppression and revolutionary struggle (*Odina*

[76] Braginskii, "Zametki o epose," p. 57.
[77] *KT,* July 17, 1945, p. 2.
[78] Braginskii, *Ocherki,* pp. 24–33.

and *Dokhunda*), appeared in the twenties. The Association of
Proletarian Writers which was formed in Tadzhikistan in 1930
was replaced in 1933 by the Union of Writers of Tadzhikistan, ad-
justing to the All-Union change. Under Aini's leadership, the
members of the writers' union concentrated on the translation of
Russian classics; some creative writing was done by the new Kom-
somol-recruited writers.[79]

Political subjugation of literature in the thirties was described
by Braginskii as "the period of the struggle with the bourgeois
nationalists, who wanted to break away from the influence of the
Russian literature and to realize the new forms of Soviet literature
in a conservative-reactionary way," [80] but he gave no details concerning the activity of the losing side. As for the winners, the most
prominent among the new prose writers was Aini, who wrote three
more novels, among them *Raby* (Slaves), a story of past oppression
in the emirate. Others included Dzhalol Ikrami (b.1909), who
wrote a novel and a collection of short stories, and Rakhim Dzhalil
(b. 1909), who wrote a novel about the life of a Tadzhik girl.
Among the poets were Aini, Lakhuti, Pairav Sulaimoni (1899–
1933), Mukhammadzhon Rakhimi (b. 1901), and others, including
the young Komsomoltsy Mirzo Tursun-Zade (b. 1911), Abdusalom
Dekhoti (b. 1911), Mirsaid Mirshakar (b. 1912), and Khabib Iusufi
(1914–43), who was killed in World War II. It was also in this
period that the first works of Tadzhik dramaturgy appeared, written by Tursun-Zade, Dekhoti, Ikrami, Satym Ulug-Zade (b. 1911),
and Pirmukhammad-Zade, who was also killed in the war.[81] The
new writers followed the programmatic Party requirements of
promoting Russian ties and approved themes (oppression under
emirate, revolution, struggle with the Basmachi, emancipation of
women, collectivization, socialist construction, and the creation of
the new Soviet man). The writers' first literary journal was *Baroi
adabiety sotsialisti* (For Socialist Literature). This was replaced
in 1940 by *Sharki Surkh* (The Red East), which survived into the
fifties.

---

[79] *Ibid.*, pp. 30–90; AN TSSR, *Istoriia*, III, Book 1, 268.

[80] Braginskii, *Ocherki*, p. 91.

[81] *Ibid.*, pp. 91–134; Braginskii *et al.*, *Antologia*, part V; AN TSSR, *Istoriia*, III,
Book 1, 268–321.

The same writers were active in the war period. It is surprising
how many of them withstood the 1938 purge, in comparison with
the members of the political elite; many of the younger ones were
drafted into the army. The dominant literary themes during the
war were the defense of the motherland, heroism, and glorious
deeds, for which examples were sought in classical literature as well
as in the feats of Tadzhik soldiers. Hitler was compared to *Shakh
Name*'s dragon tsar, for example. A large group of Russian writers
and artists came to Tadzhikistan in the war period, some of them
to stay.[82]

The end of the war saw renewed activity on the Tadzhik literary
front, with increased emphasis on ideological education of the
people and the eradication of the remnants of bourgeois nationalism. The latter seemed to have survived under the guise of the one-
stream attitude toward Tadzhik history and literary heritage, with
its proponents "idealizing the past" and at the same time trying to
minimize Russian influences in literature.[83] The directives for the
development of the Soviet Tadzhik literature in the postwar period
included the promotion of "organic ties of literature with the life
of the people"; subordination to "the leading, directing influence
by the Communist Party"; maintenance of "unity of national
form and communist content"; and utilization of "the best traditions and experiences of fraternal literature, Russian literature in
the first place, Soviet and classical."[84]

Two important ideas for Tadzhik writers to develop were the
"construction of communism," and the "friendship of the peoples."
The first comprised numerous sub-themes such as the glorification
of socialist labor, struggle for cotton cultivation, the creation of the
new Soviet man, and the emancipation of women. The theme of
friendship of the people was concerned primarily with the glorification of Russia and everything Russian. Immediately after the
war, the victory and heroism of the people was a favorite motif,
but emphasis on it gradually declined. Historical themes such as
the establishment of Communist power in Bukhara and the
struggle with the Basmachi also continued to be popular.

[82] Braginskii, *Ocherki*, pp. 138–83.
[83] *Ibid.*, pp. 185–274; *KT, passim.*
[84] Braginskii, *Ocherki*, p. 265.

The construction of communism theme required Soviet writers "to present in artistic pictures the best characteristics of the hundreds of thousands of the toilers on kolkhoz lands; to show the happiness and heroism of their creative and constructive work; . . . to uncover the sharp conflicts where the new is confronted with the old in a contemporary kolkhoz village; . . . to depict all this in a vigorous and true form." [85]

In the eyes of the Party, a good example of literary works devoted to the above theme was a poem on the trials and tribulations of a Tadzhik woman, a heroine of labor, who cultivated cotton on newly irrigated land (*On the Shores of Kafirnigan River,* by Ashirmat Nazarov). Less successful were two novels on kolkhoz life, *Shodi,* by Ikrami (see below), and *Renovated Land,* by Ulug-Zade. Mirshakar, a poet from the Pamirs, successfully specialized in depicting the happy life under Soviet rule, as in his poem *The Turbulent Piandzh,* and his adaptation of the Gurguli legend of a happy country, the Stalin-prize-winning poem *The Golden Village.*[86] In the latter, a group of Pamir peasants search for a perfect society for many years and in many lands; the one who returns is astounded to find it in his own home village, embodied in the new Soviet reality. His son greets him:

> You are at home. And all you see around
> The wreaths of roses and cotton in the fields
> And each new home, new fruit brought off the earth
> Is the result of our will and work.
> This is no paradise. Each step was hard.
> The Golden Village not yet wholly built.
> But now we know the road straight into the golden future.[87]

The theme of the creation of a new Soviet man was represented best by Aini's well-known autobiography, *Bukhara* (*Vospominaniia*), which has been translated into several western languages. Another aspect of the theme was the change in the fate of women, illustrated by a poem by Lakhuti, *The Tadzhik Woman:*

---

[85] *Ibid.,* p. 200.
[86] *Ibid., passim;* Braginskii *et al., Antologia, passim; KT, passim.*
[87] *KT,* December 5, 1946, p. 2.

Weary under the fear of God
Choked by Heavy oppression,
Beaten, under husband's tyranny,
Made light of by her son.
Ah, look at the past slavery,
Look at the sad fate of a woman!

Her garment sewn with silk
Her coat made of brocade
Her brother drives a tractor
All are happy to see her.
Ah, look at the free Tadzhik woman,
Look at a Tadzhik woman—Bolshevik! [88]

All of the prominent Tadzhik poets in the fifties engaged in the glorification of friendship with Russia. Tursun-Zade, Aini, Mirshakar, and Rakhimi were prominent among them, though Rakhimi was criticized for too much lyricism. Rakhim Dzhalil wrote about Russian friendship in prose, specializing in war-time novels and short stories. He also wrote a popular book about struggle with the Basmachi, entitled *Pulat y Gul'ru*.[89]

The strong emphasis on differentiation between the various media of literary expression resulted in the development of prose in the postwar period, though poetry still appeared to be the favorite medium. Other literary forms such as editorials and reviews, short stories, and satire were also being developed, pioneered especially by Tursun-Zade. The one genre which consistently lagged behind in quantity and quality was dramaturgy, though a number of plays were produced by some of the leading writers. These were generally described as artistically poor and lacking in depth in the presentation of the social conflicts which they attempted to portray.[90] Children's literature was pioneered by Mirshakar. Many of his stories were regarded as good enough to be

[88] Braginskii *et al., Antologiia*, p. 544.
[89] Braginskii, *Ocherki; KT, passim*. For English translations of some of the Tadzhik stories and poetry see the periodical, *Soviet Literature,* Moscow, no. 9 (1967).
[90] Braginskii, *Ocherki*, pp. 249–54. Included here were such plays as Tursun-Zade's *Arus* (a story of a Russian woman married to a Tadzhik) and his historical play *Takhir and Zukhra,* and Mirshakar's *My City*. The last dealt with a conflict between a young architect and an old one.

translated into other Soviet languages.[91] Much effort at literary
criticism was expanded under the guidance of Russian literary
critics. Here, as in the field of prose, a beginning was made by
Aini, when he started to analyze the classics from the two-stream
viewpoint.[92] Other writers followed, but not all of them were successful in meeting the demands of the current Party line and many
were strongly criticized for ideological mistakes.

THE ARTS

The cultural policy described above applied equally to the arts.
Here, however, the ground was less fruitful than in the case of
literature, because of the absence of certain types of artistic activity in the traditional culture and the difficulty involved in adaptation. Music, songs, dance, and theatrical shows and pantomimes
had always been popular, performed by traveling troupes of story-
tellers, jesters, puppeteers, acrobats, dancers, and singers. The
traditional artistic activities, however, were intimately connected
with Islamic and pre-Islamic religious rituals and festivities of the
family cycle. Their utility for Soviet purposes was limited, even
though an effort was made to fill the traditional forms with new
meaning, as in the case of converting the Iranian New Year celebration to that of the First of May. Traditional music was used
primarily as the background for poetry; polyphonic music and
orchestration were unknown. Painting, sculpture, and architecture
were all limited by the traditional Islamic proscription on the
representation of living creatures.[93]

Although a major effort was made to develop music and the
arts under Soviet rule, it had to be carried out primarily by non-

---

[91] Braginskii, *Ocherki,* pp. 255–260; *KT, passim.*

[92] AN TSSR, *Istoriia,* III, Book 1, 322; I. S. Braginskii, *Iz istorii Tadzhikskoi
narodnoi poezii* (Moscow: AN SSSR, 1956), pp. 5–7.

[93] S. P. Tolstov *et al.,* eds., *Narody Srednei Azii i Kazakhstana,* I (Moscow: AN
SSSR, 1962), pp. 637–40, 647–53; O. Dansker, "Sobiranie i izuchenie Tadzhikskoi
narodnoi pesni," pp. 87–105; "Khronika Khudozhestvennoi teatral'noi i muzykal'noi
zhizni Tadzhikskoi SSR za 1954–1955 gg.," pp. 235–42; N. Nurdzhanov, "Russkaia
klassika na stsene Tadzhikskogo Akademicheskogo Teatra," pp. 203–19, all in
Sbornik Statei posviashchenykh isskustvu Tadzhikskogo naroda, AN TaSSR, Institut
Istorii, Arkheologii i Etnografii, Works, XLII (Stalinabad: AN TaSSR, 1956); N.
Nurdzhanov, "Istoki narodnogo teatra u Tadzhikov," AN SSSR, Institut Etnografii
im. N. N. Miklukho-Maklaia, *Kratkie Soobshcheniia,* no. 18 (1953), 103–9.

Tadzhiks, because the ideas and the media were unfamiliar to the Tadzhiks and were not easily absorbed by them. The Russians collected Tadzhik songs and folk motifs in order to use them in modern musical forms such as operas and symphonies. Criticism revealed that some Tadzhiks were opposed to the introduction of polyphonic music because it was "alien" to their traditions, and all the "Tadzhik" modern composers, such as Balasanian and Lenskii, were ethnically non-Tadzhiks. In the creation of the new music and operas and ballets, the standard practice in the republic was for a Russian and a Tadzhik to cooperate, one supplying the technical mastery of the medium, the other the folk themes and melodies. This practice of "co-authorship" was frowned upon by the Party and was frequently criticized, as was the Tadzhik backwardness, regarded as yet another manifestation of bourgeois nationalism.[94]

Thematically the musical production followed the general prescriptions applied to literature. The opera, a new genre, either utilized an approved classical theme (*The Revolt of Vose, Smith Kova*) or attempted to portray the struggle with the Basmachi (the opera *Bakhtiër and Nisso*, the ballet *Two Roses*), or the new reality (*The Wife*). The Tadzhik "nationalist" contention that opera was an alien genre and hence not easily understandable to the people was officially condemned, but evidence exists that operas were not particularly popular with the Tadzhik masses.[95]

The khafiz (professional singers) were organized by the Soviet authorities; their new songs were circulated in the traditional way. In fact, the title of *khafiz* came to be bestowed on deserving singers by the Tadzhik Supreme Soviet. The best known Soviet khafiz was Bobo Iunus Khudoidod-Zade, whose songs ridiculed past oppressors and hailed the revolution and the new reality. A sample of an anti-Basmachi song follows:

> Basmachi were like wild beasts,
> But we chased them out from our land.

[94] Dansker, "Sobiranie narodnoi pesni" "Khronika khudozhestvennoi zhizni–;" *KT*, February 2, 1946, p. 3; July 19, 1949, p. 3; November 14, 1952, p. 2; and *passim*.
[95] Dansker, "Sobiranie narodnoi pesni;" Komitet po Delam Isskustv pri SNK SSSR, *Dve Rozy* (Du Gul'), ballet in 4 acts (Moscow, 1941); Dansker, *Kuznets Kova* (Kovai Oknangar), opera in 4 acts (Moscow, 1941); *KT*, April 28, 1948, p. 2; November 3, 1954, p. 4; January 15, 1955, p. 2.

Even Enver Pasha, he who sold his soul
To the devil, did not escape . . .[96]

Although archeology shows a rich Iranian heritage in the picto-
rial arts (as seen in the many newly discovered archeological sites
like the one in Pendzhikent), little progress was made in Tadzhikistan in painting and sculpture after the revolution. Most of the
artists were non-Tadzhiks, thematic development was characterized
by "one-sidedness and surface treatment," and the republic's activity in the field was considered to be among the least developed
in the USSR. One explanation given for the Tadzhik backwardness is that the ancient centers of the Tadzhik artistic activity,
Bukhara and Samarkand, were outside the republic's boundaries
in Uzbekistan.[97]

PROBLEMS AND CRITICISM

The post-1945 history of the relations between the Tadzhik intellectuals and the Communist Party was far more turbulent than
one might have been led to expect on the basis of samples of their
work. There was hardly a literary figure of any stature who escaped
Party criticism at one point or another, including Gafurov (as a
historian), Aini, and Tursun-Zade, though in all of these cases,
criticism concerned only "minor mistakes" of judgment or interpretation. In 1946 Tursun-Zade became the spokesman for the
Party line in literature as Chairman of the Tadzhik Writers'
Union and a member of the Central Committee of the KPT. Mirshakar was his second-in-command as Secretary of the Writers'
Union; he had been a candidate member of the Central Committee since 1956. Aini, who had previously played the leading role
in the affairs of the Writers' Union, was less active because of his
great age; he died in 1954.

In the implementation of the cultural policy, Party functionaries
who were in charge of the field exercised continuous vigilance.
There were, however, two high points of criticism in the postwar

[96] *KT*, August 18, 1953, p. 2; March 28, 1947, p. 2; August 30, 1955, p. 1; Dansker,
"Sobiranie narodnoi pesni."
[97] Belinskaia and Meshkeris, *Mezhrespublikanskaia vystavka; KT,* December 4,
1951, p. 2; and *passim.*

decade. The first was a part of Andrei Zhdanov's purge of the intellectuals in the fall of 1946, triggered by his concern over the "ideological purity" of Soviet artists, writers, and intellectuals. In Tadzhikistan the purge took place in September and December of 1946, and its aftermath was felt for some time. Numerous Tadzhik intellectuals were accused of ideological mistakes, inactivity, and lack of self-criticism. The chairman of the Writers' Union (Satym Ulug-Zade) lost his job, and four of the most criticized writers were expelled from the Union.[98] The second witch-hunt, which ranged more broadly and lasted longer, was caused by Stalin's linguistic decree in 1950. In Tadzhikistan the criticism continued through 1951 and centered on the question of the reevaluation of past history and the use of the language. The available evidence indicates that there was considerable resistance on the part of some Tadzhik scholars and writers toward accepting the superiority of political criteria to artistic ones and the superiority of Russian models and usages to Persian ones. The opposition centered around a few individuals. Some were members of the Language and Literature Institute of the Tadzhik Academy of Sciences, and some were members of the Writers' Union, grouped around its literary magazine, *Sharki Surkh*. These appeared to have some support in the Ministry of Education, as part of the battle was fought over the literary textbooks for the upper grades of Tadzhik middle schools. Criticism based on the charges made during this period continued through the 1950's.

The storm centered around the basic desire of the Tadzhiks to preserve their national character and on their resistance toward accepting Russian models and allowing themselves to be forced into the straitjacket of socialist realism. The dimensions of the problem were outlined by Gafurov when, in his capacity as the Party's First Secretary, he laid down the line in cultural policy for the postwar period. Referring to the "insufferable and dangerous tendencies in our midst, which, under the guise of the defense of national traditions and special characteristics, aim to limit the framework of our culture, and to isolate it from the cultures of other peoples of the Soviet Union," he described the attitude taken by those who professed the above tendencies:

[98] *KT*, October 11, 1946, p. 3; September–December, 1946, *passim*.

This kind of attitude toward the development of national culture considers it self-sustaining, closed within itself, separated from the cultural influence of other people. [It is characterized] by the struggle to preserve, especially in art, the features of primitivism and backwardness. Its source is to be found among the most backward strata of our intelligentsia . . . and also among the remnants of the hostile elements that are interested in weakening the ties with the peoples of the Soviet Union, in the weakening of the friendship of the peoples of the USSR. The hostile and destructive sermons of these people, which corrupt our youth, consist mainly in denying the need for professional mastery by cultural activists, and in an assumption that fruitful cultural activity is possible without any special preparation.[99]

The Tadzhiks' desire to preserve and develop their national heritage and their resistance to politicization manifested themselves in various ways in literary activity. The most common and straightforward was a "glorification of the past" and a desire to revive the entire Persian heritage, usually coupled with anti-Russian attitudes. Another form of resistance was formal acquiescence accompanied by the production of flat, wooden stories with heroes who were completely unconvincing. Still another was escapism; many authors ceased to create and concentrated instead on translating, editing, and performing administrative jobs.

The struggle to overcome these attitudes was referred to in the Party press as "the struggle against the manifestations of hostile bourgeois ideology, against the lack of ideology, and against apoliticism." [100] Manifestations of bourgeois nationalism included insistence on the "uniqueness of the Tadzhik culture," "scornful attitudes toward the Soviet literature" (Russian as well as Tadzhik), "nationalism," "idealization of the past," and "lack of differentiation between the progressive and reactionary elements in the national heritage" (the one-stream interpretation of history).[101] Lyrical poetry, modeled on the traditional *ghazal* (a four-verse stanza expressing the pains and pleasures of love), was also considered a bourgeois nationalist survival because it lacked social purpose and was considered degrading to women.[102]

[99] *Ibid.*, July 17, 1945, p. 2.

[100] *Ibid.*, August 22, 1953, p. 1.

[101] *Ibid.*, December 2, 1947, p. 2; July 21, 1951, p. 2; November 20, 1951, p. 2; July 25, 1951, p. 4; May 19, 1954, p. 2; and *passim;* also Braginskii *et al., Antologia.*

[102] *KT*, April 1, 1947, p. 2; July 21, 1951, p. 2; and *passim.*

An interesting illustration of the tug-of-war between the Party and the Tadzhik writers is provided by the story of the publication of a work ascribed to Amir Khisrou Dekhlevi entitled *The Adventures of the Four Dervishes*. Excerpts of the book were published by Ikrami in *Sharki Surkh* in 1940–41, but this was stopped because of criticism. Yet the whole book was published by Tadzhikgosizdat in 1951, again edited by Ikrami. The introduction was written by Aini, who characterized the work as "one of the most appealing and important national works." Unfortunately, the Party disagreed. The publication of the book was condemned as a "serious ideological mistake" because the story eulogized "religious fanaticism," "blind faith in a supreme being," "dervishism and sufism"; its heroes were "morally rotten," and large parts of it were devoted to descriptions of orgies of dervishes and the ruling classes," "drinking, opium, and debauchery," while the poor were presented "as ignorant and inert servants and slaves." [103]

The second major target of criticism was the "break between life and literature," of which the result was that few works were written on contemporary themes. Historical themes were preferred. Books concerning the "building of communism" and the "victory of the revolution" suffered from "immature and surface treatment," "blurred message," "lack of positive heroes," and failure to portray social conflict between the old and the new.[104] Escapism was also criticized; in 1954 it was disclosed that about one-half of the Tadzhik prose writers were not doing any creative work.[105] Russian writers in Tadzhikistan (who were grouped in a separate section of the Union of Writers) were also frequently criticized for a lack of creative activity.[106] All these shortcomings were blamed

[103] *Ibid.*, April 26, 1952, p. 2; May 6, 1952, p. 2; M. Riakin and N. Rodionov, "Rukovodstvo mestnymi izdatel'stvami," *Bol'shevik*, no. 15 (1952), 58–64. Any popularization of dervishes was strictly forbidden. A book by a Soviet traveler in Iran (Kolpakov), *Dervishes of Iran*, published by the Institute of Language and Literature of the TFAN, was also condemned in 1947 for "unwittingly popularizing the idealism, mysticism, and backwardness of foreign cultures alien to progressive Soviet people" (*KT*, October 10, 1947, p. 1).

[104] Criticism of this kind was expressed at the Second (November, 1947) and Third (August, 1954) Congresses of the Union of Tadzhik Writers, and at the Seventh Congress of the KPT (December, 1948). *KT*, December 2, 1947, p. 2; April 1, 1947, p. 2; January 25, 1948, p. 3; August 14, 1952, p. 1; and *passim*.

[105] *Ibid.*, August 5, 1954, p. 2; November 28, 1947, p. 1; February 5, 1949, p. 2; August 14, 1952, p. 2; December 28, 1952, p. 2; and *passim*.

[106] *Ibid.*, September 7, 1948, p. 2; and *passim*.

on the Union of Writers and the editorial board of *Sharki Surkh.* Members of both were accused of "mutual backslapping and praise," "suppression of criticism and lack of self-criticism," "poor ideological level," and "playing around with useless polemics, which generated much noise but no remedies." [107]

In the postwar decade some writers and intellectuals were often singled out for criticism. A few among them could be characterized as "nationalists": Khusein Zade, director of the Institute of History, Languages, and Literature of the Tadzhik branch of the Academy of Sciences; his deputy, and later replacement, A. M. Mirzoiev; the literary scholar Mirzo-Zade, connected with the Pedagogical Institute; B. N. Niiazmukhamedov, Vice-President of the Tadzhik Academy of Sciences; and the Minister of Education, Negmatullaev. The first three were authors of literature textbooks that the Party considered unacceptable because of their "false" interpretation of the classics, but were accepted and distributed by the Minister of Education. Niiazmukhamedov was accused of covering up for them, and also of following Marr's theories in linguistics. The writers were each accused of bourgeois nationalism in all of its ramifications. Mirzoev was also violently attacked for "Marrism" in linguistics, Pan-Iranianism, and the wrong attitude toward Jadidism, as was Mirzo-Zade. All were slow to recant, and when they were finally forced into it, their self-criticism was not well received. No one suffered more than verbal criticism, however, for his opinions.[108] It may be that Sadriddin Aini, the President of the Tadzhik Academy of Sciences until his death in 1954, was not unsympathetic to their viewpoint, and his position was strong enough to protect them from stronger reprisals. It is known that there was considerable opposition among the members of the Academy to the appointment of his successor, the mathematician Umarov, called from Uzbekistan.

Among the writers the two most frequently and most violently criticized were Satym Ulug-Zade and Dzhalol Ikrami. Ulug-Zade was forced out of the chairmanship of the Writers' Union in 1946

---

[107] *Ibid.,* October 2, 1946, p. 2; September 14, 1947, p. 2; November 30, 1947, p. 1; January 25, 1948, p. 3; May 18, 1951, p. 2; July 21, 1951, p. 2; August 20, 1954, p. 2; and *passim.*

[108] *Ibid.,* November 26, 1947, p. 1; April 24, 1949, p. 3; June 2, 1951, p. 2; July 21, 1951, p. 2; July 25, 1951, p. 4; November 20, 1951, p. 2; November 23, 1951, pp. 2–3; January 9, 1953, p. 3; January 28, 1953, p. 3; June 9, 1953, p. 2.

for a "poor ideological level," "inactivity," and "poor leadership."
The first two charges were repeated through the 1950's. Described
as "a great writer whose head was turned," with a tendency to fall
into the one-stream attitude, he was criticized for unwillingness
to listen to criticism, and for the exercise of undue influence on the
editors of *Sharki Surkh*. His most severe critic was Tursun-Zade,
who replaced him as chairman of the Writers' Union.[109]

A major stumbling block of Dzhalol Ikrami's career seems to
have been a two-volume novel of collectivization and kolkhoz life,
Shodi, the writing and rewriting of which lasted fifteen years. Delays were due to repeated criticism of "serious political mistakes"
in his interpretation of kolkhoz life. He portrayed the Soviet elements among the peasants as weak and passive, and the anti-Soviet
elements as clever and dynamic. The final acceptable version of the
novel was not produced until 1951. Ikrami was also criticized for
the use of "archaisms" in the language, for "incorrect portrayal"
of the Soviet reality, and for his editorship of *The Adventures of
the Four Dervishes*. As in the case of the social scientists discussed
above, however, the criticism did not seem to have serious consequences.[110]

The three writers repeatedly accused of inactivity were Rakhim
Dzhalil, Dekhoti, and Rakhimi.[111] Rakhimi was also accused of
lyricism and a non-socialist attitude towards women because he referred to them in his lyrics as the "ornament of the house" and
"man's honor," and described them as having "black eyes" and
"long curls." [112]

The most celebrated Tadzhik literary figures were barely
touched by the criticism. Aini was censured only for his evaluation
of the book about dervishes; Tursun-Zade blamed himself for

[109] *KT*, November 26, 1947, p. 1; November 28, 1947, p. 1; October 2, 1946, p. 2;
May 18, 1951, p. 2; July 21, 1951, p. 2; August 19, 1954, p. 2. Ulug-Zade reciprocated
in kind, criticizing Tursun-Zade for "elements of self-advertisement and self-praise"
(*KT*, August 21, 1954, p. 2). Ulug-Zade had been a front-line correspondent in the
war; his wife, Russian-born Klavdia Ulug-Zade, was also a writer and a member
of the Russian section of the Union of Writers.

[110] *KT*, October 2, 1946; August 30, 1946, p. 3; November 28, 1947, p. 1; December
3, 1947, p. 2; May 18, 1951, pp. 2, 3; December 28, 1952, p. 2; February 1, 1953,
p. 4; August 19, 1954, p. 2; and *passim*.

[111] *Ibid.*, October 2, 1946, p. 2; May 18, 1951, p. 3; July 21, 1951, p. 2; December
28, 1952, p. 2; August 19, 1954, p. 2.

[112] *Ibid.*, October 2, 1946, p. 2; July 21, 1951, p. 2.

"lyricism" in 1951 and for lack of vigilance as an editor of *Sharki Surkh;* Mirshakar was criticized in 1947 and 1953 for poor work in the drama section of the Writers' Union; Lakhuti, principal poet of the twenties and thirties, appeared to be politically in decline in the postwar decade (he died in 1957). In 1949 he was criticized for losing the theme of the revolution in misty allegories in his last work, the poem *Peri of Happiness.*[113]

CONCLUDING REMARKS

The massive effort to adapt the traditional modes of cultural expression to the reality of the new Soviet system has been impressive, and has produced some interesting results on the part of the new Tadzhik Soviet intellectuals and artists, especially in the field of literature. In response to continuous efforts, the quality of the Tadzhik cultural output has improved and the quantity has increased in the postwar period. The dominant theme, however, which emerges from a detailed study of a decade of the cultural activity has been the desire to preserve the traditional and Persian classical characteristics in as unadulterated a form as possible. This does not mean that the Soviet content has been wholly rejected; some of its features—especially those touching on the improvement in the economic and social conditions—appear to have been fully absorbed. The rejection has been focused on aspects of the new content that are clearly Russian in origin; it appears to be emotional in nature.

There is an element of doubt about whether the Persian classical heritage is really rightfully a Tadzhik one, as claimed by the Soviet historiographers. Whether or not the claim is true seems of secondary importance, in view of the fact that most of the new Tadzhik intellectuals obviously consider it so, and build on it in an effort to preserve and develop their separate national identity in response to Russian pressure. It has become an integral part in the process of growth of a new national consciousness which is not conducive to the *sblizhenie* (coming closer) or *sliianie* (merger) policies of

---

[113] *Ibid.*, November 28, 1947, p. 1; March 19, 1949, p. 3; December 15, 1953, p. 2; July 21, 1951, p. 2. Lakhuti's last poem was nevertheless praised in the sixties. See *Soviet Literature,* no. 9 (1967), 141.

the Russian leaders. The phenomenon is a new one, as there was no Tadzhik national consciousness before the Revolution. It is the by-product of the nationality policy, and it is espoused not by the traditional elite (which no longer exists), but by the new Soviet-educated intellectual and artistic group.

8

THE IMPACT AND CONCLUSIONS

THE IMPACT OF SOVIET RULE in Tadzhikistan has had far-reaching and irreversible consequences. There, as in other republics of Soviet Central Asia, modernization has been synonymous with sovietization, which, in turn, has been synonymous with Russian rule. The Tadzhik experience was also a part of the general twentieth-century phenomenon, the modernization of backward societies, that emerged as a by-product of European colonial expansion. In the "westernization" process, traditional societies were forced into a transitional stage of development. The whole process can be ascribed to the effects of the impact of modern culture (commonly referred to as "western culture," because of its European promoters) on predominantly non-western societies. Because of the eclectic character of the concept conveyed by the term western culture, some scholars prefer to refer to a "world culture" in discussing the problems of transitional societies.[1]

In general terms, the modernization pattern was unmistakably present. The political conquest by a European people stimulated rapid economic growth and induced social change which disrupted the traditional pattern of a previously stagnant society. The eco-

---

[1] See Lucian W. Pye, *Politics, Personality, and Nation Building: Burma's Search for Identity* (New Haven: Yale University Press, 1962), and other works by the same author. The use of "western culture" as a generic term was criticized by Thomas Hodgkin, in J. Roland Pennock, ed., *Self-Government in Modernizing Nations* (Englewood Cliffs, N.J.: Prentice-Hall, Inc., 1964). In the Tadzhik setting, Russian culture has been referred to as "world culture"; see Gafurov on culture, above (*KT,* February 2, 1946, p. 3).

269

nomic development, geared to supply the needs of the mother
country, was based on a typically colonial pattern of exchange of
raw materials for manufactured goods. The development was accompanied by an influx of bureaucrats, entrepreneurs, professional
people, and technicians from the mother country who acquired
a privileged status. The influx of these people was accompanied by
the introduction of ideas, political patterns, and cultural standards
of the metropolitan country, that were claimed superior to the
standards previously governing traditional society. For local nationals acculturation became a prerequisite for social, economic,
and political advancement, and led, in turn, to the readjustment
of social values and the disruption of the traditional social structure. In substituting cash crops for subsistence agriculture and in
fostering industrialization and urbanization, the economic change
aided in the breakdown of traditional social forms. The introduction of a modern educational system and new occupational opportunities favored the formation of a westernized native elite who
acted as intermediaries between the traditional masses and the
Europeans. Caught between the demands of a traditional and a
modern socialization, the elite were in a state of cultural ambivalence; their ambitions for power were frustrated by the commanding position enjoyed by the Europeans.

The experience of Soviet Central Asia differed from that of
other colonial areas in several important aspects. The "democratic
component" (in the sense of western democratic ideas and parlia-
mentary models), assumed by many to be an integral part of European influence, was lacking. Economic and social changes, which
in the colonies of the western European powers were generally the
result of uncoordinated individual enterprise followed belatedly
by metropolitan political action, were legislated and directed toward specific political goals. Economic and social reforms were
totally subordinated to political requirements, and their results
were appraised by political criteria. The superiority of the Russian
culture to traditional ones was unequivocally stated, and the realization of the benefits of westernization was made contingent on the
uprooting of traditional elements. In Central Asia the reforms
were more sweeping, the new education was more widely available
to the masses, and the influx of European immigrants was over-

whelmingly greater than in any of the western European colonies. The lands which fell to Russian colonial expansion were contiguous to the mother country and, on incorporation, became an integral part of the metropolitan political structure.

In the following pages the impact of Soviet rule in Tadzhikistan will be examined in the light of the needs and desires of the principal actors and as an indicator of future change. The goals which motivated Bolshevik leaders in extending and consolidating their power in the area will be measured by their long-range success or failure. Political, social, and economic transformation that took place in the Tadzhik society will be appraised in the light of benefits (or drawbacks) it had brought to the Tadzhik people and their approval (or rejection) of its major features. The growth of the new Tadzhik elite and their political role will be judged by the success they had in bridging the gap between the old and the new and in articulating their new national aspirations.

THE RUSSIAN GOALS

Initially, the Bolshevik Revolution was extended into Central Asia because the Russian Communist Party wanted to keep the boundaries of the Rusian empire intact. The paramount need to preserve the empire was joined inextricably with the desire to establish a revolutionary beachhead for further expansion. It was vital for the Bolsheviks to retain Central Asia because of immediate as well as long-range considerations and for ideological reasons. The short-range goal was to secure Soviet power in the area; the long-range objective was to extend the revolution, and eventually Soviet political domination, across the borders farther into Asia. In Tadzhikistan the primary objective was to consolidate power locally and to eliminate opposition; the consolidation was to be followed by economic reform and a Soviet-directed social transformation. The Party's final aim was the total integration of the area into the fabric of the Soviet state and society and the formation of a "new Soviet man," identical in perceptions, attitudes, and behavior to any "new man" in Leningrad, the Crimea, Kiev, or Chita.

The long-range vision of a Communist Asia endowed the pursuit of the short-range objective with legitimacy, and justified the means used to achieve it; but in actual application the short-range aim soon acquired a powerful *raison d'être* all its own. Through the years, the maintenance and preservation of Soviet political power ceased to require extraneous justification. This became truer as the long-range goals met with unforeseen obstacles and their realization receded into the future.

From the viewpoint of its immediate objectives in Central Asia the Party has met with unqualified success. In Tadzhikistan, this has meant the establishment of a political system of which the legitimacy is no longer in question. A new elite, whose interests can be satisfied only through the system, replaced the traditional elite, which was physically destroyed during the period of consolidation. In the economic sphere the change brought substantial achievements. The collectivization of agriculture and the construction of an extensive irrigation network permitted intensive cultivation of cotton; industrialization was made possible by harnessing the power potential of mountain streams and exploiting natural resources. Light industry developed; cities grew with the increasing population; the standard of living improved. In the social sphere the mass educational system and mass communication and indoctrination networks served the needs of a new socialization, and mass organizations mobilized the people for social and economic effort. A new system of social services complemented a social stratification in which progress depended on successful adaptation to Soviet requirements. A "national" culture based on the ancient Iranian cultural heritage of the people was developed, but it was designed to further the Soviet goals.

Have the long-range goals been attained equally well? Has the Party succeeded in extending its influence into Asia, and in merging the "new" Tadzhiks into the universal "international proletarian" culture? Here success is less evident and the answer is more difficult to discern.

The early revolutionary hopes for the expansion of Communism into India, Afghanistan, and the Middle East by means of Asian revolutionaries were dashed when it became apparent that even within the old Russian boundaries the Bolsheviks could maintain themselves in Asian areas only by force of arms. Throughout the 1930's the Soviet boundaries remained sealed off from neighboring Asia, cutting off foreign influences, and fencing in the internal upheavals of collectivization and the purges; nevertheless, from its very establishment, the Tadzhik republic was conceived as a model to attract the envy and admiration of peoples across the border and thereby to serve the spread of Communist influence abroad.

The forcible modernization of Soviet Asia began to show results in foreign policy in the fifties and sixties, as progress made compared favorably with the poverty, backwardness, and stagnation of Afghanistan, India, Iran, and other Asian areas. The inauguration of the policy of "peaceful coexistence," and the support for the "movements of national liberation" and even for their "bourgeois-nationalist" leaders, revived the hopes of extension of Soviet political influence and gave them new meaning; Afro-Asian leaders, busy with nation-building, began to eye the Soviet modernization model with new appreciation. The salesmen in the propaganda campaign of lively cultural, economic, and political exchange and aid are the smooth, well-educated, well-indoctrinated members of the new Soviet Asian elites, who bear no resemblance to the fiery revolutionaries of the early twenties; the Tadzhiks are prominent among them. In the 1960's Mirzo Tursun-Zade was President of the Soviet Committee of Solidarity with the Countries of Asia and Africa, and Bobodzhan Gafurov was Director of the Institute of the Peoples of Asia of the USSR Academy of Sciences. Both traveled widely as representatives of the Soviet government.

The effectiveness of this kind of campaign is difficult to assess. Afro-Asian leaders are willing to accept Soviet support and assistance, but are cautious not to compromise their newly won independence. Pragmatic in their policies, they attempt to maintain a maximum maneuverability in the world of the great powers and are not susceptible to ideological pressures. Even the radical leaders of one-party states failed to embrace the Soviet brand of Communism, though they borrowed many of the Soviet techniques of government and party organization and economic management. The increase in contacts has nevertheless resulted in the spread of Soviet political influence in the 1950's and 1960's, especially in the Indian subcontinent and in the Middle East, and through the latter into North and East Africa. Having reached maturity as a great power, the Soviet Union no longer insists that its client states copy the Soviet model *in toto,* but is satisfied to extend its sphere of influence in the traditional manner through aid, diplomacy, and the "show of the flag." The influence, much of it transmitted via the Soviet Asian republics, is less obvious than outright dictation but is nevertheless quite effective. The one undesirable byproduct of the lively exchange between the Soviet Union and the African and Asian countries may be the exposure of Soviet Asians to the victorious nationalism of the ex-colonies, the independence and apparent success of which renders tenuous the Soviet domestic contention that Russian leadership is the prerequisite for progress, modernization, and statehood.

Success in domestic long-range objectives has proved to be elusive despite the effective change in the economic base and the destruction of the traditional social structure. Although the Tadzhiks are happy to accept the material benefits, they have firmly resisted acquiring a new *Weltanschauung*. Their perceptions and behavior are still strongly influenced by traditional criteria and their social and cultural estrangement from the Russians has been accompanied by a new (or renewed) sense of hostility toward other Asian groups; both of these attitudes are highly detrimental to identification with broad "Soviet" interests.

Although a "new Soviet Tadzhik" (or an Uzbek or a Kirgiz) has begun to emerge within the new elites, he differs from the *Homo sovieticus* of Lenin's dream. His loyalty to the All-Union goals is weakened by his sense of separate identity, which also makes him different from his "brothers" in the other parts of the USSR.

THE DIMENSIONS OF CHANGE

Outwardly, the life of an average Tadzhik has undergone a complete transformation. His economic base is different: he may be a member of a kolkhoz, a factory worker, or a minor functionary in the state or cooperative network. If he has succeeded in graduating from a secondary or technical school or a higher educational institution, he will be found in the ranks of the new cultural, professional, and political elite. As a peasant or worker, he has been exposed to the new socialization at school,[2] at work, through the communications media, and as a participant in mass

---

[2] The dropout rate of children in rural schools in the postwar period was very high; many never progressed beyond the fourth grade. This was especially true in the case of native girls, but it also applied to native boys (*KT*, 1945–56, *passim*).

activities or politically approved cultural pursuits. If he is a member of the elite, his indoctrination has been more effective and sophisticated. Because the traditional agents of socialization have been undermined (religious practices are outlawed or discouraged, and the extended family has now become the exception rather than the rule), it would seem that the old value system should have been undermined among the people and abandoned by the elite, whose members have gradually merged with the European immigrants. A great deal of evidence, however, belies this assumption.

With few exceptions, all rural and many urban Tadzhiks live, eat, and dress in traditional styles, and, as much as possible, continue to practice traditional rituals and retain traditional attitudes. Although the material quality of their life has improved, their attitudes change gradually and reluctantly. Women and young people, who are regarded by the Party as its natural allies because of their subordinate position in the traditional society, respond poorly to efforts to place them in the vanguard of change.

By all accounts most Tadzhik rural housing still consists of adobe dwellings with flat roofs turning blind walls to the streets; the houses are divided into family compounds (whenever married sons are included) and still, in many cases, into male and female quarters. Women's quarters are screened from strangers' eyes.[3] European housing exists in urban and industrial areas, but it is occupied by Europeans and the new elite.[4] Even Stalinabad, according to a 1950 official description, still had its European and native

---

[3] *Ibid., passim;* Ul'dzhabaev, *Otchetnyi doklad XI s'ezdu,* 43–44; Pil'nyak, *Tadzhikistan, passim;* N. A. Kisliakov, *Sledy Pervobytnogo Kommunizma u Gornykh Tadzhikov Vakhio-Bolo* (Akademia Nauk SSSR, Institut Antropologii Etnografii i Arkheologii, Moscow: Akademii Nauk SSSR, 1936), X, Etnograficheskaia Seriia no. 2, *passim;* Kisliakov, "Sem'ia i brak u Tadzhikov," *Akademiia Nauk SSSR Institut Etnografii im. N. N. Miklukho—Maklaia, Kratkie Soobshcheniia,* no. 17 (1952), 74–80; Kisliakov, *Kul'tura i byt,* Chap. III. The last-mentioned study is based on the research done in one of the most advanced and modernized Tadzhik kolkhozes in the Leninabad oblast, and reflects a degree of change that is rather unusual in Tadzhikistan. Because of the bias of the author and the setting, it is reasonable to assume that life in other kolkhozes, especially in the mountains, was much more traditional. According to this study there were still many families of 8 to 10 people in the kolkhoz investigated, even though there was a general trend toward the breakup of large families *(ibid.,* pp. 163–65). See also Tolstov *et al., Narody Srednei Azii/I,* pp. 580–98.

[4] Gafurov, "V. I. Lenin i pobeda," p. 89; KPSS, *Tadzhikskaia SSR,* pp. 17–18; Salisbury, *American in Russia,* p. 211; *KT,* July 28, 1946, p. 3; December 20, 1948, p. 2; January 17, 1951, p. 3; and *passim.*

quarters.[5] Food and dress habits have also remained highly traditional among the peasants, though an improvement has been noted
in the nutritional value of foods (especially for children) and in
health habits.[6] As far as possible, despite official restrictions and
requirements, Tadzhik peasants follow traditional life cycle rituals,
particularly in funeral practices. Marriage customs have been substantially circumscribed by legal prohibitions; the rituals of preg-
nancy and confinement have been adapted and changed in response to the improvement in health habits and services.[7] In 1955,
however. Gafurov was still complaining that "harmful customary
practices in family and daily life" were "preserved and eulogized."[8]

Traditionalism also influenced agricultural methods, and made
peasants resent the introduction of new cultivation techniques.
Peasants, as well as some local Party and soviet officials, continued
to use the traditional hoe in cotton cultivation, and wooden plows
and bullocks for plowing and threshing in the mountains.[9] The
Moslem religious sanction against pork made pig breeding in
Tadzhikistan an almost exclusively Russian pursuit.[10] Among
other manifestations of feudal-bai attitudes were the apparently
widespread practices of stealing kolkhoz property (mostly sheep),
shirking kolkhoz work, and committing "other violations of kolkhoz statutes."[11] These were deplored on economic as well as at-
titudinal grounds.

Conservative traditions still abounded in kolkhoz family life,
according to the press and the testimony of Soviet ethnographers.
Kisliakov's study strongly emphasized the changes that had been
wrought in the traditional family structure, but admitted the continuation of old patterns:

[5] Chumichev, *Stalinabad,* pp. 35, 39–40, 42. Chumichev's description of Stalinabad
was criticized strongly in a review for indulging in "cheap exoticism" (*KT,* January
17, 1951, p. 3).

[6] Kisliakov, *Kul'tura i byt,* Chap. III; Tolstov *et al., Narody Srednei Azii/I,*
pp. 599–612; S. P. Rusiaikina, "Narodnaia odezhda Tadzhikov Garmskoi oblasti,"
*Akademiia Nauk SSSR, Institut Etnografii im. N. N. Miklukho-Maklaia, Kratkie
Soobshcheniia,* no. 20 (1954), 87–98.

[7] Kisliakov, *Kul'tura i byt,* pp. 190–93; Tolstov *et al., Narody Srednei Azii/I,*
pp. 612–24.

[8] Gafurov, "V. I. Lenin i pobeda," p. 88.

[9] Gafurov, *Kadry,* p. 72.

[10] *Ibid.,* p. 70.

[11] *KT,* June 23, 1948, p. 2; May 28, 1947, p. 3; and *passim;* Ul'dzhabaev, *Otchetnyi
doklad XI s'ezdu,* pp. 66–67.

Family relations still preserve some survivals of old traditions and attitudes. The bearers of those survivals are, primarily, members of the older generation who, because of their age, barely participate, or do not participate at all, in the general life of the kolkhoz, and thus are isolated from the influences which change the outlook of kolkhoz members. . . .

Feudal-bai survivals in the attitudes of some of the men, particularly the elders and heads of families who are used to regarding members of their families as inferiors, manifest themselves especially in attitudes toward women. Young men, especially those at school, have greater opportunities to emancipate themselves from the despotism of their elders, but the situation of girls and women is still difficult.[12]

Evidence relating to mountain Tadzhiks confirmed the survival of their traditional attitudes toward women, including the still extant but rapidly disappearing custom of the payment of a bride price (*kalym*).[13] One source relates that among the peasants the kalym has been replaced by the custom of the groom giving the bride substantial gifts.[14] The Tadzhik press repeatedly confirmed the existence of feudal-bai survivals in popular attitudes toward women. Complaints of the wearing of the face veil (*parandzha*), polygamy, early marriages, and wife beatings were heard often.[15] There was a virtual absence of native girls in secondary and higher education.[16] A token representation of women was found in leading Party and government positions, but their numbers were in fact minimal.[17] According to Gafurov, women who were placed in

---

[12] Kisliakov, *Kul'tura i byt*, p. 162. See also Tolstov *et al.*, *Narody Srednei Azii/I*, pp. 612–30. Tolstov agrees with Kisliakov that old customs are preserved by the older generation, and also by "some backward men," p. 613.

[13] Kisliakov, "Sem'ia i brak," pp. 74 and 79–80; Kisliakov, *Sledy Pervobytnogo Kommunizma, passim*.

[14] Tolstov *et al.*, *Narody Srednei Azii/I*, p. 616.

[15] *KT*, March 25, 1947, p. 2; January 24, 1948, p. 3; August 10, 1951, p. 2; August 12, 1951, p. 2; February 23, 1954, p. 2; and *passim;* "O rabote partiinykh organizatsii sredi zhenshchin," *Bol'shevik*, no. 1 (1951), 9–17.

[16] *KT*, December 24, 1948, p. 2; July 31, 1949, p. 2; February 10, 1951, p. 3; March 31, 1953, p. 1; March 7, 1954, p. 2; July 5, 1955, p. 3; and *passim*. Negmatullaev, the Minister of Education, disclosed at a republican conference of educators in 1953 that although in the fourth grade of primary school native girls constituted 45 per cent of all native students, in the last two grades (eighth through tenth) they made up only 19 per cent, and the number of native girls who actually graduated from the tenth grade was very small (*ibid.*, August 26, 1953, p. 2).

[17] *Ibid.*, June 28, 1947, p. 2; August 10, 1951, p. 2; February 23, 1954, p. 2; October 1, 1955, p. 1; and *passim*. See also Chap. 4 (Table 4-1) and Chap. 5.

278 IMPACT AND CONCLUSIONS

executive positions at the insistence of higher Party authorities were often subsequently quietly removed under various pretexts.[18]

Tadzhik and Uzbek members of the political elite were reported to be as guilty of feudal-bai attitudes toward women as were uneducated peasants. Cases of polygamy, child brides, wife beating, and parandzha-wearing were frequently cited in criticisms of individual Party leaders in territorial administrations and even in the central apparatus.[19] Even Stalinabad was not free of cases of this kind, but there they took "a more cultured" form; young wives who were Komsomol and Party members were not made to wear parandzha but were locked at home by their husbands. In the words of a woman Party official reporting the misdeeds: "If the leading officials keep their wives at home . . . how can we expect to achieve good results in the struggle with feudal-bai survivals!" [20] The traditional psychological conditioning of women was probably the most serious obstacle to their emancipation.[21]

The preservation of old customs is intimately connected with the survival of Islam; there have been numerous indications that the Tadzhiks have continued to practice their religion. The Party's attitude toward Islam has been hostile from the outset, and Moslem practices were proscribed, though in World War II the general relaxation of religious policy led to the reopening of a few mosques. But in practical application the regime's antireligious stand has been ambiguous, because local leaders, many of whom undoubtedly are secret believers, have apparently tolerated a whole range of religious "survivals." Antireligious propaganda is intensified, and most flagrant religious manifestations are prosecuted in the periods when the leaders in Moscow decide to step up atheistic propaganda in their concern for the ideological upbringing of the people. One such period was the mid-1950's and another began in the 1960's.

Western sources indicate that strong undercover religious ac-

[18] Gafurov, "O proverke ispolneiia," p. 69.
[19] See Chap. 5; also *KT*, March 4, 1947, p. 5; February 23, 1954, p. 2; April 20, 1947, p. 2; January 24, 1948, p. 3; and *passim*.
[20] The critic was Saidova, a secretary of Tsentral'nyi raikom in Stalinabad city. Individuals criticized by her included the Minister of Light Industry, Alimardanov, and the Minister of Communal Economy, Iusupov (*KT*, December 26, 1948, p. 2).
[21] Tolstov *et al., Narody Srednei Azii/I,* p. 613.

tivity exists in Tadzhikistan. Walter Kolarz reports that in the postwar period there was virtually no kishlak in Tadzhikistan without a secret mosque, and that itinerant mullahs (to be distinguished from the official mullahs whose activities were strictly controlled by the regime) ministered to the believers in their homes and in the market places.[22] Most embarrassing to the regime and economically most troublesome was the observance of the two great Moslem fasts (Ramadan and Kurban Bayrami), which interferred with economic activity and resulted in the wholesale slaughter of sheep, mostly stolen kolkhoz property. Pre-Islamic beliefs such as the worship of holy stones and graves (*mazars*) and the practice of magic were also widespread.[23] Remnants of fire worship were preserved in the mountains, as was the Ismailite collection of gold for the Aga Khan.[24] In 1931 a traveler described a traditional "house of fire" (*alon khona*) in the Pamirs, still used as the village meeting place.[25] An authoritative study on the Tadzhiks published in 1962 confirmed the existence of survivals of religious worship of both Islamic and pre-Islamic character including the belief in spirits, magic, amulets, and the purifying and holy qualities of fire, the veneration of mazars, and the continuation of spring celebrations welcoming the awakening of nature (the ancient Iranian *Navruz*, the New Year), now combined with the festivities of the May workers' day; other celebrations were adapted to harvest feasts.[26]

The Tadzhik press did not mention religious survivals until 1954, though the frequently criticized feudal-bai survivals included practices of religious character. An intensive antireligious campaign began in 1954; an official call was made for an increase

[22] Kolarz, *Religion*, pp. 437–38; see also Richard Pipes, "Muslims of Soviet Central Asia: Trends and Prospects," *The Middle East Journal*, no. 2 (Spring, 1955), 147–62, and no. 3 (Summer, 1955), 295–308.

[23] Kolarz, *Religion*, pp. 432–38; Briskin, *Strana Tadzhikov*, p. 18; Kisliakov, *Sledy Pervobytnogo Kommunizma*, p. 39; *KT, passim*.

[24] Kolarz, *Religion*, pp. 311, 377–78; Briskin, *Strana Tadzhikov* pp. 19, 23; Pil'nyak, *Tadzhikistan*, pp. 69–70; Kisliakov, *Sledy Pervobytnogo Kommunizma*, pp. 115–17.

[25] Kisch, *Changing Asia*, p. 177. His evidence is supported by other sources, such as Kisliakov, *Sledy Pervobytnogo Kommunizma*, pp. 116–99, and Ginzburg, *Gornye Tadzhiki, passim*. Alon khona was a room in a mosque where a fire was always burning. The room was used as the center of kishlak's social activities (for males exclusively).

[26] Tolstov *et al., Narody Srednei Azii/I*, pp. 626–30.

in broad "scientific-atheistic propaganda" against the "particularly tenacious and harmful" religious survivals in the republic:

> Servants of religious cults are trying to stupefy the people with religion, and *their special attention is turned on women and youth.* Religious survivals show in the observation of religious holidays and religious ceremonies by the backward people, in pilgrimages to the so-called sacred places . . . in drinking and stock slaughter. . . .[27]

Concern over the tenacity of Islam, and particularly over the susceptibility and participation of young people, was expressed in the press in the 1950's and 1960's.[28] In 1963 a Moscow *Izvestiia* regaled its readers with the story of a kolkhoz rest farm in Tadzhikistan which had been converted into a religious center opened only to believers; its existence was being shielded, it was intimated, by the Fourth Secretary of the Central Committee of the KPT.[29]

The local adherence to traditional ways resulted in a broad cultural gap between the Asians and the immigrant Russians and other Europeans. Their social and cultural activities were generally separate. There were few mixed marriages; of these an overwhelming majority consisted of couples in which a Tadzhik man had married a Russian girl, generally during the war. Tadzhik women were usually not allowed to marry Russian men, and only few instances of such marriages are known.[30] Kisliakov's eth-

---

[27] Reference to drinking is interesting, because Islam forbids consumption of alcoholic beverages. Can this be one manifestation of success in imitation of Russian habits? *KT,* August 26, 1954, p. 1. Italics mine.

[28] *Ibid.,* August 18, 1954, p. 2; August 10, 1954, p. 3; December 26, 1963, p. 4; April 15, 1964, p. 1; and *passim.*

[29] Feuilleton, "Assignment to Paradise," *Izvestiia,* September 26, 1963, quoted in *Current Digest,* XV, no. 39, 30–31. There was a follow-up article to the story in *Izvestiia,* January 23, 1964, quoted in *Current Digest,* XVI, no. 4, 34. The secretary in question, Nizoramo Zaripova, a Tadzhik, was then the highest ranking woman in the KPT. She was a graduate of the Higher Party School in Moscow and, since 1945, had been the head of the Department for Work with Women, first in the Komsomol obkom and later in the Kulyab obkom and the Central Committee (see Chap. 4). Zaripova was not re-elected as the Central Committee Secretary at the Sixteenth Congress of the KPT in 1966 (*Pravda,* March 9, 1966, p. 2).

[30] "Mixed Marriages in Central Asia and Kazakhstan," *Central Asian Review,* XI, no. 1 (1963), 5–12. This article is a summary of S. M. Abramzon, "Otrazhenie protsessa sblizheniia natsii na semeinobytovom uklade narodov Srednei Azii i Kazakhstana," in *Sovetskaia Etnografiia,* no. 3, 1962. Calculations based on divorce announcements collected from *Kommunist Tadzhikistana* in the ten-year period yield the following proportions among couples obtaining divorce: both partners Russian— 66 per cent; both partners local—26 per cent; local men and Russian women— 7 per cent; Russian men and local women—1 per cent (*KT,* 1946–55, *passim*).

nographic study, quoted above, flatly stated that marriages between Tadzhik girls and Russian men were unknown in the area investigated.[31]

Local attitudes toward Tadzhik veterans returning home from the wars with Russian brides are well illustrated by a poem by Mirzo Tursun-Zade. A mother of a war hero awaits him with a local bride selected in the traditional way. When the son tells her that he is engaged to a Russian girl, the mother's reaction is violent hostility:

> You made me feel bitter.
> And what am I to tell the girl?
> What reasons shall I seek?
> Everybody will reproach me . . .
> They'll laugh at me, and they'll abuse me.
> How can I survive such shame?
> If this is your decision
> Then take care of your own wedding,
> And meet your Russian wife yourself,
> That woman from Moscow![32]

When the son explains that the Russian girl saved his life in the war, the mother is mollified and consents to welcome her. The poem reveals the existence of strong social pressures against mixed marriages. The mother's primary concern is the censure of her community.

The evidence presented above leads to the conclusion that while political and economic conditions have radically changed since the revolution, Soviet political socialization in Tadzhikistan has yet to bear fruit. The nature of the available evidence prevents a meaningful comparison with other developing societies from being made, but it can be seen that cultural resistance to the Soviet type of modernization has been exceptionally strong. The preservation of the old norms is surprising because there has been no remaining traditional elite to enforce them, and traditional attitudes have

---

[31] Kisliakov, *Kul'tura i byt*, p. 174. The author also reports that it was unusual for a Tadzhik man to marry an Uzbek or a Kirgiz woman because they were considered inferior; Tatar women were preferred because of their higher cultural level.

[32] *KT*, September 30, 1945, p. 3.

been strongly discouraged by the government. One could speculate on the continuous existence of a "shadow elite" of people who enjoy prestige and power in the community by virtue of traditional criteria, and whose activities have been carefully concealed from the authorities. According to a study published by a wartime deportee, this kind of elite existed in the sister republic of Turkmenia.[33] A similar situation in French West Africa was dealt with by the people through the institution of "straw chiefs." These were the men selected by the community to deal with the French authorities in the enforcement of unpopular demands such as tax collection or labor duty. The real chiefs continued their traditional activities in secret, unknown to the colonial authorities.[34]

Evidence in the available sources is not sufficient to prove the existence of a "shadow elite" in Tadzhikistan, but there are strong indications that there was one in the 1945–55 period. Illegal mullahs undoubtedly existed. Elders, especially heads of large families, enjoyed great prestige among the rural population and, on the evidence of Soviet ethnographers, served as the custodians of traditional norms. Strong social pressures were generated in kishlaks and kolkhozes in support of the "old ways." It is significant that although the urbanization rate in Tadzhikistan has been very high, it has affected the native population to only a limited degree.

Two significant factors undoubtedly contribute to the resistance to change that exists among the Tadzhiks. One is the strength of Islam not only as a religion but also as a way of life. Another is the fact that the old way of life was forcibly attacked from outside, instead of having been left to disintegrate spontaneously under the impact of new forces in its midst, as happened in many other developing societies. An embattled belief, Islam in Tadzhikistan actually draws part of its strength from the assault, as it defends itself on two fronts, the political and the religious. It resists the imposition of Russian hegemony, and rejects Communism as a militant secular creed. The lines of the conflict are drawn between the Moslem and the Communist communities. The religion is also reinforced by ethnic divisions and a modern-traditional clash,

---

[33] Jan Dubicki, *Elements of Disloyalty, passim.*
[34] Robert Delavignette, *Freedom and Authority in French West Africa* (New York: Oxford University Press, 1950), *passim.*

because most Moslems are also Asian traditionalists, while most Communists are also modernizers and many are European. Members of the modern Tadzhik elite hover uneasily on the borderline; outwardly they belong to the modernizers, but many are still believers and traditionalists at heart.

Most rural Tadzhiks still conceive of themselves largely in local and religious terms; they have not acquired the sense of a new Tadzhik national identity or of a participation in the building of a Soviet society. Gafurov admitted in 1947 that popular attitudes still reflected the national fragmentation of pre-Soviet times and lacked a general sense of national unity.[35] Although it is a drawback to participation in the new system, this lack also provides a safeguard against the growth of a modern nationalism which might convert the peasants' resentment of Russian domination into a conscious national resistance. Most peasants do not share the sense of identity with the new elite and tend to blame them, along with the Russians, for unpopular innovations.

The gap between the modern elite and the masses which is typical of a transitional society exists also in Tadzhikistan, but the roots of the Tadzhik elite are firmly planted in popular traditions, and the dividing line between them and the masses is becoming blurred as the expanding school system produces more graduates capable of pursuing new careers, and as members of the elite continue to maintain close cultural ties to the local community.[36] The outstanding characteristics of the new elite have been its high degree of mobility and its dynamic character, reflecting the changing needs of the system. In the political sphere particularly, these needs have changed frequently. Political loyalty to the Party has remained a constant criterion, but other prerequisites have varied. In the 1930's and 1940's a "poor peasant" background was required and, it seems, political sophistication was discouraged; in the late 1940's and 1950's training in political work and formal education

[35] Gafurov, *Nekotorye voprosy*, p. 17.
[36] The term political elite is used here within the definition established in Chap. 5. Most educated Tadzhiks in social, cultural, and economic life were included in it because most were also state functionaries. The degree of acculturation of the elite varied widely as its members included local functionaries, closely identified with their environment, and such westernized members of the central leadership as Gafurov, Rasulov, and Narzikulov.

became important. In the late 1950's a new emphasis was placed on specialized technical training and better educational qualifications. As a result, the turnover in high political positions has been extensive.

The masses do not share in political activity beyond the point of "passive participation." Members of the elite, on the other hand, have been drawn into the Party and government apparatus to fill the new political roles under the watchful eyes of the Russians, for whom they serve as the necessary intermediaries with the population at large. Trained in the new political and managerial skills and allowed a share in the exercise of political power, they have been exposed to new concepts and responsibilities. In the process they have acquired a stake in the preservation of the system, and have developed new values and criteria which serve as a means of identification with it. Active participation in Soviet life notwithstanding, they still respond to traditional stimuli, with the resulting ambivalence of attitudes and behavior. In public life and in their political aspirations they tend to conform to the new Soviet norms; in their social and personal lives, however, the old norms still provide valid criteria. The cultural gap which is pronounced between the Russians and the Tadzhik peasants also exists between Russians and the elite, but it is less wide.

The new elite recognizes the value of education and economic progress. In this respect the needs of a transitional society coincide with the requirements of sovietization. Education has an intrinsic value for the elite as the means of advancement; economic development, on the other hand, builds the power base and the new technology and improves material standards. Education and economic development are objectively desirable because they furnish a means for the members of the elite to elevate themselves and their people from a backward status to a position of equality with the Europeans, and to improve their standing among other Asians in the Soviet Union and abroad. The rivalry to achieve improved standing is particularly fierce between Tadzhiks and Uzbeks, whom the Russians treat as a more advanced nationality. Economic and educational progress gives the Tadzhiks a much needed sense of achievement when they are dealing with the still "backward" Afghans or Iranians. This sense of achievement incidentally serves to reinforce commitment to the system which has made the progress possible.

As the educational requirements for the admission to the political elite increased, so did the exposure of the candidates to Russification, and their degree of acculturation. The difference is obvious when one compares the Tadzhik leaders of the thirties and forties with those of the fifties and sixties. The latter have been trained to master the Russian language and to be familiar with Russian culture and Marxist-Leninist philosophy.[37] The final distinction is conferred on a man when he goes to a higher educational institution in Moscow or Leningrad, because there he can take advantage of the best facilities available to Russians. The price of acculturation is usually alienation from the traditional community, but the benefits gained include the opportunity to ascend within the new social and political hierarchy on terms which, by training and achievement, should give an Asian equality with a European.

The process of acculturation in Tadzhikistan and in other republics of Soviet Central Asia is comparable to that the new elites in Asia and Africa had undergone under western colonial rule. As demonstrated by the Afro-Asian leaders of the new states, there is a point in the acculturation process when a basis for equality is sought in the indigenous cultural heritage, and negative reaction develops toward "superior" western cultural norms. Cultural self-assertion is another new value acquired by the Tadzhik elite as a by-product of educational advancement and the emphasis placed by the nationality policy on the development of "national forms." In Tadzhikistan this meant the modernization and daily use of the classical Farsi, the revival and adaptation of the great Samanid literature, the development of the Tadzhik "Soviet" literature, and intensive research into Tadzhik history. All of these maintain the image of the Tadzhiks as a culturally and politically advanced nation, an image which clashes with the daily reality of cultural and political hegemony of the ubiquitous Russians.

[37] Information in *Kommunist Tadzhikistana* indicated that the language of instruction in all higher educational institutions in Tadzhikistan and in most technical schools was Russian; a Russian-language examination was necessary for graduation from secondary school and admission to higher schools. Teachers in institutions of higher learning were mostly Russian (*KT*, 1945–54, *passim*). See also Chap. 7.

The cultural revival was designed to serve the purposes of the sovietization policy by disseminating new ideas in culturally acceptable guise; its by-products, however, disturb the central leadership of the Party. It has given the Tadzhik elite the means of national identification they previously lacked; it has awakened the desire to cultivate old traditions (in this case those inseparably connected with Islam) for their political value, as a basis for autonomy and as a means of appeal to the people; and it has strengthened the antagonism toward the Russians. The preoccupation of the Tadzhik elite with their newly discovered cultural heritage for something more than its sovietization value has been the target of official criticism as a manifestation of bourgeois nationalist tendencies. It has affected political as well as cultural figures accused of idealizing the "feudal past" and lacking appreciation of Russian assistance, influence, and leadership.[38] In effect, the new culture has not been able to absorb the socialist content as expected, but instead has become laden with potentially dangerous nationalistic ideas.

Acquisition of the necessary modern skills and education, training received in high positions in the administrative and political hierarchy, and cultural self-assertion inevitably lead to the ultimate demand to control one's own political destiny, the demand which, in Soviet Asia, would clash directly with the Russian leading role. As the economy improves and educated Asians participate in increasing numbers in the political process and in the social and economic functions of a modernizing society, the standard colonial argument of backwardness and the need for Russian assistance, appears less convincing.

In Tadzhikistan job market pratices do not meet the expectations of the new elite, and the Tadzhik drive for self-assertion in the political and cultural spheres is hindered by the physical presence and cultural ascendancy of the Russians. In the power structure, they assume the controlling roles within the political hierarchy; in social and economic life all positions are formally open to qualified Asians, but in practice most are pre-empted by Europeans. There is a shortage of Asians with professional skills in Ta-

[38] Gafurov, "V. I. Lenin i pobeda," p. 88. See Chap. 7.

dzhikistan but evidence exists that in recruitment to professional, technical, and administrative positions preference is shown to Europeans. Except in positions which have to be filled under the "representative aspect" of the ethnic pattern, the same is true in the political administration. This is illustrated by the predominantly European composition of administrative-clerical staffs of Party and government agencies, and especially of the republican ministries. The Russian attitude that Tadzhiks are backward is understandably a source of continuous irritation to the Tadzhiks; the continuous emphasis in the cultural sphere on the superiority of Russian models adds to their frustration.

Under the facade of druzhba narodov, tensions multiply and restiveness grows. There are among members of the current educated Tadzhik elite many who once had attained a high position but were subsequently demoted or arbitrarily removed; some of them are the most articulate and enterprising people of the new Tadzhikistan. Others, some of them in high positions, face daily frustrations inherent in the conflict between their expectations and their actual roles. In addition, the forthcoming cadres of educated Asians graduating year after year from secondary and technical schools and higher educational institutions in small but increasing numbers [39] will be confronted with *de facto* discrimination in the labor market. Many of the new graduates do not want to return to rural areas as technicians and administrators despite official encouragement to do so.[40] Facing the competition with Europeans in urban employment,[41] they are joined in pursuit of jobs by school

[39] In the 1955–56 school year, the percentage of Tadzhiks and Uzbeks in the republic's technical schools was reported to have been 59 per cent of the total, and in the higher educational institutions, 61.5 per cent of the total (*TSSR. Nar. Khoz. 1957*, pp. 312–13 and 309–10). The proportions may be somewhat misleading, because other figures found in the press indicated that the shortage of local students in higher educational establishments was considered a major problem (*KT*, 1945–46, *passim*).

[40] The press frequently complained that graduates of higher educational institutions and other schools did not want to leave urban areas to "discharge their debt to the people." They were referred to as "lily-white hands with diplomas" (*beloruchki z diplomami*) (*KT*, August 15, 1948, p. 3). In the 1950's there was a determined campaign to force employees of inflated administrative staffs back "into production" (*ibid., passim*).

[41] In 1961 First Secretary Rasulov complained of the "timidity" in promoting young specialists in the system of economic councils (*ibid.*, September 23, 1961, p. 4).

drop-outs who also do not want to return to kolkhozes.[42] The problem of school drop-outs for whom there is no work at their level of expectation, and the problem of migration into the cities of unskilled peasants (many of whom are unemployable), is a familiar one in transitional societies and carries with it the seeds of political unrest. While the economy develops rapidly in Soviet Tadzhikistan and trained manpower is speedily absorbed, there appears to be growing difficulty in the placement of Asians, especially in the placement of unskilled Asian labor. In the light of the above it appears questionable whether the Party's effort to promote education of rural masses beyond the primary level is as sincere as is publicly proclaimed. Economically it is a good policy to maintain sufficient manpower in the kolkhozes for cotton cultivation. Politically, low educational standards are a safeguard against the nationalist disease. While the survival of the traditional society stands in the way of the building of Communism, it is far less dangerous to the future of Soviet society in Tadzhikistan than would be the development of modern nationalism.

Summary and Conclusions

The picture of Soviet Tadzhikistan that emerges from this investigation does not justify the official claim that the Soviet Union is a federation of equal nationalities with equal rights, opportunities, and privileges; at any rate, the claim is not true in Tadzhikistan. An examination of the political, social, and economic structure of Tadzhik society reveals the existence of a bias against Asians in their own national areas. Definite patterns of Russian ascendancy in the power structure and of European social and economic privilege in the society at large emerge clearly. The first is

---

Similar complaints, also in the preceding period, including criticism of the failure to promote local cadres, had also appeared in the press (*ibid.*, 1945–56, *passim*). See also Chap. 5.

[42] The high dropout rate was considered a major problem in Tadzhik education (*ibid.*, September 1, 1948, p. 2; August 24, 1951, p. 2; August 20, 1954, p. 2; August 18, 1955, p. 3; and *passim*). As related by a deputy minister of education, the high dropout rate in secondary schools was the result of young Asians' failure to learn Russian well enough to pass the obligatory written Russian-language examinations in Russian literature, which was a prerequisite for being admitted to matriculation examinations in other subjects (after completion of the tenth grade) (*ibid.*, October 13, 1948, p. 3).

a matter of policy reflecting Moscow's requirements of political control and the second is the result in part of objective conditions and in part of prevalent attitudes. The gap between the Asian and European communities is reflected in their cultural alienation and is bridged only in part by the emergent native elite. The privileged position enjoyed by the Russians is reinforced by the widespread impact of Russian cultural pressures. Westernization of an eastern culture is inherent in the process of modernization; under the Soviet domination this process promotes Russification in an exceptionally heavy-handed manner.

A certain ambivalence can be seen in the attitudes of the leadership of the CPSU. On one hand, there seems to be a genuine desire to develop the Asian borderlands and to raise the local people from their economically and culturally backward status; on the other, there is a reluctance toward pursuing this goal to its logical conclusion, that is, following economic with political emancipation. The latter is not considered possible because socialization has failed in one vital respect: it has not succeeded in transforming the Tadzhiks into model Soviet men—i.e. it has not made them into good Russians. Consequently, any transfer of power from Russian to Tadzhik hands, even within the Party structure, would mean a loss of effective control from Moscow, because locally determined criteria would take precedence over All-Union ones as guidelines in local decision-making.

What success has socialization had in establishing the legitimacy of the Soviet political system and in winning popular support for Soviet goals? There is more than one answer to this query. For the masses, the system has acquired legitimacy by default, as all the alternatives to it have been eliminated. The people do not identify with the system, but they have accepted it and have adapted to it; they support projects that benefit them, and passively resist those that impose on their well-being or elude their comprehension. The members of the Tadzhik political elite identify with the system; they view the Party and government hierarchies as instruments of rule and attempt to maximize their roles within that power structure. They identify strongly with policies that promote local progress and enhance their status in relations with the central government and other republics, and resent and sabotage policies that

subordinate their interests to regional or All-Union goals. There is
no evidence, however, that they have adopted the underlying philosophical premises of Marxism-Leninism or recognized an inherent
Russian superiority. The acceptance of the legitimacy of the system has not *ipso facto* legitimized the Russians' claim to the leading role within it. Herein lies the major problem and the potential threat to political stability in the area.

It is not the survival of the old ways, vexing as they may be,
which generates a potential danger to the stability of Russian rule
in Tadzhikistan, but the new pressures awakened by the process of
sovietization and the formation of a local leadership group. Find-
ing a new sense of national identity in their rediscovered Iranian
heritage, the Tadzhiks have absorbed the values required for successful participation in the Soviet system and press for recognition
within it on equal terms with the Russians.

Although they have been absorbed into the system under an
ingenious and effective representative-control pattern, given a
share of the responsibilities and the spoils, and assured of a formal
leading role in "their" republic, the Tadzhiks have nevertheless
been denied the right to conrol their destinies and thus they suffer
the frustrations inherent in a built-in system of ethnic discrimination. The resulting pressures have been, so far, well absorbed, but
the tensions are clearly manifested in the constant pressure for
greater autonomy. The succession of scandals involving the Tadzhik leaders who attempt to circumvent Moscow's central controls,
and the ethnic hatreds, rivalries, and jealousies in local, regional,
and All-Union administration illustrate these pressures.

The postwar climate has been favorable to the recognition of
autonomous national claims within the world Communist system.
The Tadzhiks and other Soviet Asians have witnessed the growth
of "national Communism" and the succesful assertion of the right
of each country in the Soviet bloc to travel "its own road to socialism." Under the pressure of polycentrism the CPSU has lost its
position as the undisputed master of all Communist destinies, and
has barely been able to maintain its status as *primus inter pares*. In
the international arena Soviet Asians have seen the breakup of
western European colonial empires and the formation of independent Asian and African states, the leaders of which have suc-

cessfully defied European mastery and tutelage. Prominent in their representative role in Soviet delegations to Afro-Asian meetings, they have also been exposed to the Chinese challenge to Russia's status in Asia and their rejection of Russia's leading role there because of the Russians' white skin and their "imperialism."

In this study, however, no evidence suggests that a revolutionary potential exists in Tadzhikistan; instead, there is a mounting pressure for greater recognition of local requirements and more accommodation of local interests and local leaders within the power structure, and for cultural autonomy. This is not to say that centrifugal tendencies could not develop if there was a weakening of Russian political control. In Asia and Africa, violent nationalism has often been produced in only a decade, under conditions far less favorable to the formation of new states than those already in existence in Soviet Central Asia. In many ways, Soviet Asians are far more ready for a venture into independence than Afro-Asian leaders have been. Their economy is well advanced on the path of modernization; they have their own state structure and national ethos, a system of mass education, and an elite with actual experience in modern government. Should any such venture ever occur, it will probably be implemented through an adaptation of the existing political system, rather than through a return to older forms of government or an experiment in a more democratic solution. Neither their cultural heritage nor their Soviet training has made the Soviet Asians receptive to solutions other than authoritarian ones in politics.

The nationalist potential, the existence of which is undoubtedly recognized by the central Soviet leadership, is one of the reasons why the Russians cannot afford to relax the present system of political control, and why they appear to be pressing for greater integration of the border regions into the All-Union body politic. One long-range solution of the nascent national problem might be a gradual evolution of the Soviet Union toward a genuine federal relationship; the advantages of membership in it, combined with real autonomy, might prevent the emergence of disruptive nationalism in Soviet Asia. An alternative solution is that which had been used in the 1930's—suppression and destruction of the native elites, when and if they become too nationalistic, accompanied by a still greater influx of and open takeover by the Russians. This could be supplemented by the abandonment of "national forms" in favor of a unitary state and culture. Nikita Khrushchev had taken a hesitant step in the latter direction in the early 1960's.[43] The risks entailed in suppression and forcible unification would probably outweigh the advantages; moreover, it would deprive the Soviet leadership of its great asset in dealing with the Third World —their Asian republics.

The solution favored by the Party appears to be the continuation of the present political pattern, inclusive of a high rate of Slavic immigration and the intense promotion of "Soviet content." The policy is believed to lead to an eventual merger, still the ultimate goal of the leadership even though its fulfillment had to be postponed in the mid-1960's to an indefinite future date because of the pressures from the republics.[44] If the laws of dialectics are correct, the policy should result in the formation of a new Soviet nation, which would not be a sum of the component nationalities but a qualitatively new entity. The process is predicated on the full development by each Soviet nationality of its national characteristics on a common Soviet base (the stage at which union and autonomous republics are said to currently find themselves), to be subsequently transformed through a dialectical leap into a common whole, the new synthesis. Particular characteristics of the old component nationalities would then recede to the level of folklore.

As emphasized by evidence brought to bear in this analysis, however, philosophical premises frequently fail to develop in actual conditions, and a dialectical synthesis does not always bring the expected results. Contrary to the Party's expectations, its nationality policy has resulted in only a modest growth of common Soviet consciousness, while at the same time it has stimulated a growth of local nationalism at a much more rapid pace. Soviet "content" is hard pressed to hold its own against the pressure of a new national content, the embarrassing, illegitimate, and unacknowledged offspring of the nationality policy. The attraction of Soviet Russian culture is too weak and too controversial, its "proletarian internationalist" aspects are too artificial, and national frustrations

[43] See Chap. 3.
[44] *Ibid.*

inherent in the Soviet political system are too strong for the system to absorb the growth of nationalism stimulated by the process of modernization which had been imposed by a great European power on a stagnant Asian society.

It is unfortunate for the future of Soviet multinationalism that the antagonism generated on ethnic lines between the dominant Russian majority and the minority nationalities tends to complement another powerful conflict of interests, that which arises between the central and the local authorities in conditions of excessive centralization of the huge Soviet state. It is the Russians who dominate the decision-making bodies of the CPSU and the All-Union government, and it is primarily the Russians who represent the central Party and government apparatus in the borderlands. Local resentment of centrally determined policies and resource allocation, and of the proverbial All-Union disregard for local needs, requirements, and aspirations thus blends with elements of ethnic hatred and cultural alienation.

APPENDIX
PROCLAMATION OF IBRAHIM BEG, 1931 [a]

IN THE NAME OF THE MOST KIND
AND MERCIFUL ONE
APPEAL TO THE BELIEVERS OF
ALL THE WORLD

> *Near is the help of God,*
> *near is victory.*
>
> (AYAH FROM THE KORAN)

To the people of Turkestan, Tataristan, Kazakstan, Kirgizistan, Turkmenistan, Uzbekistan and Tajikistan, who dwell in Russian territory: Greetings from Divan Begi and Totsham Bashi Muchammed, from Ibrahim Beg, and His Highness Emir Olim Khan.

By these presents we remind you that in the times of the Russian Czar Nicholas and the Emir of Bokhara, Olim Khan, all your peoples dwelt peacefully and happily in their native lands and were permitted freely to practice their religion. In the years 1295 and 1298 respectively,[b] the Czar Nicholas and the Emir of Bokhara were deposed from their thrones, by acts of violence, initiated by Lenin, cursed be his name, who led the people away from the paths of duty and religion, promising them Revolution, by which

---

[a] Quoted by Egon Erwin Kisch, *Changing Asia* (New York: Alfred A. Knopf, 1935), pp. 140–46. As reported by Kisch, the proclamation was written in the Latin alphabet ("European letters"); its author was a high mullah from Kabul, Ibrahim's chief of propaganda, because Ibrahim himself was illiterate.

[b] These are Islamic dates.

they understood freedom and justice, but which was a betrayal of the subjects of the Czar Nicholas and the Emir of Bokhara.

Thereafter a few wise men, who had not submitted to Lenin, cursed be his name, instituted a campaign against the new despotic Government. Thereupon came the representatives of the Government of Lenin, cursed be his name, to these wise adversaries, and declared that the Government of Lenin, cursed be his name, would henceforth demean itself in a good and just manner; the suggestion was made that the opponents either submit or emigrate. The wise warriors followed this advice; some of them submitted to the Government, others went into foreign lands. As for our part, we too, following the request of the Government, withdrew into foreign lands.

At first the new Government granted the people the right to worship according to their religion, and every man was permitted to occupy himself in accordance with his descent, fortune, and ability. At first the new Government did demean itself in a manner that was just and merciful, but after two or three years it began to oppress its subjects in the following respects:

1. The Bolsheviks are responsible for the undermining of the honor of women in Russian Turkestan. It is their doing that women go unveiled and are thereby converted into prostitutes.

2. The new Government confiscated the land and the water from the rightful owners; obliged many dechkans to plant cotton and forbade them to plant corn, with the result that in many districts there was no bread to be had, even for as much as three roubles a pound.

3. The Government imposed useless iron ploughs upon the dechkans and made them pay a hundred roubles apiece for them. Tractors are still more useless and expensive.

4. The Government sends its tractors into the farmers' fields—tractors which, as they conceal from you, have been manufactured in foreign factories—and charges forty roubles for each batman [a current measurement] that it ploughs. With this money the Government buys from its subjects horses and cattle at low prices, for its co-operatives.

5. When the harvest chanced to be bad and the dechkan could

not fulfill the Plan, taxes were levied upon him to the amount of two thousand roubles, besides a tax in crops of anywhere from one hundred to one thousand poods—and this under the pretext that he had not delivered enough cotton. These taxes were all collected by force.

6. The Government levies taxes for the following purposes: for mutual Assistance for the Red Auxilliary Organization, for Education, for Hospitals, Loans, Co-operatives, and finally for an Orphan Fund.

7. In the time of the former Czar the markets prospered, and every poor and needy man could purchase to his heart's content at the bazaar in Gissar or Dushambe, and paid ten or fifteen kopeks for the goods he needed; but now that oppressors are at the helm of the Government, the poor dechkans can only procure goods by permitting themselves to be humiliated and insulted, and even so they must pay eighty kopeks for a yard of dress-goods.

8. The Government hoodwinks the dechkans by herding them into so-called Kolchos, depriving them of horses or cattle of their own and thereby placing them in a situation from which there is no escape.

9. At present the Government is occupied in confiscating the estates of its most distinguished subjects, only to give them to new settlers from Fergana, Tashkent, and Samarkand. This disloyal Government, together with its Party, further intends, during the coming years, to send you as exiles into far-away provinces; this it regards as one of its duties.

10. Honoured brethren, you shall further learn what the future holds in store for you: the Government plans to do away with the mosques and houses of prayer, and in their stead to found schools and clubs; dechkans who have died are to be buried without religious ceremony or even burned; the younger generation is to be brought up in the spirit of Lenin, cursed be his name; and your wives and daughters are to be sent into the streets and made into prostitutes; the Government further intends to seize the best products of the dechkans to give to alien dechkans; all religious books are to be collected on the spot and burned; and finally all those are to be destroyed who dare even to speak the name of God.

11. Brethren, be not guilty of negligence, or your women, for whom you have paid thousands of roubles and hundreds of sheep, will be seized by the Government and put into the ranks of the Komsomols; then you will be forced to grant your wives the divorce, and the result will be that your wives will become the wives of the strangers. Prostitution among women and girls will spread more and more.

12. This treacherous and horrid Government deprives its subjects of the right to be masters of their wives and property; the SAGS (registry office) compels the wives of the dechkans to bare those parts of the body (face and hands) which it is, according to the Shariat, strictly forbidden a woman to display before other men. This satanic Government has robbed the populace of all its customary wedding ceremonies and other traditional pleasures. It forbids anointments and other religious rites.

In view of the rapid spread of the above-mentioned phenomena, the meeting called by the League of Nations in Berlin, February 8th, 1928, at which representatives of the exiles from Russian Turkestan were present, as well as at the meeting of the League of Nations in December 1929, where representatives of America, France, Japan, Germany, Persia, Turkey, Italy, Afghanistan, and Poland took part, it was decided, in accordance with the declarations of the representatives of the refugees from Russian Turkestan, and, finally, by reason of the political information given in the year 1930 by the Comrades Trotsky and Zinoviev, to dissolve the Party Government in Russia and Bokhara and to put in its stead a monarchistic Government. At present the Plenipotentiary of His Highness the Emir Olim Khan has decided and proclaims the following:

We are empowered by the above-named nations to raise armies of the necessary strength on all boundaries and provide them with flying carriages and shooting weapons. But you are called upon to repair to the territory of Bokhara where you shall invite in writing the entire Red Army, the militia, the workmen's troops, and all subjects without exception to assist us with all the weapons at their disposal. Be it known that I, when I come there, in the name of God and His Prophet, will pardon all who may have served the Government of the Bolsheviks, but who have repented in time.

Our goal is completely clear.

Oppressed dechkans! We wage this war in the name of your freedom from the oppression of the Bolsheviks.

The Seal of Ibrahim Beg.

The Proclamation is an interesting document because of the light it sheds on the major popular grievances (status of women, collectivization and the use of force, freedom of religious observances, and the like), and the methods used by the Soviet government. The final part is extraordinarily naive, even for the locale in which it was written.

BIBLIOGRAPHY

BIBLIOGRAPHICAL NOTE

RUSSIAN SOURCES WERE used almost exclusively in the research for this monograph, except for background information, comparative purposes, and general reference. *Kommunist Tadzhikistana,* the daily newspaper of the Tadzhik Communist Party Central Committee published in the Tadzhik capital, was the most important single source, and provided the largest share of raw data used. The other important sources of information were the Russian-language publications of the Tadzhik and All-Union Parties and government agencies, and scholarly works issued under the auspices of the USSR Academy of Sciences and the Tadzhik Academy of Sciences. Much relevant information was found also in the All-Union political journals *Kommunist* and *Partiinaia Zhizn',* and in some specialized scholarly journals such as *Voprosy Istorii* and *Sovetskaia Etnografiia.*

Specialized periodicals in western languages were helpful, particularly the *Central Asian Review* (London), as were translations of Soviet documents, newspapers, and other publications. Works by western scholars in the field of Soviet Central Asia proved invaluable in charting the background and providing check points for analysis. Memoirs and travelogues written by recent and past visitors to Tadzhikistan were of great value in re-creating the atmosphere and the flavor of the area, and in providing the "human angle" otherwise not available.

301

The collection of data from primary Soviet sources is a tedious process, and careful matching of bits of information was necessary to form coherent patterns. Even though newspapers and publications in the period under review followed the Stalinist rule of secrecy, the local Tadzhik press yielded a wealth of data not available elsewhere. Factual information on changes in personnel and institutions, statistical indices, and daily happenings was pieced together. Their successes, failures, and changes of current policies could be charted from lead articles, press discussions, and reports to local and republican Party meetings. The shortcomings in the implementation of policies and the major areas of concern were revealed, explicitly or implicitly, in press discussion, at Party meetings, and occasionally in satirical *feuilletons* or letters to the editor. Much of the information disclosed at congresses or in press complaints contradicted official pronouncements and statistical data and frequently made rather obvious the general unreliability and confusion of Soviet statistics and official information given *ex cathedra*. Frequent campaigns to introduce a new policy, improve performance, or correct undesirable behavior often pointed to problems which normally would have been concealed. Sometimes, for lack of available data, a projection had to be made analytically on the basis of comparable situations and general background.

Raw data collected in newspapers, official pamphlets, and publications were also illuminated by political guideline articles in All-Union journals; sometimes local problems and tensions were thus placed in a broader context and given clearer focus. Scholarly publications provided an invaluable insight into historical conditions and problems of development in Tadzhikistan; ethnographic studies proved important in analyzing patterns of behavior and attitudes, especially in comparison with information gathered from the press.

The following bibliography does not include all the sources consulted, but only the sources cited in the text.

Books and Pamphlets

Agabekov, Georges. *OGPU: The Russian Secret Terror.* Translated by Henry W. Bunn. New York: Brentano's, 1931.
Aini, Sadriddin. *Bukhara: (Vospominaniia).* Authorized transla-

tion from the Tadzhik by Sergei Borodin. Moscow: Gosudarstvennoe Izdatel'stvo Khudozhestvennoi Literatury, 1952.

Akademiia Nauk Tadzhikskoi SSR. Institut Istorii im. A. Donisha. *Istoriia Tadzhikskogo Naroda,* vol. III, Book 1, *Perekhod k sotsializmu (1917–1937).* Edited by B. A. Antonenko. Moscow: Izd. "Nauka," 1964. Book 2, *Period sotsializma i perekhod k kommunizmu (1938–1963 gg.).* Edited by S. A. Radzhabov and Iu. A. Nikolaev. Moscow: Izd. "Nauka," 1965.

Aliev, G. A. *Uspekhi razvitiia ekonomiki i kul'tury Tadzhikskoi SSR. K 40-letiiu Velikoi Oktiabr'skoi Sotsialisticheskoi Revoliutsii.* (Vsesoiuznoe obshchestvo po rasprostranenii u politicheskikh i nauchnykh znanii.) Moscow: Izd. "Znanie," 1957.

Antonenko, B. A. *Podgotovka massovoi kollektivizatsii v Tadzhikistane (Ocherki po istorii Tadzhikistana,* vol. 1). Stalinabad: Ministerstvo Prosveshcheniia Tadzhikskoi SSR, Stalinabadskii Gosudarstvennyi Pedagogicheskii Institut im. T. G. Shevchenko, 1957, pp. 99–125.

Aspaturian, Vernon. *The Union Republics in Soviet Diplomacy: A Study of Soviet Federalism in the Service of Soviet Foreign Policy.* Geneva-Paris: Publications de l'Institut Universitaire des Hautes Études Internationales, no. 36, 1960.

Avtorkhanov, Abdurakhman. *The Communist Party Apparatus.* (Foundation for Foreign Affairs Series, no. 11.) Chicago: H. Regnery Co., 1966.

Barghoorn, Frederick C. *Soviet Russian Nationalism.* New York: Oxford University Press, 1956.

Barthold, V. V. *A Short History of Turkestan: History of the Semirechy'e. Four Studies on the History of Central Asia,* vol. 1. Translated from the Russian by V. and T. Minorsky. Leiden: E. J. Brill, 1956.

Berg, Lev Semenovich. *Natural Regions of the USSR.* Translated by Olga Adler Titelbaum. Edited by John A. Morrison and C. C. Nikiforoff. New York: The Macmillan Co., 1950.

Black, C. E., ed. *Rewriting Russian History: Soviet Interpretation of Russia's Past,* 2d ed., rev. New York: Vintage Books, 1962.

Black, C. E., ed. *The Transformation of Russian Society: Aspects of Social Change since 1861.* Cambridge, Mass.: Harvard University Press, 1960.

Bol'shaia Sovetskaia Entsiklopediia, 1st ed., vol. LIII, 1946; 2d ed., vol. XLI, 1956. Moscow.

Braginskii, I. S., *et al.,* eds. *Antologiia Tadzhikskoi poezii s drevnikh vremen do nashikh dnei.* Moscow: Goslitizdat, 1951.

Braginskii, I. S. *Iz istorii Tadzhikskoi narodnoi poezii.* (Akademiia Nauk SSSR, Institut Vostokovedeniia; Institut Mirovoi Literatury im. A. M. Gor'kovo.) Moscow: Izd. Akademii Nauk SSSR, 1956.

Braginskii, I. S. *Ocherki po istorii Tadzhikskoi literatury.* (Akademiia Nauk Tadzhikskoi SSR, Institut Iazyka i Literatury.) Stalinabad: Akademiia Nauk Tadzhikskoi SSR, 1956.

Briskin, Aleksandr Mikhailovich. *Strana Tadzhikov.* Moscow: Gosizdat, 1930.

Brzezinski, Zbigniew K. *The Permanent Purge: Politics of Soviet Totalitarianism.* (Russian Research Center Studies, 20.) Cambridge, Mass.: Harvard University Press, 1956.

Caroe, Olaf. *Soviet Empire: The Turks of Central Asia and Stalinism.* London: Macmillan & Co., 1953.

Chumichev, D. A. *Stalinabad, Stolitsa Tadzhikskoi SSR.* Moscow: Geografizdat, 1950.

Constitution of the Tajik Soviet Socialist Republic of March 1, 1937 (as amended through May, 1948). New York: American-Russian Institute, 1950.

Delavignette, Robert. *Freedom and Authority in French West Africa.* New York: Oxford University Press, 1950.

Douglas, William O. *Russian Journey.* New York: Doubleday and Co., Inc., 1956.

Dubicki, Jan. *Elements of Disloyalty in Turkestan.* (Research Program on the USSR, East European Fund, Inc., mimeographed series no. 53, in Russian.) New York: East European Fund, Inc., n.d.

XXIII S'ezd Kommunisticheskoi Partii Sovetskogo Soiuza, 29 Marta–8 Aprelia 1966 goda (stenographic record), vol. I. Moscow: Izd. Politicheskoi Literatury, 1966.

Eudin, Xenia Joukoff, and North, Robert C. *Soviet Russia and the East, 1920–1927: A Documentary Survey.* (The Hoover Library on War, Revolution, and Peace, publication no. 25.) Stanford, Calif.: Stanford University Press, 1957.

Ezhegodnik Bol'shoi Sovetskoi Entsiklopedii, Moscow: 1956, 1959, 1960, 1961 M, 1962 M, 1965, 1965, Issue 9.

Fainsod, Merle. *How Russia is Ruled* (Russian Research Center Studies, 11), rev. ed. Cambridge, Mass.: Harvard University Press, 1964.

Fainsod, Merle. *Smolensk under Soviet Rule.* Cambridge, Mass.: Harvard University Press, 1958.

Fanian, D. *K istorii sovetskogo stroitel'stva v Tadzhikistane (1920–1929 gg.): Sbornik dokumentov,* part I. Stalinabad: Arkhivnyi Otdel NKVD Tadzhikskoi SSR, 1940.

Florinsky, M. T., ed. *McGraw-Hill Encyclopedia of Russia and the Soviet Union.* New York: McGraw-Hill, 1961.

Formirovanie sotsialisticheskikh natsii v SSSR. Moscow: Gosudarstvennoe Izdatel'stvo Politicheskoi Literatury, 1962. I. Verkhovtsev and I. Maiatnikov, "O natsiiakh i putiakh ikh razvitiia," pp. 1–24. P. K. Khamrakulov, "O nekotorykh osobennostiiakh formirovaniia i razvitiia Tadzhikskoi sotsialisticheskoi natsii," pp. 526–51.

Frye, Richard N. *Bukhara: The Medieval Achievement.* (The Centers of Civilization Series.) Norman, Okla.: University of Oklahoma Press, 1965.

Gafurov, Bobodzhan Gafurovich. *Istoriia Tadzhikskogo naroda v kratkom izlozhenii.* vol. I. *S drevneishikh vremen do Velikoi Oktiabr'skoi Sotsialisticheskoi Revoliutsii 1917 g.,* 3d ed. rev. and enl. Moscow: Gospolitizdat, 1955.

Gafurov, Bobodzhan Gafurovich. *Nekotorye voprosy natsional' noi politiki KPSS.* Moscow: Gospolitizdat, 1959.

Ginzburg, V. V. *Gornye Tadzhiki: Materialy po antropologii Tadzhikov Karategina i Darvaza.* (Akademiia Nauk SSSR. Institut Antropologii, Etnografii i Arkheologii, Works, vol. XVI, Anthropological Series 2.) Moscow: Izd. Akademii Nauk SSSR, 1937.

Gruliow, Leo, ed. *Current Soviet Policies: The Documentary Record of the Nineteenth Communist Party Congress and the Reorganization after Stalin's death.* New York: Frederick A. Praeger, 1953.

Gruliow, Leo, ed. *Current Soviet Policies II: The Documentary*

Record of the 20th Communist Party Congress and its Aftermath. New York: Frederick A. Praeger, 1957.

Gruliow, Leo, ed. *Current Soviet Policies III: The Documentary Record of the Extraordinary 21st Communist Party Congress.* New York: Columbia University Press, 1960.

Gruliow, Leo, and Saikowski, Charlotte, eds. *Current Soviet Policies IV: The Documentary Record of the 22nd Congress of the Communist Party of the Soviet Union.* New York: Columbia University Press, 1962.

Iakovlev, Boris. *Kontsentratsionnye lageri SSSR.* (Institut po Izucheniiu Istorii i Kul'tury SSSR, Issledovaniia i Materialy, Series I, Issue 23.) Munich: Institut po Izucheniiu Istorii i Kul'tury SSSR, 1955.

Iakubovskaia, S. I. *Obrazovanie i razvitie sovetskogo mnogonatsional'nogo gosudarstva.* Moscow: Izd. "Znanie," 1966.

Karmysheva, B. Kh. *Uzbeki-Lokaitsy iuzhnogo Tadzhikistana.* Issue I. *Istoriko-etnograficheskii ocherk zhivotnovodstva v dorevoliutsionnyi period.* (Akademiia Nauk Tadzhikskoi SSR. Institut Istorii, Arkheologii i Etnografii, Works, vol. XXVIII.) Stalinabad: Izd. Akademii Nauk Tadzhikskoi SSR, 1954.

Kisch, Egon Erwin. *Changing Asia.* English version by Rita Reil. New York: Alfred A. Knopf, 1935. (Originally published as *Asien Gründlich Verändert.*)

Kisliakov, N. A. *Sledy Pervobytnogo Kommunizma u Gornykh Tadzhikov Vakhio-Bolo.* (Akademiia Nauk SSSR, Institut Antropologii, Etnografii i Arkheologii, vol. X, Ethnographic Series no. 2.) Moscow: Izd. Akademii Nauk SSSR, 1936.

Kisliakov, N. A., et al. *Kul'tura i byt Tadzhikskogo kolkhoznogo krestianstva: Po materialam kolkhoza im. G. M. Malenkova Leninabadskogo raiona Leninabadskoi oblasti Tadzhikskoi SSR.* (Akademiia Nauk SSSR, Institut Etnografii im. N. N. Miklukho-Maklaia, Works, New Series, vol. XXIV.) Moscow: Izd. Akademii Nauk SSSR, 1954.

Kolarz, Walter. *Religion in the Soviet Union.* New York: St. Martin's Press, 1962.

Kolarz, Walter. *Russia and Her Colonies.* New York: Frederick A. Praeger, 1952.

KPSS, Vysshaia Partiinaia Shkola, Kafedra ekonomicheskoi i politicheskoi geografii i zarubezhnykh gosudarstv. *Tadzhikskaia SSR: Uchebnyi Material.* Moscow: Gospolitizdat, 1953.

KP Tadzhikistana, Tsentral'nyi Komitet, Institut Istorii Partii. *Tadzhikskaia SSR za 25 let: v pomoshch propagandistam i agitatoram.* Stalinabad: Tadzhikgosizdat, 1955.

KP Tadzhikistana, Tsentral'nyi Komitet, Institut Istorii Partii. *Kommunisticheskaia partiia Tadzhikistana v dokumentakh i tsifrakh (1924–1963 gg.).* Sbornik dokumentov i materialov o roste i regulirovanii sostava partiinoi organizatsii. Edited by V. A. Kozachkovskii. Dushanbe: Izd. "Irfon," 1965.

Lorimer, Frank. *The Population of the Soviet Union: History and Prospects.* (Series of League of Nations Publications, II. Economic and Financial, 1946, II.A.3.) Geneva: League of Nations, 1946.

Luknitsky, Pavel. *Soviet Tadzhikistan.* Moscow: Foreign Languages Publishing House, 1954.

McGovern, William Montgomery. *The Early Empires of Central Asia: A Study of the Scythians and the Huns and the Part They Played in World History.* Chapel Hill, N.C.: The University of North Carolina Press, 1939.

Oshanin, L. V. *Etnogenez Tadzhikov po dannym sravnitel'noi antropologii Tiurkskikh i Iranskikh narodov Srednei Azii.* (Akademiia Nauk Tadzhikskoi SSR, Institut Istorii, Arkheologii i Etnografii, Works, vol. XXVII.) Stalinabad: Izd. Akademii Nauk Tadzhikskoi SSR, 1954.

Park, Alexander G. *Bolshevism in Turkestan, 1917–1927.* (Studies of the Russian Institute of Columbia University.) New York: Columbia University Press, 1957.

Pennock, J. Roland, ed. *Self-Government in Modernizing Nations.* Englewood Cliffs, N.J.: Prentice-Hall, 1964.

Pil'nyak, Boris (B. Wogau). *Tadzhikistan: ocherki, materialy k romanu.* Leningrad: Izd. Pisatelei, 1931.

Pipes, Richard. *The Formation of the Soviet Union: Communism and Nationalism, 1917–1923.* (Russian Research Center Studies, 13.) Cambridge, Mass.: Harvard University Press, 1954.

Pye, Lucian W. *Politics, Personality, and Nation-Building: Burma's Search for Identity.* New Haven: Yale University Press, 1962.

Rachman, V. "The Anti-Bolshevik Struggle in Turkestan," *The Strength and Weakness of Red Russia*. (Congress of Delegates of Independence Movements within the USSR, held in Edinburgh, June 12–14, 1950.) Edinburgh: Scottish League for European Freedom, 1950, pp. 106–16.

Rasulov, Dzhabar. *40 let Kommunisticheskoi Partii Tadzhikistana*. Dushanbe: Izd. "Irfon," 1964.

Rywkin, Michael. *Russia in Central Asia*. New York: Collier Books, 1963.

Salisbury, Harrison E. *American in Russia*. New York: Harper and Brothers, 1955.

Sbornik statei posviiashchenykh isskustvu Tadzhikskogo naroda. (Akademiia Nauk Tadzhikskoi SSR, Institut Istorii, Arkheologii i Etnografii, Works, vol. XLII.) Stalinabad: Akademiia Nauk Tadzhikskoi SSR, 1956.

  Belinskaia, N. A., and Meshkeris, V. A. "Mezhrespublikanskaia Vystavka Khudozhnikov Srednei Azii i Kazakhstana, 1955 g.," pp. 49–85.

  Dansker, O. "Sobiranie i izuchenie Tadzhikskoi narodnoi pesni," pp. 87–105.

  "Khronika Khudozhestvennoi teatral'noi i muzykal'noi zhizni Tadzhikskoi SSR za 1954–1955 gg.," pp. 235–42.

  Nurdzhanov, N. "Russkaia klassika na stsene Tadzhikskogo Akademicheskogo teatra," pp. 203–219.

Schlesinger, Rudolf, ed. *The Nationalities Problem and Soviet Administration. Selected Readings on the Development of Soviet Nationalities Policies.* (International Library of Sociology and Social Reconstruction.) London: Routledge & Kegan Paul, 1956.

Schwartz, Harry. *Russia's Soviet Economy*. 2d ed. New York: Prentice-Hall, 1954.

Skrine, Francis Henry, and Ross, Edward Denison. *The Heart of Asia: A History of Russian Turkestan and the Central Asian Khanates from the Earliest Times.* London: Methuen & Co., 1899.

Soviet Central Asia. 3 vols. (Subcontractor's Monograph, HRAF-49 American U.-1.) New Haven: Human Relations Area Files, Inc., 1956.

The Soviet Union in Facts and Figures, 1958 ed. London: Soviet News, 1958.

SSSR, Komitet po Delam Isskustv pri Sovete Narodnykh Kommissarov. *Dve Rozy (Du Gul').* (Ballet in four acts.) Moscow: 1941.

SSSR, Komitet po Delam Isskustv pri Sovete Narodnykh Kommissarov. *Kuznets Kova (Kovai Okhangar).* (Opera in four acts.) Moscow: 1941.

SSSR, Tsentral'noe Statisticheskoe Upravlenie pri Sovete Ministrov SSSR. *Narodnoe Khoziaistvo SSSR v 1964 g. Statisticheskii Ezhegodnik.* Moscow: Izd. "Statsitika," 1965.

SSSR, Verkhovnyi Sovet, Presidium, Otdel po voprosam raboty sovetov. *Itogi vyborov i sostav deputatov mestnykh sovetov deputatov trudiashchikhsia 1961 g.; Statisticheskii Sbornik.* Moscow: Izd. "Izvestiia Sovetov Deputatov Trudiashchikhsia SSSR," 1961.

SSSR, Verkhovnyi Sovet. *Deputaty Verkhovnogo Soveta SSSR.* vol. 6. Moscow: Izd. "Izvestiia Sovetov Deputatov Trudiashchikhsia SSSR," 1962.

Stalin, Joseph. *Marxism and the National Question. Selected Writings and Speeches.* New York: International Publishers, 1942.

Strong, John W., Ed. *The Soviet Union under Brezhnev and Kosygin.* Princeton, N. J.: D. Van Nostrand Co., *to be published.*

Tadzhikskaia SSR, Sovet Ministrov, Tsentral'noe Statisticheskoe Upravlenie. *Narodnoe Khoziaistvo Tadzhikskoi SSR v 1961 godu: Kratkii Statisticheskii Sbornik.* Dushanbe: Gosstatizdat, 1962.

Tadzhikskaia SSR, Statisticheskoe Upravlenie. *Narodnoe Khoziaistvo Tadzhikskoi SSR: Statisticheskii Sbornik.* Stalinabad: Gosstatizdat, 1957.

Tolstov, S. P., *et al.,* eds. *Narody Srednei Azii i Kazakhstana,* Vol. I. (Akademiia Nauk SSSR, Institut Etnografii im. N. N. Miklukho-Maklaia.) Moscow: Izd. Akademii Nauk SSSR, 1962.

Ul'dzhabaev, Tursunbai. *Otchetnyi doklad Tsentral'nogo Komiteta Kommunisticheskoi Partii Tadzhikistana XI S'ezdu Kompartii Tadzhikistana.* Stalinabad: Tadzhikgosizdat., 1958.

USSR, Council of Ministers, Central Statistical Administration. *The National Economy of the USSR: A Statistical Compilation.* Moscow: State Publishing House, 1956.

VKP(b), Tsentral'nyi Komitet, Statisticheskii Otdel. *Vsesoiuznaia partiinaia perepis' 1927 goda.* Issues 1–8. Moscow: Izd. Statis-ticheskogo Otdela TsK VKP(b), 1927.

Wheeler, Geoffrey. *The Modern History of Soviet Central Asia.* (Asia-Africa Series in Modern Histories.) New York: Frederick A. Praeger, 1964.

Wheeler, Geoffrey. *Racial Problems in Soviet Muslim Asia.* (Institute of Race Relations.) London: Oxford University Press, 1960.

Zenkovsky, Serge A. *Pan-Turkism and Islam in Russia.* (Russian Research Center Studies, no. 36) Cambridge, Mass.: Harvard University Press, 1960.

JOURNALS AND NEWSPAPERS

L'Afrique et l'Asie. Association des Anciens du C.H.E.A.M., Paris, 1950–1958, *passim.*

Akademiia Nauk SSSR, Institut Etnografii, Kratkie Soobshcheniia, 1947–57.

Kisliakov, N. A. "Opyt raboty kollektiva po izucheniiu byta Tadzhikskogo kolkhoznogo krestianstva," 26 (1957): 61–62.

Peshchereva, E. M. "Poezdka k gornym Tadzhikam," 3 (1947): 42–48.

Tolstov, S. P. "Rol' arkheologicheskikh i etnograficheskikh materialov v razrabotke spornykh voprosov istorii Srednei Azii nakanune prisoedineniia eë k Rossii," 26 (1957): 34–37.

Akademiia Nauk SSSR. Institut Etnografii im. N. N. Miklukho-Maklaia, Kratkie Soobshcheniia, 1950–55.

Kisliakov, N. A. "Sem'ia i brak u Tadzhikov," 17 (1952): 74–80.

Nurdzhanov, N. "Istoki narodnogo teatra u Tadzhikov," 18 (1953): 103–09.

Rusiaikina, S. P. "Narodnaia Odezhda Tadzhikov Garmskoi Oblasti, 20 (1954): 87–98.

Vinnikov, Ia. R. "Turkmeny Dzhilikul'skogo rayona Tadzhiks-koi SSR," 16 (1952): 3–13.

Akademiia Nauk SSSR, Institut Istorii Material'noi Kul'tury, Kratkie Soobshcheniia.

Ginzburg, V. V. "Antropologicheskie materialy k etnogenezu Tadzhikov," 61 (1956): 45–47.

Akademiia Nauk SSSR, Institut Vostokovedeniia, Kratkie Soobsh-cheniia.

Braginskii, I. S. "Zametki o Tadzhikskom epose 'Gurguli,' " 9 (1953): 48–57.

Akademiia Nauk Tadzhikskoi SSR, Otdelenie Obshchestvennykh Nauk, Izvestiia.

Niiazmukhammedov, B. N., and Edel'man, A. S., "Razvitie Tadzhikskoi filologii za 25 let," 6 (1954): 11–26.

American Slavic and East European Review, American Association for Advancement of Slavic Studies, Menasha, Wisc., 1950–55.

Zenkovsky, Serge A. "Kulturkampf in Pre-Revolutionary Central Asia," 1 (February, 1955): 15–41.

Bol'shevik, renamed *Kommunist* in November, 1952, theoretical organ of the CPSU Central Committee, Moscow, 1945–66.

"Druzhba narodov stroiashchikh kommunizm," 16 (November, 1965): 3–13.

Fedoseev, P. "Sotsialism i patriotism," 9 (June, 1953): 12–28.

Gafurov, Bobodzhan Gafurovich. "Ideologicheskaia rabota v partiinoi organizatsii Tadzhikistana," 2 (January, 1952): 45–55.

Gafurov, Bobodzhan Gafurovich. "O proverke ispolneniia," 12 (August, 1953): 66–77.

Gafurov, Bobodzhan Gafurovich. "V. I. Lenin i pobeda sovetskoi vlasti v Srednei Azii," 6 (April, 1955): 74–90.

Gafurov, Bobodzhan Gafurovich. "Vospityvat' kadry na preodelenii trudnostei," 18 (December, 1955): 64–74.

Gorkin, A. "Stalin—sozdatel' i rukovoditel' mnogonatsional'nogo sovetskogo gosudarstva," 23 (December, 1949): 47–65.

Gorkin, A. "Torzhestvo leninsko-stalinskoi natsional'noi politiki v SSSR," 1 (January, 1948): 9–23.

Iakovlev, N. "O prepodavanii otechestvennoi istorii," 22 (November, 1947): 26–37.

Kim, M. "Torzhestvo ideologii druzhby narodov," 22 (December, 1952): 53–68.

Mordinov, A., and Sanzheev, G. "Nekotorye voprosy razvitiia mladopis'mennykh iazykov narodov SSSR." 8 (April, 1951): 38–48.

Morozov, M. "Natsional'nye traditsii narodov SSSR i vospitanie sovetskogo patriotizma," 7 (April, 1949): 35–47.

"O rabote partiinykh organizatsii sredi zhenshchin," 1 (January, 1951): 9–17.

"O sotsialisticheskom soderzhanii i natsional'nykh formakh sovetskoi kul'tury," 22 (November, 1946): 1–8.

"Razvivat' i kul'tivirovat' sovetskii patriotizm—vazhneishaia zadacha partiinykh organizatsii," 5 (March, 1949): 3–11.

Riakin, M., and Rodionov, N. "Rukovodstvo mestnymi izdatel'-stvami," 15 (August, 1952): 58–64.

"Russkii narod—rukovodiashchaia sila sredi narodov nashei strany," 10 (May, 1945): 3–12.

"Sovetskaia politika ravnopraviia natsii," 9 (May, 1948): 1–6.

Tsamerian, I. "Natsiia i narodnost'," 6 (March, 1951): 57–62.

Vasil'ev, N. "Sovetskii patriotizm—dvizhushchaia sila stroitel'-stva kommunizma v SSSR," 17 (September, 1951): 16–26.

Central Asian Review, Central Asian Research Center, London, vols. I–XIV, 1953–1966.

Bott, Lydia, "Recent Trends in the Economy of Soviet Central Asia," 3 (1965): 199–204.

"Central Asia and the Russian People," 3 (1953): 1–8.

"Jadidism—A Current Soviet Assessment," 1 (1964): 30–39.

Khakimov, M. Kh. "O nekotorykh voprosakh razvitiia nat-sional'noi sovetskoi gosudarstvennosti v sovremennyi period," Obshchestvennye Nauki v Uzbekistane, 6, 1964; quoted in 4 (1964): 254–56.

"Mixed Marriages in Central Asia and Kazakhstan," 1 (1963): 5–12.

"Nationalism and Progress," 1 (1957): 1–5.

Sheehy, Anne. "Population Trends in Central Asia and Kazakh-stan, 1959–1965," 4 (1966): 317–29.

"Some Impressions of the Central Asian Republics," 1 (1965): 7–16.

"The Population of Central Asia and Kazakhstan," 2 (1957): 120–26.

"The Second Mother Tongue," 4 (1965): 310–22.

Current Digest of Soviet Press, Joint Committee on Slavic Studies, New York, vols. XII–XVII.

Economic Bulletin for Europe. United Nations, New York.

"Regional Economic Policy in the Soviet Union: The Case of Central Asia," 3 (November, 1957): 49–75.

Kommunist Tadzhikistana, daily organ of the Central Committee of the KPT and Council of Ministers of the TSSR, Stalinabad (Dushanbe), 1945–56.

The Middle East Journal, Middle East Institute, Washington, D.C.

Pipes, Richard, "Muslims of Soviet Central Asia: Trends and Prospects," part I, 2 (Spring, 1955): 147–62; part II, 3 (Summer, 1955): 295–308.

Partiinaia Zhizn', organ of the CPSU Central Committee, Moscow, 1945–56.

Gafurov, Bobodzhan Gafurovich. "Nekotorye voprosy vospitaniia natsional'nykh kadrov," 15 (August, 1947): 17–22.

"KPSS v tsifrakh," 1 (January, 1962): 44–54.

"KPSS v tsifrakh," 10 (May, 1965): 8–17.

Problèmes Soviétiques, Institut d'Études sur l'URSS, Munich.

Carrère d'Encausse, Helene, and Benningsen, Alexandre. "Pouvoir apparent et pouvoir réel dans les républiques musulmanes de l'URSS," 1 (April, 1958): 57–73.

Problems of Communism. U.S. Information Agency, Washington, D.C., 1952–66.

Hough, Jerry F. "Technical Elite vs. the Party: A First Hand Report," 5 (September–October, 1959): 56–59.

Pravda, organ of the CPSU Central Committee and Moscow Oblast Committee, Moscow, 1956.

Sovetskaia Etnografiia, Akademiia Nauk SSSR, Moscow, 1950–55.

Sovetskoe Gosudarstvo i Pravo, Moscow, 1966–67.

Paletskis, Iu. I. "50 let sovetskogo mnogonatsional'nogo gosudarstva," 11 (November, 1967): 13–22.

Soviet Literature (monthly), Moscow, no. 9 (1967).

Soviet Studies. University of Glasgow, Glasgow, 1959–65.

Studies on the Soviet Union, new ser., vol. IV.

Avtorkhanov, Abdurakhman, "Denationalization of the Soviet Ethnic Minorities," 1 (1964): 74–99.

Türkeli (Russian edition), Turkistan Azatlik Kamyte, Munich. 1951–52.

Chokai-Oglu, Mustafa. "Turkistan," 1 (September, 1951): 6–13.

Devlet. "Natsional'no-osvoboditel'naia bor'ba v Turkestane," 1 (September, 1951): 13–32.

Gokdepe, A. "Natsional'naia Politika Moskvy," 2–3 (October–November, 1951): 27–48.

Voprosy Istorii, Akademiia Nauk SSSR, Moscow, 1947–57.

Braginskii, I. S., Radzhabov, S., and Romodin, V. A. "K voprosu o znachenii prisoedineniia Srednei Azii k Rossii," 8 (August, 1953): 21–40.

Bromlei, Iu. V., and Lunin, B. V. "Nauchnaia sessiia po istorii Srednei Azii i Kazakhstana v dooktriabr'skoi period," 4 (April, 1954): 172–78.

Gafurov, Bobodzhan Gafurovich. "Ob Andizhanskom 'Vosstanii' 1898 goda," 2 (1953): 50–61.

"O nekotorykh voprosakh istorii narodov Srednei Azii," 4 (1951): 3–15.

Sidorov, A. L. "Nauchnaia sessiia po istorii narodov Srednei Azii i Kazakhstana sovetskogo perioda," 5 (May, 1957): 192–98.

Zevelev, A., and Abdullaev, Sh. "Diskussiia o kharaktere natsional'nykh dvizhenii v Srednei Azii i Kazakhstane v kolonial'nyi period," 9 (1951): 173–78.

Voprosy Iazykoznaniia, Moscow.

Fazylov, M. F., "Itogi perestroiki i ocherednye zadachi Instituta Iazyka i Literatury Akademii Nauk Tadzhikskoi SSSR," 6 (1953): 155–59.

INDEX

Abdullaev, N. P., 150n
Absoliutnoe zlo ("absolute evil"), 80.
    See also Historiography
Academy of Sciences, TSSR, 133, 134,
    135, 152, 265
Adventures of Four Dervishes, The, 264,
    266
Adzhizi, 240
Afghanistan, 29, 30, 33, 50, 74
Aga Khan, 9
Agitation and Propaganda, Department
    of, of KPT Central Committee, 107,
    144, 145, 150n, 153, 196
Agriculture: collectivization, 37, 38–40,
    42, 43, 56–58; continuing traditional
    attitudes in, 276; cotton, 54–55, 57,
    185–86; distribution of, 56–57; effect
    of civil war on, 57–58; ethnic pattern
    in, 57, 131–33, 134n; evaluation of,
    272; housing, 61–62, 275–76; irriga-
    tion, 8, 55; labor force, 59; living
    standards, 60–61; mechanization of,
    59; policies, 33–34, 46; private farms,
    59; publications on, 213, 217; thefts in,
    164n, 276, 279. *See also* Armed Serv-
    ices; Central Committee, KPT; Coun-
    cil of Ministers, TSSR; Economic de-
    velopment; Education; Industry; Kish-
    laks; Kolkhozes; Machine Tractor Sta-
    tions; *and under localities*
Agriculture, Bureau of, 105n
Agriculture, Ministry of, 114
Aini, S., 16, 84, 113, 134, 214, 239, 245,
    254–55, 257, 258, 259, 261, 264, 265
Akhmedov, L., 144

All Union Communist Party. *See* Com-
    munist Party of the Soviet Union
Amanullah (King of Afghanistan), 74
Architecture, 259
Architecture, Administration of, 115
Armed Services: career patterns, 147–48;
    ethnic patterns in, 122–23
Art Affairs Administration, 115
Arts: and the new culture, 233–34, 259–
    61
Arus, 258n
Ashurov, N., 152, 187
Asimov, 143
Asrorov, 191
Association of Proletarian Writers, 255
Association of Ulema, 19
Auto Transportation/Roads, Ministry of,
    114
Avicenna, 11, 238

Badakhshan principality, 12–13
Bai: definition of, 33n
Bakhtiër and Nisso, 260
Balasanian, 138, 260
Ballet, 223, 260
Baroi adabiety sotsialisti, 255
Barthold, V. V., 234, 235–36n, 244
Basmachi, 21–22, 23–25, 26, 29–30, 31,
    33, 37–38, 86: and border guards, 121;
    British assistance to, 26; defeat of, 77;
    historical interpretation of, 237–38,
    255, 256, 258, 260–61; reasons for pop-
    ular support of, 31–32
Beg, Ibrahim, 24, 25, 26, 29, 30, 38, 295–
    99

315

Donish, A., 84, 240
DOSARM/DOSAAF, 104, 125
Douglas, W. O., 126, 128
Druzhba narodov (friendship of the people), 78, 88–90, 93, 287. *See also* Nationality policy
Dukchi Ishan, 237
Dushambe (Dushanbe), 23, 25. *See also* Stalinabad city
Dva potoka or *odin potok*, 231–32, 236, 251, 256, 259. *See also* Cultural policies and programs
Dvornikov, V. S., 112, 114, 155, 188, 190
Dzhalil, R., 255, 258, 266
Dzhilikul', 216

Economic development: during consolidation, 25–27, 30; early taxes, 33; effect of civil war on, 29, 57–58; electrical power, 8, 55; ethnic patterns in, 125–38, 140–41, 147, 286–87, 288–89; evaluation of, 183, 184, 185–86, 269–70, 272, 274–75, 276, 281, 286–88; exports to European Russia, 54, 55; forced labor, 118, 119–20; "free" professions, 137; importance of raikoms in, 182–83; imports from European Russia, 54; main products, 54; and the masses, 193, 206, 207, 274–75; mining, 8, 55; and nationalism, 180; and new elite, 50, 193, 204, 284, 286–87; occupational pattern, 126–33, 135; policies and problems, 32, 33, 46, 50–59, 77, 128–30, 134, 167, 169, 171–76, 180–81; pre-revolution, 10, 11–13, 14–15, 53; pre-revolution, post-revolution, and post-World War II compared, 53–54; rates of, 54–56; resistance to, 36, 129; role of European emigrants in, 126–27, 140, 147; ruble-dollar equivalents, 60n, 61n; standards of living, 60–63, 126, 275–76; urbanization, 47–48; wages, 60–61, 126, 219–20. *See also* Agriculture; Industry; Labor force
Edinonachalie, 105
Education: development of, 27, 43–44, 64–65, 126, 152, 196, 198, 242, 247, 248–49, 284–85, 287, 288; ethnic pattern in, 133–37, 287n; evaluation of schools, 248–49, 288n; level of, 274, 277n, 287–88; literacy, 35, 44, 203, 211. *See also* Political education
Education, Ministry of, 115, 170–71, 262
Eliava, Sh. Z., 22n

Elite: Moslem, 18, 19, 21, 22; new, 14–15, 27–29, 34, 42, 50, 95–96, 133, 146–205, 226, 229, 270, 275, 278, 283–87, 289–91; political, 194–205, 275; shadow, 282; socialization of, 192–205. *See also* Political leadership
Enver Pasha, 25, 31
Ergashev, 143
Ethnic patterns, 8–9, 12, 48–51, 57, 78–79, 94–144, 146–50, 158, 223, 288–89, 293; in agriculture, 57, 131–33, 134n; in armed services, 122–23; in Council of Ministers, TSSR, 113–17, 119, 120; in economic development, 125–38, 140–41, 147, 286–89; in education, 133–37, 287n; evaluation of, 140; in industry, 125–31; in kishlaks, 133; in kolkhozes, 57, 131, 132; in Komsomol, 106, 124–25; in KPT, 41–43, 95–111; in KPT Central Committee, 102–7, 142–45; in literature, 138; at Machine Tractor Stations, 131–32; in MGB/KGB, 114, 119–20, 150, 156; in MVD, 114, 117, 119–20, 150; of population, 49–51; in power structure, definition of, 40–41, 70, 95–99; in press and publications, 137; in Stalinabad, 210n; in Supreme Soviet, TSSR, 111–13; in Tadzhik government, 35, 41–43, 95–99, 111–22, 139–40, 146–56, 179–81, 210n, 289–90
Ethnic tensions, 20, 21, 24, 28, 29, 31, 32, 36, 37, 39–41, 69, 70, 78–80, 85, 93, 176–81, 234, 240, 255, 262–65, 274, 280–84, 286–88, 290: in Tadzhik government, 29, 31, 40–41, 80, 176–81, 205, 283, 284, 287–88, 290, 293. *See also* Russians

Fadeicheva, O. P., 145, 173n, 178–79
Farsi language. *See* Linguistics
Fedoseev, I. G., 148n
Fergana Province, 14, 26
Fergana Valley, 7, 13, 22, 133, 151, 228
Finance, Ministry of, 114
Firdousi, 11, 89, 251n, 252
Five Year Plan, Second, 128
Food Industry (Products), Ministry of, 114, 170, 174
Foreign Affairs, Ministry of, 113, 114
Forestry, Ministry of, 114
Friendship of the people. *See Druzhba narodov*
Frunze, M. V., 21, 22n, 23
Frye, R. N., 236n, 241n

320   INDEX

Leninabad city: executive committee, 118; gorkom, 108, 170; *kultprosvet* in, 223, 228; living conditions, 62
Leninabad oblast: admission to Party, 166; communications media in, 220; executive committee, 118; industry in, 55; *kultprosvet* in, 225, 228; obkom, 108, 109; political schools in, 201–2; population growth, 47, 48; turnover rate of officials in, 167
Leninabad raion, 227
Lenskii, 138, 260
"Lesser evil," 80–86, 89, 90
Libraries, 225–26, 228
Light (Consumers' Goods) Industry, Ministry of, 114, 116
Linguistics: Farsi, 11, 13, 76, 78, 241, 243n, 244n, 245–46, 285; and the new culture, 241–50, 262, 265; role of Russian, 35–36, 44, 126, 136, 195, 196n, 206, 210, 211, 213, 216n, 218, 222, 242, 245–50, 285n, 288n
Literature: ethnic pattern in, 138; and the new culture, 213–14, 233, 234, 238, 250–59, 262, 264–67, 285
Local Industry, Ministry of, 115, 150n, 174
Localism. *See* Kishlaks; Kolkhozes; Nationalism; Tadzhik Communist Party (KPT); Tadzhik government
Lokai clan, 24
Lukin, A. A., 144, 145, 149n
Lychagin, A. V., 125

Machine Tractor Stations: abolition of, 182; ethnic patterns at, 131, 132; number of, 39, 59; political schools at, 196n; role of, 39; turnover rate of officials at, 168, 170
Madzhutov, 114
Main Roads Administration, 113, 115, 119, 120
Makhkamov, B., 120
Maksum, F., 37–38
Maksum, N., 40
Mangit clan, 24
Marr: linguistic theories of, 246, 265
Martov, 200–201
Marxist-Leninist University, Leninabad, 202
Mass organizations: ethnic pattern of, 123–25. *See also* Komsomol; Trade Unions, Central Council of; Union of Soviet Writers, TSSR, Council of

Matcha raion: and Basmachi, 26
Matiakin, I. Ia., 144
Mazaev, A. V., 114, 142, 143, 155, 156n, 188, 191
Meat/Dairy Industry, Ministry of, 114
Medicine, 63, 134n, 135–37
MGB. *See* State Security, Ministry of (MGB/KGB)
Mikhailov, 142
Miliutin, M. M., 119n
Minorities, 9, 132, 133, 135. *See also* Ethnic patterns; Ethnic tensions; Population
Mirshakar, M., 87, 255, 257, 258–59, 267
Mirzoiants, 113n
Mirzoiev, A. M., 265
Mirzo-Zade, 265
Miskinabad kishlak, 226
Molotovabad raion, 131, 132
Moscow Institute of Journalism, 152
Movies, 221–23, 227. *See also* Political education
Mukanna, 11, 236, 238
Municipal Economy, Ministry of, 115
Muradov, Colonel, 203
Murgab raion, 225
Music, 223, 259–61
MVD. *See* Internal Affairs, Ministry of (MVD)
My City, 258n

Naimen'sheie zlo, 80–86, 90
Narodnost' (nationality), 71, 76. *See also* Nationality policy
Narrow-gauge Railroad Administration, 115
Narzibekov, M., 143, 151, 152, 153, 187
Narzikulov, I. K., 134, 151, 152, 187
Nasrullah Khan, 83
Nationalism: bourgeois, 39–40, 41, 45, 69–70, 77, 78, 152, 194, 195n, 204, 221, 224, 231, 234, 241, 245, 250, 254, 255, 256, 260, 263, 265, 273, 286; Central Committee, CPSU, on, 180–81; and cultural policy, 221, 224, 267–68; and economic development, 180; Great Russian chauvinism, definition of, 69; and localism, 171–76, 180–81; polycentric tendencies, 40–41, 78, 271, 274, 283, 286, 290, 292–93; pre-revolution, 4, 76–77; during revolution period, 19, 22, 25
Nationality policy, 4, 42, 67–80, 90–93, 95–96, 231–34, 245, 285, 292–93: na-

Society for the Spread of Political and Scientific Knowledge, 224–25
Soiuzpechat', 216. *See also* Press and publications
Sovetabad, 48
Sovkhozes, 59, 131, 168, 170, 219
Spitsina, A., 144
Sports, Physical Education, agency of, 115
Stalin, Joseph: and Bukhara minorities, 71–72, 78; and communization of the East, 72; and education of local cadre in the Communist Party, 27–28; and importance of revolution in Tadzhikistan, 72–73; linguistic policy under, 243, 246, 247, 262; on national cultures, 231, 232; and nationality policy, 67, 80; policy toward SSR's, 88–90; on right to secede, 69; and Tadzhiks, 73n
Stalinabad city: and admission to Party, 164–65; and communications media, 217; continuing traditional attitudes in, 275–76; elections in, 210; ethnic patterns in, 210n; executive committee, 118; gorkom, 108, 109, 166; industrial development, 54; and *kultprosvet*, 223, 228; living conditions in, 62; and MVD, 119; population growth in, 47, 48; raikoms, 164–65; soviets, 112; and transportation, 8
Stalinabad garrison, 122, 123
Stalinabad Medical Institute, 136, 137
Stalinabad oblast: abolition of, 53; and admission to Party, 165, 166; economic development of, 54–55; executive committee, 118; *kultprosvet* in, 228; obkom, 107, 108, 166; political schools in, 201–2
State Control, Ministry of, 114
State Public Library im. Firdousi, 226
State Security, Ministry of (MGB/KGB), 52, 113, 114, 118–22, 147–48, 156: career patterns, 148, 150; downgrading of, 120; ethnic patterns in, 114, 119–20, 156
Stotskii, V. N., 144, 145
Sufism, 15, 237–39, 264
Sukharev, S. A., 121
Sulaimoni, P., 255
Supreme Court, TSSR, 104, 117
Supreme Soviet, TSSR: career pattern, 150n; ethnic patterns in, 111, 112–13; and KPT Central Committee, 104; Presidium, 112, 113

Supreme Soviet, USSR, 95
Sviridenko, 114

Tabari, Makhmud, 236
Tadzhibaev, 174
Tadzhik Agricultural Institute, 134n
Tadzhik Autonomous Soviet Socialist Republic (TASSR), 26, 29–37
Tadzhik Communist Party (KPT), 99–111: administrative efficiency of, 181–86; Auditing Commission, 103; career pattern in, 146–50; and collectivization, 39; and the cultural policy, 134, 138, 250, 256, 257, 259, 260, 261–67, 286; degree of autonomy in, 96–99; departments of the Central Committee, 144–45; educational characteristics of leaders, 151, 152; Eighth Congress (1952), 164, 165n, 170, 172, 174, 177, 178, 183, 201; Eleventh Congress (1957), 134n, 164, 168; early history of, 21, 31, 34–37; establishment of, 37; ethnic patterns in, 41–42, 43, 95–99, 100–111, 142–45, 147, 148, 149, 150, 163, 165, 169, 179–81; in factories, 129; Fifteenth Congress (1963), 176, 204, 225; and formation of proletarian class, 127; Fourteenth Congress (1961), 168–69, 204; gorkoms, 108–9, 111, 148–49, 166, 167, 168; "localism" in, 171–76, 177, 178, 180–81; membership in, 34–35, 40, 44, 100–101, 164–66, 181–82, 194; Ninth Congress (1954), 164, 183n, 184; obkoms, 107–8, 109–10, 147, 148, 166, 167, 168; purges of, 28, 39, 40–41, 70, 151, 155, 158, 167, 169, 256, 262; raikoms, 110–11, 147, 148–49, 164–65, 166–67, 168, 170, 171, 182–83; Second Congress (1934), 39; Seventh Congress (1948), 134–35, 164, 177–78, 194n, 195, 201, 208, 219, 220, 264n; Sixteenth Congress, 204; social composition of, 165–66; and socialization of the elite, 192–205; and socialization of the masses, 192–93, 205–8; state-Party tensions, 177–81; Tenth Congress (1956), 52–53, 164, 184, 201; Thirteenth Congress (1961), 168; turnover rate of officials in, 164, 166–71; women in, 142–45, 150n, 151, 152, 153–54, 165, 277–78. *See also* Central Committee, KPT; Komsomol; Political education; Political leadership
Tadzhik Communist Party (Regional), 21, 31, 34–35, 36, 37

 THE JOHNS HOPKINS PRESS

Designed by Arlene J. Sheer

Composed in Baskerville text and display

Printed on 60-lb. Perkins and Squier, R

Bound in Riverside Chambray, RVC-3744 by
The Colonial Press, Inc.